Nevada

A HISTORY OF THE SILVER STATE

MICHAEL S. GREEN

NEVADA

A HISTORY OF THE SILVER STATE

UNIVERSITY OF NEVADA PRESS   RENO AND LAS VEGAS

This publication is made possible in part by a grant from Nevada Humanities, a state program of the National Endowment for the Humanities.

University of Nevada Press, Reno, Nevada 89557 USA
Copyright © 2015 by University of Nevada Press
All rights reserved
Manufactured in the United States of America
Design by Kathleen Szawiola

Library of Congress Cataloging-in-Publication Data

Green, Michael S.
Nevada : a history of the Silver State / Michael S. Green.
pages cm
Includes bibliographical references and index.
ISBN 978-0-87417-980-4 (cloth : alk. paper) —
ISBN 978-0-87417-973-6 (pbk. : alk. paper) —
ISBN 978-0-87417-974-3 (e-book)
1. Nevada—History. I. Title.
F841.3.G73 2015
979.3—dc23   2014037023

The paper used in this book meets the requirements of American National Standard for Information Sciences—Permanence of Paper for Printed Library Materials, ANSI/NISO Z39.48-1992 (R2002).
Binding materials were selected for strength and durability.

FIRST PRINTING
23   22   21   20   19   18   17   16   15
10   9   8   7   6   5   4   3   2   1

To Two Ralphs and Three Bobs

CONTENTS

ILLUSTRATIONS

Photographs

Maps

PREFACE

This book marks the first completely new, in-depth survey of Nevada's history published since 1989. By 2014, Nevada's population more than doubled, with southern Nevada now boasting more than 70 percent of the state's residents, including an influx of immigrants, especially from Latin America and Asia, that reshaped the state's culture in significant ways. As gaming spread to almost every state, a spate of new resorts revitalized the Las Vegas Strip, and casino corporations exported their knowledge from Nevada across the country and around the world—and profited accordingly. Between the donations from these corporations, Nevada's growth and role in presidential caucuses, and Harry Reid's ascent to Senate leadership, the state evolved into a significant part of the national political scene. A gold mining boom enriched the rural counties, but began to recede as the Great Recession showed signs of easing for Nevada's urban areas. These strands of Nevada's recent past have received both scholarly and popular attention, but this represents the first book that weaves them into the whole of Nevada history.

The most recent histories of the state appeared before these changes. The first college-level textbook by a leading Nevada scholar, Russell Elliott's *History of Nevada,* appeared in 1973 and concentrated more on the state's mining and ranching past and their impact than on the latest history of southern Nevada and gaming; an update by Elliott and William Rowley in 1987 brought the story forward but obviously could neither foretell the changes to come nor take advantage of scholarship that has since appeared. James W. Hulse published *The Silver State* in 1989 and has updated it twice, but the need has remained for a work that considers Nevada's history both chronologically and thematically, much as a US or world history survey does, with enough attention to more recent developments. I stand on the shoulders of these fine scholars, and many others who have contributed so much to our knowledge and understanding of Nevada's past and present, in offering this volume as that work.

My research and writing have emphasized southern Nevada, where I live and teach, and my interests in political and economic history. But understanding any part of Nevada requires trying to have a grasp of every part of Nevada. I have covered the state's history broadly, but with a focus on themes that unfold throughout the text; enough information for the cursory but sufficient detail for in-depth readers, or to inspire them to further study; scholarly and interpretive enough for a professor but readable and well written enough for students and the general public to enjoy and learn from. I have organized the book chronologically, relying on other historians who argued for distinct eras in the state's history while taking a few leaps of my own and incorporating themes that flow throughout the book.

Focusing only on what interests me might make a book, but not a general history of Nevada. Consequently, I learned a lot about Nevada, and have been as comprehensive as possible, but regret that I could devote only so much space to so many subjects. Writing this book confirmed that much of Nevada's history still requires scholarly attention, and I hope it encourages further study. But this process also led to the pleasant surprise of seeing so much research, published and unpublished, on Nevada. The sheer number of works requires that the list of suggested readings exclude the many scholarly and popular articles, theses and dissertations, unpublished oral histories, newspapers, and manuscript collections and limit it to books to which readers might have easier access. Some of you may find errors or have ideas about how to improve this book; I urge you to tell me at michael.green@unlv.edu.

A wise scholar once said, "Study the historian before you begin to study the facts." This book reflects more than a quarter of a century of teaching and writing about Nevada and living in the state since age two (for the curious, 1967). While I can remember always being interested in history, I first ventured into Nevada's past at age eight, when I found Myrtle Tate Myles's *Nevada Governors from Territorial Days to the Present* at the North Las Vegas Library. Because the governor and I shared the same first name, I wanted to become governor when I grew up. Since then, I changed my mind to broadcasting for the Los Angeles Dodgers (I still want that job), then journalism (I served as a reporter and editor for the *Valley Times* and continue to dabble in that field), and finally to history while attending the University of Nevada, Las Vegas (UNLV). While working on my PhD at Columbia University, a job became available at the College of Southern Nevada (CSN). I annually taught between four and eight classes of Nevada history for nearly two decades while teaching part-time and finally full-time at UNLV, where I also teach on the subject and continue to research and write about it.

If I have failed with this book, I take the blame, but if I have succeeded, many deserve credit. To try to list everybody would ignore too many colleagues, friends, family, historians, writers, and commentators, including some I never met but learned from. Joanne O'Hare, Matt Becker, Kathleen Szawiola, Annette Wenda, and the staff of the University of Nevada Press have been marvelous to work with. For help with the photos and permissions, I am especially grateful to Delores Brownlee and Su Kim Chung of UNLV Special Collections, Tom Gorman and Rebecca Clifford-Cruz of the *Las Vegas Sun* and Greenspun Media, Melissa Warren of Faiss Foley Warren, Forrest Lewis of the North Las Vegas Library District, Kimberly Roberts of Special Collections at the University of Nevada–Reno (UNR) Library, and Lee Brumbaugh of the Nevada Historical Society. I would like to thank friends and colleagues who read all or part of this book, especially Sondra Cosgrove, Ron James, Matt Makley, and two anonymous readers for the press. Many librarians contributed, especially at UNLV's Lied Library (both Circulation and the Department of Special Collections) and the CSN Library. Without librarians, historians would be twisting in the wind.

Many others have helped more than they know. Over the years various editors and publishers, especially Marilee Joyce, Greg Miller, and Geoff Schumacher, have allowed me to air my thoughts on these subjects and helped me enormously, as have the many who discussed them with me and alternately praised and shredded them. Thousands (gulp) of students have taken classes from me and helped shape this book. Discussions at conferences, in the community, and with many instructors have affected my thinking on Nevada history. During a sabbatical from CSN, the Los Angeles Corral of Westerners Fellowship made possible a month at heaven on earth, the Henry E. Huntington Library, Art Gallery, and Botanical Gardens. As I completed this manuscript, I joined the UNLV History Department, and I thank my colleagues there for their support.

My professors at UNLV and Columbia University and the colleagues I have worked with in academe and journalism have taught me a lot, and any effort to list everybody would satisfy nobody. As I wrote, though, the voices of three mentors rang in my ears: Eric Foner, quoting his adviser Richard Hofstadter's admonition to "make war on the verb form *to be*"; Eugene Moehring of UNLV, saying, "Avoid the passive voice"; and Bruce Hasley, the managing editor at the *Valley Times,* reminding us to make news stories "short and punchy." They deserve a great deal of credit for, among other things, making me a better writer.

To explain the dedication, Ralph Roske, my adviser at UNLV, taught and wrote about Nevada history and encouraged me to do the same; among other things, he encouraged me to take history seriously but not historians. Ralph Denton schooled me in Nevada politics and law and in life; the Dentons have become family, and my gratitude to them, and to Mary Lou Foley and Michael Epling for introducing me to them, remains boundless. Bob Brown hired me as a reporter at the *Valley Times,* taught me a lot in two years, and helped inspire me to study history. Bob Faiss influenced late-twentieth-century Nevada and helped me learn how he did it and whom he joined in doing it, without ever claiming the credit he deserved. The other Bob, my father, a casino dealer for thirty years, reminds me of the importance of those who hold no high position, but simply do their jobs. He did this at the whim of mobsters and for legitimate businesspeople, while he and my mother, Marsha, had a home to keep and a son to raise, and they encouraged him to pursue whatever his dreams might be.

Without my parents, I would not have been possible. Without those mentioned above and others who will have to accept my thanks privately, this book might have been possible but would have been harder to complete. Without my wife, Deborah Young, much might be possible and completed, but none of it would be worthwhile.

Nevada

A HISTORY OF THE SILVER STATE

Overview of Nevada

1

Understanding the Place

History refers not just to the facts about the past, but to the analysis of those facts. Even what seems like a simple recitation of what happened requires interpretation: historians decide what to tell and what not to tell. These choices reflect the teller's background and biases—gender, religion, race, socioeconomic background, and cultural outlook. When the facts seem beyond dispute, their interpretation has prompted many arguments among scholars, among the general public, and between them.

Nevada and Western History

No historian has influenced how the world thinks about the American West more than Frederick Jackson Turner. In 1890 the US Census Bureau concluded that settlements had spread so much and grown so close together that it declared the frontier closed. In response, three years later, Turner, a young professor at the University of Wisconsin, wrote a paper, "The Significance of the Frontier in American History." He argued that how the nation and its institutions evolved had been due to Americans moving onto free land and adapting to new environments. On the frontier peoples and societies developed anew in an atmosphere of greater equality than in the more established Europe and eastern United States.

Yet Turner and his followers missed several key points. Turner suffered from the prejudices of his time or ignored certain issues. He barely noticed the Native people living on supposedly free lands, how settlers damaged the environment as they adapted it to their needs rather than the other way around, and how victims of racial, gender, and religious discrimination saw no signs of the frontier's alleged democracy and equality. But Turner provided a framework for western history that even his critics use today.

Open spaces and environmental change affected the West's evolution, and social mobility often proved greater on the frontier than in older communities and societies.

Other authors built on Turner's ideas, but in different ways. Writing about the area west of the Mississippi River, Walter Prescott Webb pointed to its wealth of land and lack of water, a combination that shaped a distinct West. Popular writers Bernard DeVoto and Wallace Stegner stressed the West's uniqueness as an environment. Western scholar Earl Pomeroy noted the distinctions between areas of the West, how residents of those places have adapted to their surroundings and taken advantage of them, and how visitors from the East have shaped perceptions of the West.

The 1960s movements in African American, women's, and Chicano rights reshaped American society and the study of its history. Greater racial and gender diversity among historians finally focused attention on largely ignored groups—African Americans, laborers, and women in particular. How these changes influenced western history became apparent with the 1987 publication of Patricia Limerick's book *The Legacy of Conquest,* which reversed what Turner and his followers had argued to explain the key to the West as its conquest—of its land and Native people, by groups of settlers exerting power over others. Other western scholars, on their own or under Limerick's influence, continued to move western history away from romantic notions of cowboys and Indians and the idea of "winning the West." As it turned out, winners produce both losers and lasting consequences.

While historians outside the state have interpreted and informed us about Nevada, even more useful material has come from those working inside Nevada—at colleges and universities, at historical societies and museums, in archives, and in the print and broadcast media. Some of their work has been based on the historians mentioned above, while others have focused more on what makes Nevada unique or unusual or in other ways a typical western state: its mining and ranching heritage, its reliance on gambling and tourism, its diverse and heavily immigrant population, its overwhelmingly urban population, its heritage of political corruption, and the flow of its wealth to other places.

In influencing our understanding of the West and Nevada, these authors have provided an important interpretive peg on which to hang what we know about the state. As Turner might suggest, mining discoveries in the mountains enabled settlers to prosper by adapting to the conditions there—but, as Limerick would note, with environmental and social costs. Webb might argue that Nevada's aridity affected the economy and settlement—but as many environmental historians have shown, that led to building irrigation systems and artificial places and economies that shaped where and how we live. Social mobility permitted hard-rock miners and small-time casino operators to gain wealth and power, but victims of discrimination often did unto others what had been done to them. Because history has been called an argument without end, these ideas provide the basis for arguing about Nevada's history—including some of the arguments and themes that follow.

Understanding Nevada

Several themes and trends have been crucial to Nevada's history. Luck has shaped Nevada—and not just the impact of coincidences. Despite previous failures, the belief that their luck would soon change has inspired prospectors to pan and dig for ore and gamblers to make one more wager. They have failed more than they have succeeded, and their actions have generated lore, stories of poverty and prosperity, and revenue for the state and some of its wealthiest residents and nonresidents. Their luck, good and bad, has influenced the state's economic development, and with it Nevada's politics and society. Luck also can be a risky proposition on which to build an economy, as Nevada has proved with mining boom-and-bust cycles and then with its dependence on tourism, which contributed to its economic collapse in the early twenty-first century.

A related theme, exploitation, has taken many forms. Miners and railroad builders, business and political leaders, and average citizens used and abused the land for their own purposes. Exploitation can also mean taking advantage of the weaker or discriminating against others on the basis of race, gender, religion, or nationality. While Nevada has provided opportunities for victims elsewhere to reverse their usual roles, the state has reflected national trends in dealing or not dealing with this problem. Outsiders have plundered the state to become wealthy or wealthier and taken their gains back home with them. The rise of gambling and tourism, the state's largest industries since the 1940s, exploited people's weaknesses and belief in their luck, but also exploited prosperity elsewhere to create wealth for Nevada—a reversal of the nineteenth and early twentieth centuries, when Nevada served as the colony that created wealth for others.

Tied to this theme, Nevada has been largely a one-industry state and benefited and suffered accordingly. From the "Rush to Washoe" in 1859 until the 1930s, Nevada depended on mining for its economic prosperity, and when boom times ended, as they did often and quickly, so did prosperity. During the mining period but especially afterward, Nevada looked to tourism, to outsiders willing to come to the state and spend money, for its economic well-being—and its prosperity has increased with the nation and the world and decreased in hard times. This one-note economy has bred two other trends: dominance by the one region of the state where mining or tourism has been most successful and political corruption, rooted in that one industry exercising its right to try to control policy and policy makers for its benefit, with mixed results for the industry in question and the populace. In turn, political corruption has prompted fights for political reform and change, with equally mixed but ultimately less successful results.

Another theme involves how these leaders and Nevadans in general have—or have not—gotten along with the federal government. On the one hand, federal dollars did much to build parts of Nevada, especially southern Nevada. Without the federal government's interest, statehood would have been impossible; without the efforts of Nevada's federal elected officials, mining and gambling would have been more heavily taxed and regulated. On the other hand, federal legislation to stop using silver as currency damaged Nevada's economy. Federal restrictions mean that the government owns more than 86 percent of the land within Nevada's borders, reducing Nevada's tax base and access to capital, and limits on grazing and water use have long vexed miners and ranchers. At first, many welcomed federal efforts to locate a nuclear waste repository in the state, but then that project became the subject of overwhelming opposition. Rightly or wrongly, many Nevadans believed that the federal government wanted to "get" them.

Part of that attitude reflects a deep concern with how others perceive Nevada. No state provokes more myths and criticism, and no state tries harder to promote an image of itself—at times in keeping with outside criticism, at times to counter it. Before it had a name or became a state, Nevada struck its visitors as dangerous and desolate. Their descriptions of it stuck in the public mind, and even today travelers often lament and sometimes admire its open spaces, lack of water, and varied temperatures.

Its long dependence on mining convinced many outsiders that Nevadans tended to be lawless and drifting—and slogans like "What happens here, stays here" have shaped an image from which Nevadans benefit and suffer.

Nevada has also been a laboratory for how Americans define freedom. Its first settlers—miners who wanted to get rich and Mormons who accepted their church's rules but lived in a manner that many Americans found unacceptable—wanted to be left alone. The Nevada Constitution's framers tried to provide political, individual, and economic freedom as well as freedom from government interference. Wide-open gambling, easy divorce, and limited government reflected a belief in limited government and Nevada's presumed desire to live and let live—an attitude ultimately at odds with the need to regulate gambling to keep the games and their operators as honest as possible. By the early twenty-first century, Nevada seemed to strain its ties to this tradition as its residents approved a law to define marriage and defeated an effort to make marijuana use legal—neither measure reflecting true libertarianism—while also retaining a strong antigovernment fervor.

Another important theme that informs this book concerns what unites and divides Nevadans. Nevada's history contains many broad conflicts: north and south, urban and rural, the federal government and the state, and law enforcement and criminals, to name only a few. But much has unified Nevadans, including shared elements of their history, wherever they live in the state and whatever they do, ranging from boom-and-bust economies to the origins of their communities. Nevada's boundaries, like any state's, result from various forces beyond the state's control, but they encompass a people who have much in common.

While these themes appear to owe much to Limerick, they also reflect how Nevada fits Turner's definition of a frontier society. The state's economy has offered opportunities for economic, political, and community advancement to those who otherwise lacked them, from Irish miners on the Comstock to Jewish casino operators and African American and Hispanic women in postwar Las Vegas. A sense of freedom—and room and need for experimentation on the frontier (Turner's democracy and newness)—prompted Nevada to adopt such activities as boxing, gambling, divorce, and prostitution when others frowned or still frown upon them (Limerick's conquest of land and society). Granting the presence of Native peoples on that supposedly "free" land, understanding Nevada requires an understanding of the land—how it evolved, what it contains, and what it lacks.

Shaping and Explaining the Land: Size and Climate

While Nevadans (and non-Nevadans, for that matter) claim to shape their land and fate, the land shapes them, too. Nevada's geology and geography have affected where Nevadans live and how they live. The state's economic, political, and cultural development, and sometimes the lack of it, reflects the characteristics of its land and water, its plants and animals, just as Nevadans have changed their surroundings to suit their needs.

With its size typical of western states, Nevada represents a crucial difference between the eastern and western United States. The nation's ten largest states lie west of the Mississippi River. All of New England or eight of the original thirteen colonies could easily fit inside Nevada. The driving distance from Laughlin at Nevada's southern tip to Owyhee in the northeast approximates that from Boston to Cleveland, or Washington, DC, to Atlanta. Such differences in distance and depth have often confused easterners about the West and its people. Nevada's vastness as the nation's seventh largest state (110,540 square miles) suggests how hard it can be for residents to know their state and the variety within its borders.

Its highest and lowest elevations reflect this diversity. As with other parts of the West, they differ more than those found in the East. Less than a mile from the California line, Nevada's highest point, Boundary Peak, south of the Sierra Nevada in the White Mountains in Esmeralda County, towers above thirteen thousand feet. Across the state, just west of the Utah line, Wheeler Peak in the Snake Range and the Great Basin National Park stands only about a hundred feet lower. The state's lowest point lies less than five hundred feet above sea level along the Colorado River in southernmost Nevada, outside the Great Basin.

The differences in Nevada's climate also reflect that expanse: Arctic at the state's highest peaks, desert near sea level. The hottest temperature ever recorded in Nevada, 125 degrees, rose about 10 degrees above the summertime average at Laughlin, near the state's lowest point. The lowest temperature (-50 degrees, 10–20 degrees below the winter average) came at San Jacinto, in northern Elko County, at the opposite end of the state. Reno and Las Vegas, near Nevada's northwestern and southeastern corners, have advertised the availability of both nearby skiing and warm-weather recreational opportunities, reflecting how Nevada promotes an image of itself and its diverse climate.

The statistics for Nevada's precipitation also vary, ranging annually from about five inches in the southern valleys to more than two feet at Marlette Lake in the eastern Sierra Nevada. Indeed, longtime Nevada state climatologist John James argued for describing Nevada's rain as episodes: large cloudbursts or flash floods, especially in desert areas, often as part of a monsoon season. The mountain snows create streams and occasional spring flooding, while the lesser rainfall in the valleys may come in downpours, leading to dangerous flash floods. These extremes have helped Nevadans choose where in the state to live and why tourism and agriculture succeed in some areas and fail in others. Rainfall also matters more to the economy and lifestyle of northern Nevada than southern Nevada, since the Las Vegas area's water supply depended first on an underground aquifer and later on the flow of the Colorado River.

These statistics suggest large variations in Nevada's climate, but similarities abound. Mostly arid, Nevada ranks at or near the bottom of any list of rain and snow by state. The state's many mountains, with valleys separating at least 160 distinct ranges, also contribute to differences in precipitation and temperatures throughout the state. The entire state lies within the Basin and Range Province, which extends through Arizona and New Mexico into Texas and Mexico.

The Great Basin and Its Meanings

The Great Basin encompasses all but Nevada's northeast and southeast corners, covering 165,000 square miles and alternating between mountains and deserts. It extends from the Sierra Nevada in the west to the Wasatch Mountains east of Salt Lake City. Jedediah Smith called it a "Great Sandy Plain," but another explorer, John C. Frémont, named it the Great Basin for its interior drainage, meaning its rivers and lakes empty into one another or into sinks rather than flow out of it. In the North, only a few Nevada rivers—the Owyhee, the Bruneau, and smaller streams that empty into the Columbia—drain into rivers outside the state. In the South, where part of the Mojave Desert spreads through Southern California and into Utah and

Great Basin

Arizona, the Muddy and Virgin Rivers join the Colorado. Travelers and residents in all parts of the state have long described similar challenges in the topography, whether on the mountains or in the deserts.

The presence of thirty-nine playas also distinguishes Nevada and the Great Basin. From the Spanish for "beach" or "shore," a playa refers to a dry lake. Utah's Great Salt Lake Desert constitutes North America's largest playa, with the Black Rock Desert in northwestern Nevada second at 400 square miles. Other prominent playas include part of Nellis Air Force Base in southern Nevada and the Forty-Mile Desert from the Humboldt Sink to the Lahontan Valley. In these arid, often forbidding areas, precipitation evaporates or soaks into the ground, yet playas often cover water sources that serve surrounding areas.

Water remains Nevada's most precious commodity. West of the ninety-eighth meridian, the United States differs greatly from the land to the east. The area west of that line down the nation's midsection became known as "the Great American Desert," including Nevada. With water covering fewer than 800 square miles of it, Nevada, seventh in size among states, ranks thirty-fifth in water acreage; only two states, Arizona and New Mexico, have more land and less water. In addition to the limited numbers of lakes, rivers, and streams in the Great Basin (and, outside it, the 1,450-mile Colorado River and its tributaries, including the Muddy and Virgin Rivers and the Meadow Valley and Las Vegas Washes), Nevada also has underground water, which surfaces in hot springs, prompting interest in the economic possibilities of geothermal energy and contributing to tourism. With 312 of these springs around the state, Nevada has been literally a hotbed of geologic activity. Springs like these once provided Las Vegas's water supply until growth and a lack of conservation efforts sapped it.

Nevada's Geology

These characteristics resulted from 2.5 billion years of tectonic plates shifting and crashing into one another, creating mountains and canyons. The Great Basin's oldest rocks sit just outside Nevada, in northwestern Utah, but parts of Nevada's mountains in the southern Great Basin date back about 1.7 billion years, to the pre-Paleozoic era. The bulk of the activity that created the Great Basin occurred in the past 20 million years through a combination of volcanoes and block faulting.

As recently as 13,000 years ago, Pleistocene or Ice Age glaciers filled valleys and created Donner Lake and part of Lake Tahoe. They also produced a pair of large lakes that filled most of the Great Basin. The eastern one, Lake Bonneville, mostly in present-day Utah, included Great Salt Lake and extended just across modern Nevada's eastern border. Lake Lahontan covered nearly 8,500 square miles, mainly in present-day northwestern

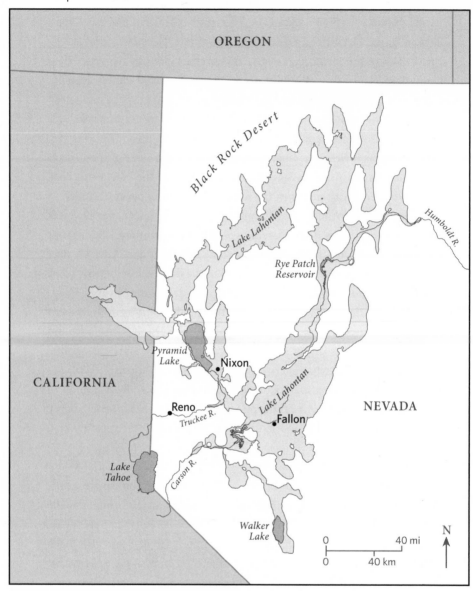

Lake Lahontan

Nevada. The remnants of Lake Lahontan include Pyramid (the deepest part of Lahontan, at about 900 feet) and Walker Lakes, the Humboldt and Carson Rivers and Sinks, and several dry lakes (also known as playas) and deserts, including the Black Rock.

While these results seem obvious, part of Nevada's geologic past may be unknowable. Its youngest igneous basement rock dates back nearly 1.5 billion years and its oldest pre-Paleozoic rocks about 650 million years, but scientists lack the evidence to determine what happened in the intervening 800 million years. The movement of tectonic plates drove dark limestones over newer sandstones to form Red Rock Canyon, west of Las Vegas. The Mesozoic era began about 250 million years ago and lasted less than 200 million years, but its impact and variety remain evident in the Valley of Fire's red sandstones, limestone, and shales and the beautiful granite of the 400-mile-long and 70-mile-wide Sierra Nevada, with its canyons that naturalist John Muir called "nature's poems carved on tablets of stone." This geologic activity has produced a variety of minerals, some eye-catching, some highly profitable, ranging from various crystals and jewels to oil, gas, and sodium. It also may have contributed to naturally occurring asbestos fibers, created 13 million years ago in volcanic rock in southeastern Clark County.

Other remnants of the past appear in rocks. Some life forms may go back 2 billion years, although most of the species can be traced to the past 500 million years; dinosaur footprints and bone fossils found in southern Nevada in the early 2010s dated back from 190 million to 230 million years. The state fossil, the ichthyosaur, lived in the ocean covering Nevada about 225 million years ago, ranged from two to fifty feet, and looked and moved like a fish. Scientists found the largest examples of the Mesozoic vertebrate's remains in present-day Berlin-Ichthyosaur State Park. Fossilized remains from another period, at Tule Springs near Las Vegas, date to nearly 200,000 years ago and include a more than six-foot-long Columbian mammoth tusk. In 2013 paleontologists announced the discovery of a horse from the Ice Age, nearly 14,000 years ago, in northwest Las Vegas.

The Modern Effects of Geology

Granting the importance of its remnants, Nevada's geologic past may seem distant, but the activity that created the Basin and Range Province continues. Faults surround many of Nevada's mountain ranges. Frequent, sometimes violent earthquakes changed the landscape millions of years ago and change it in modern times. A 7.2 quake at Gabbs in 1932 rippled throughout the Southwest. A series of 1954 temblors east of Fallon altered the state's topography, rupturing the ground in Dixie Valley and at Fairview Peak. In 2008 a 6.0 earthquake near Wells, in Elko County, damaged more than eighty buildings at a cost exceeding ten million dollars; a 4.3 rumbler less than fifteen miles from Wells early in 2012 barely attracted notice. Early in 2013 three quakes—the largest at 5.1—struck near the intersection of Highways 6 and 95 within a month of one another, and 120 minor quakes near Carson City in June 2013 raised concerns among seismologists; two months later a 4.7 quake struck Spanish Springs, northeast of Reno. Although Nevada rarely comes to mind in connection with earthquakes, only California and Alaska have reported more large earthquakes in the past 150 years.

Nevada has something else in common with those states and their geology: mineral wealth. Economically and environmentally, Nevada has felt the effects of the faulting, earthquakes, and volcanoes that made mountains—and, within them, minerals that turned Nevada into a mining state, known as the "Silver State." This makes Nevada's history similar in some ways to other western states where gold, silver, and copper have shaped the economy and society, but it also suggests some comparison with mining in other geologically active places such as Australia and the coal fields of the Appalachians in the eastern United States. Earthquakes also revealed outcroppings: in the 1840s and 1850s, emigrants sometimes saw gold and silver as they traveled, inspiring them to stay and investigate further.

The earth's movements also affect Nevada's recreational offerings, and not just such mountain activities as skiing and snowboarding. In the 1880s rancher Absalom Lehman discovered the centerpiece of White Pine County's 77,000-acre Great Basin National Park, Lehman Caves. Smaller than more famous underground sites such as the Carlsbad Caverns in New Mexico, Lehman Caves extend for just over a mile. Geochemists from the Massachusetts Institute of Technology and the Universities of Minnesota and Arizona have estimated their age at more than 1 million years old, based on samples from stalagmites and stalactites containing uranium that they measured for radioactive decay.

This conclusion links past, present, and future. The researchers worked in connection with a Southern Nevada Water Authority (SNWA) plan to pump groundwater from valleys on both sides of the park to Las Vegas. Park officials feared the plan might reduce moisture in the caves. The geochemists hoped to learn more about the effects of climate change. Thus, our knowledge of Nevada—even its earliest days—evolves, sometimes in unexpected and seemingly unrelated ways.

Plant Life

Plate tectonics have shaped not only the land, but also what grows on it and feeds off it. Humans and other forms of life have adapted to the land and adapted it to themselves, and Nevada's plant life reflects the state's diverse climate and geography. The state's forested mountain ranges cover just over 10 percent of Nevada's acreage, but even that amount of land could blanket the states of Maryland and Delaware. In addition to the firs, aspens, and junipers throughout the West, the single-leaf piñon and juniper pines cover about one-eighth of the state, especially south of the Truckee and Humboldt Rivers. The single-leaf piñon has long been used for fuel, including charcoal. Piñon nuts have been an important food source for Native Americans and an important crop for Nevada.

The bristlecone, one of the world's oldest living plants at nearly 5,000 years old, lives at higher levels, especially in the White Mountains and Snake Range. In addition to their natural beauty, these trees have been a food source for Native Americans and served the environmental purpose of helping to control flooding and water flow from the snow. Although some bristlecone pines date back thousands of years, most of Nevada's forests have stood between 100 and 150 years, because the need for lumber in nineteenth- and early-twentieth-century mining booms led to deforestation.

Wetlands, meadows, and springs dot some of the state's valleys, but the semiarid climate contributes to the mostly dry, alkaline soil at lower levels, reducing the amount of potential farmland. Mollisols—dark, thick soil rich in organic matter—develop at slightly higher elevations with more rainfall and provide rangelands, especially in a 50- to 100-mile-wide belt across northern Nevada. Less fertile soils, known as aridisols, evolve in more arid areas and, with water pumped in through irrigation, can provide potentially profitable farmland. Its soil precludes Nevada from ranking as one of the top agricultural states, with less than 2 percent of its 71 million acres being farmed. Most of Nevada's agriculture has been in hay and forage crops, with successful farming in alfalfa and cantaloupes near Fallon and cotton near Pahrump. The amount of Nevada's farm production from cattle and sheep reflects the availability and importance of grass and grazing. The state leads the West in about three-quarters of its agricultural revenue coming from livestock, with almost 90 percent of its farmland dedicated to these animals.

Most of Nevada's prominent plants have shallow root systems. Sage-brush, shadscale, greasewood, and rabbitbrush grow throughout the state because they can spread out and absorb the limited water, and mule deer, sheep, and domestic livestock rely on these plants for food. With similarly shallow root systems, desert plants such as the cactus, yucca, creosote and mesquite bushes, and Joshua tree—not actually a tree but a yucca—cover the southern valleys, while the state grass, Indian rice grass, grows in simi-lar climates in the southwestern United States and Canada; as temperatures rise and droughts become lengthier and more frequent, scientists have expressed concern that the Joshua tree may not survive climate change. The fern-like leaves and yellow flowers of the biscuitroot, also known as desert parsley, have spread through the Great Basin; the plant's name comes from its roots, which can be ground into flour, while Native Americans have used its leaves, seeds, and sprouts for food and medicine. Tules, marshland grasses, and reeds grow to eight feet and have been used for baskets and flowers, with their name often applied to such similar plants as cattails and bulrushes.

Nevada's official flower, the sagebrush, grows throughout much of the state, although most forms of it thrive in areas with more rainfall. Its sage aroma helps distinguish it from similar plants like the darker green bitter-brush, which resembles the sagebrush but lacks its smell. Some sagebrush reaches six feet in height. Native peoples have long used it (and many other Nevada plants) for everything from medicine and ceremonies to clothing and cooking, although many people develop rashes from exposure to it. Because most livestock avoid eating sagebrush due to its odor and bitter taste, many settlers and ranchers have sought to remove it.

That tactic helped spread cheatgrass, which has greatly affected Nevada without being native or welcome. Originating in Eurasia, it traveled to the United States in that land's soils. As a "winter annual" whose seeds fall late in the year, it grows rapidly in springtime, producing large numbers of seeds and thus easily spreading throughout the West, including the Great Basin. Less tasty and, with its sharp bristles and seeds, less appealing cheat-grass often replaces sagebrush, endangering animals that depend on the state flower. Because it burns easily, cheatgrass hastens and expands fires—according to one study, fires happened four times more often amid cheat-grass than in other western areas. Biologists have begun to use a fungus called "the black fingers of death" that attack the seeds to try to stop cheat-grass from spreading.

Animal Life

The Nevada Department of Wildlife reports nearly nine hundred species of amphibians, birds, fish, mammals, and reptiles in the state, with sixty-four of them exclusive to Nevada. Some of those animals live on about 117,000 acres of state wildlife habitat, while federal agencies—the Bureau of Land Management (BLM), Forest Service, and National Park System—protect more than 6.5 million acres of Nevada's 70 million–plus acres of land. Stillwater National Wildlife Refuge, created in 1948 by the Truckee-Carson Irrigation District and the Interior Department, won attention from international organizations for the hundreds of shorebirds that pass through it while migrating. These statistics attest to the importance and diversity of Nevada's land and animals, as does an effort in the early 2010s to set aside 22,650 acres as the Tule Springs Fossil Beds National Monument in southern Nevada, site of a variety of fossils, including a Pleistocene saber-toothed cat discovered in 2012.

Nevada honors the desert bighorn sheep, a subspecies of the bighorn sheep found throughout the American Southwest and northwestern Mexico, as its state animal. Named for their large horns, which may weigh up to thirty pounds, bighorn sheep have declined in number from perhaps a high of two million (before humans arrived in North America) due to a variety of factors: hunting, reduced access to food and water, changes in habitat, and diseases from livestock. The desert bighorn adapt better than other bighorn sheep to living in the desert and doing without water. Nevertheless, they fell to dangerously low numbers until environmental awareness and conservation measures beginning with the New Deal in the 1930s helped triple the number roaming the Southwest. The Sierra Nevada bighorn, found mostly in the range's western foothills, became an endangered species in 2000 and has since rebounded. Today, more than five thousand desert bighorn and fifteen hundred Sierra Nevada bighorn roam Nevada.

The wild horse or mustang long has been closely associated with Nevada. By the time the federal government set aside the first land to protect them in 1962, the estimated one hundred thousand wild horses roaming Nevada declined as the human population grew, changes in laws governing grazing affected the land available to them, and pet-food makers sought them out. Thanks largely to Velma "Wild Horse Annie" Johnston, state legislators barred mustang roundups on private property, and Congress followed suit with laws governing federal land. Nevada's mustang population has neared twenty thousand, but the federal government rounds them up, arguing that confining too many to a particular range will lead to shortages of food and water. Critics attack the destruction of the social and family structure of wild horses as more damaging, but others argue that, if not for a sentimental attachment to these horses, most would view them as an invasive species to be eradicated.

The number of animals roaming Nevada reflects the variety and limits of its geography and climate. Among its most numerous animals, coyotes prey on domestic sheep when traveling in groups, on rodents when on their own. The most populous big-game animal, the mule deer, exceeds one hundred thousand, but herds of about eighteen thousand pronghorn antelope and seventy-five hundred elk join them and bighorn sheep as big game. Native American hunters and gatherers once used the most numerous smaller animals, rabbits—including the pygmy rabbit, which relies on sagebrush—as a major food source; other common western animals in Nevada include the beaver, western badgers, porcupines, and skunks. Many varieties of reptiles, including snakes and lizards, also live in Nevada's deserts; Native Americans and travelers west sometimes survived by eating them. The state reptile, the desert tortoise, may live for a century, eating herbs, grasses, and wildflowers. The desert tortoise remains a threatened species, with conservation measures taken in response to the loss of its food sources and humans encroaching on their traditional lands.

In the Air and in the Water

Its bird population also demonstrates and reflects Nevada's diversity, with more than 450 species. Native birds include the sage grouse, which subsists largely on sagebrush—and thus, like the state flower, has declined in number and appeared headed for the endangered species list. As many as 4 million piñon jays frequent piñon pines, living off their seeds, just as Native Americans have done. The Anaho Island National Wildlife Refuge in Pyramid Lake features one of the continent's largest nesting colonies of white pelicans. Hunters introduced chukar partridges, the most prominent species brought into Nevada, in the 1930s from their native Pakistan and Afghanistan. Bald eagles have started making Lake Mead their winter home and can be found in many other places around Nevada.

Nevada's fish have been important to the state's history in a variety of ways. The state has four native game fish—the cutthroat, redband, and bull trout as well as the mountain whitefish—and four fish hatcheries place about 2 million trout a year in Nevada's waters. Nevada's only deepwater fish, the Mackinaw trout, resides in Lake Tahoe and numerous other North American lakes. The cui-ui (pronounced "kwee-wee") originates in Pyramid Lake and migrates to the Truckee River. Once a food fish for the Northern Paiute, this sucker fish became an endangered species, but has been recovering. Nevada's state fish and western Nevada's only native trout, the Lahontan cutthroat also served as a staple of the Paiute diet and almost became extinct, thanks to predators, diseases, and overfishing, but it, too, has recovered. Federal officials now consider it threatened rather than endangered.

Other Nevada fish species face graver danger. The desert or Ash Meadows Amargosa pupfish, an endangered species found in only ten spring streams in Nye County, generally grows to about six centimeters. Nearby farmers pumped groundwater from Devil's Hole until the pupfish native to that spring almost died out. Although a federal court ordered the farmers to stop, by 2013 the pupfish's numbers had dwindled to 35 from a peak of 544 in 1990, and extinction became a possibility. The endangered Moapa dace, a cyprinid (part of the carp or minnow family) that has never exceeded nine centimeters, lives only in Clark County's upper Muddy River. Groundwater pumping, nonnative species, and human population growth drove its number below 1,000, although it came back to more than 2,200 in 2014, with 6,000 considered necessary for it to leave the endangered species list.

Mussels may seem to have no connection with Nevada except in restaurants, but they exist within the state. The western pearlshell, the Pacific Northwest's most common mussel, reached Nevada, thanks to one of its major hosts, trout. Another mussel poses significant problems: the quagga mussel migrated from the Great Lakes to the Colorado River by way of recreational boats and traveled downriver to Lake Mead. They breed quickly and reduce fish populations by using so many nutrients the fish need to survive. As one ecologist said, "There's no system that's geographically isolated anymore. We're all linked."

Perceptions of Place and Nature

Pulitzer Prize–winning historian David Potter called Americans a "people of plenty." But Nevada's environment might bring to mind the Gershwins' tune from *Porgy and Bess:* "I Got Plenty o' Nuttin'." As historian Elizabeth Raymond noted, "To a country that prides itself on being a land of beauty and abundance, the Great Basin is a serious and disturbing geographic anomaly," but not lacking in beauty and abundance. Desert and playas, as writer William L. Fox said, lack the trees and water that people use to place what they see in a proper perspective: distances become harder to judge, and mirages appear. The areas seem empty due to their sparse plant life and most desert animals emerging at night rather than in the daylight. The ground itself may also be in motion, given its active geology.

Nevada can be a confusing place, not just because of its political, cultural, and social institutions. To some observers, its deserts and mountains exude beauty; to others, they represented danger to those trying to travel over them. Even within the Great Basin, perceptions of the land have differed. Some would echo Dan Carpenter, an emigrant from 1850, who wrote, "No man that never saw [it] has any idea what kind of a barren, worthless, valueless, d——d mean God forsaken country," but corrected himself: it could hardly be "God forsaken for He never had anything to do with it." The Utah portion has struck many as more beautiful and cultivated than the Nevada side, due mainly to the presence of Mormons who, as Wallace Stegner observed, found it "unthinkable that the gathering-place of the Saints should be a barren desert. It should be made to blossom."

Nevada landscape has represented many things to many people. The Great Basin's sagebrush and the Las Vegas Strip's neon lights please some and offend others. What Nevada has historically lacked—water and arable farmland—has shaped who lives there and how they live. How they use that land has varied through time, from the arrival of the first humans to the present.

SUGGESTED READINGS

Angel, Myron F., ed. *History of Nevada.* Oakland: Thompson & West, 1881.

Barber, Alicia. *Reno's Big Gamble: Image and Reputation in the Biggest Little City.* Lawrence: University Press of Kansas, 2008.

Beesley, David. *Crow's Range: An Environmental History of the Sierra Nevada.* Reno: University of Nevada Press, 2004.

Billington, Ray Allen, and Martin Ridge. *Westward Expansion: A History of the American Frontier.* Albuquerque: University of New Mexico Press, 2001.

Bowers, Michael W. *The Sagebrush State: Nevada History, Government, and Politics.* 3rd ed. Reno: University of Nevada Press, 2007.

Carlson, Helen. *Nevada Place Names: A Geographical Dictionary.* Reno: University of Nevada Press, 1974.

Castor, Stephen B., and Gregory C. Ferdock. *Minerals of Nevada.* Reno: University of Nevada Press, 2004.

Chisholm, Graham, and Larry A. Neel. *Birds of the Lahontan Valley: A Guide to Nevada's Wetland Oasis.* Reno: University of Nevada Press, 2001.

Cleere, Jan. *More than Petticoats: Remarkable Nevada Women.* Guilford, CT: Globe Pequot Press, 2005.

DeCourten, Frank L. *The Broken Land: Adventures in Great Basin Geology.* Salt Lake City: University of Utah Press, 2003.

Driggs, Don W., and Leonard E. Goodall. *Nevada Politics and Government: Conservatism in an Open Society.* Lincoln: University of Nebraska Press, 1996.

Elliott, Russell R., and William D. Rowley. *History of Nevada.* 2nd ed. Lincoln: University of Nebraska Press, 1987.

Etulain, Richard W. *Beyond the Missouri: The Story of the American West.* Albuquerque: University of New Mexico Press, 2006.

——, ed. *Writing Western History: Essays on Major Western Historians.* Reno: University of Nevada Press, 2014.

Etulain, Richard W., and Ferenc M. Szasz, eds. *The American West in 2000: Essays in Honor of Gerald D. Nash.* Albuquerque: University of New Mexico Press, 2003.

Ferrari, Michelle, and Stephen Ives. *Las Vegas: An Unconventional History.* New York: Bulfinch Press, 2005.

Fiero, G. William. *Geology of the Great Basin.* Reno: University of Nevada Press, 1986.

Findlay, John M. *People of Chance: Gambling in America from Jamestown to Las Vegas.* New York: Oxford University Press, 1986.

Floyd, Ted, Chris Elphick, Graham Chisholm, Kevin Mack, Robert Elston, Elisabeth Ammon, and John Boone. *Atlas of the Breeding Birds of Nevada.* Reno: University of Nevada Press, 2007.

Fox, William L. *The Black Rock Desert.* Tucson: University of Arizona Press, 2002.

——. *Playa Works: The Myth of the Empty.* Reno: University of Nevada Press, 2002.

——. *The Void, the Grid, and the Sign: Traversing the Great Basin.* Reno: University of Nevada Press, 2005.

Fradkin, Philip L. *A River No More: The Colorado River and the West.* Tucson: University of Arizona Press, 1984.

Francaviglia, Richard. *Believing in Place: A Spiritual Geography of the Great Basin.* Reno: University of Nevada Press, 2003.

———. *Mapping and Imagination in the Great Basin: A Cartographic History.* Reno: University of Nevada Press, 2005.

Glotfelty, Cheryll, ed. *Literary Nevada: Writings from the Silver State.* Reno: University of Nevada Press, 2008.

Goetzmann, William H., and William N. Goetzmann. *The West of the Imagination.* Norman: University of Oklahoma Press, 2009.

Goin, Peter, and Paul F. Starrs. *Black Rock.* Reno: University of Nevada Press, 2005.

Gragg, Larry. *Bright Light City: Las Vegas in Popular Culture.* Lawrence: University Press of Kansas, 2013.

Griffin, Shaun T. *The River Underground: An Anthology of Nevada Fiction.* Reno: University of Nevada Press, 2001.

Hall, E. Raymond. *Mammals of Nevada.* Reno: University of Nevada Press, 1995.

Highton, Jake. *Nevada Newspaper Days: A History of Journalism in the Silver State.* Stockton, CA: Heritage West Books, 1990.

Hopkins, A. D., and K. J. Evans, eds. *The First 100: Portraits of the Men and Women Who Shaped Las Vegas.* Las Vegas: Huntington Press, 1999.

Hulse, James W. *Forty Years in the Wilderness: Impressions of Nevada, 1940–1980.* Reno: University of Nevada Press, 1986.

———. *Nevada's Environmental Legacy: Progress or Plunder.* Reno: University of Nevada Press, 2008.

———. *The Silver State: Nevada's Heritage Reinterpreted.* 3rd ed. Reno: University of Nevada Press, 2004.

James, Ronald M. *Temples of Justice: County Court Houses of Nevada.* Reno: University of Nevada Press, 1994.

James, Ronald M., Elizabeth Harvey, and Thomas Perkins. *Nevada's Historic Buildings: A Cultural Legacy.* Reno: University of Nevada Press, 2009.

Lanner, Ronald M. *The Piñon Pine: A Natural and Cultural History.* Reno: University of Nevada Press, 1981.

———. *Trees of the Great Basin: A Natural History.* Reno: University of Nevada Press, 1984.

Laxalt, Robert. *Nevada: A Bicentennial History.* New York: W. W. Norton, 1977.

Lillard, Richard G. *Desert Challenge: An Interpretation of Nevada.* New York: Alfred A. Knopf, 1942.

Limerick, Patricia Nelson. *The Legacy of Conquest: The Unbroken Past of the American West.* New York: W. W. Norton, 1987.

———. *Something in the Soil: Legacies and Reckonings in the New West.* New York: W. W. Norton, 2000.

Lingenfelter, Richard E., and Karen Rix Gash. *The Newspapers of Nevada: A History and Bibliography, 1854–1979.* Reno: University of Nevada Press, 1984.

Makley, Michael J. *A Short History of Lake Tahoe*. Reno: University of Nevada Press, 2011.

Malone, Michael P., and Richard W. Etulain. *The American West: A Twentieth-Century History*. Lincoln: University of Nebraska Press, 1989.

Marschall, John P. *Jews in Nevada: A History*. Reno: University of Nevada Press, 2008.

McPhee, John. *Basin and Range*. New York: Farrar, Straus, and Giroux, 1981.

Mergen, Bernard. *At Pyramid Lake*. Reno: University of Nevada Press, 2014.

Miranda, M. L. *A History of Hispanics in Southern Nevada*. Reno: University of Nevada Press, 1997.

Mozingo, Hugh. *Shrubs of the Great Basin: A Natural History*. Reno: University of Nevada Press, 1987.

Nash, Gerald D. *The American West in the Twentieth Century: A Short History of an Urban Oasis*. Englewood Cliffs, NJ: Prentice Hall, 1973.

Nash, Gerald D., and Richard W. Etulain, eds. *The Twentieth-Century West: Historical Interpretations*. Albuquerque: University of New Mexico Press, 1989.

Nevada Women's History Project. *Skirts That Swept the Desert Floor: One Hundred Biographical Profiles of Nevada Women in History*. Las Vegas: Stephens Press, 2005.

Nicoletta, Julie. *Buildings of Nevada*. New York: Oxford University Press, 2000.

Nugent, Walter. *Into the West: The Story of Its People*. New York: Alfred A. Knopf, 1999.

Ostrander, Gilman M. *Nevada: The Great Rotten Borough, 1859–1964*. New York: Oxford University Press, 1966.

Pomeroy, Earl. *The Pacific Slope: A History of California, Oregon, Washington, Idaho, Utah and Nevada*. 1965. Reprint, Reno: University of Nevada Press, 2003.

Pomeroy, Earl, and Richard W. Etulain. *The American Far West in the Twentieth Century*. New Haven, CT: Yale University Press, 2008.

Reisner, Marc. *Cadillac Desert: The American West and Its Disappearing Water*. New York: Viking, 1986.

Ronald, Ann, and Stephen Trimble. *Earthtones: A Nevada Album*. Reno: University of Nevada Press, 2002.

Rothman, Hal K. *Devil's Bargains: Tourism in the Twentieth-Century American West*. Lawrence: University Press of Kansas, 1998.

———. *The Making of Modern Nevada*. Reno: University of Nevada Press, 2010.

Ryser, Fred A., Jr. *Birds of the Great Basin: A Natural History*. Reno: University of Nevada Press, 1985.

Schumacher, Geoff, ed. *Nevada: 150 Years in the Silver State*. Las Vegas: Stephens Press, 2014.

Schwartz, David G. *Roll the Bones: The History of Gambling*. New York: Gotham Books, 2006.

Shepperson, Wilbur S., ed. *East of Eden, West of Zion: Essays on Nevada*. Reno: University of Nevada Press, 1989.

———. *Mirage-Land: Images of Nevada*. Reno: University of Nevada Press, 1992.

———. *Restless Strangers: Nevada's Immigrants and Their Interpreters*. Reno: University of Nevada Press, 1970.

Sigler, William F., and John W. Sigler. *Fishes of the Great Basin: A Natural History.* Reno: University of Nevada Press, 1987.

Smith, John L. *Sharks in the Desert: The Founding Fathers and Current Kings of Las Vegas.* Fort Lee, NJ: Barricade Books, 2005.

Strong, Douglas H. *Tahoe: An Environmental History.* Lincoln: University of Nebraska Press, 1984.

Titus, A. Costandina, ed. *Battle Born: Federal-State Conflict in Nevada During the Twentieth Century.* Dubuque, Iowa: Kendall-Hunt, 1989.

Trimble, Stephen. *The Sagebrush Ocean: A Natural History of the Great Basin.* Reno: University of Nevada Press, 1989.

Webb, Walter Prescott. *The Great Frontier.* Reno: University of Nevada Press, 2003.

Wiley, Peter, and Robert Gottlieb. *Empires in the Sun: The Rise of the New American West.* New York: Putnam, 1982.

Worster, Donald. *Rivers of Empire: Water, Aridity, and the Growth of the American West.* New York: Pantheon Books, 1985.

Wrobel, David M. *Promised Lands: Promotion, Memory, and the Creation of the American West.* Lawrence: University Press of Kansas, 2002.

Young, James A., and Charlie D. Clements. *Cheatgrass: Fire and Forage on the Range.* Reno: University of Nevada Press, 2008.

Zanjani, Sally S. *Ghost Dance Winter, and Other Tales of the Frontier.* Reno: Nevada Historical Society, 1994.

2

Before Euro-American Settlement

The Washoe Indians consider Cave Rock, a 360-foot monolith at Lake Tahoe's eastern shore, sacred. Rock climbers saw it as a beautiful, daunting challenge. The Washoe sued to bar them from defacing a place of great spiritual and historical importance. In 2003 the US Forest Service banned climbing. The Access Fund, a group funded by corporations that profited from the climbers, sued; US district judge Howard McKibben upheld the prohibition, and the Ninth Circuit rejected the appeal. As Matthew Makley and Michael Makley put it in their history of Cave Rock, "Climbers had lost a valued resource; the Washoes had regained one." Never before had federal officials closed access to an area due to its importance to Native American culture. Later, the Washoe hired a contractor to help remove graffiti and other examples of human contact and defacement. But the Washoe cannot eliminate the tunnels blasted through Cave Rock to ease travel across the Sierra Nevada.

Glorifying Native Americans' ties to the land, and attacking the treatment of both the people and the land, can be easy. Understanding Native American beliefs today creates less of a challenge than knowing those generations ago. Scholars once referred to the thousands of years before humans left written records as prehistory, but now we know that many other resources can illuminate the unwritten past. Artifacts and oral traditions provide a great deal of information about that early period. It requires some extra digging—literally—and creativity, just as extra digging and creativity help figure out other aspects of history, especially Nevada's, involving politicians who left neither fingerprints nor letters and casino operators who survived by never writing down what they could keep in their heads.

Cave Rock represented an important spiritual place for Native Americans and became the center of a fight over their rights and encroachments on them. Courtesy of Special Collections, University of Nevada–Reno Library.

Digging Up the Past: The First Arrivals

About fourteen thousand years ago, the first people, hunters and gatherers known as Paleo-Indians, set foot on the North American continent. How they arrived remains open to debate, but one of the most widely accepted theories suggests by way of the Bering Strait, then a land bridge connecting present-day Russia and Alaska. After another thousand years or so, Ice Age lakes began to recede, and humans lived in Nevada—at least so far as we know. With exact dates impossible to pinpoint, estimates have to be general, and new information constantly emerges. Scientists have made educated guesses about when and where the first people lived in Nevada by using radiocarbon dating. When plants and animals have died and can no longer absorb carbon 14, a natural radioactive isotope in the atmosphere, the element begins to decay. Scientists then can measure the amount of c-14 left to determine how many centuries have passed since the life of the material ended.

The oldest evidence of people in Nevada comes from "Spirit Cave Man," the oldest mummified human remains in North America, who lived about ninety-four hundred years ago near Fallon. In 1940, working in Spirit Cave in Churchill County for the State Parks Commission, archaeologists Georgia Wheeler and Sydney Wheeler found his skeleton wrapped in matting and a rabbit-skin blanket, wearing moccasins, with skin on his back and shoulders, some dark hair, and baskets nearby. Local doctor H. W. Sawyer (whose son Grant later became Nevada's governor) determined him to be an adult male. Studies at the time estimated the mummy to be about two thousand years old, but radiocarbon dating later led scientists to a different conclusion. Further studies suggested that Spirit Cave Man probably died of a skull fracture or abscessed teeth and had been in his forties, an advanced age for that period.

Who lived in Nevada before that remains unknown. A Pleistocene-era Columbian mammoth skeleton, discovered in 1979 in the Black Rock Desert, ranged from thirteen to seventeen thousand years old. Further study found it to be about fifty years old when it died and thirteen feet tall at its shoulders. Early hunters killed mammoths, but no evidence of Paleo-Indians exists from that long ago—yet.

The Next Early Nevadans

Other evidence supports the theory that people lived near where Wheeler and Wheeler found Spirit Cave Man. In the 1950s excavations along dry Lake Winnemucca in Pershing County at five caves, especially Fishbone Cave, and Falcon Hill, found links between men, horses, and camels; fishing with nets; and baskets, bowls, and water bottles. Archaeologists concluded that people may have been there eleven thousand years ago and lived in Fishbone Cave until about six thousand years ago. They also found evidence of human life from the same period at the Humboldt Basin's Leonard Rockshelter and Hidden Cave in the vicinity of the Carson Sink. Clovis spear points, which hunters used when mammoths lived in Nevada, have been dated to about eleven thousand years ago and found in such areas as the Black Rock Desert, near Tonopah in Nye County, and in Lincoln County.

As these varied locations suggest, archaeological finds have ranged throughout Nevada. At Tule Springs, in the Sheep Range foothills at the far end of the Las Vegas Wash, archaeologists from the Southwest Museum in Los Angeles and later from the Nevada State Museum in the 1920s and 1930s found further evidence of early people even before the discovery of

Spirit Cave Man. At what became known as the "Big Dig" of 1962, scientists calibrated radiocarbon dating for the first time and found stone and bone tools as much as eleven thousand years old. The fossils of mammals from two Ice Ages included the American lion, Columbian mammoth, bison, ground sloths approximately as large as grizzly bears, and the camelops, an extinct camel species. One paleontologist estimated that the area includes more than ten thousand fossils.

About thirty miles from Tule Springs, Gypsum Cave provided more important evidence about early humans and animals in Nevada and insight into how science has changed what we know about yesterday. In the early 1930s, archaeologists discovered a large amount of dung from ground sloths and weapons that belonged to humans and guessed that they came from the same period, more than ten thousand years ago. Three decades later radiocarbon dating enabled scholars to revise this information. They concluded that some sloth droppings came from that time, but still others dated back thirty-three thousand years. The weapons found then and since could have been no more than forty-five hundred years old. Subsequent excavations located basketry from nine thousand years ago, with a weave unique to the region.

As hunter-gatherers, the people who lived in Nevada from seven to ten thousand years ago demonstrated patterns that future native Nevadans would follow in adapting to their surroundings. In addition to fishing and collecting wild plants, they used an atlatl, which combined a stick and a spear to propel a dart at greater speed and make it easier to strike small animals. Nevada's earliest residents tended to live near lakes and in grassy or forest areas and moved as the seasons changed. They often traveled barefoot but made footwear for themselves, including moccasins and sandals—and how they made them varied by region in another demonstration of how they adapted to different climates and needs.

For the next five thousand years or so, hunting and gathering continued, but Natives' lives changed in important but subtle ways. Women made baskets, nets, and sandals from plants, while men improved upon their predecessors' stone tools and clubs. Women began using stones to grind nuts and seeds and fires to cook their food, including bighorn sheep, reflecting the men's increased role in hunting.

Another new wrinkle of the period helped students of Native Americans figure out these roles and habits: rock art. These petroglyphs (cut or

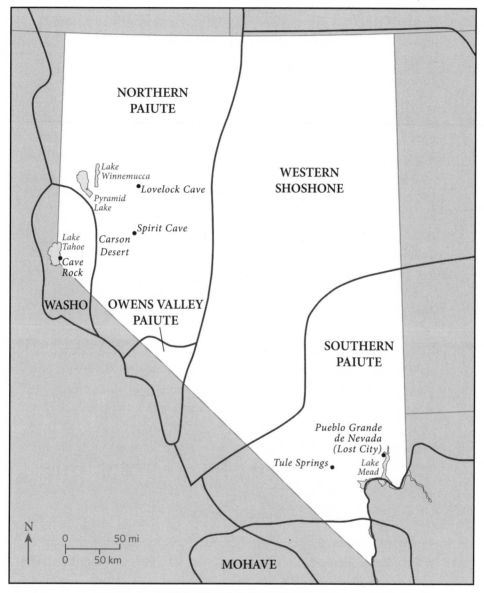

NORTHERN
PAIUTE

Lake
Winnemucca
•Lovelock Cave
Pyramid
Lake

WESTERN
SHOSHONE

•Spirit Cave

Lake
Tahoe
Carson
Desert
•Cave
Rock

WASHO

OWENS VALLEY
PAIUTE

SOUTHERN
PAIUTE

Pueblo Grande
de Nevada
(Lost City)•

Tule Springs •

Lake
Mead

N

0   50 mi
0   50 km

MOHAVE

Major Nevada Indian tribes

hammered into surfaces) and pictographs (drawn or painted onto rocks) range from lines and dots to figurines like a "monster," including fish fins and a rattlesnake tail, in Lovelock Cave. Scientists concluded that a dried lakebed just east of Pyramid Lake features North America's oldest petroglyphs—at least ten thousand years old and possibly nearly fifteen thousand years old. These artifacts remain visible at hundreds of locations around Nevada, with varied styles and implements.

Many have tried to read meaning into these remnants of the past. Rock art seems to suggest the presence of big game, especially mule deer, pronghorn antelope, and mountain sheep, since it almost always appears near springs or spots where hunters could hide to ambush their prey. Astronomers have argued that these works depict galaxies or keep a record of the sky, and other scholars have attributed "magico-religious significance" to them as part of a ritual designed to ensure a successful hunt. Shamans may have made or used them in employing or obtaining supernatural powers. Some of the art may also reflect the role that women played in Native American life and clearly reflects Native people's cultural history and oral tradition—more than the coffee mugs and T-shirts depicting rock art that have become part of modern popular culture.

Another key source of information comes from the Lovelock culture. About four thousand years ago, the climate cooled and became rainier, providing more plants and animals for Native Americans to sustain themselves. Increasing numbers of people built settlements in the Winnemucca and Pyramid Lake basins, the Carson Desert, and the Humboldt Sink, the site of Lovelock Cave. Natives relied on fish, birds, and water plants, but also appear to have traded minerals and animals with groups in California for shells and beads. The Lovelock culture left behind an array of artifacts and shelters as well as pits that suggest they may have advanced beyond hunting and gathering. The people of this group made not only baskets but also nets to catch rabbits and decoy ducks to attract birds.

Toward the Present

Around two thousand years ago, Nevada's Native groups entered a new phase. They continued to make baskets, but they became more intricate and tightly woven. They still hunted and gathered with atlatls, spears, and projectile points. But northern Nevadans started relying more on the piñon pine for its nuts. Southern Nevada's Natives began living in rock shelters and then in pit houses they built at and below the surface of the land, helping protect them against the varied desert climate. Some of them grew corn in a form of subsistence agriculture, meaning that they planted it for their survival and not to trade, and depended on rain and nearby water. Their housing and agriculture improved over the centuries.

The Basketmakers, as archaeologists call them, also gained some neighbors. Perhaps as many as twenty-three hundred years ago, the ancestral Puebloan culture developed in the Moapa Valley and remained there until around AD 1150. Residents of this area, referred to as Pueblo Grande de Nevada, became known as Virgin Anasazi because they lived close to the Muddy and Virgin Rivers in the Colorado River Plateau and shared many of the characteristics of similar people in other parts of the Southwest, especially the Four Corners of Arizona, New Mexico, Utah, and Colorado. Native Americans and students of their past no longer prefer "Anasazi": originally thought to mean "old ones," which the Anasazi would have been unlikely to call themselves, in Navajo it also means "ancient enemy," which the Anasazi never would have called themselves. Their designation as ancestral Puebloans or Puebloan people reflects their tendency to live in larger communities with more residential structures than earlier people; this group's westernmost members lived near the Virgin River, and the modern Hopi of Arizona claim them as ancestors. When the Puebloan population centers at Mesa Verde, Chaco Canyon, and in the Four Corners region broke up in the thirteenth century, many joined or established other Puebloan communities.

Nevada's Puebloan culture allowed for larger and more settled groups than that of the Basketmakers who preceded them. From about twenty-three hundred years ago until AD 500, Puebloans lived mainly in pit houses in the Moapa Valley and made baskets. Until around AD 700, they used pottery, possibly first by trading with others and then making their own. They also may have mined salt to use and to trade.

The period from AD 700 to around 1150 provides more information about the Puebloans, thanks to archaeological excavations. Multiroom, clay-floored, adobe homes dotted the landscape, with as many as twenty thousand residents at the community's peak; one of the houses excavated in the 1920s and 1930s had nearly a hundred rooms. The Puebloans grew corn, beans, squash, and cotton; ate rabbits and desert tortoises; made pottery and more elaborate coiled and twined baskets; and had dogs for pets. They obtained turquoise and shell beads from California, but also traded with other groups. In a harbinger of Nevada's and many Native Americans' future, they apparently engaged in a form of gambling similar to today's bingo games.

Their connections to Nevada's future ran even deeper. As the Puebloans turned toward agriculture and grew crops farther from bodies of water, they developed canals and dams—irrigation systems that predated by about a thousand years the Newlands Project and Hoover Dam, which did so much to shape modern Nevada. They also went into the mining business. They found a magnesite deposit about three miles from Pueblo Grande de Nevada and used it in their pottery. More crucially, they located four salt mines south of their settlement on the Lower Virgin River to use to preserve their food and meet their dietary needs and went as deep as eight feet into the earth. Estimating that mining went on as far back as two thousand years, archaeologists who excavated the area in the 1920s found picks and hammers that had been used to remove the minerals.

Mysterious Departures

The Puebloans had something else in common with more recent Nevadans, especially in the southern part of the state: they proved transient. During the mesa-house phase between AD 1100 and 1150, one of their later construction projects, a large house about 120 feet above the valley, bore some resemblance to forts built later in Europe—possibly meaning they saw the need to defend themselves against someone or something. Sometime after 1150 they left the Virgin River area.

Why they did remains unclear. Archaeologists and scientists had long argued that a drought limited farming, but more recent studies suggest the water supply declined less than previously believed—although a mega-drought in the nearby Sierra Nevada around that time dropped the amount of rain and snow, and thus the water levels of the mountain range's lakes, to much lower levels. Another group appears to have arrived in the area at about the time the Puebloans left, but further investigation revealed that they coexisted for some time—although relations could have soured, possibly over the wealth of food the Puebloans produced and stored. Additional research leads to speculation that a new religion divided the Puebloans, who may have already been fighting with one another. They belonged to a trade network stretching hundreds of miles south into Mexico, where the Toltec Empire crumbled around 1156, and those events may have triggered movement throughout the present-day Southwest. Puebloans departed from more areas than just the Moapa Valley; they vacated sites in the Four Corners as well.

Other early Nevadans disappeared. What happened to the Lovelock culture remains equally mysterious. According to the oral tradition of some Northern Paiutes, their people defeated enemies who lived in the same area around lakes and marshes, and one of their key battles took place at Lovelock Cave. This defeat, if it happened, occurred seven hundred to a thousand years ago, opening the possibility for some connection to the Puebloans' departure, hundreds of miles to the southeast.

Another ancestral Native group lived near the Puebloans; their connections remain uncertain. Known—among other names—as the Amacava, they roamed the Mohave Desert between AD 900 and 1150 and perhaps before. They ranged as far north in Nevada as Black Canyon, later the location of Hoover Dam. They left behind pottery, among other artifacts, and apparently gathered plants and built rock shelters in which to camp, but no evidence exists to suggest links between their civilization and that of the Puebloans.

Modern Native Groups

From an estimate of forty thousand Native Americans within present-day Nevada as the nineteenth century began, only about half that number remained by 1870, after exposure to European and American explorers and settlers. By then five Native American groups stood out prominently in Nevada: the Northern Paiute, Southern Paiute, Washoe, Western Shoshone, and—to a lesser extent than the other four—Mohave. The two Paiute groups and Shoshone share a Uto-Aztecan linguistic background, with the Washoe language of Hokan-Siouan origins and the Mohave's Yuman. The similarities in their ways of life have outweighed the differences, especially before their first encounters with Europeans and Americans. Several of these groups may have encountered earlier residents (as in the Northern Paiutes and the Lovelock Culture) and even gone through some form of cultural exchange. The Mohave apparently descended from the Amacava. Although their presence in southern Nevada overlapped with the Puebloans, the Southern Paiutes adapted with less involvement in agriculture and trade than their predecessors.

Each of the modern tribes also shares a deep spirituality that connects them to their lands. All of them have a creation story involving Coyote, but with varied depictions of his traits and actions. According to the Western Shoshone, the creator sent Coyote, whom they saw as having less admirable human traits, through the Great Basin with instructions not to open the lid on his basket, but he did, and they emerged and spread throughout the region. The Great Basin and Colorado Plateau peoples saw spirits in the waters, sky, and mountains, including the Mohave's ties to Spirit Mountain in far southern Nevada. To the Northern Paiutes, animals, plants, and objects had powers from which humans could benefit.

The environment also forced certain common characteristics onto Nevada's Native Americans. Whether in the Great Basin or along the Colorado Plateau, most resided in the desert, although living in the eastern Sierra Nevada gave the Washoe opportunities to harvest foods and resources from diverse regions. For the others, given how often they moved, elaborate housing required more effort than necessary. In summer Nevada's Natives built most of their homes out of branches, mud, and grass. In winter they added poles, dug a foundation, and used additional grasses and reeds for more protection against the elements and for rain and snow to run off. Because the Washoe had contact with such California Natives as the Miwok and Maidu, their housing also differed slightly, taking a more conical form than that of other Native Nevadans.

All of these Native groups hunted, fished, and gathered according to where they lived and its elevation. People in the mountains sought antelope, mountain sheep, and deer, with the Washoe at times hunting bear, all of which might be stored or skinned, while those in the valleys pursued small desert animals such as rabbits and squirrels and ate them immediately. Natives living near lakes—the Washoe near Lake Tahoe (taken from *da-ow,* the Washoe word for "lake") and the Northern Paiutes near Pyramid Lake—relied on birds, fish, and indigenous plants and dined on such insects as grasshoppers and ants. Survival required them to learn a lot about these plants (when they bloomed, which might be medicinal or poisonous) and the uses and migratory patterns of animals. They feasted on wild berries and roots, including carrots and onions, and made flour or soup from seeds and grasses. They sometimes traded with peoples in other states, especially for salt and, in the case of the Washoe and their contacts in California, acorns.

No food affected Native Nevadans more than the pine nut. High in good fats, fiber, calories, and protein, it served as an ideal source of nutrition. Each fall the harvest of piñon pine nuts determined what they ate and how much they would hunt and gather in the winter: the fewer the nuts, the more they had to seek other food. The harvests served as family and social events, often with a religious component, matchmaking, and competitions that might include dances and early forms of football and hockey. Not because they anticipated Nevada's economic future, the Washoe often bet on these sports with everything from baskets and buckskins to blankets. The Western Shoshone included a "cleansing" ceremony and round dancing in their celebration, while Washoe gatherers, mostly women, commemorated harvests and the men engaged in rituals before and after a hunt.

Animals provided not only food but also clothing. The Washoe relied heavily on rabbit-skin blankets. Other Natives used skins as they could, but they also depended on sagebrush, especially its inner bark, to help them make everything from skirts to shoes. Women wore skirts made of cattail reeds and tule and fashioned necklaces and earrings, using the bones of birds they and their families had caught and shells for which they traded with other tribes.

Natives in the Great Basin also followed in their ancestors' footsteps by coiling and weaving baskets. They varied in size and design according to need, with willows and available reeds and grasses. Women made the baskets, and mothers passed on the tradition to their daughters. When loosely woven, they served as sieves; tightly woven baskets could be used for gathering seeds, cooking, and storing food and water. Natives often preferred baskets to pottery as lighter and less breakable—an important factor for people on the move. Some basket makers did highly artistic work—but less so than those with more resources available to them—that became crucial to the Natives' economy after white contact.

Contact reshaped how Native Americans constituted themselves politically and socially. None of the groups formed anything like a tribe; a band of families of fifty to one hundred members related through blood or marriage served as the highest level of organization. Each group relied on shamans who served as middlemen between the spiritual and temporal worlds and possessed medical powers that helped cure diseases, or "headmen," usually older males related to everybody in the group who ruled, when they did, with tact and persuasion; they mediated disputes or, as needed, made command decisions. The Washoe had a ceremonial chief and a "rabbit boss" or "antelope boss" for the hunts. Perhaps because they had no table of leadership and thus no divisions over titles, Nevada's Natives had a reputation for being peaceful.

They also had to use plants more creatively than we do today and for more than just food and clothing. No germ theory of medicine existed until the nineteenth century, and medicinal plants formed a vital part of how they cured diseases and disorders. Sagebrush leaves became a tea that fought headaches and the common cold. Desert licorice eased stomach complaints. Snakeweed eased diarrhea. Natives also found other uses, such as employing yucca roots in making soap.

Contrasting the Tribes

Where they lived within the Basin and Range Province may have done more to define the major differences between Nevada's Native groups, although all of the groups in which white settlers and future anthropologists categorized them extended well beyond the state's borders. When explorers arrived in the nineteenth century, the Northern Paiutes covered more than seventy-five thousand square miles of Nevada and adjacent

A group of Shoshone women and children gathered at Ten Mile Canyon during construction of the Central Pacific Railroad. Alfred A. Hart, the railroad's official photographer, took their photo. Courtesy of Special Collections, University of Nevada–Reno Library.

states and lived in about twenty bands, each with up to two hundred members, and described themselves as "pine nut eaters" and "cui-ui eaters," for example, according to the band's main food source. They wound up sharing space with the Washoe, who descended from the Sierra Nevada to compete for food and other resources in Truckee Meadows and the Carson and Eagle Valleys.

They also encountered the Great Basin's predominant Native group, the Western Shoshone. Like the Washoe, they used resources available at higher elevations, such as the Ruby Mountains near Elko; like the Northern and Southern Paiutes, they acclimated themselves to the desert's sparseness. They entered Nevada from Idaho to the northeast and fanned out across the Great Basin and into California, creating what anthropologists have called the "Shoshonean Wedge." Whether they split the Paiutes into northern and southern groups remains debatable, but the Western Shoshone shared their characteristic of naming their bands according to what they ate, although they also designated members according to locations: the "white knives" lived north of Battle Mountain's white rock quarry, and those in Death Valley took their name from Furnace Creek.

The Paiute name originated from the Ute word for water, *pah*, the commodity that helped govern their lives. Those near water—the Moapa and Virgin River Paiutes—farmed beans, squash, and corn and may have used the rivers to irrigate crops, just as the Puebloans did. Many Southern Paiutes maintained gardens of fruit and vegetables. Most others moved through the area according to what grew or bloomed at the time they needed it, with some of them residing in the mountain ranges that ring the Las Vegas Valley. As Martha Knack, the group's leading scholar, wrote, "Virtually everywhere within this territory, Southern Paiutes could walk in a day's time to some dramatic change in elevation; much of the secret of their success in this arid land lay in their systematic exploitation" of that fact. They also stored food in grass-lined pits for when plants became even scarcer and tended to eat less appetizing fare in the springtime—thus, when John C. Frémont encountered them in the spring of 1844, he dismissed them as "lizard eaters."

The Mohave proved more agricultural than other Native Nevadans, for good reason: they lived closer to the biggest river, the Colorado. Just north of Laughlin, they took advantage of the spring flooding that later vexed many white farmers to help them with planting beans, corn, pumpkins, and

Two Southern Paiute women, sometime in the 1870s, in front of typical wickiups, when white settlement in their traditional lands remained sparse. Courtesy of Special Collections, University Libraries, University of Nevada, Las Vegas.

melons. They also made baskets and designed forms of irrigation to take advantage of the nearby water. They appear to have been more inclined to be warlike than other Nevada tribes, although only a select number of Mohave seem to have sought battle.

Perhaps the best way to contrast Natives with those of European descent may be found in how most Great Basin Indians call themselves a variation of *Nüwü,* or "the people"—Newe (Western Shoshone), Numa (Northern Paiute), Nuwuvi (Southern Paiute). They drew fewer distinctions than Euro-American settlers and cared far less about tables of organization and property rights. But all of these people confronted the same difficult environment, adapted to it, and adapted it to their needs and desires. All of them confronted a land of scarcity—even the Washoe dwelled in a less environmentally friendly section of the Sierra Nevada—and used its resources wisely and carefully. Their eating habits and the arrival of the bow and arrow sometime around AD 500 helped control the animal population, and the plants they used and ate and wood they gathered may have reduced the chance of fires spreading, but also prompted them to move to find fuel.

Rise of the Spanish Empire

When Christopher Columbus sailed for India but landed in the Caribbean in 1492, he represented Spain, a new nation-state whose rulers hoped to find markets and raw resources—the basis of an empire. Other explorers, called conquistadores, followed. So did other countries: English colonists settled the eastern United States, as the French did in Canada and the Dutch in present-day New York. But while Russia explored Alaska and established a fort in northern California in 1812, Spain became the dominant European power west of the Rockies and remained so for more than two centuries, but not easily or entirely successfully. Large numbers of early Spanish Central American and Caribbean colonists died of disease. Far more Natives died of new European diseases, combined with taking their land and forced labor and religious conversion, giving rise to the *Leyenda Negra* (black legend) of Spanish mistreatment of Natives, although some recent interpretations of the Spanish frontier of the Southwest have cast it in a less unfavorable light.

Having explored Florida, Central America, and the Caribbean in the 1490s and early 1500s, Spain established its western colony of New Spain, consisting of present-day Mexico and the American Southwest. Hernán Cortés conquered the Aztec Empire and Mexico between 1519 and 1521, but Spanish officials wanted to secure northern New Spain and find its riches. In 1540 Spanish officials sent Francisco Vázquez de Coronado north in an expedition with more than one thousand soldiers and servants and well over a thousand livestock to seek gold and silver. Over a two-year period, he explored the region from Arizona to Kansas, including the Grand Canyon and Colorado River, but found no riches. His failure dampened Spanish interest in further exploration of the Southwest until the late 1570s, when Sir Francis Drake, representing Great Britain, sailed up the coasts of South and North Americas and captured millions of dollars in gold.

Spanish leaders felt torn. Preferring to avoid the financial costs of empire, especially if their colonies proved unprofitable, they feared what other powers (especially the English and Dutch) might do. One Spanish response emphasized religion. Spanish monarchs combined with the Catholic Church to build missions from Mexico south. Franciscan and

Jesuit friars sought to convert Natives to Catholicism, teach them trades, and ensure their loyalty to Spain. Their success varied: some Natives who accepted Catholicism viewed it as one of the many religions and beliefs they shared and incorporated their new trades into existing economic systems; all too often, soldiers helped missionaries force Natives to follow their religious and economic teachings, and word spread among these groups to avoid non-Natives or face dire consequences. The mission system's success depends on who evaluates it and where it occurred, but the Spanish Empire remained intact until revolutions spread from 1810 until 1822, creating several independent countries, including Mexico and Latin American republics.

Missionaries and Nevada

Spain had built presidios and missions north from Mexico City, but only up to Tucson. After failed expeditions in the late sixteenth and early seventeenth centuries, Spain banned exploration of California for more than 150 years. In the 1760s, though, a new official, José de Gálvez, sought to expand his country's presence there, partly to block possible Russian encroachment, partly because England had just won so much land—Canada and from the Appalachians to the Mississippi River—in the French and Indian War. Unable to spare enough soldiers, Gálvez turned to Franciscan priests. In 1769 Father Junípero Serra's arrival in San Diego to found the first of twenty-one California missions extending north past San Francisco marked Spain's attempt to exert control over the Pacific Coast and ultimately conquer the land and its people. An estimated twenty-one thousand Native Americans lived in California's missions by the early 1820s, but thousands of them also died of exposure to new diseases and work habits. In turn, while striking at the Natives' communal ways, Spanish and religious authorities benefited from recruiting them as laborers and defenders of the empire. Geographer D. W. Meinig has argued that even the most innocent white conquest proved not just military, but also cultural, economic, religious, and biological—as the missions demonstrated.

None of the priests appears to have entered present-day Nevada, but their travels and reports affected where future explorers journeyed and how they viewed the land and people they encountered. In 1776 Father Francisco Garcés explored the Mojave Desert. Many priests would remain at their missions, but not Garcés, who learned Native dialects and sought converts by living among tribes. Having already traveled with Colonel Juan Bautista de Anza, a Spanish colonial official exploring from Sonora, Mexico, to Yuma, Arizona, Garcés went up the Colorado. Then some of the Mohave led him east and west. On March 4 Garcés mapped his latitude and longitude, which, he calculated, showed that he had crossed modern Nevada's southern border. A better priest than surveyor, he probably reached Needles, California. But in joining the rest of his party along the Mojave River and on to Mission San Gabriel, Garcés helped establish what became the western end of the Old Spanish Trail to southern California. He continued exploring California until his death in 1781, when Yuma Indians retaliated against California soldiers who preyed upon them, killing Garcés and several others.

De Anza's earlier trek to Monterey, California, inspired Spanish officials to seek a northern route to that port. Garcés had hoped to reach it and sent a letter that arrived at the mission at Santa Fe, outlining his travels. One of his readers, Father Silvestre Velez de Escalante, also wanted to find a route to northern California and the Pacific Ocean. Escalante and Francisco Domínguez led a dozen men northwest from Santa Fe in pursuit of that goal. They left on July 29, 1776, and crossed western Colorado and part of Utah, receiving help along the way from the native Utes. In October they arrived near present-day Cedar City to find a blizzard. Fearing a hard winter and thinking themselves just due east of Monterey (they missed by more than six hundred miles), they turned south and crossed the Virgin River. They encountered cornfields and southern Paiutes, who provided them with nuts and berries that kept them from starving after their supplies ran out. Forced to eat their horses, they worked their way through Arizona and into New Mexico, returning to Santa Fe on January 2, 1777.

The Domínguez-Escalante expedition had a lasting effect on western exploration. Escalante's journals provided valuable information about the land and people between Santa Fe and the Wasatch Front, east of Great Salt Lake. So did the maps of Captain Bernardo Miera y Pacheco, whose work marked the first time anyone who had explored near the Great Basin tried to map it. But the party also produced misinformation. Because they knew nothing about the Great Basin or the idea of interior drainage, their map depicted the Green River, which flows from Wyoming through Utah and into the Colorado, as the San Buenaventura, extending to the Pacific. Other explorers and mapmakers had made similar errors; so would later ones, most notably Alexander von Humboldt, the river's namesake, and explorers Zebulon Pike and William Clark. Future explorers, unaware that they would have to cross the Great Basin Desert and the Sierra Nevada's snows to reach the Pacific, would learn how wrong—dead wrong—these maps proved to be. But these maps helped later explorers and conquerors further clarify the geography and resources and target strategic areas for colonization and exploitation.

The missionaries and soldiers assigned to California explored much of that area and gave many of its places their names, but apparently never reached Nevada. In 1819 some Mohave Indians attacked Mission San Buenaventura in present-day Ventura, California. Spanish officer and explorer Gabriel Moraga led a group east to try to find the Mohave and headed toward the Colorado River in pursuit. They seem to have fallen short of the Mohave and Nevada and returned home, suggesting the difficulty of penetrating such a vast desert area.

The Age of Revolution

As the Spanish roamed the lands surrounding Nevada in 1776, Americans declared their independence from England and fought the Revolution. Although Thomas Jefferson and Spanish missionaries acted separately, their actions reshaped the world map. They continued the trend that European imperial ambitions began: regional, national, and international events and developments affecting what went on in a comparatively limited area—the future state of Nevada.

For the United States, its early days proved challenging. Its revolution became a world war, with France and Spain allying with the Americans to avenge losses to England in previous wars—especially the French and Indian War, which cost France a jewel of its empire, Canada. The United States won, but only with much aid and by racking up large debts. Its first government, under the Articles of Confederation, gave too much power to the states, leaving the new nation unable to meet its financial obligations or defend itself properly and prompting a group of leaders to meet at Philadelphia in 1787 and produce the Constitution and a new government. With the country extending only from the Atlantic to the Mississippi and having a tiny army and no navy, European powers exploited that weakness.

In 1789 French citizens revolted against the nobles ruling them. As the French Revolution grew more violent and swung between radical and conservative, France became a dictatorship under Napoléon, who fought England and other European countries until 1815 and his final defeat, but not before a revolution in French-controlled Haiti upset his plans for power in the Western Hemisphere. Combined with his need to fund his army in Europe, that prompted him to sell Louisiana—not the existing state but the French province, which extended to the Rocky Mountains and the border with Canada—to the United States in 1803.

In addition to doubling the country's size, the acquisition affected what became Nevada. Curious about what lay within the former French territory, Thomas Jefferson sent his secretary Meriwether Lewis and General William Clark north and west to explore it. Between 1804 and 1806 they and their Corps of Discovery traveled to the Pacific, reporting on plants, animals, and people they met. Another expedition led by General Zebulon Pike in 1806–7 investigated the southern part of the Louisiana Purchase. Their adventures inspired interest in western lands and a generation of young Americans to dream of following in their footsteps.

American expansion did nothing to ease the tensions caused by the European war. Caught between France and England, the United States finally declared war on Great Britain in 1812. That war ended in a truce, but Americans felt otherwise. Their negotiators signed the peace treaty with England on Christmas Eve in 1814 in Belgium. As news traveled more slowly then, the two sides fought one more battle, at New Orleans on January 8, 1815. General Andrew Jackson's forces repelled a larger, more experienced British army. Because news of the war's end arrived about a month later, the timing convinced many Americans that England had surrendered, further boosting national morale.

The ends of these wars brought other changes. The War of 1812 had enhanced American manufacturing, and some returning soldiers found no jobs waiting for them. Peace reopened trade between previously warring nations, and the economy expanded. So did speculation, and American agriculture suffered from being unable to sell surpluses as Europe turned from fighting to growing its own food. The panic of 1819 prompted numerous bank failures, high unemployment, and a desire among some Americans to try something new.

While Americans concentrated on battles between the English and French, events to the south affected them. A wave of revolutions swept through Spain's Latin American colonies. None of them had a bigger impact on Americans than the Mexican War of Independence against Spain, which began in 1810 and ended with local rule triumphing in 1821. Only recently, the United States had broken from an empire and become a new, weak country unable at first to defend its outlying areas against attacks. Mexico would soon face a similar problem with the United States.

SUGGESTED READINGS

Blackhawk, Ned. *Violence over the Land: Indians and Empires in the Early American West.* Cambridge, MA: Harvard University Press, 2006.

Crum, Steven J. *The Road on Which We Came: A History of the Western Shoshone.* Salt Lake City: University of Utah Press, 1994.

Down, James F. *The Two Worlds of the Washo: An Indian Tribe of California and Nevada.* New York: Holt, Rinehart, and Winston, 1966.

Forbes, Jack D. *Native Americans of California and Nevada: A Handbook.* Healdsburg, CA: Naturegraph, 1969.

Fowler, Catherine S. *In the Shadow of Fox Peak: An Ethnography of the Cattail-Eater Northern Paiute People of Stillwater Marsh.* 1992. Reprint, Fallon: Nevada Humanities Committee, 2002.

Garate, Donald T. *Juan Bautista de Anza: Basque Explorer in the New World.* Reno: University of Nevada Press, 2003.

Harney, Corbin. *The Nature Way: Wisdom from a Western Shoshone Elder.* Reno: University of Nevada Press, 2009.

Hebner, William Logan. *Southern Paiute: A Portrait.* Logan: Utah State University Press, 2010.

Hittman, Michael. *Corbett Mack: The Life of a Northern Paiute.* Reno: University of Nevada Press, 2013.

Knack, Martha C. *Boundaries Between: The Southern Paiutes, 1775–1995.* Lincoln: University of Nebraska Press, 2001.

Knack, Martha C., and Omer C. Stewart. *As Long as the River Shall Run: An Ethnohistory of the Pyramid Lake Indian Reservation.* Reno: University of Nevada Press, 1999.

Makley, Matthew S., and Michael J. Makley. *Cave Rock: Climbers, Courts, and a Washoe Indian Sacred Place.* Reno: University of Nevada Press, 2010.

Meinig, D. W. *The Shaping of America: A Geographical Perspective on 500 Years of History.* Vol. 2, *Continental America, 1800–1867.* New Haven, CT: Yale University Press, 1993.

Roberts, David. *In Search of the Old Ones: Exploring the Anasazi World of the Southwest.* New York: Touchstone Books, 1996.

3

Explorers, Emigrants, and Expansion

The first half of the nineteenth century marked an age of American expansion. The United States extended its western border from the Mississippi River to the Pacific Ocean, and Americans began filling in the area. Industrial capitalism increasingly powered the economy, requiring raw materials and different workers than traditional artisans or craftsmen. The building of canals, railroads, and telegraph lines and other innovations demonstrated the young nation's scientific know-how and determination. Politically, more white adult males won the right to vote, and elections became ingrained in everyday life. New religious movements and a sense of national destiny reshaped how Americans saw themselves, their duties, and their future, breeding an era of reform that affected everything from the spread of slavery to women's role in society. These branches of nineteenth-century America came together in the trans-Mississippi West. When the century began, the region belonged to other countries, and Americans, motivated by nationalism and a desire for territorial and capitalist expansion, redrew the map.

The Quest for Fur

Few images have been more iconic than the fur trapper alone in the wilderness, antisocial, scruffy, battling elements and Native Americans, seeking only solitude and adventure. In reality, fur traders worked mainly in groups or parties, since failing to do so could be dangerous, sometimes fatal. Excitement mingled with drudgery on the trail. Every few months they met at the "rendezvous" to exchange furs for money and supplies, see old friends, and have fun—some of which Nevada would provide, legally and illegally, in the next century.

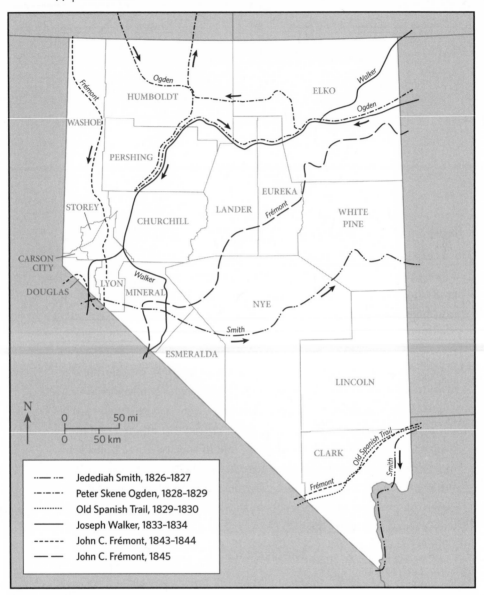

N

| | 0 | | 50 mi |
| 0 | | 50 km | |

---..--- Jedediah Smith, 1826–1827

---.-.--- Peter Skene Ogden, 1828–1829

············ Old Spanish Trail, 1829–1830

——— Joseph Walker, 1833–1834

- - - - John C. Frémont, 1843–1844

— — John C. Frémont, 1845

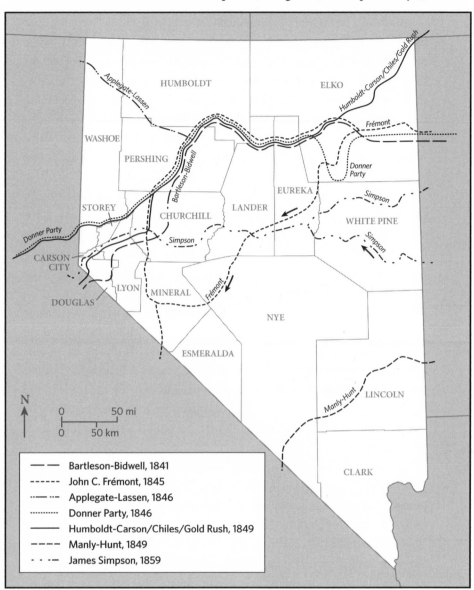

Explorer and emigrant trails

Above all, fur traders represented the capitalist ethos, trapping and trading fur as long as it remained profitable. Few became wealthy: some owned their own companies, but most worked on a salary or percentage basis. They also served as the advance guard of Manifest Destiny, the belief many Americans shared in their fate to control the continent. Detailing their encounters with (and contempt for) Mexicans and Native Americans encouraged public support for westward expansion. By taking Native American and Mexican women as wives or lovers, they helped shape the multiracial society that characterizes the West.

Nevada's role came late in the fur trade's history. In the seventeenth century, beaver pelts helped inspire French colonization of Canada, since their fur made warmer hats than the fur from other animals. The beaver's importance to English and American business grew when fur trading revived in the 1790s. John Jacob Astor, the first leading American fur-trade entrepreneur, made millions importing and exporting to Canada and as far away as China; his Fort Astoria in Oregon established American settlement on the Pacific Coast. The United States and Great Britain shared control of present-day Oregon and Washington, but in 1821 Hudson's Bay Company absorbed the North West Company to create a British fur-trading juggernaut. Until 1846 Hudson's Bay Company dominated the trade in the Pacific Northwest and surrounding regions under HBC chief executive Sir George Simpson and the chief factor or trader at Fort Vancouver, Dr. John McLoughlin.

The HBC dispatched the first non–Native Americans who explored present-day Nevada. One of its leading trappers, Peter Skene Ogden, joined it after the merger. Hotheaded and dogged, he became chief trader in the Snake River country. The HBC sent what one of its executives called "the very scum of the country and generally the outcasts" to that area, but Simpson wanted more trapping parties there in hopes of creating what historian William H. Goetzmann called "a fur desert" that would keep Americans out of the region. Ogden followed the Columbia River south in 1825 to the Snake in present-day Idaho. Along the way, he became the first known person of European descent to set foot in modern Nevada, near Denio, on the northwestern border with Oregon.

In 1828 Ogden's fifth major trip included a more substantive stop in present-day Nevada. After exploring around Great Salt Lake, he headed west, finding a river approximately where the Escalante party located the

San Buenaventura. Ogden called it the Unknown River, having never heard of it, and then Mary's River, but it became known as Ogden's River. John C. Frémont later named it the Humboldt River, and Ogden followed it to its sink, where it disappeared. Ogden's party then traveled south along the eastern Sierra Nevada into the Mojave Desert and to the Gulf of California, where Mohave Indians attacked them. Ogden lacked the scientific knowledge to grasp the Great Basin and its interior drainage, but he reported what he encountered: a harsh desert climate, few Mexicans, small bands of seemingly violent Native Americans, and American trappers annoying and interfering with British efforts to make money from fur in the Pacific Northwest.

Jedediah Smith and His Firsts

Similar reports came from Ogden's leading counterpart among American fur traders, Jedediah Smith. Born in 1799 in upstate New York, the devoutly Methodist Smith migrated west with his family to Pennsylvania and then Ohio. From an early age, especially after reading the journals of Lewis and Clark, he hoped to pursue adventure in the West. In 1822 he went to St. Louis, the jumping-off point for fur exploration in the Rocky Mountains. He took a job with the American Fur Company, run by William H. Ashley and Andrew Henry. Shrewd himself, Ashley created the "rendezvous" to bring goods and supplies to an agreed-upon location from company headquarters in St. Louis, reducing travel time and keeping his trappers in the wilderness, where they could find even more fur.

Demonstrating his abilities, Smith became captain of his own company of explorers and trappers within a year, having fought bravely in a battle with the Arikaras, a Great Plains tribe. From 1823 to 1825, he explored the Rockies south of Yellowstone, rediscovered the South Pass route through the range, trapped beaver along several rivers, and became Ashley's partner in the company. He demonstrated cunning: when some Native Americans raided a nearby HBC party, he asked for help to avoid a similar fate and gained information about his chief rival in the fur trade. He also learned the dangers of being a trapper: when he unwisely scouted alone, a grizzly knocked him down, broke several of his ribs, and nearly tore off his scalp and ear. Smith directed a friend to sew them back on, stunning his men—and those they told about it—with his bravery and calm.

In 1826 Smith and two other trappers bought out Ashley and decided to explore Mexican territory west of the Rockies. Smith led a party south along the Colorado. Entering present-day northeastern Clark County around Bunkerville, Smith and his men discovered the Muddy and Virgin Rivers, continued south into the Mojave Desert, and lost several men in a battle with the Mohave Indians. They reached Mission San Gabriel, whose priests helped the men recover from their journey; Smith later named Mount Joseph, now called the Sierra Nevada, for the mission's leader, Father José Bernardo Sánchez. Smith proved less happy with California's governor, José María Echeandía, who suspected the trapper of involvement in international intrigue and disliked foreign visitors profiting at Mexico's expense. Smith wanted permission to keep exploring. After stalling, Echeandía, tired of Smith's badgering, ordered him to go back the way he came.

Instead, Smith moved north through the San Joaquin Valley on what proved to be an incredible journey. He left most of his men and about fifteen hundred pounds of beaver fur in camp and climbed the Sierra Nevada with two trappers. First, they lost some of their animals to a late-springtime blizzard. They crossed present-day Nevada south of the Humboldt River, expecting to find the San Buenaventura. They found much desert and little water. They encountered Northern Paiutes, who, Smith feared, might massacre them, and whom he later accused of encouraging him to take the most difficult route. Near starvation and exhaustion, eventually resorting to eating their horses, they finally reached the rendezvous at Bear Lake, northeast of Great Salt Lake, and reported what they had seen and done.

Then they returned to collect the rest of their party and find more fur. Retracing their steps along the Colorado, they fought another battle with the Mohave, who killed ten of Smith's eighteen men and captured two women in the party. Smith's group made it to Mission San Gabriel, received more aid from Father Sánchez, and went north to retrieve the previous party. After Mexican officials ordered him to leave, Smith and his men ignored them—again—and hunted in the Sacramento Valley before going north to Oregon, where a fight with the Umpqua killed all but Smith and three others. They reached Fort Vancouver, where John McLoughlin and Hudson's Bay Company paid them for their fur in return for Smith's promise to concentrate his trapping east of the Rockies.

Smith never returned to the Far West. He and his partners sold the American Fur Company to another group of trappers, including Jim Bridger. Smith retired at the age of thirty-one and planned to publish his journals, but his desire to produce accurate maps and love for the trail drove him back to work. Scouting for supply wagons for his old firm, now known as the Rocky Mountain Fur Company, he went on alone. This time his mistake proved fatal: Comanches killed him sometime in May 1831 on the Santa Fe Trail.

In his short life, Jedediah Smith may have traveled more of today's American West than any of his contemporaries. Apparently the first American to enter Clark County and cross present-day Nevada, the first to travel overland to California and reach Oregon via that route, and the first to puncture the San Buenaventura myth, he discovered and pioneered trails. His reputation among other mountain men for honesty, modesty, and good relations with fellow fur traders and Native Americans enhanced his importance. His accounts of battles and troublesome Mexican officials encouraged western travelers to be cautious, perhaps even to shoot first and ask questions later. His maps provided the most accurate source of information about the regions in which he traveled. Although his writings remained unpublished for more than a century, what he did and thought became widely known among other trappers and western explorers and influenced the West's development, although no significant places in Nevada bear his name.

Trade on the Old Spanish Trail

Other capitalists besides fur traders hoped to profit in Mexican territory. A series of American and Mexican businessmen pioneered the Old Spanish Trail in search of their own profits, following roads and trails that Native Americans had used for many years. In 1829–30 fur merchant Ewing Young's expedition, which included Christopher "Kit" Carson, later a leading western scout, marked the first step toward publicizing that route, through the tip of southern Nevada.

Two other parties proved more crucial to the Old Spanish Trail's development. Late in 1829 trader Antonio Armijo led a party of sixty west from Abiquiu, about fifty miles northwest of Santa Fe, toward southern California, hoping to trade blankets and serapes for horses and mules. After the group entered present-day southern Nevada near Smith's entry point, several rode ahead. One scout, Rafael Rivera, continued and apparently traveled south on the Colorado River before rejoining Armijo's group at the mouth of the Las Vegas Wash, from which they headed through present-day Green Valley. They established the Old Spanish Trail's northern branch. William Wolfskill and George Yount led a fur-trapping brigade that completed the southern branch begun by Father Garcés by traveling from Santa Fe to Los Angeles by way of Needles, California, just south of Nevada.

While Wolfskill and Yount made their mark in other ways—Wolfskill as a Los Angeles landowner, Yount as the Napa Valley's first Euro-American settler—their part of the Old Spanish Trail attracted more travelers than the northern portion. Las Vegas had more water and grass than Needles, enhancing its appeal to horse thieves. In 1840 hundreds of horses came through the Las Vegas valley in a raid led by the Ute chief Walkara and fur trappers Bill Williams, James Beckwourth, and Thomas "Pegleg" Smith. However, the trail proved hospitable to others: in 1841 John Rowland and William Workman herded sheep from Santa Fe through Las Vegas to Mission San Gabriel and developed several ranches in southern California; they made the trip in two months but marveled at the trail's bleakness.

Government Explorers: Bonneville and Walker

The adventures of Ogden and Smith coincided with the rise of Andrew Jackson and the Democratic Party. Jackson and his followers practiced a nationalism that encouraged federal promotion of individual entrepreneurship. Not only did they protect slavery and help it expand, but they also advocated removing Native Americans from their homes in the Southeast—thus the "Trail of Tears" to modern-day Oklahoma. Believers in expansion and Manifest Destiny, they sought to plant the American flag beyond their country's borders, and possibly extend those borders to reach the places where they put the flag.

While trappers like Ogden and Smith worked for private enterprises that sometimes enjoyed government aid, future explorers who affected Nevada labored for the federal government. One group combined the public and private: a fur-trapping party led by Captain Benjamin Louis Eulalie de Bonneville. In 1831 the French-born West Point graduate received a two-year leave of absence, reportedly to trap for fur but actually to investigate the Oregon Country that the United States shared with Great Britain. He hired fur trader Joseph Walker as a scout and sent Walker southeast from the Snake River toward Great Salt Lake. They hoped to find an overland route to California and perhaps determine the degree of Mexican settlement and influence west of the Rockies.

Walker's party affected the future of Nevada and the West. He and his men followed the Humboldt (Ogden's) River west to its sink. A group of Northern Paiutes came to meet with Walker, who refused to let them enter the camp and built fortifications. When they returned a few days later, Walker ordered his men to fire, and at least thirty-nine Northern Paiutes died, in the process convincing many Native Americans that the white intruders meant harm. Walker and his men plowed onward through the northern Sierra Nevada, later part of the trail to the Gold Rush, and into California. Returning, they skirmished again with Native Americans, killing fourteen at the Humboldt Sink before rejoining Bonneville in the Bear River Valley in present-day northern Utah.

The Bonneville-Walker trek had a lasting impact. Walker mapped a route to California and added to the already troubled Native-white relations (although he stayed in the area to trap and married a Shoshone). Bonneville confirmed British control of Oregon and the lack of Mexican influence through much of that nation's territory—valuable news for Americans thinking of extending their country's boundaries. This party became one of the West's more famous trapping brigades, thanks to a meeting between Bonneville and Washington Irving. The creator of such characters as Ichabod Crane and Rip Van Winkle, Irving bought the officer's papers and wrote *The Adventures of Captain Bonneville*.

John C. Frémont, Nevada, and Manifest Destiny

Although others spread tales of adventure, no one did more to popularize the West in his time than John Charles Frémont. First called the Great Pathfinder, he became known as the Great Pathmarker to distinguish between the discoveries and discoverers preceding him and because of his skill at mapmaking and promoting himself and the lands west to the Pacific. Like his predecessors in the West, he excited interest in traveling to and acquiring the land. Entrepreneurial in his own right, he sought to serve the government, pursue adventure, and encourage westward expansion.

Frémont's life included ample adventure long before he headed into Mexican territory. Born in Georgia in 1813 to the young widow of a Virginia planter and a French tutor with whom she had an affair, Frémont

John C. Frémont, then a major general in the Union army during the Civil War. At the time Nevada, the place he put on the map in the 1840s, had just become a territory. Courtesy of the Library of Congress.

grew up in South Carolina. He entered the US Army and became an officer in its Topographical Corps, joining Jean Nicollet on explorations between the upper Mississippi and Missouri Rivers. In Washington, DC, to help Nicollet with his reports, Frémont met Jessie Benton, the sixteen-year-old daughter of Senator Thomas Hart Benton, a powerful Missouri Democrat and an exponent of Manifest Destiny. He objected to their marriage but then helped his new son-in-law win a promotion to captain, command of a unit, and funding from Congress for several mapmaking expeditions into Mexican territory. The Topographical Corps sent Frémont west to lead those explorations and promote Benton's goal of obtaining the land for the United States.

Although Frémont headed four surveys into the West between 1842 and 1853, his second and third trips proved the most important to Nevada. Diverting from the Oregon Trail in 1843, he went south and east into the Great Basin, which he named in recognition of its interior drainage. With a knowledgeable party that included guides Kit Carson and Thomas "Broken Hand" Fitzpatrick as well as surveyor and mapmaker Charles Preuss, Frémont reached Nevada's northwest corner just before Christmas (to celebrate, his men fired the howitzer they brought with them). He found a large lake and named it for a large rock in the middle that reminded him of the Great Pyramid of Cheops. Following what he called the Salmon-Trout River (later the Truckee) for its forty-pound Lahontan cut-throat trout, he camped along the river he would name for Carson and planned to cross the Sierra Nevada.

Crossing the mountains in winter took a toll on Frémont and his men. They abandoned their cannon and ate their dog and mules to survive. On Valentine's Day Frémont and Preuss looked north from Red Lake Peak and became the first Euro-Americans to see Lake Tahoe, North America's largest alpine lake and second only to Crater Lake as America's deepest lake. After reaching Sutter's ranch, they headed south, met the Old Spanish Trail, and traveled northeast to a desert oasis the Spanish called "the Meadows," or Las Vegas. They arrived on May 2, 1844, and bathed in the springs, which Frémont found too warm—at seventy-two degrees—to drink. Frémont and his party went northeast, approximating today's Interstate 15, into present-day southern Utah and then began the long trek back east.

Frémont's account of his travels, like that of his first trip, proved influential. He identified Las Vegas officially on an American map and named a nearby peak Mount Charleston, for the South Carolina city where he grew up. With Preuss's maps he described and explained the Great Basin and why interior drainage made it impossible to find an east–west river route from the Rockies to the Pacific. He named the Humboldt River for the German geographer and other landmarks for his guides: Walker River and Lake as well as Carson River and Pass.

Frémont returned to Nevada twice. In 1845, apparently with secret orders to take California from Mexico if the opportunity presented itself, Frémont split his party. Theodore Talbot commanded and Walker scouted for the group that crossed the Ruby Mountains in modern Elko County; they remained south of the Humboldt River, crossing Diamond Valley and south along the Toiyabe Range through Big Smoky Valley to meet the rest at Walker Lake before going on to California. On his last trip, in 1853, after the United States acquired the area, Frémont traveled only in present-day southern Nevada, crossing approximately from Pioche to Beatty.

Frémont remained prominent in American history, but even more so in western history. His trips produced the Southwest's most accurate maps to that time. His well-written reports guided emigrants and inspired further interest in the West that promoted Manifest Destiny and the acquisition of Mexican lands in the 1840s. Later, he became one of the first US senators from California, the Republican Party's first presidential candidate in 1856, and a controversial Civil War general. He never matched his earlier fame and importance, but he left an important legacy.

Travelers on the Trails

By the late 1830s, with the new regions explored in the past two decades largely cleared of beaver, the fur trade declined, and trappers needed new ways to survive and profit. They found work as scouts for parties of Americans headed to Oregon, which the United States shared with Great Britain, and California, where new arrivals alarmed Mexican officials concerned about American designs on the region. What attracted the emigrants to new areas depended on the group, but they shared characteristics with those who settled the original colonies on the East Coast and then moved inland: a desire for religious freedom as well as converts or new economic opportunities in land, trade with Asia or South America, and mining. Whatever their motivations, they found the road west long, hard, and sometimes deadly.

The Western Emigration Society, formed in 1840, promised to lead a group to California's Central Valley, but only sixty-nine showed up at the appointed date in Independence, Missouri. John Bidwell, then only twenty-one, organized the party for the two-thousand-mile trip with John Bartleson, who demanded to be named captain. Fortunately, they ran into Jesuit missionaries who had hired trapper and scout Broken Hand Fitzpatrick to guide them to Oregon. North of Great Salt Lake, the Jesuits headed off, with half of the Bartleson-Bidwell party joining them.

The two leaders led the rest toward California, including Nancy Kelsey and her daughter, the first Euro-American woman and child to cross the Great Basin. After struggling through the eastern Great Basin desert, they welcomed the sight of Pilot Peak in present-day Elko County, but the trail became no easier as they pushed west. With few horses in the party, most walked, shedding belongings to lighten the wagons and ease the burden on the oxen. Dissatisfied with the pace, Bartleson led away several men who wound up wandering in the desert, where Northern Paiutes saved them by giving them fish and pine nuts. They made their way back to Bidwell's group, which survived the Forty-Mile Desert between the Humboldt and Carson Rivers, and crossed the Sierra Nevada into California. His success in heading west had been due mostly to luck and reliance on others, but Bidwell founded Chico, California, and entered state politics.

The news of the Bartleson-Bidwell party's safe arrival in California—more important, without loss of life—spread back east and inspired others to follow. In 1843 Joseph Chiles, who came west with Bartleson and Bidwell, returned to Missouri, hired Joseph Walker as a scout, and headed back with the first of seven wagon trains of emigrants he brought west. Walker led them along the Humboldt and Walker Rivers and over Walker Pass, but they had to sacrifice most of the belongings that Chiles had told them they could safely take. The Humboldt Trail proved popular with emigrants, including the 1844 party led by Elisha Stevens, John Townsend, and Martin Murphy, who hired scout Caleb Greenwood, a mountain man in his eighties. They avoided going from the Humboldt Sink south to the Carson or Walker, crossing the Forty-Mile Desert to the Salmon-Trout River. Because the nearby Northern Paiute leader helped them, they named it in his honor as the Truckee River. They, too, arrived safely.

Other Trails, Other Dangers

The trails these emigrants and explorers produced led to alternative routes. Two parties developed cutoffs to California and Oregon. Encouraged by Oregon authorities, Jesse and Lindsay Applegate found a route to the Northwest from the Humboldt River, near the modern Rye Patch Reservoir. Peter Lassen took a similar approach but turned off farther west, leading a wagon train through the Black Rock Desert into California. Lassen's route added two hundred miles to the distance required in following the Carson and Truckee Rivers and made the trip more difficult for the emigrants he hoped to attract to California's Central Valley.

Other parties proved less fortunate and less organized. Lansford Hastings published a guidebook promising an easy trip to California that included misinformation about a cutoff in the northeastern Great Basin. In 1846 he agreed to lead eighty-seven emigrants west, but abandoned them on the trail. They traveled from Missouri across the Rockies, alone through the Bonneville Salt Flats and Ruby Mountains, and through hot weather along the Humboldt. The journey's length and their lack of preparation caused problems: one member of the party murdered another, others fought among themselves, and Native Americans harassed them. They made it across the Forty-Mile Desert and recovered in the Truckee Meadows.

Then the group made the mistake that gave its members their name. They climbed into the upper Truckee Canyon in October. The snows began, trapping them at Donner Lake, where they survived the winter in part by eating animals, shoe leather, and in a few cases human remains (they killed no one for food) before rescuers arrived from California. Forty-seven of them survived the trip, which became legendary: reports of the Donner Party's woes prompted a decline in westward emigration until the Gold Rush two years later and inspired Charlie Chaplin's classic *The Gold Rush* (1925), in which he eats a shoe to survive.

Another emigrant group shared the Donner Party's association with death. In 1849 William Lewis Manly and Jefferson Hunt led 107 wagons along the Old Spanish Trail in southern Utah and then split up. Hunt took seven wagons through Las Vegas to southern California. Manly's group headed west, reached Beaver Dam Canyon in present-day Lincoln County, and traversed the Meadow Valley Wash into the Mojave Desert before encountering an area they named Death Valley, but that overstated the case. Despite their hardships, including near starvation, only one member of the party died.

The Mormon Migration

The most important group of westward migrants in this period belonged to the Church of Jesus Christ of Latter-day Saints (LDS), or Mormons. They originated as part of the Second Great Awakening, a nineteenth-century revival movement that spawned many religious groups, some of them offshoots of Protestant sects, others unique. While some believed in pre-destination, the Second Great Awakening's ministers advocated the idea of "heaven on earth" and people shaping their world. These beliefs helped expand or inspire reform movements that remain well known or still rever-berate across society—abolitionism, temperance, and women's rights, for example. Others tend to be forgotten or misunderstood, most notably uto-pian socialism, the idea of a group coming together to construct a model society of its own. Combining these varied strands into a whole, the Mor-mon Church long since outlasted other organizations owing their origins to the Second Great Awakening.

The Mormon Church can trace its beginnings to upstate New York in the 1820s. According to Joseph Smith, a Vermont-born farm boy, the angel Moroni led him to golden plates that, when transcribed, told the story of true belief. Smith formed his church in Palmyra, New York, in 1830 with six members. Thus began a success story that inspired controversy, movement, and a reputation for Smith among his followers as a prophet and among his critics as a con artist. Within a year church membership jumped to one hundred, and Smith moved the Mormons to Kirtland, Ohio. They left there in 1838: the recent panic of 1837 hurt others in the area more than it harmed Mormons, creating jealousy among an already suspicious public, while the church lost enough money to incline Smith to seek a change of scenery. They went to Missouri, where residents attacked them physically over their religious and antislavery views and accused Smith in particular of promot-ing an insurrection.

Mormons moved on to Nauvoo in southern Illinois. There they pros-pered, erecting a temple and a village that resembled a New England town surrounded by farms. But Smith took two controversial steps: he sup-ported polygamy, or plural marriage, which encouraged Mormon men to take more than one wife, and declared that he would run for president in 1844 and support federally compensated emancipation. When a newspaper criticized Smith, he and the city council ordered its press destroyed, then a more common occurrence: in 1837 an anti-abolitionist mob destroyed a press and killed editor Elijah Lovejoy in Alton, about 150 miles away. Imprisoned on charges of treason after declaring martial law, Smith awaited his trial in a jail in nearby Carthage, where a mob attacked and killed him and his brother Hyrum in June 1844.

With the church divided over picking Smith's successor, Brigham Young took charge. As senior member of the Quorum of the Twelve Apostles, already known as a hard worker and master organizer, he argued that Smith viewed apostles as equal to the church president. He decided that the church would be safer beyond American borders. In 1846 he began the exodus from Illinois to the Great Basin along what became known as the Mormon Trail or Emigrant Trail, which included parts of the roads to Oregon and California. Using trappers' reports as guides, and relying in part on Frémont's account of his travels, Young led the "Vanguard Company," the first missionaries who arrived in Salt Lake Valley in July 1847. The migration of Mormons would continue along this route, often with handcarts carrying provisions, until the transcontinental railroad's completion in 1869.

By then Young had established several principles. One placed settlements near water, a scarcity in the Great Basin. Another promoted self-sufficiency, prompting colonization throughout modern Utah and Nevada in hopes of finding resources or profits. Members of the Mormon Battalion, a unit that served in the Mexican-American War, proved important in creating new towns whose names reflected Young's hopes for them— Bountiful, for one, and the county surrounding Cedar City became Iron County, since Jefferson Hunt's report on the region encouraged Mormons to mine there. Seeking an outlet to the Pacific Ocean and southern California, Young plotted missions and settlements from Salt Lake to San Bernardino, approximating today's Interstate 15. He planned to do all this far from the US and Mexican governments. As it turned out, what he tried to escape proved impossible to avoid, thanks to forces beyond his control.

The Politics of Expansion

Andrew Jackson's election in 1828 and subsequent policies led to the rise of the Democratic Party, which backed states' rights, individual freedom, and territorial expansion. Their opponents, the Whigs, sought an activist federal government with a central banking system, tariffs favorable to domestic industry, and the building of roads and canals. Democrats usually triumphed, due largely to the popularity of their views, party unity, and knack for knowing how to campaign to and for the common man. In 1844 Jackson's protégé, James Polk, defeated Whig icon Henry Clay, who tried to avoid an offensive position on the growth of slavery. Polk emphasized national expansion, whatever the impact on slavery.

First, Polk wanted Texas. Settled in the 1820s by Stephen Austin's family and other pioneers, Texas became American enough to win independence from Mexico in 1836, but Mexico refused to acknowledge losing its northern territory. Southerners worried that England might extend its empire south from Canada: since England had just abolished slavery throughout its empire, a free Texas could be a haven for runaway slaves and encourage abolitionism. Because American settlers brought slaves, northerners feared Texas would be a slave state, upsetting the balance between slave and free states and giving the South an advantage in Congress. Thus, many northerners opposed adding Texas while southerners wanted more slave territory, some politicians in both regions hoped to avoid the issue, and others saw opportunity for themselves and the nation in adding the area. Two days before Polk took office, the Senate approved the annexation of Texas.

Polk's campaign advocated taking the Oregon Country from Great Britain. Although Hudson's Bay Company ruled the fur trade with McLoughlin's iron fist, Americans had been emigrating to the Oregon Country in larger numbers for a decade. In 1844 Democrats proclaimed "Fifty-four forty or fight," referring to the line through Canada that marked Oregon's northern boundary. In negotiations Polk's administration settled for the forty-ninth parallel, just north of present-day Seattle. Without firing a shot, the United States acquired all of Washington and Oregon and part of present-day Idaho.

California and War

As the Oregon issue wound down, Polk turned his attention to California. Like most of his countrymen, Polk had no doubt that Americans would be more enterprising than the Mexicans and Native Americans in California. He offered thirty million dollars for the area, outraging Mexico's government—whose refusal to sell outraged Polk. Not only had Mexico become divided—Texas won its independence during what many historians have called a Mexican civil war—but Polk also thought too little of

Mexico to understand why a country would refuse to sell a significant portion of its territory.

A boundary dispute between the new American state of Texas and Mexico lit the fuse. The United States dispatched troops to land between the Nueces and Rio Grande, which both countries claimed. A skirmish killed eleven Americans and prompted Polk to ask Congress to approve war measures, announcing, "American blood has been shed on American soil." Congress split largely along party lines, with Polk's fellow Democrats standing by him and the skeptical Whig opposition voting no.

Between April 1846 and the Treaty of Guadalupe Hidalgo's signing on February 2, 1848, the United States defeated Mexico and acquired more than a third of that country—five hundred thousand square miles, including all or part of today's California, Arizona, Utah, New Mexico, Wyoming, Colorado, and Nevada. But achieving what so many considered the nation's Manifest Destiny came at a price. Mexicans and Native Americans living in the newly acquired territory faced consequences, many of them unpleasant. Congress fought over the Wilmot Proviso, named for David Wilmot, the congressman who introduced it. The measure said none of the land acquired in the war could contain slavery. Southerners and their northern allies kept it from passing. Nonetheless, the slavery issue soon would change the United States forever, and Nevada would feel the storm's havoc and benefits.

SUGGESTED READINGS

Arrington, Leonard. *Brigham Young: American Moses.* New York: Alfred A. Knopf, 1985.

Arrington, Leonard J., and Davis Bitton. *The Mormon Experience: A History of the Latter-Day Saints.* Urbana: University of Illinois Press, 1992.

Barbour, Barton H. *Jedediah Smith: No Ordinary Mountain Man.* Norman: University of Oklahoma Press, 2009.

Bringhurst, Newell G. *Brigham Young and the Making of the American Frontier.* New York: Little, Brown, 1986.

Bushman, Richard L. *Joseph Smith and the Beginnings of Mormonism.* Urbana: University of Illinois Press, 1984.

Bushman, Richard L., and Jed Woodworth. *Joseph Smith: Rough Stone Rolling.* New York: Alfred A. Knopf, 2005.

Chaffin, Tom. *Pathfinder: John Charles Frémont and the Course of American Empire.* New York: Hill and Wang, 2002.

Cline, Gloria Griffen. *Exploring the Great Basin.* Reno: University of Nevada Press, 1988.

———. *Peter Skene Ogden and the Hudson's Bay Company.* Norman: University of Oklahoma Press, 1974.

Curran, Harold. *Fearful Crossing: The Central Overland Trail Through Nevada.* Reno: Great Basin Press, 1983.

Denton, Sally. *Faith and Betrayal: A Pioneer Woman's Passage Through the American West.* New York: Alfred A. Knopf, 2005.

———. *Passion and Principle: John and Jessie Frémont, the Couple Whose Power, Politics, and Love Shaped Nineteenth-Century America.* New York: Bloomsbury, 2007.

DeVoto, Bernard. *The Year of Decision: 1846.* Boston: Little, Brown, 1943.

Dolin, Eric Jay. *Fur, Fortune, and Empire: The Epic History of the Fur Trade in America.* New York: W. W. Norton, 2010.

Egan, Ferol. *Frémont: Explorer for a Restless Nation.* Reno: University of Nevada Press, 1985.

Elliott, J. H. *Empires of the Atlantic World: Britain and Spain in America, 1492–1830.* New Haven, CT: Yale University Press, 2006.

Faragher, John Mack. *Women and Men on the Overland Trail.* New Haven, CT: Yale University Press, 1979.

Gilbert, Bil. *Westering Man: The Life of Joseph Walker.* New York: Atheneum, 1983.

Goetzmann, William H. *Exploration and Empire: The Explorer and the Scientist in the Winning of the American West.* New York: Alfred A. Knopf, 1966.

———. *New Lands, New Men: America and the Second Great Age of Discovery.* New York: Viking, 1986.

Hafen, LeRoy R., and Ann W. Hafen. *Old Spanish Trail: Santa Fe to Los Angeles.* Glendale, CA: Arthur H. Clark, 1954.

Hardesty, Donald L., et al. *The Archaeology of the Donner Party.* Reno: University of Nevada Press, 1997.

Horsman, Reginald. *Feast or Famine: Food and Drink in American Westward Expansion.* Columbia: University of Missouri Press, 2008.

Howard, Thomas F. *Sierra Crossing: First Roads to California.* Berkeley: University of California Press, 1998.

Lyman, Edward Leo. *The Overland Journey from Utah to California: Wagon Travel from the City of Saints to the City of Angels.* Reno: University of Nevada Press, 2004.

Moore, James Gregory. *King of the 40th Parallel: Discovery in the American West.* Stanford, CA: Stanford General Books, 2006.

Morgan, Dale L. *The Humboldt: High Road of the West.* New York: Farrar & Rinehart, 1971.

———. *Jedediah Smith and the Opening of the West.* Lincoln: University of Nebraska Press, 1953.

Mullen, Frank X., Jr. *The Donner Party Chronicles: A Day-by-Day Account of a Doomed Wagon Train, 1846–1847.* Reno: Nevada Humanities, 1997.

Rarick, Ethan. *Desperate Passage: The Donner Party's Perilous Journey West.* New York: Oxford University Press, 2008.

Reid, John Phillip. *Law for the Elephant: Property and Social Behavior on the Overland Trail.* San Marino, CA: Huntington Library Press, 1980.

———. *Policing the Elephant: Crime, Punishment, and Social Behavior on the Overland Trail.* San Marino, CA: Huntington Library Press, 1997.

Roberts, David. *A Newer World: Kit Carson, John C. Frémont, and the Claiming of the American West.* New York: Simon and Schuster, 2000.

Sánchez, Joseph P. *Explorers, Traders, and Slavers: Forging the Old Spanish Trail, 1678–1850.* Salt Lake City: University of Utah Press, 1997.

Steiner, Harold Austin. *The Old Spanish Trail Across the Mojave Desert: A History and Guide.* Las Vegas: Haldor, 1999.

Stewart, George R. *Ordeal by Hunger: The Story of the Donner Party.* 1960. Reprint, Boston: Houghton Mifflin, 1988.

Unruh, John D., Jr. *The Plains Across: The Overland Emigrants and the Trans-Mississippi West, 1840–1860.* Urbana: University of Illinois Press, 1979.

Utley, Robert M. *A Life Wild and Perilous: Mountain Men and the Paths to the Pacific.* New York: Henry Holt, 1998.

Weber, David J. *The Spanish Frontier in North America.* New Haven, CT: Yale University Press, 1992.

Wilson, Elinor. *Jim Beckwourth, Black Mountain Man and War Chief of the Crows.* Norman: University of Oklahoma Press, 1988.

Worster, Donald. *A River Running West: The Life of John Wesley Powell.* New York: Oxford University Press, 2001.

4

Building Up to a Crisis

"**H**indsight, the historian's chief asset and his main liability, has enabled all historical writers to know that the decade of the fifties terminated in a great civil war. . . . Seen this way, the decade of the fifties becomes a kind of vortex, whirling the country in ever narrower circles and more rapid revolutions into the pit of war," David Potter wrote in his Pulitzer Prize–winning *The Impending Crisis, 1848–1861*. Nevada became part of that vortex and faced local issues reminiscent of the sectional tensions plaguing the country. North and South differed strongly over slavery and its ramifications—and even divided among themselves. From 1848, when the Mexican-American War added it to the United States, until the Civil War broke out, what we now know as Nevada endured differences between and within distinct cultures. As with the Civil War, violence and change ensued.

The Dividing of America

While 1776 proved important for the new United States and Spanish explorers circling outside Nevada, 1848 became a worldwide year of revolution. Uprisings against dictatorial governments spread through Europe. Women's rights advocates met at Seneca Falls, New York, and issued a declaration of rights that described all men and women as created equal. The debate over slavery split some Democrats and Whigs from their traditional parties and drove them into the new Free-Soil Party, which called for stopping slavery from spreading into new territories—as in those acquired in the recent war. That land required some form of government, thanks to the thousands flocking to northern California after the discovery of gold—an event with revolutionary social, economic, and political effects.

Northerners and Southerners split by region (and in their regions) over whether that government should ban slavery. By 1850 California's population had grown enough to justify skipping territorial status and becoming a state. Congress passed the Compromise of 1850, including statehood for California, giving free states a numerical advantage over slave states, and a tougher Fugitive Slave Law that many Northerners found objectionable. The measure also created two territories: Utah, including all of Nevada north of Clark and southern Nye County and extending east to Wyoming, and New Mexico, which also included Arizona and southern Nevada. The residents would decide the future of slavery in these territories, but due to their anti-Mormon sentiments, few Northerners expected Utah to achieve statehood. If New Mexico grew, they reasoned, it would fill with Texans bringing their slaves, benefiting the South (they reasoned incorrectly: in 1890 Mormon Church leader Wilford Woodruff issued a manifesto disavowing polygamy, and Utah became a state in 1896, with New Mexico following in 1912).

The Compromise of 1850 only briefly eased tensions. Senator Stephen Douglas of Illinois wanted a railroad built from Chicago to the Pacific Ocean. In 1854 his Kansas-Nebraska Act allowed the two territories to vote on whether to permit slavery and repealed the Missouri Compromise of 1820, which banned slavery that far north. This issue divided Democrats and destroyed the Whig Party; antislavery Democrats and many Northern Whigs formed the Republican Party, which opposed the expansion of slavery. When Kansans fought over a proposed proslavery state constitution, the area became known as "Bleeding Kansas," culminating with abolitionist John Brown and his allies massacring a proslavery family and making Congress wary of creating any states or territories.

In 1860 seven slave states seceded from the Union in response to Republican Abraham Lincoln's election as president. Less than six weeks after Lincoln took office, Confederate States of America forces fired on Union troops in Fort Sumter in the harbor of Charleston, South Carolina, beginning the Civil War. Over the next four years, the nation's bloodiest war revolutionized American life. The need for supplies and weapons sped and improved industrialization. Americans who had never before met anyone beyond their farm or town encountered different people and places. The federal government's size and powers expanded. Three new amendments to the United States Constitution, including one freeing four million slaves, redefined civil rights. The war and its aftermath—efforts to reconstruct the South, the economic and social dislocation the war caused—inspired Northerners and Southerners alike to migrate westward. So did the prospect of greater wealth.

Winning the West: The Gold Rush

On January 24, 1848, nine days before the war ended, James Marshall found gold specks in the water as he built a mill for John Sutter, a Swiss immigrant and dominant economic force in the Sacramento area. Months passed as news traveled back across the country and by boat from San Francisco to the East Coast, inspiring an exodus of Americans and immigrants known as Forty-Niners for the year many of them reached California. Although the United States had just grown from coast to coast, its population hop-scotched from the Mississippi to the Pacific, with Mormons in between at Great Salt Lake. With the country expanding westward, settlement would radiate eastward from northern California.

The Forty-Niners traveled by three main routes, two by ship: around the tip of South America, potentially a nine-month trip, or across the Isthmus of Panama before a canal reduced the journey. While these methods appealed to families and entrepreneurs moving substantial belongings to the Far West, the overland route to California attracted aspiring gold miners out to get rich quick. But the California Trail crossed the Great Basin. Between Salt Lake and the Sierra Nevada, they found little water, much desert, few fellow whites, and hundreds of Native Americans who wished to be left alone and reacted when emigrants failed to do so.

Like earlier trappers and emigrants, most travelers viewed the Great Basin as a desert to be avoided or crossed quickly. The Forty-Mile Desert from the Humboldt Sink to the Carson River became infamous as a graveyard of wagons, animals, and personal possessions as travelers struggled across the great distance without water and vegetation. Then came the forbidding Sierra Nevada, with stories of the Donner Party making the trip even more nerve-wracking. Of the estimated one hundred thousand who navigated the California Trail in 1849, more than half trekked through the Great Basin, but left few signs that they enjoyed it.

Creating a Mining Culture

Upon arriving in California's goldfields, some stayed to dig and pan, but thousands went on to Sacramento and San Francisco. While the foundation of both cities rested on the ore that funded their rapid expansion, these urban areas and others also provided the foundation for the mining industry. Miners relied on them for supplies, recreational services ranging from sports and parks to gambling and prostitution, and such signs of civilization as churches, schools, newspapers, and businesses like stores and law offices—all requiring employees who benefited from nearby miners and their gold. Originally lacking a legal community outside the growing cities, gold seekers imposed vigilante justice, appointed a recorder of claims and discoveries, and adopted laws allowing miners to follow claims to their conclusion—actions emulated in future rushes. Technologically less creative, the Californians who panned, dug, blasted rocks with water, and built "Long Toms" and sluices to separate gold dust from dirt and water had no idea that they extracted and processed ore as Greece had done two thousand years before.

The Gold Rush had an international impact. It boosted world economies after significant downturns and increased the US role in international financial affairs. It drew immigrants from East and West: mining companies looked to Cornwall in the United Kingdom because the Cornish had vast experience as hard-rock miners, and the Chinese entered mining-related industries after leaving their war-torn land for the United States; that some came as indentured servants to Chinese merchants angered others working in the goldfields, worsening anti-Chinese sentiment that continued into the twentieth century. Immigrants already arriving in the United States headed west, including a large percentage of the more than one million Irish who had just come to the East Coast to escape the potato blight. Large numbers of these groups ended up migrating east of the Sierra Nevada after the Comstock's discovery.

Known as the Mother Lode, the Gold Rush birthed future rushes and, indeed, the nineteenth-century West. Mining booms like those in Nevada resembled northern California's: quick wealth for some and the need for greater and broader capital investment; the development of industries to serve miners, including nearby ranches and farms; and tent towns, all of which disappeared within years or even months if the ore did or gradually became more permanent and civilized, with mutually dependent towns and hinterland. This evolution meant wooden and then brick buildings, a mostly male population of miners being joined by women and children seeking to build a community, and advances in technology to reach deeper into the earth or remove ore more quickly. Those advances required more

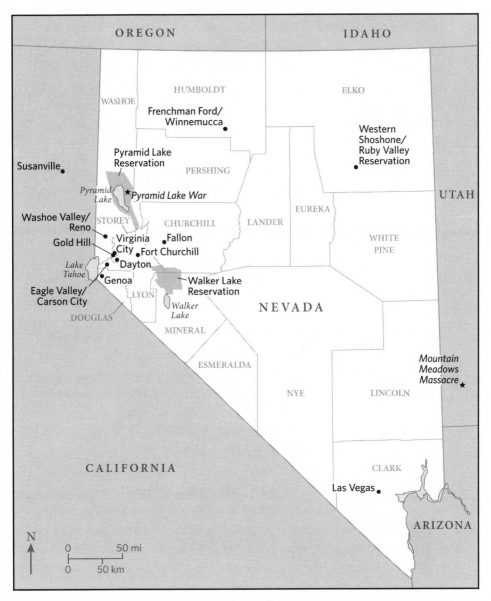

Early Nevada

money than the average miner had, leading to the rise of corporations with the capital, time, and employees to produce more material at greater profits.

The Gold Rush shaped the West's development in other ways. In the 1860s Leland Stanford, Collis Huntington, Mark Hopkins, and Charles Crocker came together as partners to build the Central Pacific portion of the transcontinental railroad. Each of them had earned considerable wealth, not as hard-rock miners working with picks and shovels, but as merchants and investors in Sacramento and the area surrounding the Gold Rush. Their railroad became central to expanding the West's wealth and population, and controlling its politics and government, for the rest of the nineteenth century. They also built or boosted towns along the route—just as the need for services on the road to the Gold Rush inspired entrepreneurs to meet those needs with trading posts and settlements.

The First Settlement(s)

Nevada's first gold discovery occurred in the spring of 1849. A group headed to the Gold Rush waited in the eastern Sierra Nevada foothills for the snow to melt. Camped at Gold Canyon, in present-day Dayton, they prospected in Gold Creek, which feeds into the Carson River. There, Abner Blackburn, a veteran of the Mormon Battalion in the Mexican-American War, used a bread pan and butcher knife to dig up gold and estimated that others in his party found ten dollars' worth. By May 1851 a California-bound emigrant reported about 200 miners prospecting in the area. What happened in Gold Canyon in the intervening two years remains uncertain; other travelers said they made the first gold discovery. But the presence of miners as of 1849 prompted Dayton's claim as Nevada's first settlement.

Blackburn had ties to the other claimant. On April 18, 1850, after returning to Salt Lake, he joined a party of about 80 led by Captain Joseph DeMont and clerk Hampton S. Beatie. As they crossed the Great Basin en route to California, Blackburn said, "The emegrants [sic] began to overtake us and said thousands and thousands were on the road." The party saw the potential in a trading post—much as other Gold Rush arrivals pursued profits by supplying miners rather than joining them in the goldfields. With his knowledge of the area, Blackburn chose to locate Mormon Station in Carson Valley when they arrived in June, and the party obtained goods from California to sell. The Mormon Battalion helped cut the Carson Trail across the Sierra Nevada through that area, providing travelers with a good road to the post, and those who had just crossed the Great Basin's deserts welcomed the sight of the valley. DeMont, Blackburn, and their party built a twenty-by-sixty-foot cabin—Nevada's first permanent structure, even if it lacked a roof and floor and its builders may not have intended it to last. Later that year, DeMont, Beatie, and the rest of the party sold out to a trader from California and split up.

Back in Salt Lake, Beatie's reports intrigued Colonel John Reese, who employed him in his general store. The Mormon hierarchy had no interest in gold mining—Mormon leader Brigham Young felt it cost more to find gold than it produced—but commerce had potential. With about a dozen wagons filled with supplies, Reese and a 17-member crew left for Carson Valley on April 5, 1851, arriving on June 4. Reese bought the cabin, expanded it, built other cabins, staked thirty acres, and began planting. Although others had been in Gold Canyon and Carson, Eagle, and Jack's Valleys, Reese became known as the area's first permanent Euro-American settler and profiteer, selling supplies at ten times the cost in Salt Lake City. Ranchers, traders, and miners grew mutually dependent for necessities and luxuries. Emigration fell amid reports of cholera and hostile Native Americans, but about 120 miners generated an estimated sixty thousand dollars in gold.

Problems with Government

They lacked a government, however. Gold Canyon's miners, and the ranchers and traders in nearby valleys, lived in Utah Territory. With the nearest government five hundred miles east in present-day Utah, they had no official way to maintain law and order or record property. On November 12, 19, and 20, 1851, settlers at Mormon Station elected officials, adopted land regulations, set up a local court, petitioned Congress for "a distinct Territorial Government," accused the Mormon-run Utah government of depriving "patriotic citizens of the Union" of justice, and vowed to protect their constitutional rights, "as our fathers did." Utah's government responded in March with a bill extending county lines throughout the territory, but that did nothing to bring any form of government closer to the Carson Valley and its environs.

Thus began a decadelong debate over government in what became western Nevada. Mormon settlers hoped to remain in Utah Territory, but with their own government entities. Reflecting prejudice against Young's followers, whom they suspected of trying to impose their values on them, non-Mormon settlers sought independence from Utah. Early in 1853 forty-three Carson Valley residents asked California legislators to annex them; California said no, and federal officials rejected the idea with the comment that California seemed large enough already. A year later, in January 1854, Utah territorial officials demonstrated concern about losing part of their land—but not too much: they sliced twenty-thousand-square-mile Carson County out of western Iron, Juab, Millard, and Tooele Counties. That they neither appointed county officials nor called for elections angered local settlers even more.

The situation satisfied no one. That summer Carson County residents hired attorney William Cornwall, who drafted a constitution for a temporary government that looked like a cross between a loyal American state and an independent republic. It included a president, a sheriff, a court, and authority to raise revenue for schools, prisons, and protection against invasion—and the admission, "This constitution, of course, possesses no validity." But it continued the pressure on Utah's territorial government, which finally acted early in 1855. Carson County became Utah's third judicial district, complete with a judge, George P. Stiles. More important, Orson Hyde, one of the twelve apostles who joined Young in governing their church, became probate and county judge and led nearly forty Mormons to the Carson Valley that May to try to organize the county.

The Mormon Mission in Las Vegas

A week before Hyde's party left Salt Lake, a church council decided to set up a settlement elsewhere in present-day Nevada. Unlike the trading post that evolved into Carson County and Genoa, this new fort-mission fitted into Young's plan to extend Mormon influence to the Pacific, exemplified by the nearly one hundred colonies his church created in a decade after arriving in Salt Lake. This protective imperialism resembled the missions built by the Spanish, who shared the Mormons' desire to spread their faith and influence. As historian Eugene Moehring has noted, it reflected a belief in "a town-based society of primarily farmers and herdsmen . . . to promote their religious idealism." It also grew from what one scholar has called "a culture of violence" and, according to another, a "siege mentality." With Mormon history full of repression toward its faith, Young sought not only an outlet to the sea and enough land to protect his flock from assault—thus his quest to create the State of Deseret from southern California to the Rockies—but also self-sufficiency, expanded farming in the wake of recent droughts, food and resources for a growing population, easier travel for missionaries and converts, and working with Native Americans religiously, economically, and militarily.

After arriving at Great Salt Lake in 1847 and acclimating themselves to it—and acclimating it to themselves—Mormons explored the eastern Great Basin and established settlements. They eventually looked southwest toward San Bernardino, California, approximating the Old Spanish Trail. Seeking to explore and settle the southern Great Basin and beyond, Young dispatched expeditions led by Colonel William Dame and George Washington Bean; Dame's party described Meadow Valley in present-day Lincoln County as ideal for settlement, while Bean's group ranged as far west as today's town of Beatty.

In May 1855 Mormon leaders ordered thirty men, led by William Bringhurst with Bean as clerk, to start a mission in Las Vegas, then in northwestern New Mexico Territory. Having colonized San Bernardino, several Mormons knew the area's difficult climate and terrain and that Southern Paiutes differed from them in their concept of property (as the communitarian Mormons did from others). Young instructed the missionaries to work with the Paiutes, especially on farming techniques, and to become self-sufficient. Using John C. Frémont's report as a guide, as Young did in coming west, they left on May 10 and arrived on June 14. When they reached the Las Vegas Springs, they found Southern Paiutes and, having heard reports of raids on travelers and battling with Utes in southern Utah, followed the creek four miles north and east to a natural bench.

There they built a fort-mission. Each missionary would be responsible for a garden and for defense: they built guard towers at opposite ends to protect against any attack. In the hot summer of 1855, they planted crops, lugged wood from the Spring Mountains about twenty miles west, and set up an experimental farm two miles north to work with Southern Paiutes. The mission's first harvest went badly: an emigrant party's cattle trampled part of their crop, and Natives took some of the rest. Bringhurst criticized his mission's "grumbling, fault finding, laziness, and cussing around." But the next harvest went better, and the missionaries enjoyed bringing their families from Salt Lake to live with them.

The mission's history proved brief and difficult. Bad harvests also afflicted the church, making it hard for Young to send aid to Las Vegas. With church leaders having sent several men who "need to learn a lesson" after working too little around Salt Lake, some missionaries may have lacked commitment. In 1856, exploring the Spring Mountains, they found lead at Mount Potosi. Encouraged by the chance to produce bullets, Young sent miner Nathaniel Jones with instructions to get the lead out. Bringhurst balked: he saw the mission's purpose as colonizing, Christianizing, and farming. Young finally removed him and replaced him with the more agreeable Samuel Thompson. But the lead proved almost impossible to refine, difficult to reach, and mixed with too much silver to be valuable; the silver had just as many problems. Mining diverted settlers from their mission and farming: their gardens wilted or suffered the effects of insects eating them and Paiutes taking them. As one missionary lamented, "The country around here looks as if the Lord had forgotten it." In 1857 Young allowed some of the missionaries to leave. The next year, with Southern Paiutes taking their crop, the rest departed.

The Mormon trek to Las Vegas had been a qualified failure. Although the mission and mining fared poorly, it established a beachhead for future settlement. One missionary, William Knapp, returned to run a general store for travelers along the Mormon Trail and miners who began digging at Mount Potosi and at Eldorado Canyon, south of present-day Boulder City. With the burning of the old Mormon Station in Genoa, the Mormon Fort remains Nevada's oldest building, a reminder of a Las Vegas unprepared to become a town or major settlement.

Mormons, Miners, and Violence

On June 15, 1855, the day after Bringhurst's group arrived in Las Vegas, Orson Hyde and his party reached Mormon Station. With non-Mormons claiming Carson County belonged to California, Hyde requested a boundary survey, which established it as part of Utah. Then Hyde called for elections at Mormon Station that September 20. Mormon candidates dominated, winning every office but one.

Hyde and his fellow Mormons sought to consolidate control, and Young's power as territorial governor and church leader helped them do so. Non-Mormons saw them as clannish and conspiratorial and feared a theocratic government might impose tithing or polygamy; they again sought annexation by California, whose legislators expressed more enthusiasm this time, but Congress again said no. The church encouraged colonizing, and in the spring of 1856 more than 200 Mormons arrived to ranch and work in Carson, Eagle, Jack's, Pleasant, and Washoe Valleys. Hyde surveyed Mormon Station, renamed it Genoa for Christopher Columbus's birthplace, and oversaw construction of a sawmill to help the local economy and improve buildings and the settling of Franktown in Washoe Valley. The valley's population swelled to more than 500.

But Mormon efforts to consolidate control and build a community screeched to a halt. In the fall of 1856, Hyde left, and 64 others followed the next July. After becoming president on March 4, 1857, James Buchanan replaced Young as territorial governor with a non-Mormon, Alfred Cumming. Gentile territorial officials saw that Mormons often ignored them and obeyed Young and church doctrine and accused the church of revolting against their authority; Mormons saw federal officials as persecuting them. Buchanan sent one-third of the US Army west, and Young readied for a fight, calling Mormons home to defend their Zion. The president sent negotiators, and the "Utah War" ended. Cumming claimed his office but proved incompetent. While Young retained most of his power over the territory, Mormons feared a repetition of the violence they faced in Missouri and Illinois and grew more suspicious of outsiders.

Thus, in September 1857, events in response to these developments changed the complexion of Carson County and affected the Mormon Church forever. On September 5 riders dispatched from church leaders arrived in Carson County and other settlements to call on Mormons to return to Salt Lake as soon and with as much ammunition as possible and to tell no one why. A train of 123 wagons and more than 400 Mormons left three weeks later, reaching Salt Lake on November 2.

By the time Mormons left Carson County on September 26, their church took an action that echoed through history. Earlier in 1857, in Arkansas, the estranged husband of one of Parley Pratt's polygamist wives killed "the Apostle Paul of Mormonism." A wagon train of California-bound emigrants from Arkansas and Missouri passed through Salt Lake and headed south. On September 7, at Mountain Meadows, a glen near Cedar City, Mormons disguised as Native Americans attacked them, killing the men and women (about 140 people) and taking the children into the church until investigators later learned what happened and returned them to their surviving relatives. Mormons blamed the Mountain Meadows Massacre on Southern Paiutes until, in the 1870s, they hanged one church member, John D. Lee, for instigating the murders. Questions remain as to who ordered the assault or deserved blame for it and what role Young played.

Disorder and War: Whites Versus Native Americans

Although events in Mountain Meadows had nothing to do with developments in far-off western Utah territory, the absence of law and order resulted in grim events. From 1850 to 1858, relations between white settlers and Native Americans had often been tense. Losing access to resources that sustained them for generations, the Great Basin's Native Americans raided emigrant trains for supplies and with hopes of dissuading further arrivals. Doing so required the tribes to organize themselves into larger bands, helping to unify Native peoples. Whites countered with attacks and trail patrols. In 1853, after Carson Valley settlers pursued Washoe attackers and killed several in Long Valley and Horseshoe Bend, Washoe depredations largely stopped, though other attacks continued—from Northern Paiutes or Western Shoshone, or "White Indians" in costume or disguise.

The situation changed in 1859. In January four miners located the Gold Hill end of the Comstock Lode. That June, in Six-Mile Canyon at Mount Davidson, came the discovery of the heart of the lode. Virginia City rapidly became a tent city, and thousands of miners and entrepreneurs began the "Rush to Washoe," through and into Indian lands. More emigrants encountered unhappy Northern Paiutes. In April 1859 would-be prospector Peter Lassen, a California rancher known for his California Trail cutoff that added two hundred miles to the trip, died near the Black Rock Desert en route to Virginia City to prospect; rumors spread that Northern Paiutes murdered him. Chief Winnemucca's death later that year removed a Northern Paiute leader who had worked to maintain peace with white settlers. The harsh winter of 1859–60 killed many Carson Valley cattle, reducing food supplies. Early in 1860 reports spread that the owners of Williams Station, at the other end of the Carson River, had kidnapped and raped two Paiute girls.

The Northern Paiutes and their Bannock allies met at Pyramid Lake to discuss their problems. Numaga, Winnemucca's son and the brother of author and activist Sarah Winnemucca, advised against fighting larger numbers of well-armed whites who would come like "sand in a whirlwind."

Then word arrived on May 6 that Northern Paiutes attacked and burned Williams Station, killing three whites. Numaga said, "There is no longer any use for counsel; we must prepare for war."

The Pyramid Lake War followed, and events proved him right. Old ties came unbound: Sarah Winnemucca learned English living in William Ormsby's home, but Major Ormsby, who had military experience in addition to his many business interests, helped form a 105-man militia that marched from Williams Station along the Truckee toward Pyramid Lake. On May 12 Numaga led more than 200 fellow Native Americans in an ambush that killed 76 members of the force, including Ormsby. In response, Colonel John Hays, a former Texas Ranger, organized the "Washoe Regiment" of thirteen militia companies from Virginia City and Carson City, with others arriving from militias and a US Army post in California. They fought Numaga and his men in late June and claimed to have killed 160 Northern Paiutes while losing only 4 of their own men.

The Pyramid Lake War resulted from diverse causes and had varied effects. Historian Sally Zanjani has suggested Ormsby may have hoped a victory in battle would promote him politically and financially; his militia's actions reflected recent tendencies in California and Nevada toward vigilante justice. Mining had recently declined, and concern about warfare temporarily stopped the economy. Late in July, after the Second Battle of Pyramid Lake, the US Army began building a fort, completed in 1861 and named for Inspector General Sylvester Churchill, to guard travelers and settlers along the Carson River. Fort Churchill also protected riders for the Pony Express, the horseback-driven mail service that crisscrossed the West in the early 1860s, and served as a supply post for the Union army during the Civil War. Native Americans kept attacking settlers and emigrants, taking livestock and sometimes killing Pony Express agents—and prompting the army to build two dozen more posts along heavily traveled trails and near settlements.

The Pyramid Lake War climaxed a decade of Native-white conflict. Native Americans viewed white travelers and settlers as taking their freedom and land; the new arrivals saw the Natives as blocking progress and lacking an understanding of the meaning of private property. Yet the war marked only one step in the evolving relations between different cultures. Starting with the Indian Appropriations Act of 1851, the federal government looked to reservations as the solution. Americans had been swarming to

California, upending the Native way of life throughout the newly acquired Intermountain West and Southwest. Moving Native Americans onto reservations would protect them against further encroachment, reduce the likelihood of violent conflicts, and enable them to learn trades such as farming—but that also would undermine their existing culture and remove them from land that might prove valuable for mining or agriculture.

In the late 1850s the Utah Territory's chief agent from the Office of Indian Affairs, Frederick Dodge, wrote, "The game is gone, and now, the steady tread of the white man is upon them, the green valleys too, once spotted with game are not theirs now. . . . Driven by destitution, they seek refuge in crime." In 1860, ordered to select land for "Indian farms" (like the one the Mormons created in the Las Vegas valley but on a larger scale), Dodge chose southern portions of the Truckee and Walker Rivers and the lakes they flowed into. Later, federal officials named them the Pyramid Lake and Walker River Reservations. Another agent set aside a small reservation for the Western Shoshone in Ruby Valley to the northeast in hopes of teaching them to farm.

The Pony Express and the Simpson Exploration

Hoping to win a federal mail contract and avoid bankruptcy, the firm of Russell, Majors, and Waddell originated the Pony Express partly to recoup losses resulting from Mormons burning their freight wagons during the Utah War. Compared with the thousands flocking to the Sierra Nevada's eastern foothills to seek gold and silver, the Pony Express added few to the trails across Nevada. But it briefly played a key role. From April 1860 to October 1861, riders carried mail over an eighteen-hundred-mile route between Sacramento and St. Joseph, Missouri. "Wanted: Young skinny, wiry fellows not over eighteen. Must be expert riders, willing to risk death daily. Orphans preferred," read the freighting company's advertisement.

The trail combined private enterprise, federal surveying, and danger. Winter snows cut off Carson Valley from California each year, and Native Americans killed or injured several mail carriers in the Great Basin, highlighting the need for better, safer travel routes. In 1854 Colonel Edward Steptoe sent two parties from Salt Lake—one led by John Reese—to find a shorter route to Carson Valley and reduce travel time; Steptoe dispatched another party to find a southern route, which generally followed the Old Spanish Trail. In 1855, seeking to drive livestock from Salt Lake to northern

California, Mormon trader Howard Egan scouted the Central Overland Trail, roughly following today's Interstate 50, the "Loneliest Road in America." He traversed the Schell Creek Range in central White Pine, Cherry Creek Range along the present-day White Pine–Elko County border, the Ruby Mountains' Overland Pass, Emigrant Pass in the Toiyabe Range, and the Desatoya Mountains at Basque Summit, near the line between Lander and Churchill Counties. Egan's route lopped off about 250 miles and two weeks of travel time from the California Trail route that followed the Humboldt River.

The federal government soon helped. In 1858 the US Army sent an expedition under Captain James H. Simpson, a longtime Topographical Corps officer, to map the trail; his findings further cut the length and time of the trip through the Great Basin. The army later dispatched Frederick Lander, another veteran of federal surveys and the county's namesake, to improve the trail for wagon travel. The Butterfield Overland Mail stagecoach line and George Chorpenning's mail route switched to this trail just as the Pony Express began. The Pony Express closed in 1861, rendered obsolete by the telegraph's arrival in San Francisco and suffering financially due to mismanagement and a bond scandal, but the trail remained heavily used until the transcontinental railroad's completion in 1869.

With young men riding at full gallop across the West, the Pony Express became mythic. Those who used its trail and then wrote about their experiences became the first in a long line of writers whose descriptions of Nevada's terrain and people have shaped how others view the place. Legendary *New York Tribune* editor Horace Greeley detailed his adventures in *An Overland Journey from New York to San Francisco in the Summer of 1859*, followed by English adventurer Sir Richard Francis Burton's *The City of the Saints, and Across the Rocky Mountains to California.* A decade later the Central Overland Route appeared a few times in *Roughing It*, Samuel Clemens's account of his trip to Nevada, where he became Mark Twain.

Other Settlers, Other Settlements

The controversy between Mormons and miners and the modern-day growth of Las Vegas and Reno have tended to obscure the existence of other settlements outside Carson Valley and the goldfields. A Mormon trader from Carson Valley, H. H. Jamison, opened a post in the eastern Truckee Meadows in 1852, apparently making him the Reno area's first white settler;

nearby Glendale began as a trading post in 1857. Frenchman Ford, opened in the early 1850s, evolved into Winnemucca. In 1854 Asa Kenyon built a general store about eight miles west of present-day Fallon near the Carson River, where he had farmed and travelers thrilled to the sight of water after crossing the Forty-Mile Desert. His outpost became known as Ragtown and then, later in the century, Leeteville. Others erected small stores nearby, and most of these earned similar reputations: one emigrant called Ragtown "the best place for catching suckers that I have ever seen."

Additional settlements radiated out from existing villages. Clear Creek Station opened about five miles south of Carson City in the late 1850s. In 1854 a small store began Sheridan, eight miles south of Genoa, with Van Sickles and Mottsville following nearby. None of these became cities or even towns, but they demonstrated the importance of urban life—the founding and building of communities—even to such seemingly rural pursuits as mining and ranching.

The stream of emigrants stopping at trading posts and minor success in the goldfields attracted a variety of settlers to western Utah territory. Gambler William "Lucky Bill" Thorington may have inspired one of legendary western writer Bret Harte's characters. Alison "Eilley" Orrum came to Carson with Hyde's party in 1855, ran a Gold Canyon boardinghouse, and married prospector Sandy Bowers; their Gold Hill mining claim enabled them to build a mansion in Washoe Valley before they lost their funds, her husband died, and she became a fortune-teller. Hannah Clapp taught in Michigan and California before organizing a school in Carson City in 1860; she later taught at the university in Reno until her death in 1908. Some of the women living in western Utah Territory at the time tried to impose the Victorian values of family, chastity, and thrift, but with limited success.

Nevada has always drawn a diverse populace, seeking the advancement often associated with the frontier and the West. Three African American families arrived, including that of Ben Palmer, later one of the valley's biggest taxpayers, while locals and visitors respected his sister Charlotte for her hospitality—for both, an unusual amount of acceptance in the nineteenth-century West. Bay Area Chinese workers arrived in Dayton in 1856 to dig a ditch and remained, creating Nevada's first "Chinatown." Dayton's Isaac Cohn and Genoa's Abraham Klauber, two of the first Jewish residents, owned stores. By the first census in 1860, immigrants accounted for 30 percent of the future Nevada Territory's populace.

Many pioneers came in hopes of finding gold but found a different metal instead. How many of them realized that they had struck silver—the silver later at the center of the Comstock Lode—remains uncertain. Several encountered what they called "the cursed black stuff," but saw it as worthless or understood its potential value and lacked the capital or desire to pursue it.

Two former Gold Rush miners recognized silver's potential and hoped to take advantage of it. Ethan Allen Grosh and Hosea Ballou Grosh failed at several enterprises in California before reaching Gold Canyon. They found silver and, from studying mining, knew it required more processing and capital than gold. They sought investors and gold to finance their operations and tried to keep their discovery secret from those who might take it from them. But in August 1857 Hosea died. Four months later, after trying to cross the Sierra Nevada as winter came, his brother died of complications from frostbite. Whether they found the Comstock Lode or the less valuable Silver City end remains uncertain, but they pioneered silver mining in Nevada—and exemplified the bad luck and decisions that affected day-to-day prospectors unable to turn their findings into wealth.

Hosea Ballou (*left*) and Ethan Allen Grosh, the brothers who may have discovered the Comstock Lode, or at least part of it, in the mid-1850s before meeting tragedy. Courtesy of the Nevada Historical Society.

The Reign of Disorder: Mormons Versus Miners, Continued

When Carson County's Mormons departed in 1857, only about two hundred residents remained. Non-Mormons happily paid low prices for or simply took the land and equipment that Young's followers left behind. A handful of Mormons, led by John Reese, chose not to obey the call to Zion. Most in the area mined in nearby Gold Canyon, but others engaged in agriculture or such services as blacksmithing.

Soon, the battle over western Utah resumed. In January 1857, anticipating changes after Hyde left, Utah lawmakers added Carson County to Great Salt Lake County judicially, financially, and electorally to avert non-Mormon control. Without courts and legislators, residents again tried to create their own government. On August 8 Reese presided at a meeting in Genoa. People came from Carson, Eagle, Hope, Humboldt River, and Lake Valleys; Ragtown, Willow Town, and the Twenty-Six-Mile Desert, all in Nevada; and Honey Lake, California. They asked Congress for a separate territory, Columbus, with Genoa as the capital, and sent Virginia native James Crane to Congress to make the request. Since leading Californians backed them, and the "Utah War" cost the territory's religious leaders what little support they might have enjoyed in national circles, the squatters felt optimistic.

Events proved them wrong. The settlement of the issues between Mormons and the federal government, coupled with divisions between the North and South, blocked action. The House Committee on Territories approved a territorial bill by Crane's ally William Smith of Virginia in May 1858, but the measure went no further. Lacking real government, Carson Valley's residents held a mass meeting and, much as San Franciscans did at the time even with state and local government, created a vigilance committee. The members dispensed justice and belied Lucky Bill Thorington's nickname by hanging him for his role in a murder.

When Utah's Gentile territorial government tried again to assert itself, it failed. In July 1858 the territorial governor sent John S. Child to serve as Carson County's probate judge, but when he called for elections that October, the voters split along Mormon and non-Mormon lines, and the anti-Mormon contingent claimed voter fraud in four of the six precincts. In January legislators tried again, restoring and expanding Carson County and naming John Cradlebaugh judge. After arriving in Genoa in the summer of 1859, he impaneled a federal grand jury whose anti-Mormon members produced a report attacking the church. That fall Child held a meeting of the probate court and scheduled elections. Although only three of the ten precincts voted, Governor Alfred Cumming and Judge Child, hoping to restore control, certified the winners, who refused to serve amid the uncertainty.

As these events unfolded, Carson County's residents kept fighting Mormon control. In June 1858, at another mass meeting, they created precincts, slated a vote, and reelected Crane as territorial delegate. They elected a constitutional convention whose delegates met in Genoa in July, wrote a constitution, and explained their need for a separate territory by accusing Mormons of trying to "reduce us under an absolute spiritual despotism" and provoking Native Americans to attack them. That September 7 voters showed their desperation: they approved a constitution, chose a legislature, and elected a governor, Isaac Roop, a politician and businessman from nearby Susanville, California.

The Impact of Outside Events

Western Utah territory showed no signs of calming down. The discovery of the Comstock Lode and the resulting "Rush to Washoe" attracted thousands of people who needed government—law enforcement and recorders especially—more than the few hundred who had been moving in and out of the region. Crane's death in September 1859 led to the election of delegate John Musser, who fared no better with Congress. The would-be territorial legislature met in December 1859, had no quorum, and adjourned. In the summer of 1860, Child oversaw elections that filled most offices and held the first court session in about three years. But in October, when President Buchanan named a new federal judge—Robert P. Flenniken, an old Pennsylvania ally—Cradlebaugh refused to give up his post, claiming the president had no right to remove a federal territorial judge. That left western Utah with a local government objectionable to Mormons and non-Mormons, and two federal judges and the governor of a nonexistent new territory claiming authority.

Just as national events worked against slicing a new territory out of western Utah, national events made it possible to achieve that goal. With seven states and their congressmen leaving the Union, and the Confederate States of America declaring itself a country on February 8, 1861, Northerners controlled Congress and could legislate more freely. On February 26 the Senate passed a bill written by James S. Green, a Missouri Democrat who chaired the Senate Committee on Territories, creating Nevada Territory. The House passed the measure on March 2, and Buchanan signed it, two days before leaving office. At the last minute Utah Territory tried to keep its western portion by moving the county seat from Genoa to the more populous Carson City, which had sprung up in Eagle Valley, and incorporating Virginia City, where miners had been flocking to look for gold and silver. But these efforts failed. Nevada Territory had been born.

That birth proved slow in coming and then arrived at breakneck speed, much like the mining rushes that inspired it and national events such as the Civil War. Colorado Territory, created the same day as Nevada, included the eastern portion of Utah Territory, to which Mormon leaders appear to have paid little attention, and resulted from the mining rush to Pikes Peak and the need for government there. After a decade of battling over slavery in new territories, Congress passed the bill without mentioning the topic—perhaps because a pro-Union Democrat from a slave state wrote the measure, or Republicans wanted to suggest their willingness to compromise, or they knew, with Lincoln taking office, antislavery forces would rule the territory anyway. Nevada had indeed been caught in the vortex of the sectional crisis; now the Civil War would affect it, too.

SUGGESTED READINGS

Arrington, Leonard. *Great Basin Kingdom: Economic History of the Latter-Day Saints, 1830–1900.* Lincoln: University of Nebraska Press, 1966.

Bagley, Will. *Blood of the Prophets: Brigham Young and the Massacre at Mountain Meadows.* Norman: University of Oklahoma Press, 2002.

Campbell, Eugene E. *Establishing Zion: The Mormon Church in the American West, 1847–1869.* Salt Lake City: Signature Books, 1988.

Denton, Sally. *American Massacre: The Tragedy at Mountain Meadows, September 1857.* New York: Alfred A. Knopf, 2003.

Egan, Ferol. *Sand in a Whirlwind: The Paiute Indian War of 1860.* Reno: University of Nevada Press, 1985.

Farmer, Jared. *On Zion's Mount: Mormons, Indians, and the American Landscape.* Cambridge, MA: Harvard University Press, 2008.

Foner, Eric. *Free Soil, Free Labor, Free Men: The Ideology of the Republican Party Before the Civil War.* 1970. Reprint, New York: Oxford University Press, 1995.

Lamar, Howard R. *The Far Southwest, 1846–1912: A Territorial History.* Rev. ed. Albuquerque: University of New Mexico Press, 2000.

Meinig, D. W. *The Shaping of America: A Geographical Perspective on 500 Years of History.* Vol. 3, *Transcontinental America, 1850–1915.* New Haven, CT: Yale University Press, 1998.

Meldahl, Keith Heyer. *Hard Road West: History and Geology Along the Gold Rush Trail.* Chicago: University of Chicago Press, 2007.

Petersen, Jesse G. *A Route for the Overland Stage: James H. Simpson's 1859 Trail Across the Great Basin.* Logan: Utah State University Press, 2008.

Potter, David M. *The Impending Crisis, 1848–1861.* New York: Harper and Row, 1976.

Reeve, W. Paul. *Making Space on the Western Frontier: Mormons, Miners, and Southern Paiutes.* Urbana: University of Illinois Press, 2006.

Richards, Leonard L. *The California Gold Rush and the Coming of the Civil War.* New York: Vintage Books, 2007.

Walker, Ronald W., Richard E. Turley Jr., and Glen M. Leonard. *Massacre at Mountain Meadows: An American Tragedy.* New York: Oxford University Press, 2008.

Woods, Fred E. *A Gamble in the Desert: The Mormon Mission in Las Vegas, 1855–1857.* Salt Lake City: Mormon Historic Sites Foundation, 2005.

Zanjani, Sally S. *Devils Will Reign: How Nevada Began.* Reno: University of Nevada Press, 2005.

5

The Civil War and Nevada

The Civil War has been called "the second American revolution." Those who study it, or reenact its battles, emphasize the war and its effects, from soldiers to politicians and the new birth of freedom the war created. "The war in the West" usually refers to battles such as Shiloh and Vicksburg, along the Mississippi River. Little fighting took place in the Far West. But in spreading industrial capitalism and expanding the scope of the federal government, the Civil War reshaped the West, and the West's mineral and agricultural resources affected the nation and the world. Nevada deserves to be called "battle born" in more ways than one.

A Territorial Government

Many of Nevada's political leaders wanted statehood as soon as possible. They understood the limits of their power in a territory and shared ambitions for national and state office. Ultimately, they achieved their goal but had little impact on how it happened. The Civil War made it possible for Nevada to become a territory on March 2, 1861, and then a state on October 31, 1864. It also affected Nevada's development through the legislation and constitutional change the war fostered.

Nevada's territorial appointees demonstrated loyalty to the Republican Party and the Union and had connections to party leaders. Like all other presidents, Abraham Lincoln used patronage to reward supporters and build his party. Governor James Warren Nye, an antislavery New Yorker allied with Secretary of State William Seward, previously a senator from that state, campaigned for Lincoln in 1860. Territorial secretary Orion Clemens worked in Attorney General Edward Bates's St. Louis law office. Minnesota's John Wesley North, a well-connected Republican, became surveyor general. In turn, Lincoln's selections wanted to build the population's commitment to the Union and their party. Organizing the territory enabled them to influence that process.

The last of the appointees to arrive, Nye headed for Nevada, hoping to ensure its loyalty to the Union and achieve statehood—and with it a US Senate seat for himself. Traveling from New York via Panama and San Francisco, he reached the territory on July 7, 1861. Congratulatory dinners and patriotic speeches consumed the next three days. On July 11 Nye settled down to business, proclaiming the territorial offices occupied and Nevada Territory established and organized. A week later, on July 18, came his proclamation for a judiciary complete with justices of the peace, district and probate courts, and a supreme court consisting of Lincoln's three appointees as territorial judges: Gordon Mott, George Turner, and Horatio M. Jones, each of whom would hear cases in different parts of the territory.

Next, Nye turned to executive and legislative matters. His third proclamation, on July 24, ordered the election of the congressional delegate and members of the territorial legislature and a census to determine electoral districts. On August 5 Nye's fellow New York transplant Henry DeGroot, a former Gold Rush miner and mapmaker, reported a populace—except for Native Americans and travelers—of 16,374 (including Honey Lake, California, which Nevadans then thought might be within their boundaries). The increase of about 10,000 from the formal federal census a year before highlighted the numbers the Comstock Lode had attracted.

Legislating a Territory

Next, Nye took steps to shape the territorial government. He called elections on August 31 for a nonvoting delegate to Congress, fifteen members of the house of representatives, and nine councilmen. The legislature would meet on the first Tuesday in October in Carson City, giving the town a potential advantage when the eventual state legislature chose a capital. While Utah's territorial legislature had moved Carson County's seat there from Genoa, the more important factor in this case may have been two former Californians who advised Nye on local issues: William Morris Stewart, a mining lawyer and politician, and Abraham Curry, a Gold Rush businessman and an early investor in Eagle Valley who represented the area in the constitutional convention to carve a new territory out of Utah. After buying a trading post and laying out the original town, Curry had built a hotel in Carson City and hoped for those visiting the capital to become part of his clientele.

The territorial legislature met on the top floor of Curry's hotel from October 1 to November 29. Reflecting California's influence and Virginia City's importance, its residents presided over both chambers—in the council J. L. Van Bokkelen, once part of San Francisco's Vigilance Committee that overrode civilian authority and doled out punishments and later commander of a similar unit in Virginia City, and Miles Mitchell, another former Californian and a Stewart ally, in the lower house. Lawmakers adopted civil and criminal codes as well as revenue measures: license fees, taxes on business and property, and a poll tax on every man between twenty-one and fifty. They created nine counties (Churchill, Douglas, Esmeralda, Humboldt, Lake, Lyon, Ormsby, Storey, and Washoe), designated county seats, and created offices. After approving six toll-road franchises to raise money from travelers, they added fifty more roads by 1864. Lawmakers ratified Nye's decision to locate the capital in Carson City, possibly in exchange for the creation of so many small counties, full of political and administrative opportunities for them and their allies.

Nye delivered a message to the legislature, suggesting a variety of actions, with mixed success. Deeming it "much cheaper to furnish school-houses and teachers than prisons and keepers," he urged lawmakers to create a school system, reflecting a movement toward public education in ethnically diverse areas to acculturate immigrants. Nye won backing for county commissioners to set aside 10 percent of all property taxes to hire teachers and funding from violations of penal laws and failure to pay poll taxes; the territorial act already required each township to set aside two sections for schools. "I particularly recommend that you pass stringent laws to prevent gambling. Of all the seductive vices extant, I regard that of gambling as the worst," Nye said, and the legislature made gambling a felony and banned theaters, cockfighting, racetracks, and "engaging in any noisy amusements" on Sundays, observing the Christian Sabbath.

Some of Nye's failures foreshadowed future problems. He suggested taxing gross profits from mining, but the legislature preferred to tax net proceeds—a debate that later roiled the territory. When he asked lawmakers to allow African Americans to testify in trials and serve in the militia, they instead prohibited both and passed laws barring black attorneys and racial intermarriage. One member declared that the legislature "met to legislate for white men." Nye privately attacked such thinking as "behind the Spirit of the Age," but his stand took courage: few places accorded African Americans these rights, Nevadans shared the nation's racial prejudice, and apparently his position prompted the only criticism his legislative agenda inspired. Nye could have endangered his political ambitions.

Negotiating with the Western Shoshone

As territorial governor, Nye held the ex-officio title of superintendent of Indian affairs for Nevada. The Pyramid Lake War and the military presence that followed seemed to ease settlers' concerns about Northern Paiutes, but the Western Shoshone, trying to preserve their way of life and discourage settlement, formed a band of three to four hundred in the Reese River Valley and preyed on emigrants. Nye hoped to resolve the dispute and dispatched federal Indian agent Warren Wasson to negotiate with the Shoshone. In December 1861 Wasson and the band's leader, Tu-tu-wa (also known as Toi-toi), reached an agreement—not a formal treaty. The Western Shoshone would stop attacking travelers and allow them to use their resources, such as land and water. In return, the Shoshone surrendered no land.

Both sides wanted more from each other. In 1862 Colonel Patrick Connor's California Volunteers arrived at Fort Ruby to protect emigrant and mail routes. They began forcing Western Shoshone to work as scouts and report on which fellow tribal members had caused problems (Connor went on to command federal troops who massacred Western Shoshone at Idaho's Bear River a year later for similar attacks on whites). The Western Shoshone sought to avoid further trouble. In turn, the federal government's plans to build a railroad through the Great Basin and promote continued emigration and settlement required a deal with them. Nye and federal Indian agents met with Newe leaders and hammered out the Treaty of Ruby Valley, signed on October 1, 1863. The Western Shoshone agreed not to attack whites and to allow forts, postal stations, mining, and settlements on their land. In return, the federal government would pay them annually for the loss of their food supply, and when they moved onto reservations, the Newe expected to be able to stay in the valleys where they had lived for generations.

Once the treaty took effect, fighting between Nevada's Western Shoshone and white emigrants and settlers declined. The bigger fight came later in the courts over the treaty's provisions. It said, "The several routes of travel through the Shoshonee country, now or hereafter used by white men, shall be forever free, and unobstructed by the said bands, for the use of the government of the United States, and of all emigrants and travellers under its authority and protection, without molestation or injury from them." Nowhere did it state that the Newe ceded land. This legal and political debate has continued into the twenty-first century.

The First Constitutional Convention

Nye and other allies had lobbied the Lincoln administration and Congress for statehood, and the Senate passed an enabling act, but the session ended before the House could act. In the tradition of western settlers used to developing their own institutions, Nevadans ignored the lack of federal authority and went ahead anyway. On December 20, 1862, the second territorial legislature passed a bill designed "to frame a Constitution and State Government for the State of Washoe." Territorial residents would vote the next September on whether they wanted statehood and on thirty-nine delegates to a constitutional convention. If they did, Carson City would host the meeting on the first Tuesday in November. On September 2, 1863, Nevadans voted 6,660–1,502 for a constitutional convention.

Two months later, the delegates spent thirty-two days drafting a constitution. All but four of Nevada's thirty-nine would-be founding fathers came from California, and only four had lived in the territory before the Comstock Lode's discovery, suggesting both California's influence and how quickly Nevada had grown. John W. North, first the surveyor general and later Lincoln's appointee as the territorial supreme court's chief justice, chaired the convention. The delegates included William Stewart, who helped maneuver the territorial capital to Carson City and an advocate in court and everywhere else for the corporate interests increasingly dominating Comstock mines; J. Neely Johnson, a former California governor whose political career there ended when he challenged the San Francisco Vigilance Committee; John Kinkead, a future governor of Nevada and later, like Stewart, closely connected to mining corporations; and such future state politicians as Thomas Fitch, an editor and later a congressman; C. N. Noteware, the first secretary of state; C. M. Brosnan, a supreme court justice; and Charles DeLong, a frequent US Senate candidate and future US minister to Japan.

Some of the discussions at the convention went quickly. Trying to settle on the proposed state's name, they agreed that "Washoe" had little appeal, and delegates suggested naming the new state Humboldt and Esmeralda (the Spanish word for "emerald" and the heroine of Victor Hugo's popular novel *The Hunchback of Notre Dame*) before settling on Nevada, Spanish for "snow-covered." They agreed on strong stands against secessionists and states' rights.

The Key Issue: Mining Taxes

Knowing the new state would have to generate revenue, delegates fought hard about that issue, with significant consequences. North led those who wanted to tax mines like any other property; Stewart's side preferred taxing only net proceeds, with depreciation and deductions first. After vigorous debate, the convention voted 21–10 for North's view. When the delegates adjourned on December 11, all, including the Stewart forces, pledged to fight for ratification. Nevadans would vote on both the constitution and a slate of candidates for state office.

An all-out political fight followed, and several issues combined to defeat the constitution. Stewart announced that his "construction" of the document permitted the state legislature to tax net proceeds instead of gross profits. Nevadans resented his implication that he and the San Francisco investors he represented would control the state and that he would be so obvious about it; as one of his rivals put it, the provision "stunk in the nostrils of the people." Prospectors and small mining companies had another concern: they backed the "multiledge theory" of mining law, which divided the ore from a vein, while Stewart's "one-ledge theory" would benefit those with enough capital to follow a vein to its end. North and Stewart fought to control the Union Party, as Republicans reconstituted themselves in response to the Civil War, and their backers split over the candidates on the ballot with the constitution. In December, when the two sides needed to unite behind statehood, Storey County's Union Party convention battled over delegates to the statewide party meeting. Stewart's slate won, kept North from serving as a delegate, and passed a resolution against North's candidacy for governor.

This combination proved deadly. Throughout the territory but especially along the Comstock Lode, Union Party members split over Stewart. They debated his views, the loyalties of the slate of candidates, and his determination to destroy North's reputation as a judge over their political ambitions and North's unwillingness to buckle to Stewart's will on the one-ledge theory. On January 19, 1864, Nevadans rejected the proposed constitution and the accompanying candidates, 8,851–2,157. In four months Nevadans had switched from voting for statehood by a 4–1 margin to rejecting it by the same percentage—for the moment.

The Second—and Final—Constitution

Federal and territorial leaders grasped that the vote had been a defeat not for statehood, but for playing politics with statehood. They pressed forward early in 1864, with several considerations in Nevada's favor. Lincoln's reelection and Union Party control might hang in the balance; a new state's three electoral votes could make the difference. Lincoln and his party hoped to pass the Thirteenth Amendment, banning slavery, and might need one more vote in the House for the two-thirds required to approve it. They also sought every possible vote in Congress for their policies on reconstructing the Union and the status of the returning Southern states and four million newly freed African Americans.

Thus, Lincoln supporters restarted the march to statehood. On February 8, 1864, Senator James Doolittle of Wisconsin, a Lincoln backer, introduced an enabling act for Nevada statehood that the president signed on March 21. The Enabling Act set certain conditions for statehood: a state constitution in line with the Declaration of Independence and the Constitution, no slavery, the cession to the federal government of any claims to public lands, the same tax rate on land owned by non-Nevadans as for the state's residents, religious toleration, and no taxation of federal property. The bill bypassed the usual requirement that Congress approve state constitutions by allowing Lincoln to accept Nevada's and declare it a state—perhaps a sign that the president wanted to guarantee Nevada's participation in his reelection bid. Accordingly, on May 2 Nye issued a proclamation for an election five weeks later to choose delegates to another constitutional convention.

The second convention took just over three weeks. Ten delegates from the previous meeting participated, and the absence of North and Stewart eased tensions. Most of the delegates had been part of the Gold Rush and its aftermath and practiced law or worked in the mining industry. J. Neely Johnson served as chair, and only one of the thirty-five who attended claimed to be a Democrat. Again mining taxes dominated the proceedings, but this time with a different outcome: the delegates agreed on a different tax system for mines, "the proceeds alone of which shall be assessed and taxed," than for other property. The convention also separated the vote on the constitution from the election of state and local officials, avoiding a rerun of that controversy.

The delegates still found issues to debate. They argued over whether to call the state Nevada until Johnson pointed out the enabling legislation referred to it that way, ending the discussion. They felt a need for a loyalty oath, given the Civil War, but then decided after considerable discussion not to, as one of them put it, "inflame men's passions." They briefly discussed whether to remove the word *white* as a limitation on voting, but a belief in black inferiority prompted them to keep the restriction in the constitution.

This time, despite the defeat for small-time miners, passage proved easier. The Civil War provided a justification: loyalty to country meant supporting statehood. More important, the Comstock Lode dipped into a depression early in 1864, and Stewart and his allies contended that a new state government, a new constitution, new tax policies, and a new judiciary would improve the economy. The minimal opposition proved caustic and similar to complaints from future Nevadans about government: William J. Forbes, an iconoclast who edited newspapers in several mining camps, announced in the *Humboldt Register*, "The Humboldt world is dead-set against engaging to help support any more lunk-heads till times get better. . . . If we have a State Government we'll have more fat-headed officers to support; and if we undertake to support them without taxing the mines, we'll run hopelessly into debt. If we do tax them, we'll stop the development of them." Despite such sentiments, on September 7, 1864, statehood won, 10,375–1,284.

A costly comedy of errors followed. Nye sent the constitution to Washington, DC, by mail, but it never arrived. His friend Seward tried to persuade Lincoln to proclaim statehood without seeing the document. When the president refused, Seward informed Nye, who then ordered it telegraphed to the nation's capital. The second-longest telegram ever transmitted, it cost more than forty-three hundred dollars to send. Lincoln received the constitution and declared Nevada a state on October 31, 1864, in time for Nevadans to vote in the November 8 election. Although Lincoln had expected during the summer to lose the election, and an aide included Nevada in the list of electoral votes that would give him a narrow victory, he defeated his Democratic opponent by an electoral vote of 212–21, including two from Nevada—the third elector, caught in a snowstorm, never made it to the vote.

Otherwise, Nevada's role in the election easily met the hopes and expectations of Lincoln and his party. Their slate swept state offices and all but two of the fifty-four assembly and state senate seats (ironically, one of the Democrats came from the county named for Nye). Virginia City mining superintendent Henry Blasdel won the governor's race. Henry Worthington, a lawyer in the mining boomtown of Austin, went to the House of Representatives, where he voted for the Thirteenth Amendment, which just passed by the required two-thirds. After legislators elected Stewart to the Senate, Nye, John Cradlebaugh, and Charles DeLong fought for the second seat. Stewart reportedly offered to support Cradlebaugh if he would obey his dictates on patronage and other matters. When Cradlebaugh refused, Stewart backed Nye, who won. As senators, Stewart and Nye proved loyal Republicans, fighting the efforts of Lincoln's successor, Andrew Johnson, to limit civil rights and to ease the Southern states' return to the Union.

Myth and Reality

Nevada's constitution and statehood, like so much about the state, inspired myths. According to one of them, Nevada became a state illegally: the Northwest Ordinance of 1787 stipulated that a territory's population must reach sixty thousand before it could seek statehood, and Nevada fell at least thirty-five thousand short. But other states entered the Union in unusual ways, including Texas (annexed as an independent republic), Maine (carved out of Massachusetts in a compromise over slavery), and West Virginia (originally called Virginia and part of that state; Lincoln guided it into the Union because the western part of the seceded state had remained loyal). Whatever the wisdom of Nevada's statehood, the federal government acted legally, or at least consistently.

The myth of why Nevada enjoyed federal support for statehood has been more important and lasting. The Comstock's wealth attracted the population to justify territorial and statehood status, prompting the belief that Lincoln saw statehood as a means of securing that revenue for the Union cause—a myth perpetuated by an episode of the popular *Bonanza* television series, set in and near Virginia City. Since Nevada had been a federal territory, its gold and silver already belonged to the Union. Lincoln and his party sought statehood for Nevada for political and policy reasons tied to the Civil War, but not out of a need for its gold and silver.

Politics proved decisive. Whether Lincoln paid much attention to statehood out of hope for his reelection remains uncertain, but, as a shrewd and veteran politician, he knew how to count votes. Representative James Ashley of Ohio, the Thirteenth Amendment's floor manager in the House, wanted Nevada's support for that measure and to help him in "negativing states' rights," as he put it, by adding another pro-Union state and enhancing federal power. But Ashley also realized that if Lincoln lacked an electoral majority, the election would wind up in the House of Representatives, where the new state of Nevada could help their party.

Economic factors played a role—just less excitingly than the myth suggests. Responding to the Comstock's downturn, delegates argued that statehood would restore prosperity by creating a stronger government and settling mining litigation they viewed as detrimental to development and investment. Those from ranching areas resented the different tax structure for mining and complained about "foreign capitalists" from California and other states; one delegate said, "I am in favor of taxing the mines, because I want to make those gentlemen who are rolling in wealth in San Francisco, pay something for the support of our government." Mining leaders hailed "the lone, struggling prospector," as historian David A. Johnson noted, but offered "a corporate vision of Nevada's mining economy" that would unfold for decades to come. What the Comstock had produced attracted the population to justify a vote on statehood; its future prospects justified voting yes.

The Nevada Constitution: Influences

The Nevada Constitution reflects its times. Three documents most directly influenced it. Two other state constitutions helped guide Nevada's framers: that of New York, Nye's home state, and of California, where the overwhelming majority of the delegates came from. Then, and most important, came the United States Constitution. Both the US and Nevada Constitutions contain a preamble and a bill of rights (in Nevada's case a Declaration of Rights), exemplify the political theory of federalism (a separation of powers and checks and balances among three branches of government), emphasize the legislature's powers more than the executive and the judicial, and leave much of the detail to legislators to explain and expand upon through laws and statutes.

In addition to providing the purpose for writing it, no event affected the Nevada Constitution's tone and content more than the Civil War. The constitution barred slavery, banned former Confederates from voting, and provided for soldiers and sailors away from home to be able to vote—an accommodation related to the war. Article I, Section 2, declared that "the Paramount Allegiance of every citizen is due to the Federal Government in the exercise of all its Constitutional powers," repudiating Southern secession. Another provision in the opening ordinance said Nevadans "forever disclaim all right and title to the unappropriated public lands lying within said territory, and that the same shall be and remain at the sole and entire disposition of the United States." Future western states faced similar restrictions, rooted in the expansion of federal power that the war fostered. Ever since, Nevadans have objected to the federal government controlling more than 86 percent of their state and tried to change that relationship.

Early-nineteenth-century reform movements also shaped the document. Nevadans imposed few limits on voting, except for racial minorities, and the US Constitution soon affected that provision. They bowed to early-nineteenth-century reforms by prohibiting dueling, which struck them as too southern and barbaric, and allowing women to own property separately from men, a goal of the women's rights movement. Mormonism had been an outgrowth of the religious and communitarian reforms of the time, and the Nevada Constitution, written after a decade of conflict between Mormons and miners, included a slap at that faith (and perhaps at Native American practices) when it said that religious freedom "shall not be so construed, as to excuse acts of licentiousness or justify practices inconsistent with the peace, or safety of this State"—as in polygamy.

The expansion of democracy and its frontier influences also affected the Nevada Constitution. Requiring a six-month residency for voting reflected the Jacksonian commitment to suffrage and the frontier's transient population. Scheduling the legislature to meet biennially and limiting members' pay to sixty-day sessions demonstrated a Jeffersonian and Jacksonian desire for limited government, but growth and government services led to a weaker legislature and a stronger governor, thanks to the former's fewer meetings and the latter's power over state agencies. More democratic Nevadans believed in electing judges rather than appointing them, as the US Constitution stipulates at the federal level. Because the delegates included old Jacksonian Democrats who prized individual freedom over government interference, their Declaration of Rights restricted the state more than the federal Bill of Rights does the US government. Other efforts to expand democracy and reform, including the early-twentieth-century Progressive Era and the civil rights revolution of the 1960s, shaped the Nevada Constitution in the future.

The Constitution the War Made

The Civil War changed the US Constitution, prompting its first amendments in sixty years and the last three for nearly a half century. Nevada helped pass the Thirteenth Amendment in 1865. Its members of Congress voted for the Fourteenth Amendment, which took effect in 1868 and sought to define American citizenship and the rights it entails. Its Equal Protection Clause and the Supreme Court's gradual "incorporation" of rights covered in the Constitution's first ten amendments at the state level affected Nevada law and society.

The Fifteenth Amendment had significant ties to Nevada. Stewart wrote it, but considerable debate and compromise reduced it to two sentences: "The right of citizens of the United States to vote shall not be denied or abridged by the United States or by any State on account of race, color, or previous condition of servitude" and "The Congress shall have power to enforce this article by appropriate legislation." Whether or not he had this in mind, states and courts found ways around the amendment to limit black suffrage, such as poll taxes (outlawed in 1964 by the Twenty-Fourth Amendment); literacy tests, which newly freed, mostly illiterate former slaves found hard to pass; and grandfather clauses, which limited the vote to those whose grandfathers voted before 1860. These measures also targeted recent immigrants and the poor, and the power of state and local governments over elections remains an issue.

Nevada became the first state to endorse the amendment, but with little pleasure. Legislators balked until Stewart reassured them the amendment would have no effect on their efforts to deny voting rights to the Chinese and apparently warned that his colleagues would look unfavorably on the state in case of a no vote. Nevada's constitution had included a ban on black suffrage until the Fifteenth Amendment and barred women who had been slaves from voting. It also provided for a poll tax, based on the logic of one delegate: if the four-dollar fee proved too high, there were "always plenty of politicians to pay it for him the days before election." Nevada repealed this measure only after the change in the US Constitution, nearly a century after it endorsed the Fifteenth Amendment.

Setting Boundaries

During the territorial period and early days of statehood, a question lingered: what constituted Nevada? The territorial legislation of 1861 set the western boundary at the "dividing ridge separating the waters of Carson Valley from those that flow into the Pacific." While that meant the Sierra Nevada's crest, the act said that "so much of the Territory within the present limits of the state of California, shall not be included within this Territory until the State of California, shall assent to the same by an act irrevocable without the consent of the United States." Despite Nevada's lobbying, California lawmakers declined to "assent," hoping to benefit from an unsettled boundary. Not only did they covet the Comstock's silver, but they also learned of a boom at Aurora in Esmeralda County, close enough to the California line to give the Golden State hope.

Settling the issue involved violence and negotiation. The violence broke out between Roop County, Nevada, and Plumas County, California, when officials from the two jurisdictions claimed the same land. After some shootings, both sides agreed to leave the matter to higher-ups. A joint boundary survey concluded that Honey Lake lay in California, ending efforts by that area's residents to participate in Nevada affairs. Aurora, it concluded, belonged to Nevada, but because it had been the seats of both Mono County, California, and Esmeralda County, Nevada, it held two elections on the same day and elected legislators in both areas. Only Nevada's vote counted.

While Nevada battled and negotiated with California over its western boundary, its eastern side evolved due to legislation and national prejudice against Mormons and their polygamist practices. In 1862 Congress agreed to Nevada's request to add land from Utah Territory. In 1866 it passed a bill extending Nevada's eastern boundary to its present location, completing the addition of present-day Lincoln, White Pine, and Elko Counties as well as eastern Nye County. In 1867 Congress shifted Nevada's border south, adding all of Clark and southern Nye County from Arizona Territory.

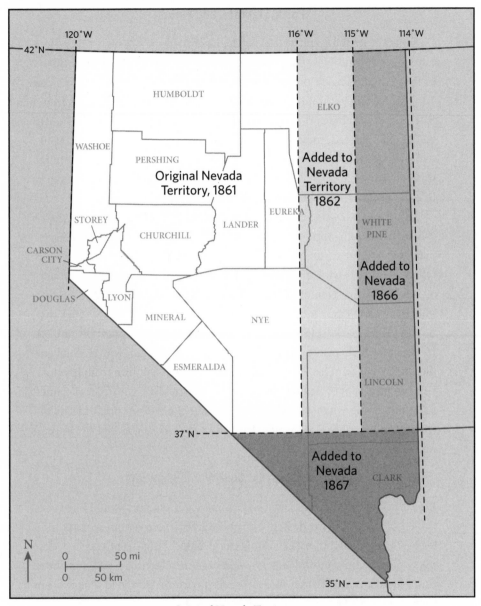

Original Nevada Territory

These acts reflected a territory's inability to control its internal affairs as a state does. They also showed that the federal government wanted to encourage its supporters in a state at the expense of territories—especially, in Utah Territory's case, Mormons they refused to trust.

Forts, Fighters, and Flour

Completion of the coast-to-coast telegraph made it possible to find out news quickly, and Nevadans followed developments in the war as closely as they could. Nevada played a military role in the Civil War, but a small one. About twelve hundred Nevadans fought for the North, including a battalion of cavalry and another of infantry, but not on the better-known battlefields. Instead, they protected travelers on overland roads and trails, mainly from Native Americans. They also served in several forts scattered throughout the area, including at Fort Churchill, which provided supplies to Union soldiers stationed in the vicinity.

Nevadans also worried about what Lincoln called "the fire in the rear": the war's domestic opponents. The US Army jailed a few Confederate sympathizers at Fort Churchill, and random violence chilled the opposition. Other Nevadans who disagreed politically helped the war effort. A store owner in Austin, Democrat Reuel Gridley, lost a bet on a mayoral election and had to carry a fifty-pound sack of flour through town. After that, he carried the sack to towns around the country, auctioning it off until he raised more than $250,000 for the Sanitary Commission, which aided soldiers and their families. His patriotism and charity kept him from his store, ruining him economically. His story became widely known and gained additional fame when it became the subject of part of a book by his old friend from Hannibal, Missouri, Sam Clemens, writing as Mark Twain in *Roughing It*.

Making Nevada: Civil War Legislation

Had the South not seceded, its congressmen and senators would have controlled Congress. Instead, Republicans enjoyed the freedom to pass their legislation, which otherwise would have failed. This trend started during the secession winter, when Nevada became a territory, and continued throughout the war. Three measures, all passed in 1862, had a significant impact on Nevada.

The Homestead Act grew from Thomas Jefferson's celebration of yeomen or self-sufficient farmers, the heart of American agriculture into the mid-nineteenth century, and the Republican belief in making free soil available instead of forcing slaves to work the land. The Homestead Act allowed any male over age twenty-one, single woman, or former slave to file a claim. After living on the 160 acres for five years and improving it, the homesteader could then file paperwork to own it. The law enabled Nevada ranchers to expand their land and livestock holdings, but, as in many other states, it also helped land speculators make huge profits.

Also in 1862 Congress passed and Lincoln signed the Morrill Land-Grant College Act, based on a decades-old movement to create agricultural colleges and make a college education available outside of private or church-funded schools. Republicans ultimately wanted to go beyond the original goal and promote learning among immigrants and industrial workers and thus, "without excluding other scientific and classical studies and including military tactics, to teach such branches of learning as are related to agriculture and the mechanic arts." To build a college or university, each state—and, after further legislation, territory—would receive 30,000 acres of federal land for each member of Congress it had as of 1860; in Nevada's case, since Congress had yet to create it, the state would receive credit for one representative and two senators. Writing the Nevada Constitution in

The women students at the Normal School, created to train teachers, in a drawing class in 1908. In the background, Morrill Hall, the University of Nevada–Reno's first building, honors the congressman who introduced the Land Grant Act that gave rise to the school. Courtesy of Special Collections, University of Nevada–Reno Library.

1864, the convention delegates provided for an eventual state university with departments in agriculture, mechanical arts, and mining.

The Morrill Act ultimately funded more than seventy colleges and universities. Nevada finally took advantage of it in 1873. Thanks to pressure from Governor Lewis Bradley, an Elko rancher, the school opened the next year as Nevada State University in the northeastern community, with a dozen students. It moved to Reno in 1886 and into its first building, Morrill Hall, named for the congressman. Subsequent expansions of the Morrill Act prompted the creation of the University of Nevada Cooperative Extension Service, and the university's growth into southern Nevada in 1951 eventually led to an independent school, the University of Nevada, Las Vegas.

Working on the Railroad

The third major act in 1862 culminated years of debate and effort. Without Southerners to fight for their own route, Northerners passed a law to build a transcontinental railroad. The Pacific Railroad Act approved land grants, rights-of-way, and bonds for the Union Pacific to build west from Omaha, Nebraska, and the Central Pacific to meet it coming east from Sacramento, California. Eventually, the UP built nearly eleven hundred miles of track and the CP nearly seven hundred miles. The road's completion, celebrated with the golden spike at Promontory Summit, Utah, on May 10, 1869, linked the Atlantic and Pacific Oceans by rail. The laws made the railroads second only to the federal government among landowners in the West, set up a public-private partnership that changed industry and government, created large businesses that transcended socioeconomic lines, and opened trade routes for the United States with Asia. The railroad also continued a series of nineteenth-century technological innovations, including the invention of the telegraph and advances in transportation ranging from the steamboat to the Erie Canal, all making parts of the country less remote from one another and promoting national and international involvement in seemingly exotic places like Nevada.

Although a transcontinental railroad had long been discussed, a group of Californians teamed with the federal government to plan the western branch. The Central Pacific's chief advocate and lobbyist, Theodore Judah, realized the Sierra Nevada would be the major obstacle and worked with a miner who had surveyed a route for a wagon road that would also work for a railroad. When Judah interested Collis Huntington in financing the road, the Sacramento merchant used his eastern connections to win support and brought in three other investors to form the Big Four: his business partner Mark Hopkins and merchants Leland Stanford and Charles Crocker. By the time construction began in 1863, Judah had died and Crocker became superintendent. Climbing the Sierra Nevada proved as hard as expected, but they blasted through with dynamite and imported Chinese laborers more willing than the largely Irish labor force to work twelve-hour days in cold and dangerous conditions for thirty to thirty-five dollars a month; at times whites constituted only about one-fifth of the construction workers, mostly in supervisory or skilled jobs. This approach produced results: the railroad reached the California-Nevada line in December 1867, more than four years after construction began.

In addition to easing immigration laws to bring in more Chinese, federal and state governments helped the project. Huntington and his lobbyists constantly worked to obtain favorable legislation. As California's governor, Stanford ignored any concerns about conflicts of interest and urged his state legislature to support bond and stock issues. In the original act and future laws, the US government subsidized construction at sixteen thousand dollars per mile over flat lands, thirty-two thousand in the high plains, and forty-eight thousand in the mountains, benefiting Union Pacific investors as their line climbed the Rockies and the Big Four as they went through the Sierra Nevada and the mountainous Great Basin. Land grants topped 175 million acres, more than twice the size of Nevada and a source of great profit to Huntington, Hopkins, Crocker, and Stanford when the UP and CP sold off the most valuable acreage. Each line received a four-hundred-foot right-of-way on either side of the tracks and ten alternating sections of 160 acres of land per mile of track.

Building the line also proved expensive. The Big Four had to ship most of what they needed for construction from California into Nevada. The cost of iron rails more than doubled from the start to the end of construction. One engineer said, "Water was scarce after leaving the Truckee and Humboldt Rivers. . . . There was not a tree that would make a board on over 500 miles of the route, no satisfactory quality of building stone. The country afforded nothing." But the CP began carrying passengers and freight where it could, between Sacramento and Reno, and then to points east. Profits began to grow, although Huntington sensed displeasure: "I notice that everybody is in favor of a railroad until they get it built and then everyone is against it unless the railroad company will carry them and theirs for nothing." The future brought little sympathy with his point of view.

A Political Machine

Nationally, the Union Pacific's political activities invited more attention and criticism when the Crédit Mobilier scandal of 1873 revealed that its operators bought off elected officials with stock deals. The Central Pacific also proved both questionable and questioned. The railroad paid off government loans and liens, but its leaders, especially Huntington, sought to limit federal or state interference in its operations through taxes, regulations, or setting passenger and freight rates. Thus, the Central Pacific became a key player in Gilded Age politics, nationally and in Nevada. Until the Seventeenth Amendment to the US Constitution in 1913, state legislatures elected US senators. If the railroad controlled enough legislatures, it could avoid interference at both the state and the federal levels.

Huntington and his lobbyists—a term coined in the late nineteenth century—used a variety of techniques. They committed bribery, with Nevada's senator William M. Stewart receiving fifty thousand acres of land. As Huntington told Crocker without a hint of irony, "He is peculiar, but thoroughly honest, and will bear no dictation, but I know he must live, and we must fix it so that he can make one or two hundred thousand dollars. It is to our interest and I think his right." They liberally distributed passes, allowing politicians and editors and their families to travel on the CP and its feeder lines for free. They pressured politicians by giving or withholding contributions and did the same to editors with advertising.

The iron horse became one of the ironies of history. "Honest Abe" Lincoln signed the act for the transcontinental railroad, whose investors and operators then engaged in a variety of dishonest business and political activities. As beneficiaries of government aid, the Union Pacific and Central Pacific did their best and worst to limit government action. While its builders became known as titans of business, their line went through sparsely populated areas that may not yet have wanted or needed such a significant project. In Nevada the Central Pacific worked with—and sometimes against—equally important mining industrialists in pursuit of similar purposes and gains. As historian Heather Cox Richardson has written, "The same ideas and optimism that shaped the Republicans' plans for a strong and prosperous nation caused them unwittingly to lay the groundwork for the turmoil of the late nineteenth century." Nevada would be at the heart of the turmoil.

The Railroad Shapes Nevada

Many Nevada towns owed their existence or expansion to the Central Pacific. As superintendent, Crocker usually chose sites already settled or with ample water available. The tough job of building over the Sierra Nevada and through the Great Basin's mountains and desert led to the creation of new towns and the expansion of old ones for workers, construction supplies, repair yards, and related industries. With the railroad constructed from west to east, its towns encouraged building roads north and south through valley networks, and mining and ranching hinterlands grew accordingly. The railroad's presence in these towns also promoted warehousing and travel, both key components of Nevada's economy long after surrounding mining areas turned from boom to bust.

The first town the railroad developed, Reno, expanded from Myron Lake's inn and toll bridge (later the Virginia Street Bridge) into a city. Lake sold land north of the Truckee to the CP, which auctioned it on May 9, 1868—thirty-seven years and six days before a similar auction began Las Vegas—and named the town for a Civil War casualty, General Jesse Reno. Reno soon became a distribution point for the CP, the nearby Comstock Lode, and an agricultural hinterland. Protected from the mining economy's boom-and-bust cycles, Reno became Washoe's county seat by 1870 and the state's major city by the 1880s.

As the Central Pacific pushed east, it built or promoted other towns. Nearby Wadsworth, the site of trading posts for emigrants in the 1850s that Crocker named for another Civil War general, became the CP's Truckee Division headquarters. After Welsh-born rancher George Lovelock donated land, the CP built a station and named the town for him, and Lovelock grew to serve other nearby farmers and ranchers. Already mushrooming from a trading post to a small town catering to miners, and intersecting with north–south stage lines, Winnemucca benefited when Crocker made it a division point, with an icehouse and a roundhouse. Golconda's hot springs had drawn emigrants, and the CP's arrival turned it into a resort and a shipping and telegraph station. Crocker built Argenta (Latin for "silver"), but settlers preferred Battle Mountain, where the Reese and Humboldt Rivers

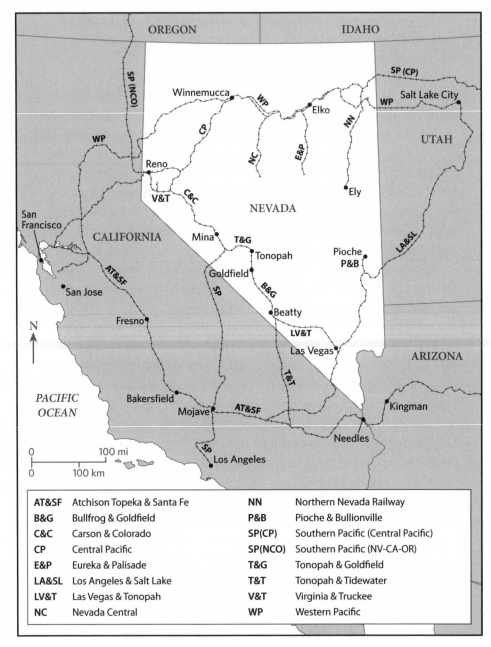

Nineteenth- and twentieth-century railroads

meet, and the railroad went along, building a siding to supply nearby mining camps.

The Central Pacific developed four towns in Elko County. About seventy miles apart, Carlin and Wells became freight distribution points, though Carlin had originally been a settlement for Chinese railroad workers. Elko's origins resembled Reno's, with the CP platting it and auctioning parcels and the town growing quickly, relying on an agricultural hinterland that added to the benefits of mining but also offset it during economic downturns. Like Reno, Elko combined culture, cowboys, and carousing, with forty-five saloons open in its first six months, and developed ties to the closest big city—Reno to San Francisco and Elko to Salt Lake. Farther northeast, Toano, linked to southwestern Idaho and eastern Nevada, served as a division point but became a ghost town in the early twentieth century.

With the federal government easing immigration laws to help the CP obtain cheaper labor, additional Chinese migrants joined earlier arrivals from the Far East, Union Army veterans, former slaves and free blacks, and Irish who had recently come west or previously joined mining rushes. After helping to build the railroad, some continued to work for the CP after its completion. As they settled mainly in towns near the line, their presence further diversified Nevada's varied population, although people of color usually wound up segregated, especially the Chinese.

Just as the Central Pacific's construction fostered towns and population, it also encouraged other transportation after its completion. Stage and wagon companies appeared to transport people and freight to railroad stations. Following in the footsteps of the CP's operators in California, where they consolidated rail links to their road, feeder lines from various towns flowed into the CP, most notably the Virginia & Truckee (V&T), which originated in Virginia City and later served nearby agricultural communities like Minden and Gardnerville. Anson Phelps Stokes, an eastern developer who invested in mining, built a short line from Battle Mountain to Austin in the late 1870s to reduce travel time and the cost of transporting ore. Darius O. Mills, the president of the Bank of California and one of the V&T's builders, completed the Eureka & Palisade Railroad in 1875 to tie that mining boomtown to the CP and the Carson & Colorado to link western Nevada with the Colorado River in California, with unrealized hopes of building farther east and west. What Mills said of the C&C may have been true of railroad building in the West: "We built this line either 300 miles too long or 300 years too soon."

Historian Richard White has noted, "Building the transcontinentals and fighting the Civil War both involved great risk, immense expenditures of money, a sense of national purpose, and the organizational efforts of a newly powerful national state. Yet, as in a mirror, the resemblance was reversed. The Civil War demanded personal sacrifice for concrete collective goals; the railroads promised personal gain for projected public purposes." As part of that mirror, Nevada probably became a state too soon, considering its volatile economy and transient populace. White and other scholars have argued that the men behind the railroads that remapped the West, including Nevada, built them too soon. Yet both Nevada's existence—its status as a territory and state, its political culture, its constitution—and the railroad construction that affected Nevada and the nation reflected the opportunities and changes the Civil War created and the West's geography made possible. That geography also led to the mining rushes that shaped Nevada in tandem with and sometimes in opposition to the railroads and the government.

SUGGESTED READINGS

Ambrose, Stephen E. *Nothing Like It in the World: The Men Who Built the Transcontinental Railroad, 1863–1869.* New York: Simon and Schuster, 2000.

Etulain, Richard W., ed. *Lincoln Looks West: From the Mississippi to the Pacific.* Carbondale: Southern Illinois University Press, 2010.

James, Ronald M., and Robert E. Stewart, eds. *The Gold Rush Letters of E. Allen Grosh and Hosea B. Grosh.* Reno: University of Nevada Press / Nevada Historical Society, 2012.

Johnson, David A. *Founding the Far West: California, Oregon, and Nevada, 1840–1890.* Berkeley: University of California Press, 1992.

Lewis, Oscar. *The Big Four: The Story of Huntington, Stanford, Hopkins, and Crocker, and the Building of the Central Pacific.* New York: Alfred A. Knopf, 1938 and reprints.

Long, E. B. *The Saints and the Union: Utah Territory During the Civil War.* Urbana: University of Illinois Press, 1981.

Matthews, Glenna. *The Golden State in the Civil War: Thomas Starr King, the Republican Party, and the Birth of Modern California.* New York: Cambridge University Press, 2012.

Miller, William C., Russell W. McDonald, and Ann Rollins, eds. *Letters from Nevada Territory, 1861–1862, by Andrew J. Marsh.* Carson City: Legislative Counsel Bureau, 1972.

Moody, Eric N., ed. *Western Carpetbagger: The Life and Extraordinary Memoirs of "Senator" Thomas Fitch*. Reno: University of Nevada Press, 1978.

Moreno, Richard. *A Short History of Carson City*. Reno: University of Nevada Press, 2009.

Myrick, David F. *Railroads of Nevada and Eastern California*. Reno: University of Nevada Press, 1992.

Orsi, Richard J. *Sunset Limited: The Southern Pacific Railroad and the Development of the American West, 1850–1930*. Berkeley: University of California Press, 2005.

Richardson, Heather Cox. *The Greatest Nation of the Earth: Republican Economic Policies During the Civil War*. Cambridge, MA: Harvard University Press, 1997.

Stonehouse, Merlin. *John Wesley North and the Reform Frontier*. Minneapolis: University of Minnesota Press, 1965.

Tutorow, Norman E. *The Governor: The Life and Legacy of Leland Stanford, a California Colossus*. 2 vols. Spokane, WA: Arthur H. Clark, 2004.

White, Richard. *Railroaded: The Transcontinentals and the Making of Modern America*. New York: W. W. Norton, 2011.

6

The Nineteenth-Century Mining Boom

In 1873 Mark Twain and Charles Dudley Warner's novel, *The Gilded Age: A Tale of Today* (as in Shakespeare's *King John:* "To gild refined gold, to paint the lily . . . is wasteful and ridiculous excess"), defined an era. Most Americans associate the period from the Civil War to 1900 with developments in the eastern United States. But Nevada exemplified the Gilded Age, and not merely because Samuel Clemens became Mark Twain there and his reporting in the *Virginia City Territorial Enterprise* and book *Roughing It* brought his experiences to the masses. The Gilded Age reflected national and international events, but perhaps nowhere so clearly as in Nevada during a nineteenth-century mining boom that spread throughout the state and displayed many of the era's characteristics.

Gilded Age America

Admirers and critics of Andrew Carnegie's steel company, Standard Oil's John D. Rockefeller, and other Gilded Age giants have debated what to call them: visionaries who built the United States into an economic giant or robber barons who took advantage of the less fortunate to gain great wealth and power. Both descriptions fit them and help explain America—and Nevada—in the Gilded Age. Although the Industrial Revolution had remade European and American life since the late eighteenth century, technological advances between 1860 and 1900 marked a new industrial age for the United States. The Civil War—the weapons to fight it and the logistics of equipping and moving soldiers—sped the process. From Thomas Edison's lightbulb to Henry Bessemer's steam engine, inventions and improvements generated products more quickly and cheaply. By developing vertical integration to control their products, industrialists owned the factories and the resources that made their factories hum and then often transported and sold the results themselves.

Expanding and upgrading those factories intensified the reshaping of American life. Changes in farming reduced the need for labor, and new factory jobs accelerated urbanization. Immigration from southern and eastern Europe—Greece and Italy as well as Slavic Jews, most escaping oppression and turmoil—provided more residents for cities and labor for factories. They often wound up in ethnic enclaves due to segregation, limited finances, or the need to be close to work: while prejudice played a role, their numbers made it hard for workers to organize for better pay and conditions. But the American Federation of Labor (AFL) organized skilled craftsmen and the Knights of Labor the unskilled, and some local unions enjoyed successes. Demands for reform and better working conditions inspired movements, strikes, and violence such as the Haymarket Riot in Chicago in 1886 and the Homestead Steel Strike of 1892 against Carnegie.

These changes promoted corruption, even beyond the railroads (see chapter 5). In 1873 stock manipulation and speculation crashed financial markets, causing a six-year depression. Urban bosses found immigrants susceptible to control as they tried to adjust to a new way of life. Northerners largely gave up on Reconstruction and efforts to protect African Americans' constitutional rights. Industries developed political machines to make sure that if government interfered in the economy, it did so to help them. The Gilded Age also became known for gridlock: with several close presidential races and the two major parties often sharing power, changes in policy became hard to make or sustain, especially compared with the freer hand Republicans enjoyed during and right after the Civil War.

Birth of a Lode

The Comstock Lode's beginnings reflected the larger role of industrialization and investment in American business. From 1850 to 1858, Gold Canyon miners found about $642,000 worth of ore amid a darker, less fine, less solid material that many, with the exception of the ill-fated Groshes, dismissed as worthless. Their error suggested an absence of vision, but they lacked the funds to extract and refine what they found—like the lode's discoverers, who found large veins in two phases and wound up selling out and giving way to corporations that grew larger, as finding gold and silver demanded more capital and technology.

The Gold Hill discovery began the first phase in January 1859. John Bishop, Alexander Henderson, John Yount, and longtime area miner James "Ol' Virginny" Finney found gold at the head of Gold Canyon. They set up a camp and named it Gold Hill. Nearby miners swarmed in, sank other shafts, determined the gold ran at least eight feet deep, and produced enough money to generate reports of immense riches. Prospectors also began diverting needed water from a stream on the side of Sun Mountain, adapting to technology and adapting it to their needs.

To the east, Six-Mile Canyon attracted other miners hoping the riches extended that way. Two of them, Patrick McLaughlin and Peter O'Riley, moved uphill and, on June 8, built a dam to harness the water they found. The soil they threw in their rocker contained gold, along with black rock that turned out to be silver. By that evening, with ample gold piled up, Henry Comstock arrived. A camp veteran, he told McLaughlin and O'Riley that he had claimed the area—maybe a ruse, maybe the truth, since some miners filed multiple claims. They agreed to a partnership with him and his friend Immanuel Penrod. Three days later, on June 11, they and other prospectors met to enact rules to govern their mining district, including elective offices and record keeping.

Soon, McLaughlin, O'Riley, Penrod, and Comstock gained some idea of what they had. They found the black material congealing into a thick vein but had trouble extracting it. They brought in two more partners, rancher John D. Winters Jr. and a newly elected local justice of the peace, J. A. Osborn, in return for building two mills with horses and mules. Less than three weeks after their discovery, an assayer judged its value per ton at $876 in gold and $3,000 in silver.

The Rush to Washoe loomed, but others profited more than the founders, who sold their interests early and reaped few of the rewards that more savvy investors and mining experts would. Finney apparently sold his share for a horse and either cash or whiskey and kept prospecting. The other partners received money for their holdings, including Comstock, who invested in a mercantile and lost his riches. His name became inseparable from the rush as he traveled the West, mining and talking about "my" lode. In 1870, suffering from mental illness, he committed suicide in Montana, site of a rush similar to the one in Nevada. By then, the Comstock Lode had become enormously wealthy, with more and better to come.

The Early Comstock, 1859–64

In the five years after the Gold Canyon and Six-Mile Canyon discoveries, Virginia City and its environs evolved from a canvas-covered boomtown to an urban industrial center serving and being served by a hinterland of farms and timber. By 1860 Virginia City and Gold Hill attracted a population of more than three thousand; it increased within two years to nearly forty-five hundred, including miners, every imaginable variety of related businesses, and other artisans, craftspeople, and entrepreneurs. Teamsters and packers hauled ore and various goods; carpenters helped shore up mines and built businesses; merchants provided an assortment of goods. The towns consisted almost entirely of single young men, yet, contrary to legend, proved no more violent than places with a similar population. Indeed, local residents quickly sought to ensure law and order through government institutions and churches that promoted good behavior.

Contrary to another legend, few of the limited number of women along the Comstock in 1860—perhaps 4 percent of the population—involved themselves in prostitution. Most women identified themselves as keeping house, as wives, or as domestic servants. By 1864 a religious order, the Daughters of Charity, had arrived in Virginia City and started such social services as a hospital, a school, and an orphanage, reflecting Comstock society's maturity and its problems. Not that Virginia City lacked for misbehavior: it included at least a hundred saloons at various points in the 1860s and 1870s and a Temperance League dedicated to barring alcohol. In 1867 Julia Bulette's murder turned her into the lode's most famous prostitute and bred the image of the wealthy, tainted lady with the heart of gold—local firemen named her an honorary member of their engine company, and other attention came her way after her death—but most Comstock prostitutes did low-paying work that the community saw as disreputable.

In the lode's early years, immigrants constituted more than 30 percent of its residents—a greater average than in most of the country at the time. The presence of diverse societies led to varied cultural opportunities, from ethnic organizations to food. From the start, new or recently arrived Irish migrants outnumbered other groups, although Cornish who came from Wales in significant numbers due to their experience with mining made their presence felt. Although Hispanics proved few in number, the Maldonado brothers filed several claims near the Ophir, the most profitable mine of the early Comstock. By 1880 just over a quarter of the nearly twenty-eight hundred men employed in the declining Comstock mining industry had been born in the United States—fewer than the number of Irish.

Almost every imaginable church and denomination sprang up as the Comstock grew, including African American efforts to form their own churches, but two religious leaders stood out. Rabbi Herman Bien started a Jewish day school, served in the legislature (where he tried and failed to abolish the death penalty), and exposed corruption in Storey County's educational system before departing to head a congregation in Chicago. Father Patrick Manogue served as Virginia City's priest for more than two decades before leaving and rising to bishop; while on the Comstock, he gained notice for both good works and, given the large Irish Catholic population, his congregation's size.

Comstock Culture

Early Virginia City also developed social and cultural institutions, none more important to the town than its newspapers, especially the *Territorial Enterprise*. It set such a unique standard that literary scholar Lawrence Berkove coined the term "the Sagebrush School" to describe the style its writers used there and in more literary offerings. Editor Joseph Goodman's editorials infuriated fellow Republican Thomas Fitch enough to challenge him to a duel; Goodman shot him, and they wound up friends. Other *Enterprise* writers such as Rollin Daggett, Charles C. Goodwin, "Lyin' Jim" Townsend, and Wells Drury went on to long careers in journalism and, sometimes, politics and literature. Onetime contributor Alfred Doten edited the *Gold Hill Daily News* and kept detailed journals of local life that legendary Nevada writer Walter Van Tilburg Clark edited into a three-volume collection that remains an important source of information about the lode.

The longest-tenured *Enterprise* reporter, William Wright, adopted the pen name of Dan DeQuille—and wielded a dandy quill. His book *The Big Bonanza,* the first major history of the lode, combined facts known only to a longtime local reporter and fiction of the sort that he inserted into *Enterprise* columns when the mood struck him or local news proved scarce. These hoaxes ranged from blind fish in Virginia City mine shafts to what he called "The Traveling Stones of Pahranagat," magnetic stones in southeastern Nevada that could form a circle. Some of his articles also satirized his roommate, fellow *Enterprise* reporter Samuel Clemens.

While living in Virginia City, Clemens began using the pen name of Mark Twain and joined Wright in covering and inventing news. Besides clerking at the territorial legislature, he criticized it in print and in satirical programs called "The Third House," which became a Carson City tradition. Eventually, he left for San Francisco—according to rumors, after the subject of one of his hoaxes challenged him to a duel. Although Twain's combination of satire, dialect, and dark humor accompanied him from Missouri, his Nevada adventures helped shape the future author of *The Adventures of Tom Sawyer, Huckleberry Finn,* and one of the most important works of Nevada literature, *Roughing It,* his long and sometimes uproarious account of his trip to and life in the West.

The Comstock's—indeed, nineteenth-century Nevada's—cultural opportunities extended beyond journalism and literature. Piper's Opera House became a cultural center, hosting leading performers and lecturers. Traveling theatrical troupes and circuses toured Nevada mining towns. As with any community, residents of the Comstock's towns formed an array of ethnic and literary clubs and societies.

Comstock Technology

The Gold Rush bred innovations, but the Comstock proved more advanced technologically. Mining silver and preparing it for the market required more complex processes than gold, and the geography of Virginia City and surrounding areas made transporting ore and supplies harder than in California's goldfields. New inventions drove industrialization in late-nineteenth-century America, and Nevada stood at the forefront of these developments in mining. In turn, these highlighted the need for capital, sped the transition from prospectors to corporate ownership, and increased the reliance on outside money to fund technology and wage labor to work in the mining "factories" of Gilded Age Nevada.

Mill owner Almarin Paul originated the first major change in technology to separate ore from the rock. After iron hammers or stamps pounded the gold and silver, workers shoveled them into iron pans, mixing the ore with water, mercury, salt, and copper sulfate. Once the heavier gold, silver, and mercury dropped to the bottom, mill hands strained them through a buckskin bag, and heat separated the mercury from the ore. Paul's idea evolved into the Washoe Pan Process, which still fell short in reckoning with dividing the silver and gold. But by late 1861, seventy-six mills with twelve hundred stamps pounded away daily—too many mills, which, historian Ronald James noted, "left part of the mining infrastructure overinvested and underemployed, vulnerable to financial takeover and manipulation."

Whatever the financial dangers, physical ones outweighed them. Wide veins went deep into the earth, where clay and water made underground shafts unstable, even deadly. In 1860 the Ophir Mining Company, the lode's first San Francisco–based corporation, called in German engineer Philipp Deidesheimer. Only twenty-eight years old, he spent a decade in California before arriving in Virginia City, but in a month he devised the solution: square-set timbering, which framed timbers in rectangles and joined them, with the cavities packed with dirt as miners removed the ore. Although imperfect (timbers eventually cracked under the pressure), this system proved life-saving and profitable for owners who could dig deeper, miners who could thus earn more pay, and lumber companies providing the needed wood—but not Deidesheimer, who never patented it. Still, it made his reputation, and although stock speculation eventually bankrupted him, he regained wealth as a mine owner and superintendent.

Unfortunately, Deidesheimer's brilliance had unintended consequences: it fed an insatiable need for wood, enhancing the economy and harming the environment. The town of Glenbrook sprouted on Lake Tahoe's eastern shore to process the trees that lumber companies cut. Duane Bliss and W. S. Hobart became wealthy chopping lumber—about six hundred million feet as well as two million cords of firewood by 1880. Square-set timbering required wood, but so did railroads, roads, and buildings—and the prevalence of fire led to the need for lumber for reconstruction, too. Thus, the Comstock's success denuded the forests on the mountains around Virginia City and up toward Lake Tahoe.

Square-set timbering contributed to the existing problem of obtaining lumber and water. Steep roads to the top of the Sierra Nevada proved hard to travel, and damming the waters to wash timber downstream rarely worked. In 1867 James W. Haines perfected the V-flume, named for its shape. He joined boards at right angles, each section under the one above it, with props and trestles to hold them up, ran water, and more easily washed the trees down to Virginia City. One such flume extended fifteen miles and could move more than three million feet of lumber per week— further boosting the lumber industry and damaging the nearby forests. German immigrant Hermann Schussler's engineering knowledge enabled him to develop the inverted siphon, a system of flumes and tunnels that made it possible to make water flow uphill to the Comstock.

Cornish miners shared a belief in "Tommyknockers," ghosts rapping on timbers in the shafts and, more important, a fear of the hemp ropes used to lower them into the mines. Andrew Hallidie adapted his iron rope to create a braided wire belt that proved safer and spread to other camps. Hallidie took his invention back to San Francisco, where he used it in creating the city's cable-car system.

Adolph Sutro and His Tunnel

New technology helped, but corporations and engineers still faced the problem of clearing water out of their mines for the sake of extracting ore and protecting miners against cave-ins. In 1865 the Belcher Mine pumped more than one million gallons out of its shaft. Machines known as Cornish Pumps, complete with steam engines and flywheels sometimes weighing more than one hundred tons, removed water, but proved large, loud, and costly.

Local mill owner Adolph Sutro, a former San Francisco merchant, de- vised a solution: an enormous drainage tunnel under the Comstock. Start- ing in 1865 he incorporated his company, won legislative support, raised $3 million from mine owners, and began plotting a nearly four-mile tun- nel from the Carson River Valley to the Comstock's mines, about one-third of a mile underground. He promoted construction of a town, modestly called Sutro, at the entrance, and vowed it would replace Virginia City as the Comstock's business center. Those promises, and the threat he posed to their influence, soon prompted bankers and politicians who had once supported him—the chairman of his company had been Senator William Stewart, who represented many of them as an attorney—to abandon him.

Sutro accomplished part of his goal. He finished the tunnel in the late 1870s; by then the Comstock had declined, and the necessity for his idea diminished. The tunnel cost about $3.5 million, with salaries during con- struction adding up to about $1,000 a day. While most tunnel contractors and investors lost money, Sutro gained ample wealth from the funds they poured in. He took his money to San Francisco, bought land, and eventually won election as mayor—one of many to benefit financially from Nevada and leave the state.

The Rise of the Bank Crowd

Early in the Comstock's history, California-based investors began to play a significant role in its evolution. Less than a year after the Six-Mile Canyon discovery, the Ophir Silver Mining Company incorporated at a value of more than $5 million. Its owners included George Hearst, a miner and businessman from the western Sierra Nevada foothills who started the nation's largest private mining firm, laying the foundation of his financial empire and that of his son, publisher William Randolph Hearst. Even then, the Ophir and other companies formed to operate Comstock mines proved too small and conservative to develop the area to its fullest, and the boom-and-bust cycle of mining overtook the region by early 1864.

The Ophir mining works and shaft in Virginia City. The extensive mining operation depicted in this photo, taken sometime in the 1860s or early 1870s, suggests why the individual prospector had to give way to the corporation. Courtesy of Special Collections, University of Nevada–Reno Library.

That year supporters of statehood argued that it could ease or end the downturn afflicting the Comstock Lode. The best ore had been reached, and whatever lurked below the surface sat too far underground to be reached easily or profitably. Production, revenues, and stocks began falling in 1863 and continued to do so over the next two years, with the Comstock's estimated value plummeting from $40 million to $4 million. Up to ten thousand residents may have left Virginia City and the surrounding area for other mining boomtowns, in Nevada and elsewhere.

For some, though, depression meant opportunity—especially the San Francisco–based Bank of California. Its president, William Ralston, invested in Comstock mines as early as 1860; his partner, Sacramento banker D. O. Mills, benefited from and helped finance the Gold Rush. They opened a Virginia City branch in the summer of 1864, with William Sharon as manager. As a Gold Rush merchant and real estate investor who lost his fortune speculating in mining stocks, Sharon knew the aspirations and failings of his customers and the industry they relied on. He ordered a geological survey that convinced him of the lode's value and depth. With more capital than other bankers, he undercut competitors with lower-interest loans—2 percent instead of 5 percent. Using call loans enabled him to demand payment at the least-convenient time for the borrower, who then had to surrender his collateral: his mine or mill or claim. California investor Alvinza Hayward helped the bank take over two leading mines (the Yellow Jacket and Chollar-Potosi) and form the Union Mill and Mining Company. By 1867 Sharon and the Bank Crowd owned every important Comstock mine and seventeen mills.

Vertical Integration

While eastern industrialists often receive credit for vertical integration, Sharon may have been more masterful at it. The Bank Crowd owned mines that produced vast amounts of ore, major mills to process it, about fifty thousand acres of timberland to shore up the mines, a V-flume for transporting the timber, and a water company to provide pumps to remove water from the mines and a supply for drinking and milling. Sharon bought a majority interest in the *Territorial Enterprise,* controlling information and advertising through a powerful newspaper to the benefit of the bank and its related businesses. But he purchased it mainly for political purposes, reflecting his desire for office and power: Sharon wanted to avoid unfavorable taxes and regulations as much as the Central Pacific's Big Four did.

More important, Sharon and the bank's owners saw a need for efficient and profitable freight transportation, and the financial possibilities of passenger service that went with it. With the Central Pacific built through Reno, Sharon hired an engineer to plot a route there from Virginia City by way of Carson City. To help finance construction, he and his partners persuaded Washoe and Ormsby Counties to float $500,000 in bonds and mining companies to put up $700,000. By the time the Virginia & Truckee Railroad began operating in 1869, it had to climb nearby mountains, requiring six major tunnels and twenty-one miles of track to Carson City—and a famous five-hundred-foot-long, eighty-five-foot-high trestle across the Crown Point Ravine near Gold Hill. An extension to Reno in 1871 linked the v&t to the Central Pacific. By 1873 additional silver discoveries and population growth drove the v&t's monthly profits to a reported $100,000 and the number of daily runs to forty. Due to its six thousand degrees of turns—the mountains require the v&t to turn in seventeen circles throughout its route—the line became known as "the crookedest railroad in the world." The Bank Crowd's business and political practices also had something to do with that nickname.

The Bank Crowd's reputation—and that of other Comstock entrepreneurs—suffered due to stock speculation. Prospectors believed in luck and chance, and those tied to the market knew how to manipulate them. Sharon and Hayward excelled at starting rumors of new finds to drive up values, then selling their shares at a profit before the market collapsed. At one point, Hayward's efforts increased shares in the Savage mine, which he co-owned, from $62 to $725 in three months. Nor did such stock scandals stay confined to Nevada: representing one of the group of British investors who paid $5 million for Utah's depleted Emma Silver Mine, William Stewart involved the US minister to England and Ulysses Grant's administration in his efforts to profit, may have swindled clients and shareholders, and wound up having to deny wrongdoing before a congressional investigating committee.

Labor and Mining

Few industrial workers enjoyed better benefits or suffered harsher conditions than Nevada miners, especially on the Comstock. They often could work no more than fifteen minutes at a time and, one estimate found, used nearly one hundred pounds of ice per shift to combat the intense heat. In 1863 they formed a Miners Protective Association that later became the Miner's League of Storey County—another sign that Comstock mines had become corporate, industrial complexes employing wage labor. Miners hoped to preserve the $4-a-day scale, which mine owners tried to cut during economic dips. The miners failed: not only did their pay drop to $3.50, but after local mine owners teamed to work against them, territorial governor James Nye called in troops from Fort Churchill to suppress labor agitation. Similar actions produced similar results in Nevada mining towns in the twentieth century.

Later unions fared better. Labor groups formed in 1866 and 1867 focused not only on wages and benefits, but also on elections, especially for law enforcement. Thus, when they struck, mine owners who wanted the authorities to help them break the strike found no sympathy and gave in. And it paid for them to do so: the Comstock's growing wealth and the need for capable miners made it easier and wiser for mine owners to accede to demands for a $4 daily wage, just as Las Vegas resort owners would accede to many union demands during the tourism boom of the 1990s and early 2000s.

The unions flexed their muscles in other ways. Like the Central Pacific Big Four, Sharon, Ralston, and Mills, the triumvirate running the V&T, relied heavily on Chinese labor—at first. When a slight downturn before V&T construction began in February 1869 reduced employment, miners resented their lack of work and the lower pay for which the Chinese worked. They even confronted Chinese laborers in Gold Hill and refused to back down when the sheriff ordered them to do so. Sharon agreed to their demands and replaced the Chinese workers. For Sharon and his partners, considering their profits, that proved a small price to pay.

Industrial Communities

Mining boomtowns often proved short-lived. But the ones that lasted evolved into industrial cities and towns. Like Carnegie's Homestead,

Pennsylvania, or railroad towns along the Union and Central Pacific tracks, they often relied on one industry—a trend that continued into twentieth-century Nevada, as military spending and tourism joined mining as economic drivers. In a decade, as the Comstock's population swelled, the percentage working in mining declined and the number of women and children skyrocketed—evidence of an increasingly diverse urban region. The Irish and Cornish presence expanded, especially in mining, while the Chinese formed ethnically segregated enclaves.

The Comstock's communities also set precedents for future Nevada cities. For one, they combined residential living with vice. Some of the Comstock's Chinese catered to those interested in drugs, especially opium, and prostitution, although racism and language barriers may have prompted census takers to count as prostitutes Chinese women who had nothing to do with that profession (the same may have been true of Mexican women). Also, the mines at Virginia City and its surrounding communities employed three shifts of workers who sought necessities and entertainment—especially the latter and often the more sinful, the better. Most of the economic activity flourished by day, but enough went on after dark for Nevada to have twenty-four-hour towns long before gambling in Las Vegas and Reno.

Just as eastern industrial towns boasted a pastiche of ethnic groups and suffered from various forms of bigotry, so did Nevada. Although income level and land values also determined location, black Nevadans often lived in segregated areas. W. H. C. Stephenson may have been Nevada's first African American doctor, living in Virginia City and registering to vote soon after the Fifteenth Amendment's passage, and other people of color worked at a variety of occupations. Segregation limited the number working in the mines to a few, but federal measures and pressure from newly enfranchised black voters and enlightened whites prompted the state to lift bans on jury service and court testimony. The Nevada Supreme Court held segregated schools unconstitutional, due mainly to the financial expense involved, but laws against racial intermarriage remained in force.

As in the heavily immigrant eastern cities, segregation and traditional roles combined with the opportunities that Turner saw on the frontier. Discrimination affected others who lacked the organization or support from whites to be able to combat it. Most of the Comstock's Mexican immigrants worked as miners at first and then found it harder to obtain such well-paying jobs. The Chinese found profit in stereotypical occupations, running laundries that competed with Irish women who washed clothes. Some Northern Paiutes lived in similarly segregated sections of the Comstock and fitted gender stereotypes—men as laborers, women as domestics.

The Big Bonanza

Competitors eventually bent the Bank Crowd's power over the Comstock, but never broke it. In 1870 bank board member Alvinza Hayward and Crown Point superintendent John P. Jones, his brother-in-law, bought the mine's stock and took it over. The mine had yet to produce high-grade ore, but it soon did, making Jones and Hayward still wealthier. Forming a mining and milling company, they began competing with Sharon and his allies, including when Jones defeated Sharon for a US Senate seat in 1873. But both groups sought the same goals financially and politically, meaning their economic competition did nothing to breed real differences or changes at the federal, state, and local levels. Sharon negotiated a swap, obtaining their stock in another mine that produced ample dividends.

The Bonanza Firm provides a better example of competition and community. Just as California had a Big Four (the Central Pacific), Nevada had its own powerful quartet. John Mackay, James Fair, James Flood, and William O'Brien shared Irish ancestry (all but Flood immigrated to the United States) and involvement in the Gold Rush. Flood and O'Brien became saloon keepers and stockbrokers. Mackay and Fair remained in mining, moving separately to the Comstock, where both rose to superintendent and Mackay grew wealthy. Their big chance came in 1869 when Sharon and the Bank of California drove up stock prices on the Hale & Norcross, a mine they invested heavily in with little success. Mackay and Fair teamed with Flood and O'Brien to take over through stock purchases, won election as directors, and made the mine profitable. In 1872 they obtained the Best and Belcher, a productive claim that had never been fully explored. With Fair supervising, they searched until, in 1873, they hit "the Big Bonanza," following a vein twelve feet wide. The "Bonanza Firm," as it became known, had struck it rich. Over the next decade, the four partners split dividends of more than seventy-four million dollars.

Their success changed the lode. The amount of ore produced and the revenue generated topped previous records, enriching the Bonanza Firm and distributing increased wealth throughout the area. Thousands returned or came to the region to reap what Mackay and Fair had sown; by 1875 the population in Virginia City and Gold Hill reached about twenty-five thousand, making the Comstock one of the West's largest urban areas. Miners earned the four dollars a day they saw as the ideal wage, and entrepreneurs took advantage of opportunities to equip and serve them.

Meanwhile, Mackay and Fair practiced vertical integration. Imitating the Bank Crowd's approach, they started a bank, opened milling and lumber firms, and bought a water company from Sharon. They never built a railroad but won special rates from the Virginia & Truckee by threatening to do so. Nor did they start their own publication to ensure favorable publicity: Mackay became a minority owner of the *Territorial Enterprise*. Whatever Sharon and Mackay thought of each other, their mutual interests united them. While Sharon and Fair won few friends with their business practices, Mackay supported many causes and needy individuals, and some of his family wealth endowed buildings on Reno's university campus.

The Dangers of Mining and Boomtowns

Mining makes heavy physical demands on all of its employees, especially in the shafts. At least nine hundred miners died or suffered injuries on the Comstock in the 1860s and 1870s (with more in other parts of Nevada), and mill workers suffered due to exposure to mercury, used to process ore. Beyond falls, broken cables, and extremes in heat and cold, fire posed another danger: the vast amount of wood and poor ventilation encouraged the spread of fumes. Several fires closed mines and killed miners, but mostly in isolated incidents. On April 7, 1869, the most famous fire, at the Yellow Jacket mine in Gold Hill, began about eight hundred feet down, killed as many as forty-five miners, and prompted new financial and popular support for Adolph Sutro's proposed tunnel. The Bank Crowd won unwanted publicity and wild accusations that speculators started the fire— a charge that Sharon later directed at Jones when they faced off for the US Senate in 1873, prompting a dive in the stock market and helping to elect Jones.

Another dangerous fire originated not in the mines, but in one of the industries mining produced: a boardinghouse, made of wood, like so many other buildings in a mining boomtown's get-rich-quick atmosphere. On October 26, 1875, amid the Big Bonanza, a fire began, and the combination

These miners on the Comstock in the 1870s understood that they did dirty, treacherous work—and what Ulysses Grant meant when he said after going down among them that now he understood what hell must be like. Courtesy of Special Collections, University of Nevada–Reno Library.

of winds, wooden buildings, and a lack of rain spread it throughout town. The fire claimed few lives but leveled hundreds of buildings, destroyed millions of feet of timber, and entered several mines. Virginia City quickly rebuilt, most memorably its Catholic church, whose priest, Patrick Manogue, comforted the afflicted, and one of whose parishioners, Mackay, contributed large sums to help restore it. But area residents little realized their town's best days had passed: the national panic of 1873, new federal monetary policy that culminated in the demonetization of silver, and the expenses of rebuilding led to tougher times for Virginia City and the Comstock.

Not Just the Comstock

From 1859 to 1880, mines associated with the Comstock Lode generated about two-thirds of the almost $450 million in mineral production statewide. Those figures neglect revenue from industries tied to mining or in communities dependent on it. Although the Comstock dominated the state, other booms dotted Nevada, affecting and reflecting developments in Virginia City and other towns. Several originated with miners exploring the region or traveling to or from the Comstock.

One of the most prominent, if short-lived, booms began ninety miles southeast of Virginia City, four miles inside Nevada from the California border. Three veteran miners found gold in the Wassuck Range in late August 1860. With other prospectors, they organized the Esmeralda Mining District and the town of Aurora, which soon included wood and brick buildings—usually a sign of permanence, but not this time. Thousands moved in and out of the area over the next decade, including a small Chinese population the town sought to segregate. The district produced nearly $30 million in ore and a newspaperman: Samuel Clemens started sending articles to the *Territorial Enterprise* after joining the rush. Aurora became known for violence, including its own vigilante committee. Major fires in 1866 and 1873 leveled much of the community, hastening its decline.

A trading post serving emigrants to the Comstock laid groundwork for a rush in the West Humboldt Range. In the spring of 1860, the post's two proprietors found gold on the range's west side, and a small rush began after the clamor surrounding the Pyramid Lake War receded. Unionville became the central town for silver prospectors in Star and Buena Vista Canyons. Perhaps a couple of thousand prospectors and businesspeople worked there before its decline in the late 1860s.

Austin and the Reese River boom began, as mining along the Comstock did, largely as an afterthought. Just as Gold Canyon miners had been traveling to or from the Gold Rush, William Talcott made the Austin discovery in May 1862 while working at Jacobs Station, first a Pony Express stop but by then an Overland Telegraph office. Almost at once, prospectors formed a mining district and chose a recorder to monitor claims. The rush began in January 1863, with up to ten thousand arriving in the next two years, setting up canvas tents that housed miners and the usual cross-section of entrepreneurs catering to their needs at work and play. Like the Comstock,

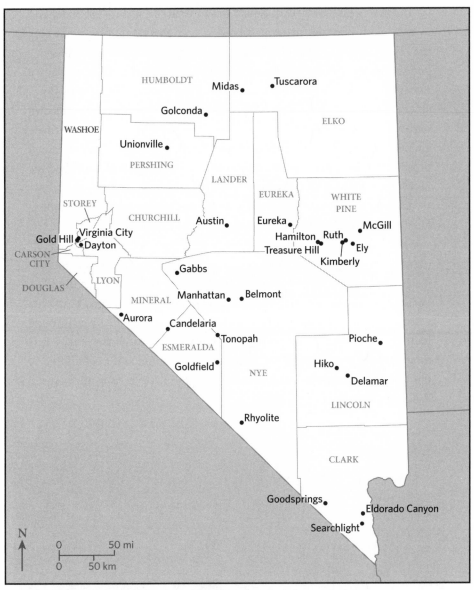

Nevada's mining towns

Austin endured a downturn in 1864, due partly to a San Francisco stock market collapse. Austin rebounded more quickly, though, due to news of discoveries there and an influx of stable capital from a variety of outside sources.

In Austin's case New York capital began to arrive just before statehood in 1864, with London investors following and outside money controlling the region. The big mining petered out by 1870, but during its life as a boomtown, Austin drew diverse ethnic groups and attempts to organize a miners' union as wage labor replaced individual prospecting. Like its Comstock counterparts, Austin veered between the dichotomy of having its own well-written newspaper (the *Reese River Reveille*) and visiting performers and lecturers such as humorist Artemus Ward to a range of gambling and prostitution dens. Austin also contributed to technology with what became known as the Reese River Process, using the Stetefeldt furnace, which lowered milling costs while eliminating arsenic and other chemicals that interfered with separating out central Nevada's more complex silver ore.

As the nucleus of a mining and ranching region, Austin became a milling and freighting center, but its glory days proved brief. A decline in mining ended the district's booming status, with the state even carving Elko, White Pine, and Eureka Counties out of Lander County by 1873. It suffered when the Central Pacific ran its tracks along the Humboldt River through Battle Mountain. In the late 1870s, the arrival of Anson Phelps Stokes, heir to and operator of the Phelps Dodge mining empire, and his building of the Nevada Central Railroad to link the Reese River area to the Central Pacific did little to revive mining.

When a mining town survived the early boom, it tended to grow fast and up the nearest mountainside, as Eureka, Nevada, did during the 1860s and 1870s. Courtesy of Special Collections, University of Nevada–Reno Library.

But, like Virginia City, Austin also served as a regional nerve center. It provided and received services from a nearby hinterland, and Austin miners fanned out and started booms at Belmont, Eureka, Hamilton, Treasure Hill, and Tuscarora. Austin miners exploring about a hundred miles east in the western foothills of the White Pine range found silver in the fall of 1865 and organized the White Pine mining district, complete with recorder. By 1870 perhaps thirty thousand rushed to eastern Nevada, created large towns like Hamilton, planned mining communities they never built, attracted California speculators who floated capital and stock of up to $250 million, and left disappointed, with a decade of effort yielding minimal revenue and the population declining fast. English entrepreneurs, part of a large group from across the Atlantic sinking money into American investments after the Civil War (including in Austin), maintained the search for ore for another two decades, with little success.

Another nearby camp originated with Austin miners and prospered much longer than White Pine's towns and mines did. In 1864 prospectors organized Eureka, about seventy miles east of Austin. As Mormons discovered in southern Nevada, the interspersing of silver and lead reduced the value of both and made them hard to mine and mill. In 1869 two Welsh miners reworked the furnace developed by engineer Carl Stetefeldt to roast silver before extracting it and made it possible to smelt Eureka's ore, launching that boom. Capitalists from San Francisco (Eureka Consolidated Mining Company) and London (Richmond Consolidated) invested and helped generate about $2 million a year in production from 1872 until 1885, making Eureka almost certainly Nevada's most productive mining area outside of the Comstock in the Gilded Age. Typical of other mining towns, it created a varied economy and society, including a beautiful opera house that stands today, and needed a system to transport ore—in its case the Eureka and Palisade, which linked the town to the Central Pacific in 1875.

Eureka distinguished itself in other ways. The cold and snow prompted construction of a network of tunnels under the town. The black smoke belching from its smelters made it the Nevada mining town that most resembled eastern factory cities. The smelters required charcoal to operate, and the Charcoal Burners Association attracted a significant population of Italian immigrants, known as Carbonari, to work them. When a downturn followed flooding in 1879, smelter owners cut what they paid for the charcoal. The Carbonari responded with a boycott and threatened to burn Eureka, prompting a sheriff's posse to ambush the strikers, killing five, wounding several others, and ending the labor action.

Mormons and Miners in Southern Nevada

Encounters between Mormons and miners in southern Nevada never replicated their conflict to the north, but they affected one another. After Mormons left Las Vegas, the mission served as a general store for travelers in northwestern New Mexico and then, as of 1863, Arizona Territory. Gold at Eldorado Canyon, south of present-day Boulder City, and silver and lead at Mount Potosi attracted a few dozen miners in thte early 1860s. One of them, Octavius Decatur Gass, took over the old mission in 1865 and converted it into a farming operation, serving miners, travelers, and military posts in southern California and northwestern Arizona; he also won several terms in Arizona's territorial legislature, where he pushed through the creation of Pah-Ute County.

Pah-Ute's county seat, Callville, reflected Mormon influence in the region. In 1864 missionary William Hamblin found silver (himself or with a Southern Paiute's aid) near present-day Pioche and then led prospectors to the area. Brigham Young sent Francis Lee to colonize land south of the mining district at Panaca, prompting miners to object to the church's presence. Ore discoveries in Pahranagat Valley in March 1865 and the founding of Hiko to serve miners only exacerbated the conflict. Both Nevada and Utah asserted control: the legislature created Lincoln County, with Hiko as the county seat, while Young ordered missions at Moapa, St. Thomas, St. Joseph, Overton, and West Point on the Muddy River and sent Bishop Anson Call to plat a town for warehousing and shipping. Gass won county-seat status for Callville, which briefly served as an army fort and as a port for steamboats traveling up and down the Colorado.

Young thought much of this territory belonged to Utah, but Nevadans asked Congress to extend their border east in 1866 and south in 1867. Not until a federal boundary survey in early 1871 did both sides accept that the mining and missions lay inside Nevada. Then, Muddy River Mormons returned to Utah but others near Panaca and the Pahranagat mines stayed and profited from the market for crops and goods. Refusing to acknowledge his Nevada residency until then, Gass remained in the Arizona Legislature and paid no Nevada taxes, digging a financial hole. Still, his fate could have been worse: interested in learning more about the region, in

1866 Governor Henry Blasdel of Nevada led a party toward Pahranagat that nearly starved in the desert; one member of the group died.

Others struck it rich. The Meadow Valley Mining District produced little until, in 1870, mills began using the Washoe Pan Process. San Francisco capitalists led by François L. A. Pioche invested in a mill, as did the Raymond and Ely company, set up by two Pahranagat miners. The area's production skyrocketed from less than $3,000 in 1869 to a peak of nearly $5.5 million in 1872. By mid-1870 the town of Pioche had more than eleven hundred inhabitants, half of them foreign born, populating one of the West's most diverse, violent, and isolated mining camps, more than two hundred miles from the nearest railroad. Their prosperity proved short-lived: mining revenues fell to about $7,600 by 1880 and declined from there.

Mining and the Federal Government

The Comstock shaped the laws governing mining during the lode's heyday—and to this day. From the beginnings of the silver discovery, miners and then corporations debated what constituted the boundaries of a claim. Most legal documents, based on California mining laws that William Stewart codified in federal legislation, referred to a claim as including a vein with "all its dips, angles, and spurs." But what if gold and silver running through Virginia City consisted of one vein and one claim, to be followed from beginning to end? Representing mining corporations, Stewart argued the "one-ledge" theory. Territorial judge John North at first ruled the opposite way, pleasing prospectors who then would have a chance to profit: only corporations could amass the capital to sustain the mining of one large ledge. Eventually, amid Stewart's accusations that he took bribes, North reversed himself, citing a geological report describing the Comstock as one giant vein. But his actions and the growing power of mining corporations destroyed North's hopes for a political future in Nevada. Settling the issue mattered more: Stewart estimated the lawsuits that various miners and companies filed during the territorial period cost about $10 million that might have been invested and alleviated the downturn by 1864.

Nevadans long have both appreciated and resented the federal government, and the nineteenth-century boom offered ample cause for those conflicting emotions. In 1869, due mainly to Stewart's efforts in the Senate, a United States Mint opened in Carson City, the first of Nevada's many significant federal projects. This benefited his friends and clients in the Bank

Crowd, whose new v&t Railroad could easily ship bullion from Virginia City, but it also cut freight costs, encouraged mining development, and provided jobs for Nevadans, including assayers and watchmen, for example. In turn, such measures aided the growth of the ranching and lumber industries, which supplied mines and miners.

The national mining laws of 1866, often called "the miners' Magna Carta," and 1872 represented Stewart's most important contributions to the industry. Congress had long debated what limits, if any, to place on the search for ore. The California Gold Rush prompted Senator Thomas Hart Benton of Missouri, an expansionist and John C. Frémont's father-in-law, to call for "free mining": open public lands to the search for wealth, in the interest of promoting settlement. In 1866, thwarting eastern opposition, Stewart and other westerners added a provision to a bill for digging ditches and canals on public lands to include mining. The measure acknowledged the legality of actions creating mining districts, permitting more local control. The 1872 law cleared up the 1866 measure by instituting the one-ledge theory and expanding the number of minerals that could be mined on public land. Environmentalists and critics have long tried to change it to reduce mining on federal land and increase taxes and regulations on the industry, but Nevada's and other western states' officials have fended off these attempts.

The End of an Era

From a high of more than $38 million in 1876, the Comstock's mineral output plummeted to $1.4 million in 1881. The Comstock had generated just under $300 million in two decades, but the boom times had passed. The mining booms in central, eastern, and southern Nevada proved less productive and petered out even faster. Although their population leveled off or usually declined, several mining towns continued to produce a limited amount of ore and revenue and tended to survive as the nucleus for smaller surrounding camps and ranches and as county seats. But Nevada and its political economy and society, tied so closely to mining, could be endangered in a variety of ways.

SUGGESTED READINGS

Abbe, Donald R. *Austin and the Reese River Mining District: Nevada's Forgotten Frontier.* Reno: University of Nevada Press, 1985.

Ahmad, Diana L. *The Opium Debate and Chinese Exclusion Laws in the Nineteenth-Century American West.* Reno: University of Nevada Press, 2007.

Ashbaugh, Don. *Nevada's Turbulent Yesterday: A Study in Ghost Towns.* Los Angeles: Westernlore Press, 1963.

Bakken, Gordon Morris. *The Mining Law of 1872: Past, Politics, and Prospects.* Albuquerque: University of New Mexico Press, 2008.

Brands, H. W. *The Age of Gold: The California Gold Rush and the Birth of Modern America.* New York: Doubleday, 2002.

Browne, J. Ross. *A Peep at Washoe and Washoe Revisited.* Contemporary account available in several editions.

Chung, Sue Fawn. *In Pursuit of Gold: Chinese American Miners and Merchants in the American West.* Urbana: University of Illinois Press, 2011.

DeQuille, Dan [William Wright]. *The Big Bonanza: An Authentic Account of the Discovery, History, and Working of the World-Renowned Comstock Lode.* Originally published in 1876 and in several editions since.

Dixon, Kelly J. *Boomtown Saloons: Archaeology and History in Virginia City.* Reno: University of Nevada Press, 2005.

Drabelle, Dennis. *Mile-High Fever: Silver Mines, Boom Towns and High Living on the Comstock Lode.* New York: St. Martin's Press, 2009.

Drury, Wells. *An Editor on the Comstock Lode.* Reno: University of Nevada Press, 1984.

Dwyer, Richard A., and Richard E. Lingenfelter. *Lying on the Eastern Slope: James Townsend's Comic Journalism and the Mining Frontier.* Miami: University Presses of Florida, 1984.

Elliott, Russell R. *Servant of Power: A Political Biography of Senator William M. Stewart of Nevada.* Reno: University of Nevada Press, 1983.

Ford, Victoria. *Silver Peak: Never a Ghost Town.* Reno: University of Nevada Oral History Program, 2002.

Frady, Steven R. *Red Shirts and Leather Helmets: Volunteer Firefighting on the Comstock Lode.* Reno: University of Nevada Press, 1984.

Goldman, Marion S. *Gold Diggers & Silver Miners: Prostitution and Social Life on the Comstock Lode.* Ann Arbor: University of Michigan Press, 1981.

Hall, Shawn. *Old Heart of Nevada: The Ghost Towns and Mining Camps of Elko County, Nevada.* Reno: University of Nevada Press, 1998.

———. *Romancing the Past: Ghost Towns and Historic Sites of Eureka, Lander, and White Pine Counties.* Reno: University of Nevada Press, 1994.

Hardesty, Donald L. *Mining Archaeology in the American West: A View from the Silver State.* Lincoln: University of Nebraska Press, 2010.

Hulse, James W. *Lincoln County, Nevada: The History of a Mining Region, 1864–1909.* Reno: University of Nevada Press, 1971.

Jackson, W. Turrentine. *Treasure Hill: Portrait of a Silver Mining Camp.* Reno: University of Nevada Press, 2000.

James, Ronald M. *The Roar and the Silence: A History of Virginia City and the Comstock Lode*. Reno: University of Nevada Press, 1998.

———. *Virginia City: Secrets of a Western Past*. Lincoln: University of Nebraska Press, 2012.

James, Ronald M., and Susan James. *A Short History of Virginia City*. Reno: University of Nevada Press, 2014.

James, Ronald M., and C. Elizabeth Raymond, eds. *Comstock Women: The Making of a Mining Community*. Reno: University of Nevada Press, 1998.

Johnson, Susan Lee. *Roaring Camp: The Social World of the California Gold Rush*. New York: W. W. Norton, 2000.

Lewis, Oscar. *Silver Kings: The Lives and Times of Mackay, Fair, Flood, and O'Brien, Lords of the Nevada Comstock Lode*. New York: Alfred A. Knopf, 1947.

———. *The Town That Died Laughing: The Story of Austin, Nevada, Rambunctious Early-Day Mining Camp, and of Its Renowned Newspaper, the "Reese River Reveille."* Reno: University of Nevada Press, 1986.

Lingenfelter, Richard E. *Bonanzas & Borrascas: Gold Lust and Silver Sharks, 1848–1884*. Norman, OK: Arthur H. Clark, 2012.

———. *The Hardrock Miners: A History of the Mining Labor Movement in the American West, 1863–1893*. Berkeley: University of California Press, 1974.

Lyman, George. *Ralston's Ring: California Plunders the Comstock Lode*. New York: Charles Scribner's Sons, 1937.

Makley, Michael J. *The Infamous King of the Comstock Lode: William Sharon and the Gilded Age in the West*. Reno: University of Nevada Press, 2006.

—-. *John Mackay: Silver King in the Gilded Age*. Reno: University of Nevada Press, 2008.

McGrath, Roger D. *Gunfighters, Highwaymen, and Vigilantes: Violence on the Frontier*. Berkeley: University of California Press, 1984.

Moehring, Eugene P. *Urbanism and Empire in the Far West, 1840–1890*. Reno: University of Nevada Press, 2004.

Nystrom, Eric C. *Seeing Underground: Maps, Models, and Mining Engineering in America*. Reno: University of Nevada Press, 2014.

Paher, Stanley W. *Nevada Ghost Towns and Mining Camps*. 1970. Reprint, Las Vegas: Nevada Publications, 1984.

Paul, Rodman W. *Mining Frontiers of the Far West, 1848–1880*. New York: Holt, Rinehart, and Winston, 1963.

Sohn, Anton P. *The Healers of Nineteenth-Century Nevada*. Reno: Greasewood Press, 1997.

Sprague, Marguerite. *Bodie's Gold: Tall Tales and True History from a California Mining Town*. Reno: University of Nevada Press, 2003.

Starr, Kevin, and Richard J. Orsi, eds. *Rooted in Barbarous Soil: People, Culture, and Community in Gold Rush California*. Berkeley: University of California Press, 2000.

Townley, John M. *Reno: Tough Little Town on the Truckee, 1868–1900*. Reno: Great Basin Studies Center, 1983.

Twain, Mark. *The Autobiography of Mark Twain*. Vol. 1. Berkeley: University of California Press, 2010.

———. *Roughing It*. Numerous publishers.

Waldorf, John Taylor. *A Kid on the Comstock: Reminiscences of a Virginia City Childhood*. Reno: University of Nevada Press, 1991.

Watson, Margaret G. *Silver Theatre: Amusements of the Mining Frontier in Early Nevada, 1850 to 1864*. Glendale, CA: Arthur H. Clark, 1964.

Wheeler, Sessions S., and William W. Bliss. *Tahoe Heritage: The Bliss Family of Glenbrook Nevada*. Reno: University of Nevada Press, 1997.

Zanjani, Sally S. *A Mine of Her Own: Woman Prospectors in the American West, 1850–1950*. Lincoln: University of Nebraska Press, 1997.

7

Boom, Bust, and Reform

An offshoot of the Civil War and Reconstruction, the Gilded Age broke with that era but also continued it. The war and the effort to rebuild the South expanded federal power and responsibilities. Historically, reform movements last only so long before they exhaust themselves, but aspects of them survive and breed still other movements and responses. Just as Nevada reflected the industrialization in Gilded Age America, it also ended up at the center of its political ferment.

From Bonanza to *Borrasca*

After the bonanza of the 1860s and 1870s, the 1880s and 1890s brought the opposite, *borrasca*—a Spanish term for prosperous mines turned unproductive and unprofitable. From a peak gross yield of more than forty-six million dollars in 1876, statewide production bottomed out at just under two million in 1894. The Comstock and Reese River stopped booming, and few new discoveries eased the pain. Candelaria in Mineral County enjoyed brief bursts in the 1880s but never came close to matching the earlier booms. Tuscarora in Elko County flared briefly, then fizzled.

The southern portion of the state offered the most hope during the depression. About ten million dollars emerged in the 1890s from a new boomtown in Lincoln County begun in 1891, when John Ferguson and Joseph Sharp found gold about forty miles southwest of Pioche. Named for Joseph R. DeLamar, its major investor, it proved too short-lived to sustain Nevada's economy, and the dust kicked up from the quartzite or sandstone in the mines caused an assortment of lung problems for those living there. In Belmont discoveries and investments by Anson Phelps Stokes of New York built up hopes in the late 1890s, as did George Colton's

Mine developer Anson Phelps Stokes built his "castle," modeled on an Italian tower, outside Austin in the 1890s. Molly Flagg Knudtsen helped save it from further decay, and it became part of the National Register of Historic Places in 2003. Courtesy of Special Collections, University of Nevada–Reno Library.

gold find in what became Searchlight. But by 1900 little had materialized, Nevada's population had fallen from sixty thousand to forty-two thousand in twenty years, and critics discussed the merits of revoking statehood on the grounds that so small a population had no right to representation in Congress. The state immigration bureau tried to attract new residents with salesmanship—it called Nevada's climate "the most delightful and salubrious in the known world"—but with little success.

Building a Ranching State

Nor did agriculture, which benefited from and contributed to the mining boom, end the depression. A brief livestock boom in the first half of the 1880s stirred hopes for a burgeoning ranching industry, but the number of cattle and sheep grew slowly, while their market value declined. Drought and other weather problems, especially blizzards between 1888 and 1890, only made matters worse.

Still, several large ranching families became important to Nevada's economy and society. In the 1850s Henry Fred Dangberg arrived in Carson Valley, H. N. A. "Hock" Mason in the valley named for him along the Walker River, and R. B. Smith, T. B. Smith, and two partners in the Sierra Nevada foothills in Smith Valley. Several others entered the Washoe Valley around Reno. Future governor Lewis Bradley worked his way from Mason Valley to Reese River and finally to Elko, and another governor, Jewett Adams, ran cattle and sheep in White Pine and Lincoln Counties. Elko-area rancher Jasper Harrell sold his operations in 1883 to two Texans, John Sparks and John Tinnan, whose cattle spread through northeastern Nevada; their ranching success helped elect Sparks governor in 1902.

Just as California mining corporations often dominated the Comstock Lode, California ranching operations became a presence in Nevada. Henry Miller and Charles Lux arrived from the San Joaquin Valley to buy water rights in Mason Valley and the Humboldt Basin. They eventually hired Hock Mason, bought up seventy thousand acres, and controlled grazing rights on hundreds of thousands more. But overgrazing combined with bad weather to devastate Nevada ranching: at one point Sparks lost more than half of his herd, and Mason lost almost all of his.

All of these ranchers served nearby railroad or mining towns and suffered the effects of market forces and drought, a constant threat in the Great Basin. They found other markets: by 1870 Nevada ranchers reportedly shipped thirty thousand animals to California's butchers each year. But in the mid-1880s, cattle prices dropped, and the San Francisco market had no need for Nevada's livestock, forcing ranchers to look east, increasing their dependence on railroads. Nevada's farmers had that in common with their counterparts around the country, except others had even worse problems. Farmers and miners eventually decided to take political action.

Inflation and the Money Supply

During and after the Civil War, inflation and its effects worried political and financial leaders. To finance the war effort, the federal government issued bonds and, for the first time, printed paper money, called "greenbacks" for their color. With so much paper on the market, its value declined—but not that of gold. During Reconstruction Republicans passed a law to pay off war bonds with gold and, in 1875, added the Resumption Act to start retiring all greenbacks from circulation in 1879. These policies sought deflation—the smaller the money supply, the greater the value of existing money, or specie. This policy benefited creditors and harmed debtors: if a loan of one hundred dollars made in inflationary times came due after deflation increased the value of currency, the repayment would be worth more than the original loan. Thus, the more money in circulation, the less its value, and the easier debtors found it to pay what they owed. But that meant the creditor who loaned the money would raise interest rates to make greater profits.

These issues pitted several groups against one another. Businessmen might be creditors (especially in the eastern United States) and debtors (likelier in the West), or verge on becoming either. Farmers and workers usually ended up in debt, but divided on what to do about it. Widespread political corruption during the Gilded Age limited their means and ability to act against policies they opposed. More important, their interests differed: both wanted inflation to help with debts, but farmers sought it to increase the prices they received for their crops. Industrial workers nationally and in Nevada's mines and mills had no desire to create higher prices for the food they needed to buy rather than growing it themselves.

Making the mix more combustible, farming changed during and after the Civil War. The Morrill Act of 1862 to start agricultural colleges and the government's creation of the Department of Agriculture encouraged scientific farming and reduced the need for farm laborers. Many of Jefferson's yeoman or subsistence farmers moved to the city for industrial jobs or concentrated on cash crops and became dependent on the market. Meanwhile, the South sought to revive its economy after the devastation the Civil War caused and to retain its African American labor force. Plantation owners turned to sharecropping, meaning black farmers would continue to do the work, in return for a percentage of profits. But southern planters also relied on the market and aid from the government and bankers.

A debt spiral followed for the nation's farmers. Expanding or retooling their farms required loans or liens on their crops from bankers and merchants who sought collateral: either their land or their next crop. When markets failed to yield profits or crop prices remained low, they lost their collateral or went deeper into debt in hopes of improving their lot. Thus, they wound up so indebted that they had no hopes of paying off their creditors for years, or they lost their farms. They blamed a variety of forces, but especially bankers and merchants.

The Railroad Problem

Farmers and ranchers around the country, including in Nevada, also blamed railroads. They depended on the transcontinental railroad and various feeder lines to bring their crops to market, besides carrying them and assorted freight. In Nevada those with grievances against the railroad included mining companies that also relied on the Union Pacific and Central Pacific, landowners who grazed cattle and sheep, and individual miners and ranchers.

Many Nevadans resented the state's tax policies toward railroads, but short-haul/long-haul discrimination angered them above all. The Central Pacific charged to carry goods for the longer haul, even if the train dropped off the goods before reaching the more distant destination. In 1881 Rollin Daggett, a *Territorial Enterprise* editor elected to Congress with Bank Crowd support, made a famous speech accusing the CP of overcharging his constituents by $30 million in the past decade and citing evidence of the discrimination: from New York a carload of coal oil cost $300 to San Francisco, $536 to Reno, and $716 to Winnemucca. Two years later departing governor John Kinkead, who also received backing from mining corporations, urged the legislature to take action against the CP.

Their efforts proved fruitless at the federal and state levels, because the Central Pacific lobbied and curried favor with state legislators who, in turn, elected US senators and often rose to higher office. In Nevada the CP appointed agents who handled an assortment of duties, especially politics. They worked with Henry Yerington, manager of the Bank of California's Virginia & Truckee Railroad, and his colleague Abner C. Cleveland, a White Pine rancher who tended to eastern counties. The Nevada-based group wanted taxes and regulations no more than the CP did and usually dealt with state matters, while the CP stressed national affairs. Both sides underwrote candidates and their campaigns—Yerington even described one county's elected officials as "*all friendly to us* (and God knows they ought to be) and so we have Washoe in the hollow of our hand for many a year to come if desirable." Then they lubricated the machinery as needed at Carson City and tried to control party conventions, which wrote platforms and nominated candidates who heeded them. When the 1891 legislature succumbed to pressure from ranchers and created a state board of assessors and equalization that increased taxes on railroads, lobbyists pressured the 1893 session into abolishing it. Reform-minded politicians learned their lesson.

The Power of Mining and Railroads: The Senate

Mining and railroad interests almost completely dominated Nevada politics from statehood until well into the twentieth century. From the first territorial election in 1861 until the 1890s, Republicans controlled most federal and state offices. The combination meant that few Democrats who won office either proved more reform minded than the Republicans, who, after all, had no reason to want to change the status quo, or, more likely, had enough wealth to overcome the Republican advantage in voter registration and access to mining and railroad funds.

The first state legislature elected William Stewart and James Nye to the Senate in 1865. Stewart distinguished himself, at least with the CP and the Bank Crowd, with the national mining law and prorailroad measures and won a second term. So did Nye, who took stands for civil rights. But when his second term ended in 1873, Nye lacked an impressive record and financial support and showed signs of senility. Crown Point mine co-owner John P. Jones outbribed William Sharon at the legislature to win and served five terms in the Senate, defending mining interests. At first, his independence frightened railroad operators, but his California investments—Jones joined with Stewart in mine deals and later developed Santa Monica—required him to get along with the Central Pacific.

As his reelection bid loomed in 1874, Stewart announced his retirement from politics to pursue opportunities in mining and law. The Bank Crowd had long been Stewart's main Nevada supporters, and Sharon had made his ambitions known, so his declaration of candidacy proved unsurprising. Adolph Sutro, who correctly saw Sharon and Stewart as enemies, announced his interest, began a newspaper to compete with Sharon's *Territorial Enterprise,* claimed to belong to a new independent political party, and then backed out when he saw no hope. Sharon won, but his six-year term proved disastrous for Nevada: he voted less than 1 percent of the time and never introduced any legislation, even to help himself. He visited Nevada only while en route to San Francisco, where he lived.

Sharon also had an excuse. In 1875 the Bank of California collapsed due to the panic of 1873 and bad investments by founder William Ralston. Ralston deeded ownership to Sharon and admitted his culpability to the board of directors, which fired him as president. Then he died while swimming, due to a stroke or a suicide. Sharon returned to San Francisco, and he and partner D. O. Mills revived the bank and restored order. The bank's success ultimately may have helped Nevadans more than Sharon's effectiveness or lack of it on Capitol Hill.

After one six-year term, Sharon wanted more, but Nevadans had had enough. In 1880 Democrats found a candidate with deep-enough pockets to outspend any Republican: James Fair of the Bonanza Firm. He and his party emulated Republicans tied to the CP and Bank Crowd, spreading money around the state as campaign funds or bribes. Democrats swept Nevada for the first time, including the presidential race. Sensing an opportunity, Sutro tried to run as a reformer, promised to spend as much as necessary, and then hatched a plan to accuse Fair of buying the election and swear out warrants to arrest those he bribed—all to no avail. Fair won the six-year term and did almost as little as Sharon did.

By 1886, when Fair declared for reelection, Nevadans had wearied of poor representation and Stewart had tired of sitting on the sidelines. When Stewart announced his plans to run, the presence of Charles C. "Black" Wallace, the Eureka County assessor turned Central Pacific agent for Nevada, as his campaign manager signaled the extent of his support. John Mackay helped fund Stewart's race, in part out of anger at Fair for divorcing his wife to marry his mistress, which offended Mackay's Catholicism and decorum. Stewart's return to the Senate in 1887 meant mining and railroad interests retained power to choose officeholders, but at least Jones had a competent colleague and Nevadans had a full-time senator.

While Fair's scandal curtailed his political career, a scandal involving Sharon launched another. Sharon's mistress, Sarah Hill, claimed he promised to marry her after his wife's death. The case wound up in the California courts, since both lived there, and seemed to favor Hill and her lawyer, David Terry, a longtime California politician and judge she married.

Sharon's attorney, Stewart, suggested his client claim Nevada residency to shift the matter to the federal courts, where appointed judges—including US Supreme Court justice Stephen J. Field, a onetime Gold Rush attorney—might prove more sympathetic. Eventually, Field's rulings for his old friend Sharon prompted Terry to attack him, and Field's bodyguard shot and killed Terry. By then, Sharon had died, and to maintain Nevada residency for the case, his son-in-law moved there and entered politics at Stewart's suggestion. As fate would have it, Francis Newlands became a thorn in Stewart's side.

The "Crime" of '73 and the Decline in Nevada Silver

Referring to the "act of John Sherman smuggling the silver dollar out of the list of coins in the Mint Act of '73," Stewart wrote, "I felt it my duty to return to the Senate and do what I could to rectify the crime which was clandestinely committed without my knowledge." Stewart had voted for the act, suggesting a complex bill or dishonesty. Granting Stewart's dishonesty, the evidence leans toward the former. Sherman introduced the act in 1870 as part of a policy of deflation and to emphasize specie, especially gold. When it emerged from the Senate Finance Committee, which Sherman chaired, the Mint Act demonetized silver in favor of gold. Although some constituents sounded the alarm, Stewart remained quiet and even endorsed the gold standard in future Senate speeches.

How much the Mint Act of 1873 deepened the depression that devastated Nevada's economy remains debatable. At the time, the Big Bonanza's discovery began several years of prosperity, but the Comstock and other mining booms soon petered out, while the panic of 1873 sent the national economy into a tailspin. Silver prices fell more than 21 percent in the three years after the Mint Act passed, making it a scapegoat for miners, mining corporations, and politicians.

Nevadans and their allies tried to remonetize silver. In 1876 Richard "Silver Dick" Bland, a congressman from Missouri who had practiced law in Nevada, introduced a bill to coin silver at a ratio of sixteen units of silver to one of gold, but settled for a Silver Commission to study the matter. Jones's membership helped ensure a favorable report, but the best silver's supporters could do—the Bland-Allison Act, cosponsored by Bland and Senator William Allison of Iowa and passed over President Rutherford Hayes's veto in 1878—bought two to four million dollars' worth of silver monthly. In the 1880s, with silver lacking support in the two major parties—in 1885 President Grover Cleveland even suspended coinage at the Carson City Mint—Nevadans kept accusing the rest of the country of being out to get them. They also acted: in 1885 they and other states held a National Silver Convention to promote remonetization by setting up state silver groups. The Nevada Silver Association met only once, but in 1886, for the first time, both major parties in Nevada called for free silver coinage in their election platforms.

The census of 1890 reported the closure of the frontier—the event that inspired Frederick Jackson Turner's frontier hypothesis—but that year the West achieved new political status. For the first time since the 1870s, Republicans controlled the White House and Congress and hoped to keep it that way. Some of their actions reflected old allegiances and their decline: they tried and failed to pass a bill to enforce voting rights guaranteed by the Fifteenth Amendment, partly through the opposition of none other than Stewart, the amendment's author. But Republicans granted statehood to several western territories, hoping, as Lincoln did with Nevada in 1864, to win votes. Washington, Montana, North Dakota, and South Dakota became states in November 1889, with Idaho and Wyoming following the next July—all heavily involved in mining or agriculture or both.

Western silver interests saw their opportunity. In November 1889 a National Silver Convention urged the return of free coinage. In 1890 Sherman, the villain in the Crime of '73, introduced a Silver Purchase Act: the Treasury Department would buy 4.5 million ounces per month at market prices. The measure passed, not because Republicans suddenly heeded Nevada's pleas, but because western congressmen traded support for a tariff hike to pass the bill.

Then, in 1893, an economic panic resulted from stock speculation, inflation and credit problems, and overbuilt railroads unable to meet obligations. President Cleveland blamed the silver-purchase measure and persuaded Congress to repeal it. Nevada's elected officials fought him hard—Stewart delivered a three-day speech, and Jones topped that with a seven-day effort that filled one hundred pages of the *Congressional Record*. But instead, Nevada wound up back where it had been, stuck in a deep recession and losing population.

The Populist Movement

Some historians have argued that Populists sought to stop the forward march of capitalism and turn back the clock—in some cases displaying anti-Semitism in their criticism of those shaping the market. Others have called them radical reformers with a thoughtful critique of American society. As usual, the reality proved subtle and complex. The Populist movement evolved from several factors. In the late 1860s, unhappy that industrial capitalism increased their dependence on markets and consumers, farmers formed the Grange to promote unity as they went through debt, bankruptcy, and foreclosure. They sought state regulation of railroads, with mixed results, and federal programs to aid them; one of them, the Cooperative Extension Service, moved to the state level and continues in Nevada. Those seeking political action, especially against railroads and the crop-lien system, shifted from the Grange to Farmers Alliances, which began in 1875. By the late 1880s, these groups became more united, despite regional and racial differences.

In 1889 the alliances reconstituted themselves, with some support from the Knights of Labor in the industrial Northeast, as the People's or Populist Party. Its members believed that the wealthy, especially in the railroad industry, controlled the Democratic and Republican Parties, necessitating a third party. In 1892 the members met in Nebraska, nominated James B. Weaver for president, and issued the Omaha Platform. They demanded a host of reforms: a graduated income tax, direct election of US senators rather than leaving it to the legislatures, eight-hour workdays, and even broader civil service reform than the Pendleton Act, passed in 1883 to professionalize the federal government.

Other provisions reverberated in the West. By seeking government ownership of railroads, the Populists hoped to eliminate short-haul/long-haul discrimination. Their proposed independent subtreasury would warehouse crops and require the government to pay them market value and then take responsibility for selling the rest. The Populists also sought to inflate the currency, reducing the debts they owed to bankers and merchants by having the government print money—which they would use to pay those debts. But the Populists saw a way to win western support they otherwise would have lacked in industrial mining areas by suggesting inflating the currency by remonetizing silver. Weaver won the electoral votes of four states that year, and three of them—Colorado, Idaho, and Nevada—depended on silver. The silver and Populist movements seemed to have met and merged.

Silver Clubs and the Silver Party

In 1892 George Nixon had just turned thirty-two. In the early 1880s he started as a railroad telegrapher in Nevada, and by 1886 he had organized a bank, taken over several Humboldt County mines, and started the Winnemucca *Silver State*. As early as 1889, he suggested, "The friends of silver must place the interest of the metal above party, or better yet, organize a party." Imitating the farmers' movement, he called for Nevadans to create silver clubs to promote mining issues. He set up the first one in April 1892; a week later Eureka followed, with former congressman Thomas Wren and future governor Reinhold Sadler as its leaders. The silver-club movement spread, thanks partly to anger at the two national parties: Republicans tried to avoid offending anyone, and Democrats nominated Cleveland, who backed the gold standard and sought repeal of the silver-purchase bill. In June the state's silver clubs met in Reno, formed the Silver League, made plans to turn it into a political party, and called for remonetization. That September the Silverites met in Winnemucca, nominated candidates for state offices, and endorsed Weaver's election on the People's or Populist platform.

Over the next decade, Nevada became a one-party state, with the Silver Party supporting whichever national party showed any inclination to help it. In 1892 the first Silver convention endorsed the Populist platform and Stewart's reelection; given his ties to the Central Pacific and that his campaign manager, C. C. Wallace, served as its Nevada agent, to call that a contradiction would be an understatement. Wise to Washington's ways, Stewart had opposed the third-party movement as dangerous to Nevada and himself, but he and Wallace saw the light and helped organize the Silver Party, with the Central Pacific apparently reasoning that maintaining control of Nevada would be easier through infiltration rather than opposition—and, as historian Mary Ellen Glass put it, the railroad owners "allowed the politicians and the parties to *say* anything they pleased about the company and its practices. The important item was that [they] *act* correctly when it was time to vote." The Bank of California felt similarly: the Silverites supported Newlands's successful first race for the House.

The Silver Party's influence and contradictions became more apparent as the 1890s unfolded. In 1894, seeking reelection, Newlands spoke at the Silver convention against government ownership of railroads, irking delegates, including Wallace, who discouraged him from voicing that position. Yerington, a Newlands ally and the lobbyist for the Bank of California and the Virginia & Truckee Railroad, broke with Wallace and the CP over their abandoning the Republican Party for the Silverites. That year a fourth party materialized, the People's Party, claiming it wanted to lay the groundwork for a presidential campaign two years later and had no faith in the Silver Party as long as railroad executives approved of it and played a role in it. Yerington and the People's Party would be disappointed: the Silver Party won a landslide victory in 1894, and candidates running under its banner dominated the ballot into the next decade. Yet the People's Party's message resonated with some voters: its candidates attacked railroad domination and won significant minority votes.

Silver Party leaders understood the need for national support. In July 1896 Stewart and Newlands hoped to form a national silver party. Before they could, young Nebraskan William Jennings Bryan electrified the Democratic National Convention by declaring that "we shall answer their demands for a gold standard by saying to them, you shall not press down upon the brow of labor this crown of thorns. You shall not crucify mankind upon a cross of gold." Prosilver Democrats stampeded the convention, called for remonetization, and nominated Bryan for president. The People's and Silver Parties ratified the choice. Bryan easily won Nevada but lost nationally to Republican William McKinley, and fusion in Nevada proved short-lived: in 1898 Silverites won every major office, but in a few cases by a small majority, and Republicans came within sixty-three votes of defeating Silverite Reinhold Sadler for governor.

The Battles for the Senate

The failure to fuse resulted not from policy but from battles between ambitious Silver Party leaders. By 1896 Senators Stewart and John P. Jones had served more than two decades. Younger politicians had ambitions and, granting Stewart's CP support and Jones's wealth, the money to satisfy them. In 1897 Silverites and Democrats seemed united behind Jones for a fifth term, but Nixon, who had formed an alliance with Newlands, ran on a platform of "home rule" and "Nevada for Nevadans," suggesting the unpleasant truth: Jones lived in California. Jones won easily, due partly to support from Stewart and Wallace, who saw Newlands and Nixon as a threat.

The next election proved them right. As the 1899 legislature met, after winning reelection to his House seat and trying to lull the opposition, Newlands ran against Stewart. Stewart had a stronger record than Jones and support from the Central Pacific, but critics questioned his Nevada residency and fidelity to the silver movement, noted his advancing age, and resented his power over patronage in Nevada. Worse for Stewart, Yerington and the Bank Crowd backed Newlands.

The race grew ugly. Stewart and Wallace imported lobbyists and gun-slingers to provide physical intimidation if needed. Speaking in Carson City, Newlands sought to exert pressure by—with unintended irony—accusing Stewart and his backers of corruption designed to turn Nevada into a colony for California and demanding that Nevadans take control of their state and restore "integrity to the law-making and elective process." The day after a test vote showed the assembly tied, Storey County's W. A. Gillespie, reputedly a Newlands supporter, failed to show up, and Stewart won by one vote. One report accused Gillespie of accepting a bribe, while Sam Davis, the pro-Stewart editor of the *Carson City Appeal,* claimed Jones's brother invited Gillespie to ride to Carson City and instead kidnapped him and kept him locked up at another Stewart supporter's home in Empire.

Many Nevadans agreed that this election proved the need for reform. The previous legislature had passed a "purity of elections" law to improve reporting of contributions, but in 1899 lawmakers repealed it, realizing the Stewart-Newlands fight made it look ridiculous. That election inspired a law creating a preferential primary: Senate candidates would appear on the ballot, and voters could advise legislators, who would be wise to heed them or pay for it at their next election.

A Culture of Corruption

From the territorial period on, Nevadans appeared conscious of their state's political corruption and interested in doing something about it. Several factors worked against real reform. Mining (like gaming later) bred transience, movement from one boom to another as each went bust, and thus reduced the chances of a population uniting behind change or united long enough to effect change. Also, the need for capital and transportation to make a mining economy function empowered mine and railroad owners more than workers and increased the state's dependence on a particular industry. These factors combined to produce a small power elite without many or much to rule and thus a culture of corruption.

The case of Nevada's first state treasurer, Eben Rhoades, exemplified the worst of the problem. He hired his brother as his deputy and spent a great deal of time in San Francisco, reportedly trying to sell state bonds, before dying there in 1869. Apparently, he committed suicide, and after his death auditors found Rhoades embezzled or had no record of more than $106,000 in state revenue. When Nevada tried to recover the money, the state Board of Examiners—the governor, attorney general, and secretary of state—claimed ignorance, as did those who "bonded" his salary (ensuring its payment and vouching for his good behavior), including Sharon and *Territorial Enterprise* editor Joe Goodman. Governor Henry Blasdel, a Virginia City mine superintendent and Republican, had received a loan from Rhoades; the next governor, Lewis Bradley, a Democratic Elko rancher with few ties to Blasdel's supporters, vetoed a bill to try to recoup some of the funds from the people who bonded Rhoades. According to one estimate, the state revenue loss, with accrued interest to the present, may have topped $300 million.

Yet Bradley stood up to mining interests. Ever since the Nevada Constitution mandated taxing net proceeds of mines, revenue measures caused controversy as too generous to mining or, the industry said, not generous enough. For example, the first state legislature's Revenue Act of 1865 set property taxes at $2.75 per $100 of assessed valuation, but mining paid $1, with further deductions. In 1875, as Bradley's second term began, legislators approved changes in the tax structure that increased what corporations would pay. Because it had to pay more than the Bank Crowd did, the Bonanza Firm questioned the law's legality and refused to comply. In response, in 1876 both major parties vowed not to change the taxes, but the "Silver Kings" had learned from Sharon and his lobbyists, who viewed the tax hike similarly. The 1877 session passed a bill to cut the tax by about one-third. Bradley vetoed it, declaring that "it does not become the dignity of a State to be dictated to by a couple of non-resident corporations." The

Territorial Enterprise, co-owned by Sharon and Mackay, replied, "He is old and decrepit, and it would be cowardice to abuse or insult him. . . . But would to God that he was a young man that we might publish how much we wish that he was dead."

In 1878, backed by ranching and eastern Nevada mining interests, Bradley sought a third term and lost to John Kinkead, who ran with support from Comstock corporations. Mackay and Fair and their allies agreed to pay nearly $300,000 in back taxes, but, at their request, the legislature passed and the governor signed a bill excusing penalties of more than $75,000 for their earlier refusal to pay. After the Nevada Supreme Court declared this unconstitutional as a "special act," the Bonanza Firm asked the legislature to try again. This time Kinkead vetoed the bill as unconstitutional, and the US Supreme Court agreed. The mine owners finally paid their bill in 1883. Kinkead chose not to run again and faced a mini scandal: his uncle managed the Reno Savings Bank, whose owners included the state treasurer, who almost went to prison for shifting state funds to the bank.

The Legacy of Discrimination

Nevadans, like most Americans of the time, discriminated against people of color. From what an Elko observer called a policy of "no proscription" toward blacks in the 1870s, Elmer Rusco wrote of Nevada's African Americans that "the economic decline that caused a drop in white population was evidently felt even more severely among the black population," manifested in "more hostility toward them from the white community than had been the case earlier." As the number of whites—especially middle-class whites—declined during the *borrasca,* African Americans' economic status, already less secure than that of whites, fell even more noticeably. So did their social status: more derogatory language began appearing in the press, and by the early twentieth century several communities had become "sundown towns," where authorities barred African Americans from living there or forced them to leave—as they did with other minorities.

The Chinese faced segregation, bias, and violence in many areas, especially during economic troubles, which Nevada had in abundance. Politicians appealed to voters by singling out the Chinese as a threat, partly on moral grounds, mainly as endangering white people's jobs. After Virginia City's miners union blocked the Chinese from working on Virginia

& Truckee Railroad construction in 1869, the legislature followed with a ban on Chinese labor on state projects. Future legislative sessions endorsed efforts to reduce immigration until the federal Chinese Exclusion Act of 1882 prohibited "skilled and unskilled labor employed in mining" from entering the United States. Meanwhile, as others did in the West, Nevadans punctuated their opposition by creating anti-Chinese clubs from Carson City to Austin to Tuscarora; in 1878 some Reno residents ordered Chinatown emptied out within forty-eight hours and then rioted, but local authorities stepped in and the Chinese stayed. But the combination of the exclusionary law and Nevada's economic decline reduced the Chinese population enough to ease tensions.

Other tensions remained over Mormons. Few Mormons lived in Nevada late in the nineteenth century. In 1877, under Edward Bunker's leadership, twenty-three Saints moved to southern Nevada as the "United Order" to farm near the Virgin River. They tried the kind of communal living that helped inspire the church's founding and earlier utopian settlements. They ate, stored crops, and raised animals together. After about two years, that plan failed amid squabbling, but they continued on their own in their town, Bunkerville. In 1880 another group of Mormons settled five miles northwest, in Mesquite Flat, later the city of Mesquite.

Nevadans debated an expanded Mormon presence. In the 1880s, two decades after Congress approved the expansion that created Nevada's present boundaries, Stewart led an effort to annex Idaho Territory's southern tip to Nevada. Conflicts similar to those in Nevada in the 1850s broke out in Idaho between Mormons and non-Mormons. Stewart and other Nevadans felt anti-Mormon legislation would aid their chances of capturing southern Idaho. In the spirit of the federal Edmunds Act of 1882, which banned polygamy, the 1887 legislature required any would-be voter to take an oath denying membership in the Mormon Church. A year later a Mormon resident of Panaca tried to vote and sued over his denial. Stewart said, "It would be very dangerous to allow the Mormons to vote in our State. The proposition to colonize and take possession of our State Government is seriously considered by the Mormon Church." Instead, in 1888 the state high court held the law violated the Nevada Constitution's definition of eligible voters. Nevada fared no better at the national level: Idaho Territory remained intact. In 1890 LDS president Wilford Woodruff announced the end of church support for polygamy.

These events fostered new Mormon communities. In the 1880s antipolygamy laws permitted the federal seizure of Mormon property, and some livestock wound up with an eastern Nevada company that then proved unable to account for some of it. After Utah became a state in 1896, as part of an attempt at redress, Mormons received the White River Valley Ranch, about 15,000 acres in southern White Pine and northern Nye Counties. In 1898 Mormons began farming the area and soon settled the towns of Lund and Preston.

The Debate over Native American Rights

Republicans and Democrats tried a variety of policies toward Native Americans in the nineteenth century, with disastrous results. The reservation system provided tribes with land, but Southern Paiutes along the Muddy River demonstrated the problem: they received nearly 2 million acres, mostly desert, but nearby settlers refused to leave the arable land and the federal government reduced the Moapa Reservation to about 1,000 acres. Ending the reservation system won support for several reasons: continuing Native efforts to stop encroachment and eliminate whatever power Native groups still enjoyed, the Euro-American desire for land, and the view of capitalism and traditional religion as superior to Native beliefs. The Dawes Severalty Act or General Allotment Act of 1887 granted Native Americans land—160 acres to a family head, 80 to a single person or orphan, 40 to minors—in hopes of ending the reservation system, encouraging assimilation, and opening land to whites. In 1898 the Curtis Act followed by trying to eliminate tribal courts and governments, subjecting Native Americans to the regular US government.

Stewart's record displayed the contradictory impulses of Nevadans—indeed, Americans—on these issues. In addition to backing a national mining college, a national college to train teachers, and the Second Morrill Act of 1890 to expand the original measure of 1862, he won federal support for an Indian school for which the state and Ormsby County contributed land and money. It opened in December 1890 southeast of Carson City with thirty-seven students and remained Nevada's only boarding school for Native Americans. It sought to teach them trades and assimilate them into American culture, but, before the school closed in 1980 and became a historic site, the Bureau of Indian Affairs (BIA) allowed students to speak their Native languages and learn more about their culture.

Yet even as he sought aid for the Washoe, Stewart tried to eliminate Northern Paiute title to the Walker River Reservation and part of the Pyramid Lake Reservation. These efforts resulted in part from rumors in the 1880s of mineral deposits on the Walker River Reservation; during the *borrasca*, Nevadans sought ore wherever it might exist. Nevadans wanted access to the Walker Reservation's farming and lumber resources and hoped to use Pyramid Lake for commercial purposes rather than allowing Northern Paiutes to keep relying on it for fishing and thus their survival. Nor did Stewart object when his allies at a Bank of California subsidiary, the Carson & Colorado Railroad, tried to break a contract to provide free transportation to Walker River Paiutes in return for the right-of-way.

Native Americans also faced difficulties with whites in eastern Nevada. In 1873 those living near Ely heard about northern California's Modoc War and feared that nearby Shoshone and Goshutes in the Snake and Spring Valleys planned to attack them. Their fear went unrealized, but in September 1875 the White Pine War ensued when a Goshute killed a mining prospector and settlers responded by killing three Indians and then hanging the Goshute. The Bureau of Indian Affairs moved about 160 Shoshone and Goshutes north to Deep Creek, emptying the two valleys, which became open to grazing for white-owned ranches.

Native American Leaders

Few Native American reformers gained greater fame and importance than Sarah Winnemucca, a Northern Paiute born around 1844 as Thocmentony, or "Shell Flower." Her grandfather Captain Truckee and father, Chief Winnemucca, got along with white explorers and emigrants. Educated at the home of William Ormsby (later killed in the Pyramid Lake War against Northern Paiutes led by her cousin) and a Catholic school in California, she joined her family at the Malheur Reservation, set up on President Ulysses Grant's orders for the Northern Paiutes and Bannock (Northern Paiutes liked this no better than the Western Shoshone, who expected to relocate to the Duck Valley Reservation near the Nevada-Idaho line in 1877). She taught in a local school and worked as an interpreter for the resident Indian agent. But his replacement began refusing to pay the Northern Paiutes for their work and sold supplies intended for them. The Bannock rebelled, and although Winnemucca claimed they took her family and others hostage, they became part of a relocation near Yakima, Washington.

Few Native Americans worked harder to promote peace between their people and whites than Sarah Winnemucca on the left, next to her father, Chief Winnemucca; her brother, Natchez; and Captain Jim, another Northern Paiute chief, beside an unidentified boy. Courtesy of Special Collections, University Libraries, University of Nevada, Las Vegas.

During the war she helped her family escape from an enemy encampment and worked as a translator and scout for US Army officers, who developed great respect for her and her abilities.

These events made her a public figure. She began to lecture in California and Nevada on Native American issues and went to Washington, DC, in 1880, to meet with Secretary of the Interior Carl Schurz on issues affecting Natives; as she put it, he made "promises which, like the wind, were heard no more." Back in California, she married a Bureau of Indian Affairs employee and continued lecturing; they went east, where she spoke on her life in the West more than four hundred times, often condemning the reservation system. She began publishing articles, and reformers she met in Boston helped her bring out *Life Among the Piutes: Their Wrongs and Claims,* in 1883—the first book by a Native American woman. Back in Nevada, she built a school, Peabody's Institute, near Lovelock to educate Native American children in their language and culture, but lack of support and health problems forced her to join her family in Idaho, where she died of tuberculosis in 1891. She dedicated much of her life to Native rights and trying to work with whites to protect them—often to no avail. But she brought attention to major issues and demonstrated the ability of a woman and a Native American to fight for justice in a time when neither could easily do so.

Another Northern Paiute had a far-reaching impact. Born circa 1856 in present-day Esmeralda County, Wovoka grew up in a white rancher's family, took the name Jack Wilson, and learned English. Around 1870 Tävibo, a Mason Valley Northern Paiute, prophesied the earth would swallow up whites and dead Natives would return; Native Americans could speed these events by dancing in circles, singing religious songs, and seeking spiritual and moral renewal. In the late 1880s, Wovoka, sometimes reputed to be Tävibo's son, had a similar vision, perhaps combining Native thought

Wovoka, the Northern Paiute who became widely known for the Ghost Dance, with his grandson Dennis Bender, possibly outside the Carson Indian School early in the twentieth century. Courtesy of Special Collections, University of Nevada–Reno Library.

with a form of Christian mysticism. Winnemucca dismissed his claims as "nonsense," and when the Western Shoshone at the Duck Valley Reservation held a Ghost Dance that attracted one thousand visitors, the crowd lost interest when no Indian messiah appeared. After this Ghost Dance religion spread in the West, the Lakota Sioux sent a delegation in 1889 to meet Wovoka and returned to their Dakota homes convinced of the coming millennium.

Cruel disappointment and violence followed. Wovoka hated war and the Sioux hoped to avoid it, but they believed that sacred or magic shirts would protect them from attack. When the Sioux conducted the Ghost Dance at Wounded Knee Creek in South Dakota in 1890, the Seventh Cavalry saw it as an opportunity to disarm the group—and, historian Heather Cox Richardson has argued, Republican politicians saw a way to demonstrate their commitment to opening western lands for mining and agriculture. The firing of a shot led to the massacre of three hundred Native Americans. Wounded Knee became a sacred place for Native American rights and a reminder of the injustices done to an entire people. Despite his pacifism, Wovoka lost some of his luster, although Native Americans and anthropologists continued to visit and learn from him until his death in 1932.

Women's Rights

Sarah Winnemucca's advocacy for her people sometimes obscures her role in promoting women's rights. Other late-nineteenth-century Nevadans also supported women's rights in a variety of ways, reflecting changes in the state: as mining and migration into the state subsided, the percentage of women approached half and average ages rose. Despite the folklore, few women worked as prostitutes, and most women who settled in Nevada worked to build a family life and a better community. The spread of Victorian values and the "cult of domesticity," which emphasized the home as women's sphere and their duty to play a civilizing role in their communities and the lives of their families, provided an avenue for them to try to shape policies that would improve morals and education. But Nevada women found this difficult to accomplish in so economically depressed a state.

Nevada became one of the first western states to discuss women's suffrage. In 1869, before Wyoming Territory approved it later that year, Assemblyman Curtis Hillyer of Storey County introduced legislation to amend the state constitution to allow the vote. He reasoned, "The politics of the country is corrupt," and women's traditional role as tribunes of morality and civilization would elevate public discourse. The legislature agreed, but amending the Nevada Constitution requires two consecutive sessions to act. Despite the state's first women's suffrage convention at Battle Mountain and campaigning by women's rights advocate Laura DeForce Gordon, the 1871 legislature said no. A significant turnover in membership and controversy that had grown since the previous vote apparently caused its downfall. On several occasions, apparently believing Nevada's suffering economy required them to do something, lawmakers came close to allowing a vote on amending the constitution. After the 1895 legislature approved a similar measure, it failed in 1897 in a close vote, despite visits from Susan B. Anthony and the formation of the Nevada Women's Equal Suffrage League.

Women found other outlets to improve Nevada society. Eliza Cook, one of Nevada's first trained women doctors, practiced in Reno and, belonging to suffrage and temperance organizations, recalled that she "talked on both subjects when opportunity offered and made myself very objectionable at times, I've no doubt." Mila Tupper Maynard supported suffrage from her position as a Unitarian minister in Reno, where she conducted classes on social reform and set up the Twentieth Century Club, which helped start her community's first kindergarten and public library. Hannah Clapp and Eliza Babcock operated the Sierra Seminary, a private school in Carson City; after it closed, Clapp became one of the university's first professors in Reno. There she worked for suffrage and helped educate Anne Martin, who would become Nevada's most famous advocate of social reform.

Some Nevada women found an outlet through the written word. Married to editors Henry Mighels and then Sam Davis, Nellie Mighels Davis organized the first Red Cross in Nevada during the Spanish-American War and served as its first president, but achieved greater fame with the *Carson City Morning Appeal,* which she briefly published and wrote for, including as the only woman to cover the Corbett-Fitzsimmons fight in 1897. Idah Meacham Strobridge grew up in Lassen Meadows between Winnemucca and Lovelock, but her husband and three sons died during blizzards in 1888–89. She left Nevada and began writing, publishing several books and becoming known as "the first woman of Nevada letters" for her folktales, short stories, and essays.

Helen Stewart and Southern Nevada

After Mormon missionaries left Las Vegas, their old fort became a ranch. Octavius Decatur Gass had taken over the mission, by then a general store for miners like himself, and expanded his holdings to about a thousand acres by the mid-1870s. But Gass ran into problems: boundary changes cost him tax money and his political influence; he upset Mojave Desert military camps, which accused him of overcharging for his fruits, vegetables, and meats; and he kept suing southern California land baron Abel Stearns over ownership of tin mines in the Temescal Mountains. Constantly mortgaging his ranch finally cost him ownership of it in 1881—not typical of Populists, but, like them, caught in his own debt spiral.

The ranch's new owner, Archibald Stewart, a Pioche merchant, moved there with his wife, Helen, and their children. The Kiels, neighboring ranchers known for welcoming gunslingers, resented Stewart, whom they saw as having swindled their friend Gass. This mixture became combustible in the summer of 1884. A Stewart ranch hand went to work for the Kiels, insulting Helen Stewart as he left. Upon returning, her husband rode over to the Kiel Ranch. Two hours later she received a note from Conrad Kiel telling her to "take Mr. Sturd away he is dead." One of the gunslingers shot him, claiming self-defense, although she remained convinced that they had ambushed him.

She faced a difficult situation, to say the least. With four children, a fifth on the way, her neighbors tied to her husband's shooting, and little business experience, she stayed. Stewart operated the ranch, ran a roadside rest for travelers, and hoped someday to sell it to developers. She had to wait until 1902 and Senator William Andrews Clark of Montana, who paid fifty-five thousand dollars for her land and the water rights for his proposed railroad from Los Angeles to Salt Lake. After that she remained active as Las Vegas grew around her, holding educational offices, studying local history, amassing a collection of Paiute baskets, and deeding ten acres of her land to the local Southern Paiutes for a colony where they still live in downtown Las Vegas. Thus did Helen Stewart strike a blow for women as a ranch owner, aid Native Americans, and help build what became Nevada's largest city. For good reason, she became known as "the first lady of Las Vegas."

Helen Jane Wiser Stewart reluctantly came to Las Vegas with her husband and stayed to raise a family, run a ranch, serve as postmaster, and ultimately become the "first lady of Las Vegas." Courtesy of Special Collections, University Libraries, University of Nevada, Las Vegas.

The Panic and the Unemployed

The panic of 1893 caused high unemployment and induced businesses to tighten their belts. Angry over the downturn and disparities in wealth, "General" Jacob Coxey proposed public works projects to provide jobs. Rebuffed by Congress, he organized an "Industrial Army" to march across the country to help unemployed workers bring attention to their plight. Urged to find a way to stop them, Governor Roswell Colcord dismissed concerns: "It would be madness for such an army to subsist while marching this sparsely settled State." The Central Pacific hurried the approximately 1,000-man "army" across Nevada in twenty-three cattle cars, but the unemployed miners and other laborers who tried and failed to join them in Reno paraded and demonstrated until the sheriff ordered them to leave town or go to jail. Coxey's Army went on to Washington, DC, where authorities arrested him for marching on the White House lawn, ending the demonstrations.

The railroads they rode faced labor problems. In June 1894 Eugene Debs led an American Railway Union strike against Pullman, which made railroad cars, and other companies. When President Grover Cleveland sent troops, about 250 soldiers took over railroad operations in Winnemucca, where demonstrations had been peaceful. In Wadsworth a crowd damaged some of the railroad equipment, and troops attacked strikers and their sympathizers. In Reno, by contrast, demonstrators threw eggs at the army. When Nevadans who objected to the federal soldiers asked Colcord to seek their removal, his negative reply prompted Nixon in the *Silver State* to encourage government ownership of railroads to avert any such future "expenditure of public force for private benefit."

Federal involvement broke the strike, but Nevadans made their sympathies clear. Both Coxey's Army and the Pullman strikers supported inflation and free silver, attacked Cleveland over the gold standard, and received aid in Nevada from several Silver Party leaders. The Silver Party's advocacy of mining interests, rich and poor, helped its slate coast to victory in the elections that fall. Nationally and in Nevada, the demonstrations and the government response to them helped fire support for William Jennings Bryan's presidential candidacy in 1896.

The Limits of Reform

As the role of Stewart and Newlands in the Silver and Populist movements and the difficulty in passing women's suffrage demonstrated the limits of reform in Nevada, so did actions that stamped the state as immoral, even if it shared the prejudices of the time and permitted activities that have become common. In 1897 "Gentleman Jim" Corbett and Bob Fitzsimmons wanted to fight for the world heavyweight boxing championship, but several states barred them from doing so because they viewed prizefighting as no more than organized mayhem. Granting that recent rule changes had eliminated some of the bloodiness, their struggling economy meant Nevadans could ill afford to be choosy and the match would bring them publicity and business. The legislation to permit the fight, which Fitzsimmons won, proved controversial: church officials divided over its morality, and some critics directed anti-Semitism at Carson City businessman Al Livingston, one of its supporters. It also foreshadowed the future: Nevada legalized what other places would not and hoped those visiting the state to indulge in dubious behavior would like the place enough to move there and become taxpayers.

Gambling provided another means of generating revenue. Soon after statehood, the legislature tried to make it legal, at least partly because it went on anyway. But Governor Blasdel, a Methodist known as "the coffee and chocolate governor" for his opposition to serving alcohol at state functions, vetoed it in 1867 and 1869. The second time, lawmakers overrode him, and gambling remained legal for the rest of the century. But the state avoided interfering in local operations, letting local sheriffs regulate the games and collect the fees, which counties divided with the state. With boxing and gambling, Nevada erected a system of limited regulation and relying on outsiders for prosperity that came back to haunt it later and made clear that its commitment to moral reform depended on what its economy could afford—as it proved as the twentieth century began, Nevada's economy revived, and moral reform loomed on the horizon.

SUGGESTED READINGS

Canfield, Gae Whitney. *Sarah Winnemucca of the Northern Paiutes.* Norman: University of Oklahoma Press, 1983.

Davies, Richard O. *The Main Event: Boxing in Nevada from the Mining Camps to the Las Vegas Strip.* Reno: University of Nevada Press, 2014.

Glass, Mary Ellen. *Silver and Politics in Nevada, 1892–1902.* Reno: University of Nevada Press, 1970.

Goodwyn, Lawrence. *The Populist Moment: A Short History of the Agrarian Revolt in America.* New York: Oxford University Press, 1978.

Hittman, Michael, and Don Lynch. *Wovoka and the Ghost Dance.* Lincoln: University of Nebraska Press, 1997.

Hopkins, Sarah Winnemucca. *Life Among the Piutes: Their Wrongs and Claims,* 1883. Reprint, Reno: University of Nevada Press, 1994.

McArthur, Aaron. *St. Thomas, Nevada: A History Uncovered.* Reno: University of Nevada Press, 2013.

Paher, Stanley W. *Las Vegas: As It Began—as It Grew.* Las Vegas: Nevada Publications, 1971.

Patterson, Edna B., Louise A. Ulph, and Victor Goodwin. *Nevada's Northeast Frontier.* Sparks, NV: Western, 1969.

Pisani, Donald J. *To Reclaim a Divided West: Water, Law, and Public Policy, 1848–1902.* Albuquerque: University of New Mexico Press, 1992.

———. *Water, Land, and Law in the West: The Limits of Public Policy, 1850–1920.* Lawrence: University Press of Kansas, 1996.

Postel, Charles. *The Populist Vision.* New York: Oxford University Press, 2007.

Richardson, Heather Cox. *West from Appomattox: The Reconstruction of America After the Civil War.* New Haven, CT: Yale University Press, 2007.

———. *Wounded Knee: Party Politics and the Road to an American Massacre.* New York: Basic Books, 2010.

Roske, Ralph J. *Las Vegas: A Desert Paradise.* Tulsa, OK: Continental Heritage Press, 1986.

Rusco, Elmer R. *"Good Time Coming?": Black Nevadans in the Nineteenth Century.* Westport, CT: Greenwood Press, 1975.

Smoak, Gregory E. *Ghost Dances and Identity: Prophetic Religion and American Indian Ethnogenesis in the Nineteenth Century.* Berkeley: University of California Press, 2006.

Starrs, Paul F. *Let the Cowboy Ride: Cattle Ranching in the American West.* Baltimore: Johns Hopkins University Press, 2000.

Stegner, Wallace. *Beyond the Hundredth Meridian: John Wesley Powell and the Second Opening of the West.* Boston: Houghton Mifflin, 1954.

Taylor, Quintard. *In Search of the Racial Frontier: African Americans in the American West, 1528–1990.* New York: W. W. Norton, 1998.

Taylor, Quintard, and Shirley Ann Wilson Moore, eds. *African American Women Confront the West, 1600–2000.* Norman: University of Oklahoma Press, 2003.

Townley, John M. *Alfalfa Country: Nevada Land, Water and Politics in the Nineteenth Century.* Reno: University of Nevada Agricultural Experiment Station, 1981.

Utley, Robert M. *The Indian Frontier of the American West, 1846–1890.* Albuquerque: University of New Mexico Press, 1984.

Wallace, Anthony F. C., ed. *James Mooney, the Ghost Dance Religion and the Sioux Outbreak of 1890.* Chicago: University of Chicago Press, 1965.

Watson, Anita. *Into Their Own: Nevada Women Emerging into Public Life.* Reno: Nevada Humanities Committee, 2000.

Worster, Donald. *A River Running West: The Life of John Wesley Powell.* New York: Oxford University Press, 2001.

Young, James A., and B. Abbott Sparks. *Cattle in the Cold Desert.* Reno: University of Nevada Press, 2002.

Zanjani, Sally S. *Sarah Winnemucca.* Lincoln: University of Nebraska Press, 2001.

Zanjani, Sally S., and Carrie Townley Porter. *Helen J. Stewart: First Lady of Las Vegas.* Las Vegas: Stephens Press, 2012.

8

A New Century, a New Boom

L ike a new year, a new century marks a turning point. In American history, the controversial election of 1800 prompted the first transfer of government power, from John Adams to Thomas Jefferson; the more controversial 2000 election, with Al Gore's popular-vote lead and George W. Bush's Electoral College victory, took place in the shadow of Y2K and concerns about computers upending civilization. By contrast, the 1900 presidential election seemed quiet—William Jennings Bryan disappointed Nevada Silverites, losing again to Republican William McKinley—but the twentieth century's first decades brought different responses to change throughout the United States and the world. Nevada evolved similarly. Its government and political system changed in important ways, but it did so amid an economic revival created by a mining boom in the south-central and eastern portions of Nevada that reshaped the state's society and culture in almost every way.

Births of the Booms

As 1900 arrived, Nevada's two-decade depression continued, and prospectors searched and hoped. In the San Antonio Mountains southwest of Belmont, one story says, Western Shoshone Tom Fisherman led miner, rancher, and attorney Jim Butler to a new bonanza. According to legend—and perhaps some reality—a windstorm that May 19 forced Butler to seek shelter. His quest to find his burro, which had wandered away, led him to an outcropping of gold and silver, but he had no funds to assay it. He turned to county recorder Wilson Brougher and Belmont lawyer Tasker Oddie, a New Yorker representing mining investor Anson Phelps Stokes. Also short of money, Oddie traded part of his interest in the ore to local science teacher Walter Gayhart in return for an assay. A month later, Gayhart reported 640 ounces in silver and $200 in gold per ton. Not until August 25, after finishing with clients and harvesting, did Butler return to the site and file claims for himself and his two partners—and apparently he acted only at the behest of his wife, Belle, who discovered the largest Butler claim and ran their ranch.

Their new camp, Tonopah, never approached Virginia City in importance or wealth (production peaked at $9 million in 1914), but it ended Nevada's two decades of depression. Just as mining booms begat other towns—Virginia City and Austin had been "mother camps," for example—Tonopah fostered other booms and boomtowns. Late in 1902 Jim Butler and Tom Kendall grubstaked prospectors Harry Stimler and William Marsh in exchange for a percentage of what they found. On December 4, in the Columbia Mountains about thirty miles south of Tonopah, they found gold—and Fisherman, who may have been related to Stimler's Shoshone mother, probably led them there. Additional exploration, especially in January 1904, gave birth to Goldfield. That year Frank "Shorty" Harris and Ernest Cross found gold in southern Nye County's Amargosa Valley, just east of Death Valley. This area became the Bullfrog District, home of the mining boomtown of Rhyolite and a nearby freighting center, Beatty.

Butler's original find led to about a hundred discoveries and, with them, the creation of numerous boomtowns that served, as nineteenth-century towns did, as hubs for mining and ranching hinterlands. Cattlemen located gold north of Tonopah at an old camp, Manhattan, in 1905, and the population reached about four thousand in a year—until the San Francisco earthquake also shook investors and delayed development, although the camp revived and produced into the 1920s. Almost concurrently, gold discoveries to the north triggered another mining town, Round Mountain, which generated $1 million by 1909, while other short-lived camps sprang to life near Tonopah and Goldfield. Like their predecessors, they boasted large numbers of saloons (one in Rawhide rented floor space as beds) as well as newspapers, schools, and community organizations. Tonopah and Goldfield residents suffered through a great deal of disease, due partly to unsanitary conditions, yet Tonopah in particular became civilized more speedily than other, earlier, camps, with more families moving in and wives forming clubs and societies.

Also in 1900 eastern Nevada joined in the revival. In 1870 White Pine's Robinson District yielded low-grade copper, but that exploration proved brief due to minimal demand and a lack of transportation and technology. By the late 1890s investors expressed renewed interest, thanks to the need for electric wiring created by Thomas Edison inventing the DC generator and George Westinghouse and Nikola Tesla perfecting the AC, a technological change perhaps as influential in its time as computers and cellular phones in the late twentieth and early twenty-first centuries. Thus, young miners Edwin Gray and Dave Bartley tried their luck. Grubstaked by a grocer, they filed two claims near Ely, tunneled into the mountain, found copper on all sides at 145 feet down, and kept going deeper. The rush to Ely and the surrounding area would follow, but not right away.

The Discoverers

The early days of Nevada's nineteenth- and twentieth-century mining booms revealed a series of similarities and differences. The latter's founders generally emerged with more substantial funds, and capital traveled different routes to central and eastern Nevada than it did to the Comstock, although it produced similar results. In October 1902 Gray and Bartley optioned their Ely claims for $150,000 in stock to Eureka and Palisade Railroad owner Mark Requa, son of a Comstock mining engineer. Requa took over another company, incorporated the Nevada Consolidated Copper Company in November 1904, and won backing from eastern investors. He also prompted competition from the Guggenheim family, which had entered western mining with Colorado lead and silver and expanded into copper there and in Arizona until, by the late 1910s, they controlled three-quarters of the world's silver, copper, and lead production. They obtained a site for water and a smelter, incorporated the Cumberland-Ely Copper Company, and helped finance construction of Requa's planned Northern Nevada Railway. But the Guggenheims eventually took over Requa's company. Requa may have expected to play a role in managing their White Pine claims; he proved mistaken.

The Guggenheims acted much as the Bank Crowd did in Virginia City. They took over Requa's railroad and mining claims. Just as William Sharon ordered studies of the Comstock and responded to a downturn, the Guggenheims spent $4 million on preparation and continued as the panic of 1907 choked off investment and reduced stock prices. No ore shipped out of the district until August 1908, but staggering results followed: production skyrocketed from nearly $625,000 in 1908 to $6.5 million in 1909. The Guggenheims later incorporated Kennecott Copper, which controlled most White Pine production into the 1980s. Just as Comstock gold and silver profits went west to San Francisco, White Pine copper earnings traveled to other company holdings in Utah and Arizona and back east to finance a family of investors and philanthropists.

Tonopah fed off local ownership and outside development. Butler and Oddie filed every claim they could but realized they lacked the capital, time, or personnel to work them. When San Francisco investors, suspicious of speculating in Nevada due to so many recent failures there, declined their overtures, Tonopah's founders developed the lease system, enabling them to retain ownership, employ miners to handle the work, and share the profits. Butler and Oddie granted each lessee one hundred feet of the vein and fifty feet on each side and received 25 percent of the revenue produced, ensuring employment for others and profits for themselves.

Finally, Butler and Oddie attracted buyers. The publicity about their leasing system drew interest from outside investors, led by Philadelphia's Brock family, whose members controlled numerous eastern businesses,

Tonopah's discovery in 1900 revitalized Nevada's economy and created a boomtown where few Nevadans had previously lived or traveled. Courtesy of Special Collections, University Libraries, University of Nevada, Las Vegas.

including coal mining. In July 1901, a year after the discovery, Butler and Oddie sold their portions for more than $300,000, but their lives took different trajectories. Whereas Butler concentrated on other businesses and held on to his money, Oddie felt he sold too low and too soon, but went to work for the new investors and made hundreds of thousands of dollars on stock transactions. Then he lost his fortune in mining speculation and the panic of 1907 and ran for governor because he needed the job—and won. The Brocks incorporated the Tonopah Mining Company and followed in the footsteps of earlier Nevada mine owners such as the Bank Crowd and Bonanza Kings. They vertically integrated, adding milling and water companies and banks to their holdings, but for additional reasons: private water companies sought to serve homes and local businesses rather than mines, and they needed power lines run from California to be able to build modern mills.

The Bullfrog District resembled such earlier booms as Hamilton and Treasure Hill: intense but brief. Because Bullfrog, Rhyolite, and nearby camps materialized after Tonopah and Goldfield, which proved Nevada had come back to life, the rush began quickly. In 1905 miner E. A. "Bob" Montgomery incorporated the Montgomery-Shoshone company and soon sold most of it to Charles M. Schwab, president of US Steel and an investor and a stock speculator in the Tonopah area (and no relation to the modern broker). But its mines and others soon petered out, leaving mostly ghost towns and ghosts: old buildings and, most notably in Rhyolite, a house made of bottles, which the local saloon industry, always a beneficiary of mining capital, helped supply. One of Rhyolite's buildings housed the law offices of William Morris Stewart, who moved there after leaving the Senate in 1905 and even became a member of the local school board.

Goldfield and Wingfield

Like Tonopah, Goldfield operated at first under the leasing system. One lease, the Hayes-Monnette, generated a carload of ore worth nearly $575,000. This had two effects: the Monnettes took their profits out of Nevada and put them into what became Bank of America, and outside investment in Goldfield's one-hundred-plus mining companies became inevitable. Nevadans George Nixon and George Wingfield became the catalysts and beneficiaries. After investigating the region, and busy with a US Senate seat he had won in 1905, Nixon provided capital. Wingfield, an

Arkansas native, did most of the work. A cowboy, gambler, and saloon-keeper who lived in Winnemucca and Golconda before arriving in Tonopah in 1901, he moved around central Nevada, investing in mines, manipulating and speculating in stock, and looking for luck to strike. In 1906 Wingfield moved on to Goldfield and bought the Jumbo, Red Top, and Mohawk mines. He and Nixon incorporated what historian Sally Zanjani has called "the economic juggernaut that dominated the district": the Goldfield Consolidated Mines Company, capitalized at $50 million and the first Nevada mining firm on the New York Stock Exchange, complete with financing from legendary Wall Street financier Bernard Baruch (who had a Nevada link through marriage to the Olcoviches, a pioneer Jewish family in Carson City).

Nixon and Wingfield became the early-twentieth-century equivalents of the Bank Crowd. They bought additional properties throughout the year and, by early 1907, owned almost every producing mine in Goldfield. Then they vertically integrated with a vengeance, especially in banking and milling. Wingfield oversaw a one-hundred-stamp mill that used the "all-sliming" technique, which relied more heavily on cyanide and improved production and profits. Within two years Nixon and Wingfield bought out the Brocks and took over Tonopah.

Wingfield's takeover involved even more than that. In 1909 he and Nixon dissolved their partnership so that Nixon could concentrate on banking and Wingfield on mining. Wingfield said, "I have took over everything." That year his company generated $10 million in gold and $7 million in stock dividends. But after Nixon's death in 1912, despite Governor Tasker Oddie's description of him as having "a wonderfully strong and pleasing personality, an iron nerve, unexcelled business ability and integrity and an intimate knowledge of the general condition and needs of the State," Wingfield declined the offer of an appointment as his successor, claiming responsibilities in and to Nevada. He then bought out Nixon's widow and ended up owning most of the major mines outside of the White Pine copper boom, most of the state's leading banks, large ranches in northern and central Nevada as well as several California enterprises, and several hotels.

Boomtown Life

The twentieth-century boomtowns resembled and diverged from their earlier counterparts. With any mining discovery, a district soon followed with a recorder, and the local saloon usually became the central meeting place—Wyatt Earp owned one saloon in Tonopah, the Northern. Unlike the Comstock, originating in mostly ungoverned western Utah territory, Tonopah, Goldfield, Ely, and other towns began in existing counties and thus had some form of government in place. These factors contributed to the earlier arrival of families and such institutions as schools, churches, and public libraries, first in tents and then in wood buildings; if the boomtown survived, brick structures followed quickly. Town boards concentrated on problems ranging from sanitation to imposing monthly $5 licensing fees for prostitutes. Most of the communities also included tennis courts, and Searchlight reported a bowling alley. Social events sometimes depended on class and status: at the peak of his wealth and influence in Tonopah, Oddie held a dance party three hundred feet down in his Mizpah Mine, while miners often participated in drilling competitions, often as part of bigger community-wide celebrations, that allowed them to display their prowess, speed, and strength.

Journalism in early 1900s Nevada never competed with the *Territorial Enterprise*'s brilliant staff of the 1860s and 1870s. While editors and publishers in Nevada's largest city, Reno, promoted civic betterment and influenced policy in the *Nevada State Journal* and the *Reno Evening Gazette,* mining-camp editors served a different but still important function. Their information contributed to the boom-and-bust cycle, depending on their accuracy and, sometimes, the editors' involvement in the industry, stock speculation, and politics. One of the era's leading editors, Frank Garside, owned several mining-camp newspapers, including Tonopah's, and later published Las Vegas's largest daily. Arthur Buel spent three years as an editorial cartoonist in Tonopah before moving on to Reno for three years and then to a long career in northern California newspapers.

The populations of Tonopah and Goldfield both shot above ten thousand, although the lack of a census until 1910 leaves such numbers open to debate. Within two years of its founding, Tonopah boasted an estimated three thousand residents, thirty-two saloons, a church, a school, and two weekly newspapers; Goldfield grew rapidly, too. As with the Comstock, not

Goldfield became not just a boomtown but a community with mining at the center of it. Miners often participated in parades like this one as a relief from their work. Courtesy of Special Collections, University Libraries, University of Nevada, Las Vegas.

only investors and entrepreneurs but also attorneys flocked to the region. From the Klondike came Key Pittman, who practiced law, mined, and entered politics. George Bartlett arrived from Eureka, spent two terms in Congress during the boom, and became a US attorney and a judge, enjoying ties to Wingfield throughout his career. Son of an Irish immigrant sheepherder, Pat McCarran moved down after representing Reno in the assembly for a term and became Nye County district attorney and, eventually, an almost constant annoyance to Wingfield and Pittman.

Humboldt and Elko County always relied more on railroads and ranching than on mining, but the rebirth of Nevada mining prompted a population influx, more markets for livestock, and the urbanization that always accompanied discoveries. Tuscarora generated half of Elko County's nineteenth-century mining production, and investment spiked in 1907, but that year's national depression ended that effort. That year, northwest of Elko, a gold discovery led to the founding of Midas, a platted town site, and about two thousand residents within a year; it went through ups and downs, prospering again from 1915 into the early 1920s. A gold discovery in the western Bull Run Mountains led to Edgemont, a large mill, and substantial production until an avalanche destroyed most of the area in 1917.

Jarbidge grew to more than fifteen hundred amid rumors of gold in 1910 but went through on-and-off development over the next decade. Near Winnemucca discovery of several ores led to the founding of Golconda in 1898 and a decade of production, but it became more famous for its celebrities: Wingfield invested in the boom and befriended a young mining engineer named Herbert Hoover, who later became a friend of Mark Requa, the early Ely promoter and, during World War I, a member of Hoover's staff in the US Food Administration.

New Railroads and Towns: The Rise of Las Vegas

Mining developments in southern and central Nevada enticed Nevadans such as Nixon and Requa as well as outside investors. In 1902 Senator William Andrews Clark, a Montana copper baron who had just invested in Ely, bought Helen Stewart's acreage and water rights in the Las Vegas Valley for his proposed San Pedro, Los Angeles & Salt Lake Railroad. He planned to transport his copper to California markets and overseas, especially with the spread of electricity and the accompanying need for copper wire. Edward Henry Harriman, the New York stockbroker running the Union Pacific and Southern Pacific (SP), planned the Oregon Short Line along the same route, also attracted by the burgeoning southern California market. Construction began on both lines, at times yards apart, with brawls between the workers ensuing. Finally, the two companies merged; split ownership, with Clark responsible for the railroad's operations; and completed construction. Shortly thereafter, on May 15, 1905, officials auctioned off a town site, now the heart of downtown Las Vegas.

While Tonopah, Goldfield, Ely, and others relied mainly on mining, and mining officials even created company towns, Las Vegas resembled the nineteenth-century railroad towns, especially those the Central Pacific created. Like Carlin, Lovelock, and Wadsworth, Las Vegas served as a railroad division point—a storage facility, a repair center and housing spot for train crews, and a shipping and transportation depot for those in the hinterland who sent resources to it, obtained others from it, and connected through it to national and international markets. The railroad made Las Vegas function almost as a company town and, from its beginnings, as a twenty-four-hour community catering to travelers and railroad workers. The railroad's subsidiary, the Las Vegas Land & Water Company, largely controlled local utilities and services, thanks to its water rights, prompting entrepreneurs to dig their own wells outside of the town site, leading to considerable waste. The railroad also limited activities in town: it barred liquor sales outside of one block, but exempted hotels, prompting saloon owners to compete by installing brothels, which operated on Block 16 until World War II. The railroad affected the economy in other ways: flooding along various parts of the line virtually shut down Las Vegas on several occasions for lack of employment and supplies.

As in the mining towns, and in earlier incarnations, power prompted dissent and civic responses. J. T. McWilliams had been a railroad surveyor before trying to start a competing town site west of the tracks. Because McWilliams lacked water rights and the capital to take on the Clark and Union Pacific interests, most residents moved to the new town. After a fire all but leveled Ragtown, as it became known for its canvas buildings, late in 1905, McWilliams alternately worked for and annoyed the railroad while trying to develop nearby Lee Canyon into a recreational and tourist area. Yet the railroad's presence also promoted a sense of permanence, so early Las Vegans set out to build a community. In 1911 Helen Stewart helped start the Mesquite Club, a women's organization still involved in community education and civic activities, and businessmen created the Las Vegas Chamber of Commerce, which promotes the town and eventually bridged the gap between established community members and businesses that struck them as catering to vice.

Thanks to the railroad, Las Vegas wound up playing a role similar to Reno: central hub for a mining hinterland. The boom to the north and the railroad construction that built Las Vegas encouraged nearby mining in the town's early years. Searchlight, founded as a mining district in 1898, competed with Las Vegas for population but declined after 1908. Although it had ties to Las Vegas, Searchlight boasted its own nearby ranches, attracted eastern investment, and enjoyed a decade of growth that resembled most significant Nevada mining areas. Potosi revived, becoming Nevada's top zinc producer during the 1910s. Goodsprings had been known for lead, gold, and zinc, but production quadrupled with the railroad's completion, which eased transportation. Eldorado Canyon stirred again, with the town of Nelson platted nearby.

Like Reno, Elko, Winnemucca, and other northern towns, Las Vegas owed its growth to railroad building—as do other early-twentieth-century communities (see map on page 104). The central and eastern Nevada boomtowns would have prospered less without railroads. Serving the new rushes, the Carson & Colorado stirred to life and benefited Southern Pacific coffers—Collis Huntington bought it cheap in the late 1890s—but not politically, as the railroad's influence declined in Nevada. The sp also emulated the cp in creating communities along its tracks. During a rebuilding phase in the early 1900s that altered the direction of its tracks, the sp bought ranches in the Truckee Meadows to replace its older or obsolete repair shops at Wadsworth. Just as the up and Clark created a town site in Las Vegas, the sp set up a town for its shops just east of Reno and named it for Governor John Sparks. The doubling of Reno's population from 1900 to 1910 demonstrated the impact of the revival of mining and railroad building outside their immediate areas.

The economic revival prompted new construction. The v&t's expansion south from Carson City—expected to extend into California—went through Carson Valley. The Dangbergs, the area's leading ranching family, proposed and planned a town along the tracks and named it for Minden, the German town from which H. F. Dangberg came. The Western Pacific Railroad, created in 1903, extended from California through northern Washoe County to Winnemucca, paralleling the sp until crossing into Utah at Wendover; it later built a branch line to Reno. The Atchison, Topeka & Santa Fe, one of the nation's largest lines, entered Searchlight from Barnwell, one of its sidings in southern California—and managed to offend locals by employing hundreds of Mexicans in helping to build it. When the train stopped operating, the Searchlight residents who used the ties to build homes included the parents of Harry Reid, later a US senator.

Labor Problems: Goldfield

Although nineteenth-century miners tried to counter companies' efforts to control them or increase profits at their expense, the twentieth-century boom led to greater labor strife. In 1905 the Western Federation of Miners (wfm) helped start the Industrial Workers of the World, a radical union that stressed "industrial unionism" over the American Federation of Labor's "craft unionism." For unknown reasons, iww members became known as Wobblies. Critics claimed iww stood for "I Won't Work" and expressed concern over the iww's beliefs: that workers should unite as a class, capital sought to divide labor, and the wage system should be abolished.

Although the wfm organized miners in 1903 in Searchlight, causing a mostly unsuccessful strike, Goldfield marked the IWW's first foray into large-scale organizing in Nevada. In 1904 the AFL and WFM tried to start unions there. In 1906 organizer Vincent St. John won IWW membership from local workers ranging from dishwashers to teamsters. The union held a radical parade, and St. John announced, "We will sweep the capitalist class out of the life of this nation and then out of the whole world." By 1907 new arrivals from Cripple Creek, Colorado, site of recent organizing and violence, bolstered the WFM and IWW.

Yet mine owners refused to concede easily and won support from other local businessmen affected by the IWW's actions. Not only did they form a Goldfield Business Men's and Mine Operators' Association to work together, but Wingfield also decreed two new policies, both for profits and in response to the panic of 1907, which temporarily dried up capital investment. One sought to stop "high-grading," a practice through which miners smuggled valuable gold out of the mines in their work clothes, by putting security guards in the changing rooms. The other replaced paychecks with scrip, effectively making Goldfield a company town.

Violence contributed to and resulted from the controversy. In November the shooting of St. John prompted him to leave Goldfield to become a national IWW leader. But earlier in 1907, another shooting had more lasting effects. Restaurant owner John Silva's killing led to the arrest, trial, and conviction of organizers Morrie Preston and Joseph Smith. The fairness of the trial raised suspicions and fitted a pattern that other labor radicals faced throughout the West: their convictions followed a failed attempt to convict IWW leader "Big Bill" Haywood of murder in Idaho, Utah executed Joe Hill in 1915 after a dubious trial, and San Francisco organizer Tom Mooney received a life sentence on doubtful bombing charges in 1916. In Nevada future efforts, especially by Preston (as a prisoner the Socialist Labor Party's choice for president, the only Nevadan ever to be a national party's nominee), to win pardons failed amid rumors that Wingfield intimidated members of the pardons board. Nearly eighty years later, in their book *The Ignoble Conspiracy,* historians Sally Zanjani and Guy Louis Rocha concluded that Preston shot Silva in self-defense and Wingfield allies may have perjured themselves. The state pardons board responded by posthumously pardoning Preston and Smith.

Goldfield and Labor: Long-Term Effects

At the time, though, the combination of events, culminating in a general strike on November 27 and the closure of local mines, gave the mine owners their chance to break unionizing efforts in Goldfield. They asked Governor John Sparks to request federal troops; the longtime rancher owed Wingfield for loans and complied. He wired President Theodore Roosevelt that amid "unlawful combinations and conspiracies . . . the constituted authorities of the State of Nevada are now and continue to be unable to protect the people." Roosevelt responded with soldiers on December 6. Mine owners cut wages one dollar a day and soon began recruiting nonunion workers from out of state. The mines reopened in January.

These events had long-term ramifications. Suspicious, Roosevelt sent an investigating committee that reported no need for federal troops. The president told Sparks that he would remove the troops unless Nevada created its own police force, which it did in a special session the governor quickly called. The army left in March, and the state police stepped in. The miners gave up and returned to their jobs. Up for reelection to the Senate that fall, Francis Newlands worked behind the scenes to help Sparks pass the bill while seeking to maintain labor support and unity in the Democratic Party. That fall a majority of the legislators seeking reelection lost, paying the price for aiding mine owners such as Wingfield, whom the Goldfield labor troubles established as the dominant player in Nevada politics.

One problem for Wingfield refused to go away. Nye County district attorney Pat McCarran criticized the federal intervention and the state police force's creation. That increased Wingfield's enmity, which McCarran originally earned by representing his wife, May, in a divorce that included charges that Wingfield suffered from a venereal disease (McCarran lost the case anyway). When Wingfield tried to silence him with the offer of a judgeship, McCarran not only declined it but also ran futilely for Congress against one of the magnate's allies and then unsuccessfully challenged other Wingfield-backed candidates in US Senate races during the 1910s. This relationship would affect Nevada in years to come, as McCarran warred against Wingfield and the political establishment.

Company Towns

Surrounded by towns dependent on mining or railroads, the Guggenheims went one step further. Ely had survived since the late 1870s, but barely. As the county seat, it remained the center of White Pine County, but, as it did in other states, the copper company wanted more control over its workforce. The Guggenheims built three company towns: Ruth near the mine, Kimberly to the west, and, more than twenty miles north, McGill, named for a longtime rancher whose land the company bought to build a smelter. Guggenheim executives served as the local government.

On the one hand, workers and their families found much about company-town life appealing. Because residents paid no taxes, they received municipal services free or at reduced rates. The company provided low-cost medical services, including a hospital in nearby East Ely, and a variety of community events. Historian Russell Elliott, who grew up in McGill, called the company "a benevolent although slow-moving landlord," since it built row houses that resembled modern suburban developments and maintained them and the residential streets. It also provided schools for the children of miners and other laborers.

On the other hand, control could be absolute. With no local government, residents had no say. Because they designed the towns to ensure sobriety and stability, the companies regulated behavior, including approval of saloons (McGill originally had only one) and pool halls where employees could sign over their paychecks to ensure payment of debts. The companies segregated immigrants—mainly from Japan, Greece, and Austria-Hungary—but also tried to foster assimilation. Despite the company's efforts, workers still found ways to amuse themselves in what Elliott called "fringe" towns such as Ragdump and Steptoe City outside of McGill as well as Riepetown between Ruth and Kimberly. White Pine County commissioners generally allowed drinking, prostitution, and gambling to flourish in those hamlets—foreshadowing how a federal company town, Boulder City, interacted with a nearby open city, Las Vegas.

Strikes and violence rarely upset labor peace in White Pine before 1912. That September miners struck at Guggenheim copper facilities in Bingham, Utah, partly over an attempt to start a chapter of the Western Federation of Miners. They won a wage hike, but the family refused to recognize the union. In October the WFM called sympathy strikes at other Guggenheim properties, and workers at Ruth and McGill walked out. Nevada Consolidated Copper Company responded by bringing in thirty armed men as guards (said the company) or as strikebreakers (according to the miners). The new arrivals killed two strikers and wounded others. Mine officials called on Governor Tasker Oddie, who arrived, tried to work out a settlement, and finally declared martial law. The state police arrived, swore in a posse, and disarmed both sides. Finally, the strike ended, the miners returned to work, and a local grand jury refused to indict the accused murderers. The strikers called for arresting two company managers as accessories, but Oddie wrote that he "compelled the withdrawal of the warrants charging the managers of the Company with murder, as I knew they were not guilty."

While these events helped shape how Nevadans viewed labor and unions, the copper towns may have had greater technological and environmental effects. Although a few used it on the Comstock, the Guggenheims introduced large-scale open-pit mining to Nevada, a far cry from the tunneling common around the state. Open-pit mining involved a large hole or burrow, made possible by advances in equipment and transportation; one in the Ruth area went one thousand feet down and a mile across. The use and constant improvement of open pits meant low-grade ores became more profitable than they had been through costlier tunneling. Historian Gerald Nash called it "a technological breakthrough . . . hardly less important for the mining industry in the twentieth century than the development of the factory system was for the industrial revolution of the nineteenth century."

Transportation and Technology

Just as reaching Virginia City required an arduous journey, the new boomtowns sat almost literally in the middle of nowhere. Just as Comstock transportation evolved from freighting to V-flumes to railroads, Tonopah's founders started by digging out two tons of ore and shipping them by wagon to Austin before it went on to Salt Lake City. Freight routes to Carson & Colorado Railroad stations (from Tonopah to Sodaville, where one conductor told train passengers, "Change for all points in the world," and from Goldfield to Candelaria) eased the difficulty of moving ore to market and reduced the market for freighting companies, just as the V&T Railroad limited the need for them in Virginia City.

Outside investors seeking profits in Nevada had a similar effect. Southern California's growth helped inspire construction of a road to Salt Lake. But so did the Tonopah-Goldfield boom, prompting Clark's Las Vegas & Tonopah, which ran to Beatty and Goldfield, linking the Los Angeles area to Nevada mining, though less profitably than San Francisco in the previous century. Arriving in Nevada in the 1860s, Francis Marion Smith found wealth by mining borax, a compound used in detergent, in Mineral and Esmeralda Counties. He used mules to move his goods to market and later promoted 20 Mule Team Borax, but also built the Tonopah & Tidewater and Bullfrog & Goldfield Railroads. The Brocks backed a line linking Tonopah and Goldfield to the Carson & Colorado, and thus to the Southern Pacific and San Francisco. The Guggenheims helped Requa set up the Northern Nevada Railway, which went through Steptoe Valley to meet the SP at the newly created Elko County town of Cobre—Spanish for "copper." Yet these entrepreneurs may have missed an opportunity: Russell Elliott observed that a line from the Tonopah-Goldfield area to Ely would have united the two mining regions and "in so doing . . . redirected the entire economic structure of the state." But geography probably played a role: north–south mountain ranges made it difficult to build a northeast-southwest line.

Appropriately for a new century, Nevada mining also relied on a new vehicle: the automobile. Trucks began hauling ore around 1913, the same year the state started requiring automobile licenses: a minimum fee of $1.88, with future fees based on the car's horsepower. Before those changes cars had begun competing with railroads and stage lines to connect major Nevada towns, prompting laws setting speed limits: four in Tonopah and six in Goldfield, whose officials stipulated that "vehicles drawn by horse, at all times, have the right of way." Running for governor in 1910, Oddie campaigned almost entirely by car, saw the need for better roads, and, when he could, followed through.

The mining boom made no real contribution to these technological advances, and the Comstock Lode had indeed been more innovative than its successor in central and eastern Nevada. But mine and mill operators adopted new techniques and adapted to different circumstances. University of Nevada professor Robert Jackson had begun using cyanide to help extract metals at Washoe Lake, and the process worked its way to Tonopah and Goldfield. Those areas also started using a sliming process: grinding the ore as much as possible until it approximates slime, improving the ability to extract ore. But like the mercury used earlier, cyanide polluted the Carson River, causing long-term environmental problems.

Speculation and Society

Speculators preyed on nineteenth-century investors, and the twentieth-century boom proved little different—but at times more colorful. Shortly after veteran schemer George Graham Rice arrived in Goldfield in 1904, his stock promotions sank a local bank. Then he and two friends invented a mining district, Rawhide, turned it into a boomtown, and publicized it by holding an ostentatious funeral for horse-racing gambler Riley Grannan. A fire destroyed Rawhide, and, unlike Virginia City after its blaze, it never recovered. But Rice went on to quintuple the stock value of a failed Ely copper mine before his arrest for mail fraud. Rice went to prison and wrote a book, *My Adventures with Your Money,* before disappearing.

Rice also worked closely with Tex Rickard, whose success led him to much bigger things. Rice and Rickard promoted the Battling Nelson–Joe Gans boxing championship match in Goldfield in September 1906, and Rickard expanded on that and other fights to go to New York as a promoter and build the original Madison Square Garden. Rickard's success in boxing, then considered uncivilized, reflected how the boom resembled its forebears in another way: towns developed parallel societies. Goldfield's saloons topped one hundred in 1906, but the capital pouring into central and eastern Nevada led to stone and brick buildings, schools, and churches, many of them taller than in earlier boomtowns. Residents sought entertainment both proper and improper, with a new twist: movie theaters. Hotels provided more luxury than anything envisioned on the Comstock. Tonopah's Mizpah offered steam heat and the town's first elevator, while the Goldfield Hotel, complete with crystal chandeliers and the latest fire escapes, allegedly opened with champagne flowing down the front steps—and Wingfield co-owned both of them.

The south-central and eastern Nevada mining regions also drew a large number of immigrants, but from different groups than earlier booms. Again they ended up segregated residentially, and not just in the company towns, where Guggenheim officials segregated them. Whereas the Irish had been the most prominent immigrant group in Comstock shafts, Greeks and Italians formed the backbone of miners' unions in several towns, while Goldfield proved more heterogeneous and Caucasian than usual in mining communities. As in Virginia City and its environs, women trailed men in arriving, and fewer entered the sex trade than legend and myth suggest; they varied from waitresses to schoolteachers, but those who became prostitutes encountered the same unhappiness as others throughout the West: about one-third of the prostitutes who died in Goldfield committed suicide, usually around age twenty-one, about the average in mining country.

The Inevitable Decline

Russell Elliott, the boom's preeminent historian, called it "the touch of the decay that was inevitable in these isolated mining booms once the ore petered out." Small mining camps rose and fell quickly, often inside five years. Rhyolite's estimated population of eight thousand in 1908 plummeted by 1920 to fourteen—still better than several other early-twentieth-century camps. Goldfield's production began falling after a 1910 peak of more than $10 million until, a decade later, it generated only about $350,000, and the population of perhaps ten thousand around 1906 had dipped to nearly five thousand in 1910 and a little more than fifteen hundred by 1920. If others dropped like a stone, Tonopah coasted downhill, benefiting from wartime silver needs and the Pittman Silver Act of 1918, which set a minimum price of a dollar an ounce, but still gradually losing population and production. Tonopah and Goldfield benefited from their status as county seats and eventually the highways that went through them, but by 1920 their glory days had ended.

White Pine had better luck. Between 1908 and 1920, its revenues fell just short of the production from Tonopah and Goldfield combined, and Nevada ranked fifth among states in copper production. The Guggenheims still prospered from the district for decades afterward, although the Ely area, too, would suffer a decline.

The twentieth-century mining boom not only revived Nevada but also changed it significantly. Nevada's connections to California deepened through its southern and central boomtowns, while eastern Nevada became more closely tied to Salt Lake City and Utah's copper towns. Although few major political figures started out in White Pine, the south-central axis produced or influenced many of Nevada's key politicians to the present. They would affect how the state functioned and Nevada's relationship with the federal government, which evolved just as the mining boom reshaped the state—and reshaped the state in different ways.

SUGGESTED READINGS

Brown, Mrs. Hugh. *Lady in Boomtown: Miners and Manners on the Nevada Frontier.* Palo Alto, CA: American West, 1968.

Coles, Kathleen, and Victoria Ford, eds. *Nevada Mining Oral History Project.* Reno: University of Nevada Oral History Program, 2008.

Douglass, William A., and Robert A. Nylen, eds. *Letters from the Nevada Frontier: Correspondence of Tasker L. Oddie, 1898–1902.* Reno: University of Nevada Press, 2004.

Elliott, Russell R. *Growing Up in a Company Town: A Family in the Copper Camp of McGill, Nevada.* Reno: Nevada Historical Society, 1990.

———. *Nevada's Twentieth-Century Mining Boom: Tonopah-Goldfield-Ely.* 1966. Reprint, Reno: University of Nevada Press, 1988.

Fleming, Jack. *Copper Times: An Animated Chronicle of White Pine County, Nevada.* Seattle: Jack Fleming, 1987.

Goin, Peter, and C. Elizabeth Raymond. *Changing Mines in America.* Santa Fe, NM: Center for American Places, 2004.

Hall, Shawn. *Preserving the Glory Days: The Ghost Towns and Mining Camps of Nye County, Nevada.* Reno: University of Nevada Press, 1999.

Jones, Florence Lee, and John F. Cahlan. *Water: A History of Las Vegas.* 2 vols. Las Vegas: Las Vegas Valley Water District, 1975.

Limbaugh, Ronald H. *Tungsten in Peace and War, 1918–1946.* Reno: University of Nevada Press, 2010.

Lingenfelter, Richard E. *Bonanzas & Borrascas: Copper Kings and Stock Frenzies, 1885–1918.* Norman, OK: Arthur H. Clark, 2012.

McCracken, Robert D. *A History of Beatty, Nevada.* Tonopah, NV: Nye County Press, 1992.

———. *A History of Tonopah, Nevada.* Tonopah, NV: Nye County Press, 1990.

Olds, Sarah E. *Twenty Miles from a Match: Homesteading in Western Nevada.* Reno: University of Nevada Press, 1990.

Patterson, Edna B., and Louise A. Beebe. *Halleck Country, Nevada: The Story of the Land and Its People.* Reno: University of Nevada Press, 1982.

Raymond, C. Elizabeth. *George Wingfield: Owner and Operator of Nevada.* Reno: University of Nevada Press, 1992.

Read, Effie O. *White Pine Lang Syne: A True History of White Pine County, Nevada.* Denver: Big Mountain Press, 1963.

Reid, Harry. *Searchlight: The Camp That Didn't Fail.* Reno: University of Nevada Press, 1998.

Whitely, Joan Burkhart. *Young Las Vegas, 1905–1931: Before the Future Found Us.* Las Vegas: Stephens Press, 2005.

Zanjani, Sally S. *The Glory Days in Goldfield, Nevada.* Reno: University of Nevada Press, 2002.

———. *Goldfield: The Last Gold Rush on the Western Frontier.* Athens: Swallow Press / Ohio University Press, 1992.

Zanjani, Sally S., and Guy Louis Rocha. *The Ignoble Conspiracy: Radicalism on Trial in Nevada.* Reno: University of Nevada Press, 1986.

9

Making Progress

Progressives "caught the Populists in swimming," Kansas editor William Allen White said, "and stole all of their clothing except the frayed underdrawers of free silver." While some Populists became Progressives as the twentieth century began, the two groups of reformers differed in key ways. Nevada's Progressives proved the rule and the exception. Although many involved in the fight for silver joined the Progressives, both movements underscored the same problem for Nevadans: how reform minded they could be when their economy depended on the boom-and-bust cycle of mining, whom to ally themselves with regionally and nationally to achieve their economic goals, and whether those goals fitted with Progressivism.

The Origins of Progressivism

Like the Populists, Progressives reacted to social issues—corporate expansion, industrialization, urbanization, immigration, and corrupt politics—but in different ways. Generally, while Populists advocated that government take over industries such as railroads, Progressives preferred to regulate them. Populists hoped to control and even harness industrialization; Progressives wanted to embrace and use it to promote scientific management of the government, economy, and environment, but divided on whether to allow large business or, like the Populists, encourage small producers. Rural Populists and urban Progressives saw cities differently, although they felt similarly about the evils of the corruption and social inequality in them.

How Populists and Progressives viewed all but nonwhite males suggested their contradictions. Both struggled with racism, especially as immigration from the East (southern and eastern Europe) and West

(Japan) increased. While Progressives advocated restrictions and assimilation, Populists worried more about African Americans than about foreigners. Their view of women differed: in promoting the small farmer, Populists saw them as part of a family economic unit; Progressives included growing numbers of wage-earning women seeking rights of their own. Reformers varied in how they viewed those rights, but women became a Progressive force, pursuing better working conditions, social services, and new kinds of personal freedom, including not just the vote, but also birth control and less restrictive definitions of art and freedom.

The two movements' origins also differed. The Populist movement started among small farmers after the Civil War. By contrast, Progressivism had no single birthplace and many parents, but resulted partly from the triumph of Alexander Hamilton's industrial state over Thomas Jefferson's subsistence farmer. With new laws to regulate interstate commerce and trusts to limit monopolies and ensure competition, the Gilded Age foreshadowed the Progressive desire for government activism. But Progressives saw these measures as lacking teeth or accomplishing too little. The era's large-scale immigration also heightened Progressive concerns about immigrants and how they affected American politics, culture, and society.

Populists numbered mostly small-town editors among their supporters, but Progressives gained ammunition from larger-scale media and writers known as "muckrakers" for their investigative reports. Several mass-circulation magazines helped build support for Progressive reform by publishing Lincoln Steffens's series on urban machine corruption, which inspired government and political change, and Ida Tarbell's exposé of the business practices of John D. Rockefeller's Standard Oil, prompting new demands for trust busting and an end to monopolies. Fiction also aided Progressive efforts. Upton Sinclair's *The Jungle,* on the meatpacking industry's horrors, aided passage of the Pure Food and Drug Act of 1906 and federal inspection of meat and dairy products. Frank Norris's *The Octopus* attacked the Southern Pacific, the new corporation that absorbed the Central Pacific in 1899, and generated calls for reform, especially in California.

While Populism started among the lower and middle classes, the middle and upper classes more directly shaped Progressivism, as did reform-minded elected officials. Wage earners backed the eight-hour workday and limits on immigration, but their bosses hoped to impose order and management on government and the economy. The era's three presidents—Republicans

Theodore Roosevelt (1901–9) and William Howard Taft (1909–13) and Democrat Woodrow Wilson (1913–21)—demonstrated the best and worst of the movement, especially on race, culminating with Wilson segregating federal offices. Several states elected Progressive governors, most notably Republicans Robert La Follette in Wisconsin and Hiram Johnson in California, and sent them and other Progressives to Congress.

The Nevada Progressives

While producing no presidents or renowned leaders, Nevada reflected Progressive goals and lived up to them in its own way. Progressives generally advocated democracy and social justice, conservation and wise use of resources, better management in business and government, and assimilation into American or Anglo culture and society. Nationally, Nevada's Francis Newlands earned less attention than he deserved for his Progressivism: his reclamation law affected the West more than the East, where reputations have always been shaped; he proposed a corporate tax to control trusts and a federal law that would have adopted some Populist goals in connection with railroads; he attacked the power of railroads, although mainly out of anger at the Southern Pacific for backing his political opponents; and he worked behind the scenes on numerous measures, aiding women's suffrage at home and becoming an adviser to Wilson. Historian Gilman Ostrander called Newlands "a unique phenomenon in Nevada politics: the man who bought his way into Congress in order to serve the nation."

Progressive governors enjoyed some success. Due to his popularity around the state, especially among cattlemen, Silverites and Democrats supported rancher John Sparks for two terms, despite his support for gold instead of silver. Before Sparks's death in 1908, Nevada approved the creation of several new regulatory boards. His successor, Denver Dickerson, became the first of many politicians from the new mining towns; an Ely editor, he sired a political family that included a future attorney general and district attorney. He recommended numerous Progressive laws to the 1909 legislature, whose members included many elected as a rebuke to the state's role in putting down the Goldfield strike. Dickerson won a fight to increase tax assessments on railroads, but also battled fellow Democrats over policy and patronage appointments.

When Dickerson sought a full term in 1910, Nevadans chose between two avowed Progressives. Tasker Oddie declared for governor in June and faced a primary against Judge W. A. Massey, the Republican establishment's—and George Wingfield's—candidate. Emulating Californian Hiram Johnson, Oddie accused the Southern Pacific of controlling Nevada and the GOP, although it no longer did so; also, when Oddie had run for office before, the SP supported him. He vowed, "I will have no strings or pledges of any kind to hamper me in doing what I think is right." Although Oddie criticized Nixon for opposing him, the candidate's brother-in-law served as Wingfield's top mining engineer. As a state senator, Oddie had backed Nixon's first Senate campaign and been a director of Nixon's Tonopah bank—but with Oddie deep in debt, Nixon sold his holdings. Thus motivated, touring the state by car, refusing contributions other than meals and gasoline from friends, Oddie eked out a 189-vote win. Then he joined his party's caravan around Nevada, tempered his criticisms, beat Dickerson in the general election, and pushed through several Progressive measures, including banking and tax commissions and protection and compensation for railroad workers injured on the job.

Other Progressives won no major office but became influential. Women still lacked the vote in Nevada but fought for candidates, suffrage, and various reforms. The son of German immigrant ranchers in Carson Valley, Progressive Republican George Springmeyer sought to build on his record as a prosecutor in Goldfield and ran for attorney general in 1910. Akin to Oddie, he won the primary with the slogan "The Unspiked Rail in the Path of Railroad Domination" and pushed through a party platform that read like a Progressive manifesto. But in the general election, Nixon and Wingfield considered him too independent and, as Nixon told him, "turned loose a river of gold against [him]," instead backing the eventual and narrow winner, Democrat Cleveland Baker, the son of a Southern Pacific attorney, son-in-law of a senator from California involved in the railroad industry, and brother of a future state prison warden and director of the United States Mint.

The dilemmas of Nevada Progressives became clear in the 1912 presidential race. Roosevelt challenged incumbent and onetime friend Taft's renomination and then opposed him as the Progressive or Bull Moose Party nominee. Divisions in Nevada mirrored national events: at the state Republican convention, Nixon, Wingfield, and their operatives passed resolutions favoring Taft and Nixon but defeated Roosevelt supporters such as

Springmeyer, who backed an endorsement of Oddie's record as governor. Taking the hint and pressured by Wingfield—he even borrowed money from the magnate while in office—Oddie remained silent in the general election, won in Nevada and nationally by Democrat Woodrow Wilson. With one group—Wingfield and his allies—so economically and politically dominant, Nevada Progressives won fewer electoral or legislative victories than they might have wished. That they won as many as they did suggests the depth of support for Progressivism at the time and the ability of Wingfield and other political powers to limit the scope of those victories.

Participatory Democracy

Progressives sought to expand democracy to promote civic engagement, gut political machines, and force politicians to heed public opinion. Numerous states created the initiative, referendum, and recall so that voters could bypass corrupt or unresponsive officials. Responding to voter demand, Nevada's legislature passed the referendum in 1905 and the initiative and recall in 1909. The state constitution requires any amendment to be approved twice before taking effect, and the electorate overwhelmingly did so in each case. Under state law any initiative or referendum petition must include only one subject. For an initiative to go on the ballot, the law required signatures from 10 percent of the voters in 75 percent of Nevada's counties, but future legal battles led to a different stipulation: 10 percent of the voters in each of the state's House districts. A recall petition requires signatures from 25 percent of those who voted in the last election of the targeted officeholder. Thus, for a statewide official, it takes a quarter of those who voted across the state, but for a legislator or county or city official, it requires a quarter of the voters in his or her district. After that the special election may be a vote on whether to retain the official, or others may file to run against him or her.

These measures met some Progressive goals. Nevada originally used the initiative and referendum sparingly. Ironically, the first initiative to become law, in 1918, embodied Progressive moral reform by banning the sale of alcohol, demonstrating the power of some Protestant churches, educational reformers, and women's groups. Years passed between votes on initiatives, but the pace quickened in the 1950s with a "right-to-work" law that passed despite opposition from unions and two failed repeal efforts. Several initiatives appeared on every ballot in the 1990s and 2000s, perhaps reflecting Nevada's rapid population growth and limits on how long and often the legislature meets (120 days every two years). Recalls have been rare and rarely successful—never statewide and only occasionally in cities and counties.

Yet Progressive intentions differed from results. Instead of the public using the initiative to control officials, politicians used petitions for pet issues: in the 1990s, when Jim Gibbons, running for governor, backed a measure to require two-thirds approval in the legislature to raise taxes and when political consultant Sig Rogich led the effort to pass legislative term limits—both successfully. Some recall supporters have sought revenge or advancement: the North Las Vegas police helped engineer the recall of the majority of the local city council in 1976 for opposing a pay raise, and basketball coach Jerry Tarkanian's supporters tried to recall two regents who backed his forced departure from UNLV in the early 1990s.

Amending the US Constitution

Progressives supported several constitutional changes. Nevada joined other states in ratifying amendments for a federal income tax (the Sixteenth) and Prohibition (the Eighteenth). Two other amendments reflected the Progressive belief in expanding democracy: the Seventeenth, to elect US senators directly rather than through the legislature, and the Nineteenth, giving suffrage to women.

Nevadans long backed direct Senate elections, before, during, and after a series of bribery scandals involving legislators selling their votes. In 1885 Governor Jewett Adams, a rancher irked at the mining companies' power, urged lawmakers to ask Congress to amend the Constitution. Finally, in 1893 they put an advisory question on the ballot. After Nevadans overwhelmingly backed direct Senate elections—7,208 to 443—seven of the next eight legislatures endorsed an amendment. In 1908 the two state parties agreed to a preferential vote and that legislators must accept the outcome. The next year legislators passed the Direct Primary Law, requiring the same nominating system for federal elected officials as for those running for state office and for legislative candidates to declare whether they planned to obey the results or use them only as a recommendation.

In the early twentieth century, Nevada's Senate elections reflected the effects of Progressive ideology and the state's evolving political leadership. In 1903 Senator John P. Jones retired after five terms due to age and the political alliance between Francis Newlands and the Bank Crowd with George Nixon and his Silver Party and Southern Pacific allies. Targeting Newlands after their Senate battle, William M. Stewart recruited longtime state and federal judge Thomas Hawley to oppose him for Jones's seat. Asked about the septuagenarian's age, Stewart shot back, "I never heard of Mr. Newlands being well a week at a time; it is either rheumatism, gout from English high living, bladder trouble, headache, indigestion, or all these combined . . . and any person who will examine the Congressional record of Mr. Newlands will be unable to determine from anything they find there whether he has been dead or alive." Newlands won, and, in another sign of Nevada's political evolution, his machine underwrote legislative candidates to aid his candidacy, including a Washoe County sheepherder's son, Pat McCarran, who would reflect, represent, and fight the state's new leadership.

In 1905 Stewart retired. Several factors made his departure inevitable: his age (nearing eighty), C. C. "Black" Wallace's death in 1901, the SP's declining desire and ability to control Nevada politics, his unpopularity after his battles with Newlands, a power shift to the central Nevada boom, and Nixon's wealth and ambition. A mine owner who stayed in Nevada rather than relocating to California as earlier entrepreneurs did, a friend of the Southern Pacific who kept their ties quiet, and the Silver Party's founding father, Nixon completed several transitions: from nineteenth-century Nevada to the twentieth, from Republican control to Silver-Democrats to a more balanced party system, from dominance by Comstock and Central Pacific magnates to a new set of powers.

These democratic impulses also affected the new senators: bribing legislators would no longer elect them. Newlands, the first senator to face a preferential vote, had no trouble in 1908; also, he had run statewide five times for the House. Nixon's situation differed in 1910, when the Direct Primary Law bound legislators. He and his Democratic opponent, Tonopah lawyer Key Pittman, agreed that the loser would refuse to allow his nomination in the legislature, bowing to public will. Nixon won by fewer than fifteen hundred votes out of the more than eighteen thousand cast, but Democrats took over the legislature, jangling Republican nerves until Pittman kept the bargain.

When Nixon died in 1912, Pittman had another chance. Oddie offered the post to Wingfield, who declined, becoming known as a "cowboy who refused a toga." Instead, Oddie chose his 1910 primary opponent, Massey. In the general election, Pittman beat Massey by eighty-nine votes. By retaining the legislature, Democrats ensured Pittman's safe election. Pittman remained in the Senate until 1940, rising to chairman of the Foreign Relations Committee and power in the Senate and his party. Before another election, the Seventeenth Amendment had taken effect, removing the legislature from any role in choosing senators.

Votes for Women

After considering women's suffrage in 1869, when Wyoming Territory became the first jurisdiction to approve it, Nevada became one of the last states to ratify the Nineteenth Amendment. After efforts fell short in 1897, the battle subsided, but in 1911 the fight began anew with the creation of the new Nevada Equal Franchise Society, headed by Jeanne Elizabeth Wier, a professor at the university and the Nevada Historical Society's founding director. The next year Wier's predecessor as a history professor, Anne Martin, succeeded her as president, with Bird Wilson as vice president. The daughter of a Reno businessman and educated at Stanford and overseas, Martin became involved in reform, including women's rights and Fabian socialism, while traveling in England, then its own reform movement.

Despite movement in their direction across the country, their quest proved difficult. Wier and Martin pushed for an amendment through several legislative sessions, with support from Oddie. Martin organized groups in each Nevada county and welcomed nationally prominent speakers such as social reformer Jane Addams. Suffragists overcame opposition from Wingfield, who threatened to leave Nevada if the amendment passed and an antiwomen's suffrage group that included two former Nevada first ladies and the wife of prominent Reno businessman and publisher Robert Fulton. Expecting cities to oppose suffrage under pressure from casino and saloon operators, Martin targeted rural voters, and events proved her right: mostly on their strength, Nevada endorsed the Nineteenth Amendment in the 1914 election, 10,936–7,258.

Martin would do far more. She served on commissions and as president of the Nevada Women's Civic League. She wrote extensively on the need for women's equality and rights, including helping to pass federal laws to fund maternal and infant health care. She became a member of the National American Woman Suffrage Association executive committee,

Anne Martin led Nevada's movement for women's suffrage and ran for the Senate in 1918—two years before the Nineteenth Amendment to the US Constitution enabled her to vote for president. Courtesy of Special Collections, University Libraries, University of Nevada, Las Vegas.

national chair of the Woman's Party, Addams's ally in seeking world peace, and an independent US Senate candidate from Nevada in 1918 and 1920. Then she left the state, but not before describing it as backward, concluding, "She will continue to lie, inert and helpless, like an exhausted Titan in the sun—a beautiful desert of homeseekers' buried hopes."

Martin benefited from and influenced other Nevada women leaders. Wilson practiced law in central Nevada and lobbied lawmakers for married women's equality, easier divorce laws, and industrial schools for delinquents. One of the suffrage group's founders, Felice Cohn, the granddaughter of a Carson City rabbi, became the fourth woman admitted to practice before the US Supreme Court. After running the franchise group's Washoe County branch, Sadie Hurst became the first woman legislator when she won an assembly seat in 1918 and introduced bills for animal rights and aid to families, reflecting the Nevada Federation of Women's Clubs platform. Delphine Squires helped her husband publish the *Las Vegas Age* and aided the movement in southern Nevada, including hosting a visit from sociologist and reformer Charlotte Perkins Gilman during the suffrage campaign. Some of these women turned the Equal Franchise Society, its goal accomplished, into the Nevada Women's Civic League, an educational group to help women vote, and started Nevada's chapter of the League of Women Voters. In the first session after suffrage passed in 1914, lawmakers approved better pensions for teachers and mothers, kindergartens, and a change in inheritance laws to aid women—all lobbied for by women and all a sign of their influence.

"Good" Government

By instituting civil service reform, better building codes, and more attention to wastewater treatment, Nevadans followed in the footsteps of Progressives known as "Goo-Goos" for their quest for Good Government. Although the Guggenheims and Wingfield reigned in their towns, no Nevada area lived under crooked "boss" rule like New York City's Tammany Hall, due partly to preventative action. Knowing the ephemeral nature of boomtowns, the 1881 legislature empowered county commissioners to create town governments. In the early 1900s county commissioners set up local boards to govern Tonopah, Goldfield, and Rhyolite, but officials could do only so much. When Tonopah won Nye County's seat from Belmont in 1905 and Goldfield did the same to Hawthorne in Esmeralda County two years later, government in the new boomtowns benefited. So did the construction industry, which built courthouses—and helped prompt Mineral County's creation with Hawthorne as county seat. Reno incorporated in 1903 and Las Vegas in 1911, thus governing themselves rather than relying on county commissions and following in the footsteps of Galveston, Texas, which turned to a commission system after a disastrous government response to a hurricane in 1900.

Efforts to improve government took other forms. In 1915 legislators instituted major changes. To combat judicial politicking, they passed a law making judges nonpartisan. Lawmakers reduced the legislature's membership—it had reached the constitutional maximum of seventy-five members—presumably to save money, possibly for efficiency. The legislature also began a half century of operating under the "little federal plan," which emulated Congress: a lower house based on population and an upper house with one senator per county. That violated the Nevada Constitution's requirement to determine representation by population, but smaller counties wanted to protect their power in relation to larger urban areas.

Following Progressives nationally, the state created or enhanced regulatory boards. As of 1907 the state Board of Education received more power to enforce higher standards for teachers and students, and the Banking Commission kept tabs on financial institutions—and became controversial when Oddie named a Tonopah banker with links to Wingfield to conduct audits. In 1909 Dickerson won a fight to employ a state mine inspector to enforce workplace safety. Oddie backed a state office to promote agriculture and irrigation and two new agencies. Starting in 1911 the Railroad Commission regulated rates and safety as well as telephone, telegraph, and electric companies, with members tied to those being regulated; it evolved into the Public Utilities Commission. As of 1913 the Tax Commission began studying assessments to ensure their fairness, with some of its duties spun off in 1959 into the Gaming Commission to oversee that industry. Locally, more cities, led by the new city of Las Vegas, turned to "commission" governments, with experts replacing politicians to run departments such as police and fire—another Progressive goal to improve management and reduce corruption.

Progressive or not, Las Vegas wound up in a fight over county division and governance soon after its 1905 founding. With the county seat, Pioche, more than 150 miles away by train and stage, Las Vegans wanted their own government. Worse, Lincoln County decided to build a courthouse in 1872, and through bad investments, overruns, and corruption, the sixty-thousand-dollar building became a boondoggle costing eight hundred thousand dollars, and Las Vegans feared getting stuck with the bill. Southern Nevadans formed a division club and succeeded at the 1909 legislature, allegedly thanks to two Clarks: William, the railroad owner, who looked favorably on naming the new county for him, and Ed, a Las Vegas businessman and politician who supposedly helped persuade lawmakers by sending them a case of whiskey.

The Management Culture Managing Culture

Progressives believed in perfecting business and society, nationally and in Nevada. They intended federal agencies like the Food and Drug Administration and the Federal Trade Commission (which Newlands helped design) to regulate industries and help them function better. Nevada

Progressives approved the eight-hour workday in 1903, workmen's compensation in 1911, and railroad safety rules; more controversially, in 1911 they also won a "closed-shop" act that could force workers to join unions to have jobs. Yet Oddie vetoed a law to mandate an eight-hour day for women, contending that Japanese men would take their jobs as domestics; the 1917 legislature passed a similar measure, and Governor Emmet Boyle signed it. Oddie combined the Progressive passion for reform with concern about Nevada's roads by backing a bill to use convicts to build roads in return for compensation and time off. But Oddie stepped in when the IWW tried to organize White Pine and prepared to send in the state police amid threats of labor trouble in Las Vegas.

Progressives also took actions ranging from insensitive to blatantly racist. Across the nation they sought compulsory public education, partly to assimilate immigrants, and passed "blue laws," banning business or recreation on Sundays to encourage churchgoing. Nevada chapters of the Women's Christian Temperance Union advocated Prohibition, antismoking laws, and uniform divorce rules. State lawmakers passed a bill requiring miners to speak English at work, reflecting a belief in safer workplaces or a desire to bar immigrants from jobs—or both. After California barred Japanese people from owning land, Nevada tried to follow suit. A. Grant Miller, Nevada's leading Socialist, joined other westerners in his party to attack "the immigration of all these people from the orient." In 1912 Newlands, who suggested colonizing African Americans in the Caribbean, urged Democrats to seek repeal of the Fifteenth Amendment and limit immigration to whites—perhaps a remnant of his Mississippi youth, but exemplifying Progressives' belief in Anglo-Saxon superiority. That could be politically dangerous in Nevada, where immigrants numbered nearly a quarter of the population in the 1910 census.

Other Progressive efforts did prove politically dangerous. In 1909 lawmakers passed a measure to ban gambling, which had been legal since 1869. They heeded educational, religious, and women's groups and because in Reno, as historian Alicia Barber puts it, "in order to attract . . . long-term investment, many residents were convinced that the town needed to purge itself of its depravities." But gambling's supporters triumphed: the law took effect just before the next election, and the 1911 legislature immediately restored some poker games. Oddie pushed the next session to make

When Jack Johnson fought Jim Jeffries in Reno on July 4, 1910, it marked a major moment in Nevada's history of catering to people's pleasures and desires—and in the history of African Americans. Courtesy of Special Collections, University of Nevada–Reno Library.

it illegal again and succeeded: in 1914 *Sunset* magazine reported, "Today there is not a single open gambling place in the West." Wanting to head off Nevada's growing reputation as a divorce capital, Oddie also persuaded the 1913 legislature to lengthen the residency requirement to a year.

But money trumped morals. The corresponding falloff in Nevada's economy, especially in Reno, helped cause Oddie's defeat in 1914 by Democrat Emmet Boyle, and the restoration of card games and the six-month residency. "I'm on my way to Reno" became a refrain for the unhappily married, and they brought money with them, fostering a reputation for Reno and the rise of dude ranches in the surrounding area and at Lake Tahoe. National condemnation of Nevada's morals continued when Reno hosted the July 4, 1910, heavyweight championship fight between Jack Johnson and Jim Jeffries, especially after Johnson, an African American attacked for his flamboyant lifestyle (including white girlfriends), won; print and visual reports on the fight displayed a vibrant community dependent on economic activities that many claimed to shun. One writer called Reno "a progressive little country town surrounding a peculiar nucleus of human puzzles"—a fitting description of many Nevada communities.

Progressives and Race

Johnson's win upset Progressives and others who believed in white supremacy. These attitudes reflected Progressive ideology and what residents already believed. Rawhide branded itself a "white man's camp" and banished African Americans, as did other towns; a sign at Fallon's depot declared, "No Niggers or Japs allowed"; Reno's police chief lamented the presence of "too many worthless negroes in this city"; and Goldfield's sheriff declared the town off-limits to any "Chink visitor." An Ely editor charged that an immigrant's "mission is to cut wages to a point where an American cannot live, to save a few dollars and return home." Attitudes underscored actions: Reno leveled the Chinatown east of Virginia Street and north of the Truckee over the land's value to the area's growth, and in 1915 the superintendent of the state orphans' home urged the legislature to bar Native American, African American, and Chinese children from the facility.

Progressives added to past racism in segregating Nevada's African Americans. The year of Johnson's victory, black residents of Reno built the Bethel African Methodist Episcopal Church between the Truckee River and the railroad tracks for what has become the state's oldest African American congregation. The agent for the railroad's Las Vegas town site sought to make one area "a cheap residence district for undesirable classes" by "locating colored people and foreigners in this block." Instead, African Americans and other people of color—and some whites—began moving west of the railroad tracks into the old McWilliams town site.

The Progressives also continued long-standing efforts to assimilate Native Americans into Euro-American society. On the Duck Valley Reservation, Western Shoshone largely adopted American names in public, and men turned to American hairstyles. Superintendents pushed to end traditional celebrations in favor of the Fourth of July, which the Western Shoshone combined with their own fandangos, featuring feasts, dancing, songs, and games. Efforts to force the Western Shoshone and the Moapa Reservation's Southern Paiutes to farm—including a 1909 law requiring them to buy hunting and fishing licenses—ran into trouble, thanks to short growing seasons and poor land. Sadly, these actions had the effect of driving more Indians to drink; since the federal government banned them from buying alcohol, the Shoshone turned to white bootleggers in nearby Mountain City. Other Western Shoshone moved to towns or Northern

Paiute reservations, sometimes for school, but returned to their own culture when they could. Southern Paiutes benefited when Helen Stewart provided them with ten acres of land in Las Vegas.

Some Native Americans became successful at basket making. The work of Mary Hall of Beowawe, southwest of Elko, earned great attention, and her daughters followed her into the craft. The era's most famous basket maker, Dat-So-La-Lee, lived in the Carson City area. Born as Debuda and known by the Americanized name Louisa Keyser, the Washoe created circular baskets (*degikups*) with the same-size top and bottom and a bellied middle for the Cohn family from 1895 until her death in 1925. While Carson City merchant Abe Cohn supported her and marketed her wares, Native American basket makers then and later imitated, adapted, and refined her techniques. Dat-So-La-Lee originally cooked and cleaned clothes for miners, which reflected another aspect of Progressive thought about Native Americans: exposing them to white families as domestics would both teach them a trade and help them assimilate.

Nevada's Basque Culture

Although a few migrated earlier, the early 1900s marked the first major influx of Basques. They came from the Pyrenees Mountains of France and northern Spain, escaping demands from both countries that they assimilate. Previous arrivals concentrated on ranching—the Altube and Garat families built substantial holdings around Elko, as did a few Basque ranchers near Winnemucca. Similarly, the newer Basques often herded sheep in the mountains for months or years at a time. Mostly single males in their teens, they earned thirty to forty dollars per month, saved their money, and revisited the Pyrenees before returning. One of them recalled arriving with a sign around his neck directing him to an Elko County ranch and then spending a decade in the hills until he said he "couldn't speak English, no Basque, just 'baaaaaa.'" Some turned to mining or to other forms of agriculture, and Basque-owned businesses emerged in the Elko area during the first decade of the century.

Basques became swept up in the controversy over how Progressives viewed immigrants. Newlands defended them, joining his Republican opponents to help livestock companies seeking cheap labor. But Key Pittman attacked the sheep industry for hiring them and Basques as having no intention of becoming citizens and "lacking in intelligence, independence, or anything else. They are just about as near a slave as anybody could be." The latter part of his statement had merit: many Basques wound up almost totally under the control of large livestock owners and firms, earning minimal wages.

Basques also became victims of the discrimination common to Progressivism. They faced accusations of being "tramp" shepherds, grazing stock on others' land and destroying too much grass, yet found it harder to obtain land or permits than did native-born ranchers. Their efforts to return home inspired criticism: William Douglass and Jon Bilbao wrote, "In the vigorous but underdeveloped economy of the American West, the Basque who siphoned off wealth to Europe was viewed as a distinct threat." In a far worse case of anti-Basque sentiment, three sheepherders died in an attack in Washoe County. In 1911 a posse chased a group of Native Americans

Basque tree carvings like this one provided a means for immigrants from the Pyrenees to communicate their feelings, and with one another. Courtesy of J. Mallea-Olaetxe.

led by "Shoshone Mike," who had refused to settle on a reservation and resorted to cattle rustling, and killed them near Golconda. White cowboys probably committed the crime, reflecting opposition to the Basques' presence, and the assault on the Shoshone provided a grim reminder of earlier Euro-American concerns about Native American violence and overreacting to it.

Basques also influenced Nevada's society and culture. Their festivals expanded beyond the group that started them to become tourist attractions and community events, and Basque restaurants dot northern Nevada, with the popular refreshment Picon Punch. Some of the hotels they opened early in the 1900s still operate. Basques invented jai alai, an indoor sport with a wicker basket tied to the player's wrist for hitting the ball, that became an attraction in MGM hotels in Las Vegas and Reno. In rural areas Basque aspen tree carvings serve as art and historical sources—in a sense, modern petroglyphs and pictographs. One sheepherder who arrived in this era, Dominique Laxalt, changed Nevada: his wife ran a hotel in Carson City; one of their sons, Paul, served as a governor and US senator, and another son, Robert, became one of the state's leading authors.

The Cultural Progressives

Early-twentieth-century Nevada produced no literary movement to rival the Sagebrush School of the Comstock era, but the state affected and reflected other cultural developments. A resident of the Sierra Nevada's eastern slope in the 1890s and early 1900s, Mary Austin produced a lengthy list of fiction and nonfiction. Her literary themes, based on her life, often fitted in with important themes of Nevada and Progressivism: an understanding of the desert and the struggle to live in it and women trying to lead fulfilling lives in a male-dominated society.

Progressives also influenced architecture with a different sort of house: the bungalow/craftsman. Meant to encourage handcrafted construction and integrate with their environment, these became popular in California. The bungalow style, low-rise houses with verandas or porches, spread through Nevada, as the growth driven by mining caused a corresponding construction boom. The railroad in Las Vegas built sixty-four such homes for its workers between 1909 and 1912, and successful entrepreneurs around the state tended to build larger examples of them.

Public buildings also reflected Progressivism. Born in Reno in 1882,

Completed in 1909 and first occupied by the family of Denver Dickerson, the Nevada Governor's Mansion remains a Carson City landmark and symbol of state pride. Courtesy of Special Collections, University of Nevada–Reno Library.

Frederic DeLongchamps became Nevada's finest, best-known architect, designing more than five hundred buildings in a six-decade career. He began with Washoe County's courthouse in 1909 and continued with seven of the eight county courthouses built from 1911 to 1922, mansions for some of the wealthiest Nevadans, and buildings on the university campus in Reno. Following the late-nineteenth-century empire-revival style, seen in legendary structures such as UNR's Morrill Hall and Virginia City's Fourth Ward school, his work extended through numerous trends in design, starting with neoclassical structures large enough to suggest permanence, with elaborate entrances and classical columns. Similar to his Progressive-style combination of artistry and practicality, George Ferris's design of Carson City's Governor's Mansion, opened in 1909, fitted the neoclassical revival style and a Progressive mentality in appearance and in its first occupant, Denver Dickerson.

Newlands and Reclamation

Historians vary in explaining how Progressives approached conservation —especially reclamation. Donald Worster has written that "it promised to augment American wealth and muscle"; new uses of land and water would "promote the accumulation of profit and power, two conservative ends served by innovative means." The acquisition of Hawaii, followed by Guam and the Philippines and the control over Cuba that resulted from the Spanish-American War of 1898, had been the nation's first major imperial steps beyond the continent. Improving the West would enhance access to these markets and others—and the droughts afflicting the West in the 1880s and 1890s suggested an obvious need for improvement.

While Progressives hailed nature, their attitude combined and conflicted with their managerial goals. They believed in using land and water wisely: preserve it if possible, but without making economic development impossible. Thus, Sierra Club founder John Muir waged a successful campaign to protect Yosemite National Park and other wonders, but many of his Progressive allies broke with him to support sacrificing the beauty of Yosemite's Hetch Hetchy Valley to provide water to San Francisco and diverting water from the Owens Valley to irrigate southern California and help Los Angeles grow. In 1907 Progressives had no problem setting aside 2.1 million acres between Austin and Tonopah to form the Toiyabe National Forest, since few whites used the land—but the Western Shoshone did. The federal government's newly imposed limits on and fees for grazing livestock, designed to finance federal programs but also manage the environment, hurt the Natives economically.

Nevadans advocated irrigation projects "to make the desert bloom" long before Progressive conservationists controlled federal policy. Colorado River explorer John Wesley Powell, the US Geological Survey's first director, popularized the idea with his 1878 *Report on the Lands of the Arid Region of the United States* and calls for irrigation. Senator William Stewart wanted to bolster Nevada through irrigation but grasped the West's limitations: its inconsistent economy, thanks to mining's boom-and-bust cycles, and inability to develop and tax the large expanses of federal land. Reclamation supporters saw that with advances in electricity, hydroelectric power generated by dams could provide profits and needed services.

On returning to the Senate in 1887, Stewart backed creating a committee on irrigation and became its chair. He supported more surveys of land and water and "reclaiming" public lands for irrigation, including dams and reservoirs. In 1889 Nevada legislators set up a Board of Reclamation and Internal Improvements and asked, "Can the general government refuse to render assistance or will it allow one of its sovereign states to languish?"— reflecting recent droughts and Nevada's seesaw relationship with the

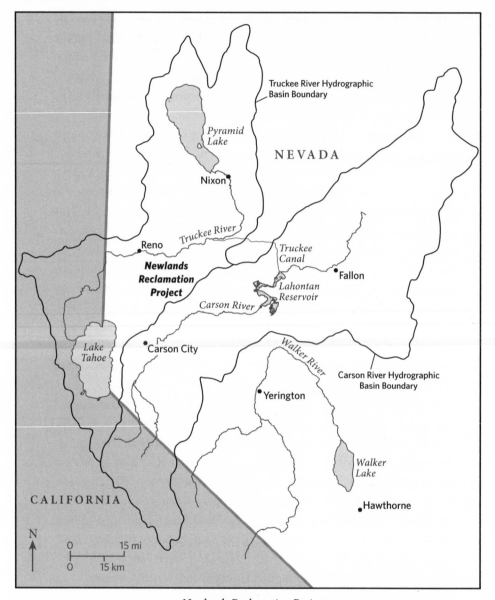

Newlands Reclamation Project

federal government. With Stewart's encouragement, Newlands adopted the issue, serving as a delegate to irrigation congresses and introducing legislation that turned him into the national voice of reclamation.

When Theodore Roosevelt, a onetime Dakota rancher who loved the outdoors, became president in 1901, Newlands and other advocates saw their chance. That December Roosevelt called for building dams and reservoirs to ensure proper water flow and conservation of resources, paying for them by selling public lands to settlers, and government action because private funding would be inadequate. Anticipating and echoing those plans, Newlands built on Powell's original argument by contending that with western river systems extending beyond state borders, only the federal government could manage a reclamation program.

The next year the Newlands Reclamation Act of 1902 became law. The measure stipulated how the acreage would be distributed, instituted an eight-hour workday on all projects, and barred Chinese labor—a perfect Progressive storm of racism and management. Critics claimed the projects would never pay for themselves, leaving the East to foot the bill—which proved correct, but westerners saw it as fair, since their ore financed so much development back east. The measure also promised 160 acres of land to anyone who irrigated the land within five years—a throwback to the Homestead Act and similar in enabling speculators and owners of large farms to snap up land and profits. Unexpectedly, the hydroelectric power the dams made possible paid for more of the costs and became a new source of government and private revenue. The agency that evolved into the Bureau of Reclamation would become involved in more than a thousand reclamation projects and irrigating about 38 million acres of western farmland and ranchland.

Nevada benefited from Newlands's efforts. The new Reclamation Service soon began work on the Derby Dam, about 20 miles south of Reno on the Truckee River, and completed the dam and about 32 miles of the Truckee Canal by 1905. In 1911 four years of construction began on the Lahontan Dam on the Carson River. In 1913 completion of a dam at Lake Tahoe to control the flow into the Truckee increased the water's elevation by six feet and allowed for additional water storage. Created in 1918, the Truckee-Carson Irrigation District (TCID) signed with the federal government to manage the two projects, about 380 miles of canals, irrigating more than 72,000 acres and diverting 400,000-plus acre-feet of water. It connected the two rivers to deliver the greatest possible amount of water to their hinterlands, led to the agricultural town of Fernley, expanded Fallon, and promoted growth of alfalfa, cantaloupes, and other products in Churchill and Lyon Counties.

Yet the reclamation measure also caused problems. Promoters convinced some that quick and easy riches waited in verdant Nevada farmlands and increased land speculation. It reduced wetlands, caused the water level to drop significantly in Pyramid Lake, and led to a protracted battle between Northern Paiutes and the federal government over water rights. With the state's population just starting to grow again and 20,000 acres of Nevada being farmed at the time, the Newlands Act worsened water shortages. Nor did all Nevadans appreciate the federal power and bureaucracy that accompanied it, even when they benefited from it.

Reclamation and its environmental effects also affected the fledgling tourism industry. As part of a plan for further logging and turning the area into a resort, Duane Bliss and his family, who grew wealthy supplying lumber to the Comstock, built a steamboat, a railroad from the Southern Pacific to Tahoe, and a hotel. But an eastern syndicate proposed to use the lake as a reservoir in connection with the hydroelectric power generated by the Newlands Project, and the legislature agreed in 1913 to let the federal government use Lake Tahoe water "in such manner and to such extent" as necessary. Neither these actions nor ensuing highway construction destroyed the lake, but both fitted into a pattern that would lead to a combination of cooperation and conflict between California and Nevada, and between the two states and the federal government, that continues to the present.

While Newlands sought to aid his state—and took excessive credit for the bill's passage—he approached reclamation from a national and Progressive perspective. In 1917 he proposed an "enlarged policy": a commission to control all river development, including irrigation, dam building, electricity, and conservation. The bill to create it passed that summer, but Wilson never chose the commissioners, and Newlands died that Christmas Eve—as did his plans. Beyond the resentment his idea caused in various departments of government and private enterprise, as Newlands's biographer William Rowley noted, "Most of all Congress recognized that its control over pet projects for constituents stood in peril if authority escaped to the all-powerful commission." Some of Newlands's successors took full advantage of the power Congress retained.

The War to End All Wars

Newlands's plan also suffered from bad timing: the United States had just entered World War I. Europeans went to war in August 1914 after a Serbian shot the heir to the throne of Austria-Hungary, an empire collapsing over nationalism: while Austrians and Hungarians dominated it, Croats, Serbs, Czechs, Slovaks, and other central Europeans wanted power in it or independence from it. European powers signed various treaties—some secret—to defend one another. Besides promising to aid Serbia, Russia had an alliance with France, which had an agreement with England. Germany had long since agreed to assist Austria. When Europeans wandered into war, Wilson announced American neutrality while conceding the difficulties caused by family and ethnic backgrounds. For nearly three years, the United States avoided war—indeed, Wilson's narrow reelection in 1916 resulted in part from campaigning on that issue. But a combination of factors—Germans sinking a luxury liner, the *Lusitania,* with Americans aboard; the country's links to western Europe; the democratic overthrow of the Russian czar, which seemed to define the war more clearly as representative government versus autocracies—finally prompted Wilson to seek a declaration of war on April 6, 1917.

Nevada's economy benefited greatly. Higher prices and more markets for fruits, vegetables, and meats heartened ranchers and farmers. Demand for sugar and honey promoted beekeeping and sugar beets. When England needed to repay notes to India in silver and ran out of it, only the United States could meet the demand. The resulting Pittman Act of 1918 marked the first federal silver purchases since the Sherman Act of 1890. Copper production more than tripled from 1914 to 1916, with older mines reopening and existing mines boosting jobs and revenue until in 1918 the state's mines generated more than forty-eight million dollars, more than the Comstock's best year. But with the war's end, mining and agricultural revenue declined.

The state's preparation for military involvement lagged. Responding to federal legislation, Governor Boyle found little support for organizing a National Guard and blamed labor opposition, but the legislature also acted slowly. Thus, as the war began, the state's entire defense consisted of the university Reserve Officers' Training Corps (ROTC) unit and nine "Government Civilian Rifle Clubs." A legislative appropriation of twenty-five thousand dollars early in 1917 led to the Nevada State Council of Defense, which set up county and school district organizations and helped the Red Cross and federal agencies.

Nevada's large immigrant population both aided the war and aroused suspicion. Some of Douglas County's leading Germans served on the local defense council, but the local Lutheran Church stopped holding services in German and the school board agreed to student requests to end classes in the German language. Newer German arrivals encountered harassment, and Nevadans eagerly backed Prohibition laws, which reflected Progressive views on assimilation and morals but took aim at German and Irish dis-tillers. Ely's Serbian Benevolent Society assured Wilson of its loyalty, and forty-two of its members joined their group's army in the Balkans to fight against the Austro-Hungarian Empire, with promises from the Nevada Consolidated Copper Company that their jobs would await them on their return. Wilson and Congress legislated against espionage and prosecuted some critics of the war, but none in Nevada.

World War I presented opportunities for women in the workplace and civic life, and they made the most of them. Nevada sent 3,384 draftees and 1,447 volunteers to war (per capita among states, one of the nation's top rates for military service, and 120 died), and women replaced some of them in their jobs. Families planted gardens and collected shoes and clothes, and Mormon women running a relief society in Lund sent their fruits and vege-tables to Europe. Women remained active politically by backing Prohibi-tion laws, including the Progressive idea of temperance education in public schools. The women of several towns formed chapters of the American Red Cross and led the charge in meeting quotas for bond drives and observing meatless days to provide food for the military.

Socialists in Nevada

During the Progressive Era, Socialists found more support in Nevada than most states—and displayed political savvy. Many in the state's foreign-born populace, especially from central and eastern Europe, endorsed the party's ideology, which found some support among miners all too familiar with the dangerous but low-paying work that Socialists blamed on the capital-ist system. In 1908 Eugene Debs's percentage of the presidential vote ran three times higher in Nevada than nationally, and the state party platform adopted a Progressive tone and avoided harsh rhetoric. Many Socialist

candidates won double-digit percentages in general elections and did especially well in the Mountain West, between California and the Rockies. In
1912, capitalizing on Oddie's use of the state police to break the White Pine
strike, Debs won 17 percent of Nevada's presidential vote, the nation's highest Socialist percentage, and nearly one-third in Nye County.

In 1914 Socialists mounted their greatest political challenge, with
A. Grant Miller, a Reno lawyer and former miner and Knights of Labor
member, opposing Democrat Newlands and Republican Samuel Platt for
the Senate. With Socialists accusing Newlands of being a Southern Pacific
toady and personally profiting from owning land near the Truckee-Carson
project, he outpolled Platt by forty votes, 8,078–8,038, with Miller winning
5,451. Newlands found plenty of blame to go around: Republicans for backing the Socialist to draw votes from him, Wingfield for resenting his vote
for a tariff bill the magnate disliked, and Churchill County for failing to
appreciate his irrigation project. Future senators from Nevada who won by
small margins or lost reelection bids complained similarly, but Newlands
underrated the popularity of socialism around the country and in his state.
So did Oddie: had he won the bulk of the Socialist gubernatorial candidate's 15 percent of the vote, he would have defeated Boyle.

Early in the twentieth century, Nevada's wide-open spaces attracted
would-be colonizers, acting in the spirit of nineteenth-century utopian
communities in the East and Mormon settlements in the West. Although
promoters announced plans for 1,000 Irish to move near the Carson Sink
and 400 Polish families near Fort Halleck in Elko County, Socialists became
the most prominent group to attempt a utopia in Nevada. The founders of
Nevada City, four miles east of Fallon, hoped to attract at least 5,000 voters and sold stock in the company, trying to make a decidedly unsocialist
profit. They planned an agricultural community to take advantage of the
nearby Truckee-Carson Irrigation District. The population peaked at 550,
although another 2,000 announced plans to move there.

American entry into the war crippled the colony and socialism in
Nevada. In 1916 Miller won almost 30 percent of the Senate vote, as Pittman squeaked past him and Platt to a second term, but in 1918 the Socialist
Senate candidate won only 710 out of 25,563 votes cast. In between, patriotism overwhelmed Socialist sentiment, and the Socialists imploded. When
the local draft board listed Nevada City resident Paul Walters as an evader,
Churchill County sheriff Mark Wildes tried to arrest him. Walters shot

him. A posse tracked down Walters and killed him, and Nevada City residents either left or declared their support for the war. Elsewhere in Nevada, socialism declined for other reasons. When Nye County's sheriff hired an unemployed Socialist mine worker as his deputy, the Loyalty League's complaint prompted county commissioners to remove the new officer, who later went to prison on charges of sedition; Nye County voters then voted out the sheriff. Miller left the party out of opposition to German autocracy and became the head of Nevada's Defense Council, where he sought out and questioned subversives. As a Nevada political force, socialism had ended.

Enough Progress

Nationally, the Progressive Era wobbled to an end after World War I. In Nevada remnants survived into the 1920s, reflecting the desire to reform the state and the economic factors making that difficult. Mining remained central to the economy, but boom-and-bust cycles convinced some of the state's residents of the dangers of relying on it. Newlands saw how to promote agriculture, but it fostered a reliance on federal projects that ran counter to the belief of Nevadans accustomed to viewing the government as an enemy or at best uninterested in helping them.

Thus, the future that Progressives brought to Nevada produced some ironies. Newlands's reclamation projects became even more crucial to state and regional development and set a precedent for the federal scope of action and Nevada's dependence on it. The limits of national involvement in state activity ultimately freed Nevada to develop new industries that encouraged what Progressives considered immoral behavior: gambling, drinking, and prostitution. Consequently, as many historians have pointed out about the West, a defining characteristic of its history has been colonialism—its dependence on or service to other places. The mining boom had included Nevada's first real steps toward keeping its riches, but its next major economic redefinition required it to depend on outside money, from the federal government and elsewhere.

SUGGESTED READINGS

Barkan, Elliott Robert. *From All Points: America's Immigrants West, 1870–1952*. Bloomington: Indiana University Press, 2006.

Chan, Loren B. *Sagebrush Statesman: Tasker L. Oddie of Nevada*. Reno: University of Nevada Press, 1973.

Dangberg, Grace. *Conflict on the Carson: A Study of Water Litigation in Western Nevada*. Minden, NV: Carson Valley Historical Society, 1975.

Douglass, William A., and Jon Bilbao. *Amerikanuak: Basques in the New World*. Reno: University of Nevada Press, 1975.

Echeverria, Jeronima. *Home Away from Home: A History of Basque Boardinghouses*. Reno: University of Nevada Press, 1999.

Greenwood, Robert. *Jack Johnson vs. James Jeffries: The Prize Fight of the Century—Reno, Nevada, July 4, 1910*. Reno: Jack Bacon, 2004.

Harpster, Jack. *100 Years in the Nevada Governor's Mansion*. Las Vegas: Stephens Press, 2009.

Howard, Anne Bail. *The Long Campaign: A Biography of Anne Martin*. Reno: University of Nevada Press, 1985.

Mallea-Olaetxe, J. *Speaking Through the Aspens: Basque Tree Carvings in California and Nevada*. Reno: University of Nevada Press, 2000.

Pisani, Donald J. *Water and American Government: The Reclamation Bureau, National Water Policy, and the West, 1902–1935*. Berkeley: University of California Press, 2002.

Rowley, William D. *Reclaiming the Arid West: The Career of Francis G. Newlands*. Bloomington: Indiana University Press, 1996.

Shepperson, Wilbur S. *Retreat to Nevada: A Socialist Colony of World War I*. Reno: University of Nevada Press, 1966.

Townley, John M. *Turn This Water into Gold: The Story of the Newlands Project*. Reno: Nevada Historical Society, 1977.

Worster, Donald. *A Passion for Nature: The Life of John Muir*. New York: Oxford University Press, 2008.

Zanjani, Sally S. *The Unspiked Rail: Memoir of a Nevada Rebel*. Reno: University of Nevada Press, 1981.

10

From Roaring Twenties
to Depression and Change

I n November 1932, routed in his bid for reelection, President Herbert Hoover visited the Boulder Canyon Project to see the dam being built. As secretary of commerce, he had been at the center of the negotiations that led to its construction. After becoming president and continuing a hands-off approach to government regulation that characterized most of the 1920s, he bore the brunt of the blame for the Great Depression. That cataclysm drove thousands of jobless Americans west to seek work at the dam project named for him and contributed to a reshaping of Nevada's economy that reflected a laissez-faire approach to government and the changes in American society and culture during the 1920s.

The Roaring Twenties

When Warren Harding ran for president in 1920, he sought a "return to normalcy." This meant recovering from the war and that Progressivism, with its emphasis on government regulation of business and guarantees of wages and safety for labor, had been an exception, not a rule. Republicans controlled the White House under Harding (1921–23) and his successors Calvin Coolidge (1923–29) and Hoover (1929–33) as well as Congress for most of the period. Usually committed to keeping government out of the economy, they retained regulatory bodies created in previous decades but filled them with probusiness appointees. They reduced the nation's involvement around the world, perhaps reacting to former allies unwilling to defer to American power and failing to pay war debts.

The prosperity inspired by World War I continued—to a degree. In the 1920s consumption reached new heights as industry directed its wartime gains toward consumer products, but generating products such as automobiles did little good if consumers had no need or money to buy them. Farmers who benefited from feeding armies and civilians overseas during the war found prices dropping but kept growing crops at the same rate. Between favorable tax policies and limited regulation, the distribution of wealth increasingly favored the richest Americans, while wages for laborers remained the same or fell. Woodrow Wilson's administration canceled all government war production contracts after the fighting ended, and his successors proposed few programs to make up the difference.

While pursuing these policies, Coolidge and Hoover cleaned up after Harding's corrupt administration. His interior secretary Albert Fall became the first cabinet member convicted of a felony for taking money from oil companies leasing federal reserves at Teapot Dome, Wyoming. His attorney general Harry Daugherty resigned over various scandals. As his successor, Harlan Fiske Stone made an appointment that ultimately affected Nevada: to run what became the Federal Bureau of Investigation (FBI), he chose Justice Department attorney J. Edgar Hoover.

Americans in the 1920s sought freedom from government, but also different kinds of freedom. Some women's rights advocates demanded an equal rights amendment and an end to special protection. Many women's groups feared the ERA might kill programs that aided mothers and children. The amendment failed, and Congress repealed or defeated several laws its opponents supported. But women expressed themselves in other ways—especially younger women who began to marry later, go on dates without chaperones, use birth control, ignore Prohibition, and wear more revealing clothing. Actress Clara Bow exemplified these "flappers" as Hollywood's "It Girl"; she later married cowboy actor Rex Bell, and they became residents of Searchlight, buying the Walking Box Ranch, previously the property of a leading Southwest ranching firm.

Others indulged in freedom by breaking a law. Republican leaders endorsed Prohibition but underfunded enforcement. Federal agents fought a losing battle to stop liquor sales and profiteers—and not only in Nevada, where California agents often conducted raids. The main suppliers of alcohol, mostly Italian and Jewish organized crime interests, invested their ill-gotten gains in other illegal activities such as prostitution and drugs. Those profits would mean a great deal to Nevada's future development: they also invested in gambling.

Increased sexual openness, flouting of Prohibition, and leftover concern from the Progressive Era about immigration prompted a backlash. In 1924 the federal government imposed new quotas limiting nonwhite and non-Protestant migration to the United States. Some right-wing fundamentalists engaged in vigilante efforts to enforce Prohibition and drive nonwhites and immigrants from their communities. More important, they helped revive the Ku Klux Klan (KKK), which still targeted African Americans in the South but shifted its emphasis north and tried to enhance its appeal as a fraternal organization. As membership grew, a new generation of Klansmen and women allies harassed and attacked Catholics and Jews. The Bolshevik Revolution of 1917 that turned Russia into the Soviet Union inspired the Great Red Scare and concerns about communism spreading in the United States; under the direction of Attorney General A. Mitchell Palmer and his aide Hoover, federal raids deported about four thousand suspected Communists and anarchists.

Peace and Labor War

After the war labor unions expected to benefit from accommodating the federal government during the war by refraining from striking. They proved mistaken. Strikes spread across the country, culminating in a national railroad strike in 1921 and 1922. Rising unemployment and stagnant or declining wages contributed to these actions, but so may have the Industrial Workers of the World. More crucially, Americans suspected labor of ties to communism, whose growth in Europe as it went through economic woes did nothing to ease those concerns.

Nevada became caught in the swirl of labor's revival and the Great Red Scare. Nevadans supported traditional labor unions and strikes but, encouraged by business and political leaders, questioned groups linked to radicalism, and local unions declared their desire to "fight iwwism and Bolshevism." In 1919 Governor Emmet Boyle expressed concern about the iww returning amid the expected postwar drop in mining and ranching revenue. Mining companies had begun cutting back due to declining demand, ample supplies, and the desire of stockholders for dividends and saw no logic in increasing wages.

Lawmakers heeded Boyle's call to avert "the danger to harmonious relations between employer and employee." The Criminal Syndicalism Act of 1919 punished "doctrine which advocates or teaches crime, sabotage, violence or unlawful methods of terrorism as a means of accomplishing industrial or political reform" with ten years in prison, a five-thousand-dollar fine, or both. A recent wildcat strike by 150 copper miners at Ruth, where demands for higher pay and memories of the iww led to charges of socialist involvement, helped inspire the law. Indeed, some Ruth miners belonged to an organization tied to the iww, but the union and the strike had been unrelated, and the workers conceded defeat. Nevada Northern Railway employees also failed to obtain a pay hike; railroad officials declined to meet with them and cut the pay of those workers not laid off.

Other strikes involving the iww followed. That July in McGill, Boyle and a federal mediator helped settle a strike; although the iww played no role, the action involved workers from earlier battles. The next month iww organizers came to Tonopah, where miners had tried to persuade their employers, led by George Wingfield, to raise wages. After the miners walked out, federal and state officials negotiated a settlement and submitted it to the miners; a secret ballot revealed the iww voted no, but other workers supported it. When the iww stayed out, other unions honored the picket lines until October, when the owners talked the craft unions into dropping the radical union, forming the new Tonopah-Divide Mine and Millmen's Union and accepting the agreement.

The iww refused to give up and suffered for it. With the Wobblies still striking, Boyle obtained an injunction under the Criminal Syndicalism Act. In November the mine operators agreed to sell coal to employees at cost, set up a commissary, and pay them a fifty-cent daily bonus until the cost of living fell enough to justify eliminating the commissary. The strike ended. The iww forged ahead, shutting down Tonopah mines twice in 1920 and encouraging a strike at Elko, but the iww became anathema to Nevadans—enough for Nevada's US attorney to accuse the union of infecting cattle with hoof-and-mouth disease to hurt ranchers.

One more major strike affected Nevada. In 1921 Senator William A. Clark sold his half of the Los Angeles & Salt Lake Railroad to his partners at the Union Pacific. Las Vegas's economy relied on the line's repair yards, but after the up took over and fired sixty shop workers in October 1921, a wildcat strike began. No radical unions became involved, but the six-month strike grew heated: the railroad imported strikebreakers who became the target of violence, while the up's control of the town prompted retribution against union supporters. Boyle sent state police, imposing martial law when local officials proved unable or unwilling to protect either the strikers who elected them or the replacement workers. The railroads eventually triumphed, and the UP responded by removing its repair shops from Las Vegas to Caliente. The line still stopped at the local depot with passengers and freight, but Las Vegas would have to find a new means of prosperity—and did.

Labor and political unrest had other effects. Legislators tried and failed to make strikes and lockouts illegal and submit all labor disputes to arbitration. They promoted patriotism by mandating that all college students study the US and Nevada Constitutions before graduating. In 1919, fearing violent socialist labor groups, Nevadans advocated approving the death penalty. Boyle vetoed the legislature's first attempt but not a second effort after the public made its support clear. The next legislature ordered the gas chamber used for executions. In 1924 Gee Jon, accused of killing another Chinese man in Mina, became the first person in America executed in that way.

Highway to Success

In the 1920s the bust cycle arrived for Nevada mining. By 1920 production fell to one-half of its inflated wartime level of 1918, and a national downturn in 1921 further depressed ore markets. Thus, Nevada looked for new means of prosperity and found a possible route: highway construction that also promoted travel to the state. The success of Henry Ford's Model T inspired other automobile makers, and federal and state governments saw the need for better roads. In 1916 the Federal Aid Road Act set up a dollar-matching plan for states to build roads, provided that they established a highway department. Boyle acted, and legislators created the department and the office of state highway engineer, determined four highway routes, and instituted a tax to raise funds.

But with Nevada lacking the tax base and revenue flow to match federal funds, Tasker Oddie paved the way to a solution. In 1920, after Wingfield backed him in a crowded Republican primary for the US Senate, Oddie won the general election (he benefited from independent Anne Martin drawing votes from the incumbent Democrat, Elko lawyer Charles Henderson, the grandson of Nevada's second governor, Lewis Bradley). In the Senate, remembering early Tonopah and driving around the state while running for governor, Oddie turned his attention to road building. In 1921, partly through his and Pittman's efforts, the second Federal Aid Road

Nevada's highways

Act rejiggered the dollar-matching plan to aid states where public lands numbered more than 5 percent, leading to more than $1 billion in government support. With at least 86 percent of its land federally owned, Nevada needed to raise only $16.32 for every federal dollar. In 1930 the Oddie-Colton Act required the federal government to pay for all interstate highways that crossed public land and Indian reservations, thereby tripling the federal funds that Nevada received for highway construction in the ensuing decade.

State officials also took the lead. In 1922, after two terms, Boyle supported a friend as his successor: fellow Democrat and mining engineer James Scrugham, a World War I veteran and founder of the American Legion. Although Wingfield preferred Republicans, Scrugham cruised to victory on the strong endorsement from Boyle, who continued to influence the state as publisher of Reno's *Nevada State Journal,* and with Key Pittman easily winning reelection to the Senate atop the ticket. Scrugham shared Oddie's belief in good roads, but his mining experience convinced him the state's economy needed a larger foundation. Tourism encouraged by easy transportation would provide the answer, and California might provide the market: the population of Los Angeles doubled during the 1920s, but the number of cars in that area quintupled.

In his first legislative session in 1923, Scrugham took action. Others had backed highway construction: in the late 1910s, E. W. Griffith, a businessman and state senator from Las Vegas, had pushed for the Arrowhead Highway through southern Nevada. Scrugham went much further. In 1923 the legislature approved a two-cent-per-gallon gasoline tax to fund road building, and by 1926 the state spent $10 million a year—the largest percentage of the budget—on one thousand miles of roads, especially Highway 50, Nevada's portion of the national Lincoln Highway. In 1925 the Union Pacific, following through on a promise Clark made in 1905, paved Fremont Street in Las Vegas from Main Street to the highway—now Las Vegas Boulevard. Many roads remained to be paved during the 1930s, but at least they had been graveled, and communities through which Highways 6 and 50 passed had to do the same, increasing government spending and creating jobs. The original interstate highway went through Searchlight, so Clark County commissioner James Cashman, a Las Vegas auto dealer, led a local crew that built a road approximating Interstate 15 through Las Vegas to Southern California.

Believing these roads would make it easier for tourists to traverse the state, Scrugham wanted to give them something to see. He backed better highways to bring visitors from Yosemite through Nevada and won the power to set aside recreational and wilderness areas. Although the Nevada Land and Livestock Association objected to "sentimental" land policies, he created fifteen recreation areas for the Nevada Fish and Game Commission to administer, including what became the first official state park, Valley of Fire in southern Nevada. An academic—he came to Nevada as a university professor—Scrugham also took a great interest in archaeology. His efforts led to Mark Harrington of the Museum of the American Indian studying Lovelock Cave and Pueblo Grande de Nevada, the basis of significant anthropological research; the latter prompted the creation of the Lost City Museum in Overton. For his trouble, when Scrugham sought a second term, his opponent adopted a slogan: "Live cities instead of dead ones."

Scrugham also hoped to capitalize on federal actions but became neither the first nor the last Nevada politician to have to bow to the power of ranching and mining interests. In 1922 President Harding established Lehman Caves National Monument northeast of Ely at a site discovered in 1885 by Absalom Lehman, who had been charging admission to see the caves. Scrugham pushed to convert the monument into a national park, and Pittman tried to use his influence. Ranchers and miners bemoaned the loss of land, but the National Park Service did their work for them: although its leaders had embarked on an expansion, they took no action due to the caves' remoteness and the likelihood of few visitors, despite a new highway to the area. When Scrugham lost his reelection bid amid complaints that he cared more about attracting visitors to Nevada than about the ranchers and miners living there, efforts to create a national park subsided. But they would return—as would battles over what to use the land for, and who would control it.

Prohibition, Organized Crime, and Tourism

Other parts of the country became better known than Nevada for flouting Prohibition and aiding the rise of organized crime. In New York bootlegging helped underwrite the "Bug and Meyer Mob," led by boyhood friends Benjamin "Bugsy" Siegel and Meyer Lansky, who eventually teamed with Italian gangsters led by Frank Costello and Charles "Lucky" Luciano. In Chicago Al Capone performed similar services, battling Bugs Moran's competing organization until his crew killed several of Moran's lieutenants in the St. Valentine's Day Massacre in 1929 and consolidated his organization's power. California bootleggers profited throughout the state, but none more than Tony Cornero Stralla, who went to federal prison for his activities. Each group later entered Nevada's tourism industry.

Before their arrival, Nevada benefited from visitors seeking opportunities for vice. Nineteenth-century Virginia City and other towns had been known for their casinos, brothels, and opium dens. In 1915 legislators approved betting on horse races and a state racing commission to regulate it, to the delight of Wingfield, a racing fan. In 1919 Boyle, reflecting Progressive ideology, dismissed the existing antigambling law as a failure and called unsuccessfully for "a rigid enforceable law designed to prohibit gambling in all forms." After Frederic DeLongchamps's redesign in 1927, Wingfield's Riverside Hotel catered to the divorce trade—the legislature had just halved the residency requirement, from six months to three—while Wingfield invested in other hotels and in casinos operated by Bill Graham and Jim McKay, who reportedly laundered money for mobsters and ran Reno's brothels. In Las Vegas Block 16, near the railroad depot, offered prostitution and illegal gambling. Ely boasted enough gambling to persuade White Pine Copper Company mining engineer J. Kell Houssels to enter the business; he eventually became a key figure in Las Vegas gaming and other industries.

Government officials tended to encourage such behavior, responding to voters who passed two initiatives calling for an end to Prohibition. Wingfield's desire to be left alone dovetailed with Nevada's libertarian views. Lawmakers passed bills overturning state Prohibition laws, but Nevada's Supreme Court held them unconstitutional for conflicting with the Eighteenth Amendment. State officials battled US Attorney George Springmeyer's attempts to enforce antidrinking laws. Wingfield supported the Reno mayoral race of E. E. Roberts, a former congressman who won in 1923 in opposition to Prohibition and announced his goal of placing a barrel of whiskey, complete with a dipper, on every local street corner.

Most Las Vegans opposed Prohibition, and local law enforcement declined to enforce it, even warning when federal agents planned a raid. Officials arrested Las Vegas mayor Fred Hesse for bootlegging, opened a Block 16 speakeasy called Liberty's Last Stand to conduct a sting operation, and raided violators outside of town, arresting more than a hundred bootleggers and police officers. In 1917 Utah rancher Thomas Williams bought 140 acres north of present-day downtown Las Vegas and began selling home sites that had only one rule: no African Americans could live there. Many buyers took advantage of the artesian wells to turn the new settlement, North Las Vegas, into a haven for bootlegging.

While Reno's divorce trade and nearby ranches attracted visitors, Las Vegas found other ways to cater to tourists. An investor sought to convert the old Kiel Ranch in North Las Vegas into a dude ranch. New local fairgrounds attracted the county fair, rodeos, and other events. Complementing the Arrowhead Highway's construction and the beginnings of Highway 91 from Los Angeles to Salt Lake, daily air service between Las Vegas and those two cities began in 1926. David Lorenzi created the Twin Lakes Resort at the western end of town, and local businessmen focused on developing skiing and small resorts at nearby Kyle and Lee Canyons. From these tiny beginnings, a dominant industry later grew.

Wingfield and His "Bipartisan Machine"

In the 1920s Wingfield consolidated his influence over Nevada. The extent of his power remains open to debate. That he ran a political machine seems clear, but, without written evidence, not what he did and how he did it. He worked from his office in the Reno National Bank, which he owned. The same building housed Nevada's leading law firm, headed by Frank Norcross, later a federal judge; William Woodburn, of a longtime political family; and former attorney general George Thatcher. Woodburn served in the 1910s and 1920s as Democratic national committeeman, followed by Thatcher, while Wingfield held the same post for Republicans, raising money, recruiting candidates, setting policy, and arbitrating disputes. Thus, Nevada's leading behind-the-scenes operatives shared space in what observers called "the Cave"; they said to know what went on politically in Nevada, dial "4111," the phone number for their offices. The Reno Chamber of Commerce's decision to relocate into the bank seemed to confirm his importance.

Wingfield—and most Nevadans in that era—supported Republicans. Yet Democrats retained a number of offices, especially when their views meshed with Wingfield's or a Democrat's popularity proved insurmountable even for the state's boss. Wingfield voiced no major objections to Scrugham's election in 1922, but disliked his quest to increase government spending—even though his advocacy of better roads and tourism figured to benefit Wingfield, who declined entreaties from Republicans to seek the job himself in 1926. Instead, Wingfield backed Fred Balzar, a popular state GOP chair and former Mineral County state senator, against Scrugham—and Balzar still won by only about 1,850 votes out of nearly 31,000 cast. Democrat Key Pittman won reelection to the Senate in 1922 and 1928; voters clearly liked him, and the senator supported Nevada's interests and Wingfield's. Also, Pittman gave Nevada entrée into the Democratic leadership: he declined the vice presidential nomination in 1924 and played important behind-the-scenes roles in the 1928 and 1932 campaigns. Wingfield grasped the value of that access.

Wingfield believed that he had Nevada's best interests at heart. Limited government, he felt, made Nevada a better place to live and invest. By supporting Oddie, whom he worked with on patronage issues and loaned money to on several occasions, and at least tolerating Pittman, he ensured Nevada a member from each party in the US Senate. With Nevada's small population—only seventy-seven thousand in 1920, a slight decrease from a

The *Sacramento Bee* won a Pulitzer Prize for its reporting on George Wingfield, depicted here by the *Bee*'s cartoonist as the king of Nevada, stretching to reach different parts of his domain. Courtesy of the Nevada State Library and Archives.

decade before—it had no hope for power in the House of Representatives, where population determined membership. Throughout its history, with seniority usually deciding Senate committee chairmanships, Nevada benefited from retaining incumbents who gave it entrée to the White House and other bastions of federal power, first with Senators William Stewart and Francis Newlands and down to the early twenty-first century with Senate Democratic leader Harry Reid. As part of the Republican majority throughout his two terms (1921–33), Oddie enjoyed valuable connections, while Pittman gained seniority.

Wingfield also flexed his muscle in Reno. Francis Newlands and university presidents Joseph Stubbs and Walter Clark had promoted education, culture, and municipal improvements with help from Mayor H. E. Stewart, who targeted the red-light district for elimination. In 1923, when Stewart ran again, Wingfield backed fellow Republican Roberts, who won three terms as mayor by promoting gambling, prostitution, and alcohol. During Roberts's administration, Virginia Street became adorned with its famous arch, declaring Reno "The Biggest Little City in the World," celebrating the Lincoln Highway's completion but also suggesting a combination of small-town friendliness and big-city attractions. Like many other growing Nevada towns then and later, Reno often found itself divided between its quest for tourist dollars and its desire for respectability—much like Wingfield, the cowboy and gambler turned capitalist.

The Cole-Malley Case: McCarran Versus Wingfield

The proof of Wingfield's influence may exist not in whom he helped elect, but in whom he helped defeat. After battling Wingfield in the Tonopah-Goldfield area, Pat McCarran returned to Reno and became a successful attorney. He won a term on the Nevada Supreme Court and wrote several important decisions. But McCarran saw the court as "a political burying place" and lost a reelection bid in which he barely campaigned. He returned to private practice, where he earned his greatest fame representing actress Mary Pickford, known as "America's sweetheart," in a divorce case, but probably encouraged perjured testimony to establish her residency. McCarran also kept trying to fulfill his ambition of becoming a US senator, but lost both serious and halfhearted races in 1914, 1916, 1918, 1920, and 1926. Defeating him required little from Wingfield, since Pittman hated McCarran for challenging his reelection in 1916 and few Democratic regulars trusted him. But Wingfield's distaste for McCarran did nothing to discourage those views.

McCarran's outsider status involved him in a court case that demonstrated how insiders controlled Nevada. In May 1927 an Ormsby County grand jury charged two Democratic former officials, controller George Cole and treasurer Ed Malley, and former Carson Valley Bank cashier H. C. Clapp with embezzling more than $500,000 from the state to invest in mining and oil stocks. For eight years they hid their actions from state banking officials. Wingfield owned the bank and company that bonded Malley's salary. Worse, state law limited government deposits in any bank to $75,000, and the bank lacked the funds to cover the loss. Although he deposited $500,000 in the bank to make up for what they had embezzled, Wingfield requested that Balzar call a special legislative session to raise taxes to account for the loss. After Balzar complied, lawmakers discussed requiring Wingfield to pay for the whole amount since he had bonded Malley, making him legally responsible. Instead, they set up a board that determined Wingfield should pay for 30 percent, or more than $150,000.

Meanwhile, Cole and Malley needed a lawyer. McCarran took the job and argued that they expected Wingfield's power to protect them, stressing Wingfield's comment about state officials: "they know what I want." With great pleasure, he badgered Wingfield on the witness stand. In the end jurors convicted Cole and Malley, and several legislators who voted for the tax hike lost their bids for reelection over it. Wingfield suffered embarrassment, but not enough to deter him from campaigning openly in 1928 for his friend Herbert Hoover's election as president and for himself to a ten-year term on the university Board of Regents. McCarran enjoyed some vengeance and little more, but when a better opportunity followed, he made the most of it.

The Klan and Bigotry

In the early 1920s, after gains in the South and Midwest, and in West Coast cities with more significant African American populations, the Ku Klux Klan targeted the Intermountain West. Ten Klaverns spread across Nevada between 1924 and 1926. A cross burning announced the Klan's arrival in a community, but the response varied. The Klan enjoyed success in Nevada's largest city, Reno, but failed miserably in areas (mostly mining towns) with a large percentage of immigrants. Some Klan events attracted curious Jews and Catholics, and because most members seemed to view themselves as forming a social club, no violence resulted. With more than one-third of Nevada's population foreign born, the Klan's message often fell on deaf ears.

Although Reno's Klavern may have reached 1,800 members, the KKK proved more successful in southern Nevada than in the North. In 1922 the KKK called off an effort in Las Vegas when Clark County's district attorney obtained a list of their names and threatened to publish them, destroying the anonymity they prized. The Klan tried again in 1925, marching up Fremont Street to the county fairgrounds for a public initiation, and became successful enough to advertise its meetings and set up a women's branch (a similar effort failed in Fallon). But success bred trouble: the Klark Kounty Klan, as it styled itself, turned vigilante, using pressure and violence against prostitution and Prohibition violators. Conducting show trials discouraged adultery, but a grand jury report that encouraged shutting down vice to improve young people's morals led nowhere.

The Klan also affected national and state politics. At the 1924 Democratic National Convention, it helped block the nomination of Al Smith, the Catholic governor of New York; Nevada's delegation backed a platform that avoided even mentioning the Klan, although a minority, led by McCarran, a devout Catholic, disagreed, seeking a condemnation of the group. Critics tried to persuade a legislator to introduce a bill implicitly barring the wearing of Klan regalia but failed. In Las Vegas members openly campaigned for and against candidates, usually losing and then harassing the victors. Criticism from local editors and other organizations, counterattacks from Klan targets, and a lack of deep and widespread local hostility toward immigrant groups combined to send the KKK into decline throughout Nevada by 1926.

Bigotry spread in other ways. Legislators passed laws barring teaching German and other foreign languages in elementary schools, noncitizens from working on government projects, the foreign born from filing for mining claims or grazing and water rights, and, long after the Johnson-Jeffries fight, interracial boxing matches. The "Yellow Peril," the fear of Nevada's 750 Japanese residents, led to several Nevada towns excluding them by ordinance or force, while Governor Emmet Boyle urged a constitutional amendment to ban Japanese landownership, as California had done. Yet after it passed, joining a similar prohibition against the Chinese, the legislature never acted on it, and it went largely unnoticed; indeed, one of southern Nevada's leading farms belonged to Nanyu Tomiyasu, who supplied area markets and restaurants. Reno demonstrated similar contradictions in Nevada's attitudes: the state's first permanent synagogue, Temple Emanu-El, opened there in 1922 and added a full-time rabbi in 1931, and the community elected a Jewish city councilman, Sam Frank, for more than two decades. But Sam Platt, the synagogue's attorney, fought anti-Semitism in losing three bids for the US Senate.

Planning a Dam

In the 1850s officials discussed irrigating the Southern California desert and controlling the Colorado, which writer Marc Reisner called "unrivaled for sheer orneriness. . . . Its flow varied psychotically between a few thousand cubic feet per second and a couple of hundred thousand, sometimes within a few days." In 1905, in the latest of a series of disasters for those dependent on the river, it flooded the Imperial Valley, restoring the prehistoric Salton Sea. With the Bureau of Reclamation building small dams and diverting small rivers, erecting a large dam to manage a large river gained appeal. Theodore Roosevelt advocated the Progressive ideal of "diversion dams and distribution systems in the Colorado River Valley . . . so that none of the water of this great river which can be put to beneficial use will be allowed to go to waste."

But several problems intervened. Roosevelt proposed compensating the Southern Pacific for its efforts to control flooding; Congress balked. World War I diverted attention. Other investments concerned Southern California developers more. When bureau engineers began examining the locations, costs, and work involved in building a dam, they faced flash floods and bad weather. Finally, they settled on the ideal location on the Nevada-Arizona line, in Boulder Canyon or Black Canyon; engineer Walker Young decided the latter's lower elevation, downstream location, and ability to store more water made it the better choice. Besides recommending paying for the project with hydroelectric power sales, Reclamation director Arthur Powell Davis (Colorado River explorer John Wesley Powell's nephew) argued that because the Colorado flowed between several states and to Mexico, interstate and international issues required the federal government to take responsibility for building a dam and the irrigation system.

Deciding the location proved easier than dividing the results. In 1920 the League of the Southwest, a promotional group, met in Los Angeles to discuss a dam, and southern Nevadans played a key role in supporting an interstate compact to bring it to fruition. In 1922 Harding chose Hoover, an engineer and his secretary of commerce, to broker a deal between the seven states where the nearly two-thousand-mile river flowed. Each state had different interests (for example, the least water went through California, which needed it most). They debated federal authority, what to do about sixty thousand Native Americans on thirty reservations in the river's basin, and Mexico receiving less water, potentially affecting international affairs and land owned by leading Southern California businessmen.

Legal questions further muddied the waters. Under riparian rights, owners of land bordering water enjoyed it equally if they did nothing to limit others' access. But most western states adopted the doctrine of prior appropriation, "first in time, first in right," which historian Norris Hundley Jr. called "swift commandeering of water resources and rapid economic development." In 1922 in *Wyoming v. Colorado*, the US Supreme Court ruled that prior appropriation applied to the states. This threw a wrench into dividing the Colorado because California's greater needs would enable it to control the bulk of its waters. Several other states, especially Arizona, recoiled at the thought.

Nevadans avoided divisions. They sought little of the water, given their small population and the aquifer serving Las Vegas, but the prospect of electricity and construction excited them. They wanted the dam in Nevada and for the federal government to respect states' rights. Devising an agreement took six years, as Hoover and state officials varied between patience and hostility. Boyle sent Scrugham to negotiate; Charles P. Squires, the Republican owner of the *Las Vegas Age,* and businessman and southern Nevada Democratic leader Ed W. Clark helped. Wingfield encouraged them but complained, "The Las Vegas crowd don't care whether Nevada gets anything out of it or not as long as the Dam is built and they get a temporary boom." Joining other Nevadans in chafing at their western neighbor's power, he added, "I don't want to see Southern California steal everything that belongs to Nevada."

Nevada proved to be the least of the problems with reaching an agreement. Approved by negotiators in November 1922, the Colorado River Compact would apply to the Upper Colorado's four states (Colorado, Wyoming, New Mexico, and Utah) and the three on the Lower Colorado (California, Nevada, and Arizona). But all seven state legislatures had to approve, and California and Arizona fought over their share of the water, with Southern Californians knowing their future depended on increasing the local water supply. The investments and personal and political rivalries of California leaders also hamstrung two key dam supporters: Senator Hiram Johnson and Representative Phil Swing of the Imperial Valley.

Finally, events conspired to drive the dam forward—and almost scuttle it. The Mississippi River flood of 1927, which killed 246 people, pushed Congress to act on flood control. A Federal Trade Commission investigation revealed opponents of publicly controlled hydroelectric power, which a dam would produce, received money from the utility industry—including Scrugham, a project supporter. North of Los Angeles, the St. Francis Dam burst, killing more than 450 Californians; it could have derailed the Boulder Canyon Project, but, instead, safety concerns prompted the creation of a board of experts to oversee planning other dams.

At last, the Swing-Johnson or Boulder Canyon Project Act, appropriating $165 million overall, passed Congress, and President Calvin Coolidge signed it on December 21, 1928. Significantly, it required only six of the seven states to approve the compact, thereby countering Arizona, which had refused to join the agreement over its water allotment. The other states signed the compact, with Nevada accepting 300,000 acre-feet of the Lower Colorado's expected yearly output of 7.5 million acre-feet (the amount required to cover an acre with a foot of water). Congress soon approved another $10.6 million to build 22.6 miles of railroad from the existing Union Pacific line to the top of the proposed dam site.

A Depressed World, a Depressed State

In October 1929, in two days of trading, the New York Stock Exchange lost about one-fifth of its value, destroying $10 billion in real and imagined wealth. The crash climaxed a decade of speculation and overproduction, farm depression, widening income disparities, and Europe's limited recovery from World War I. Just a few months into his presidency, Hoover preferred to avoid calling it a panic or recession, so he branded it a "depression." It became the Great Depression. By 1932 the gross national product fell by one-third and prices by about 40 percent, unemployment reached 25 percent, and thousands of World War I veterans formed a "Bonus Army" and marched on Washington, DC, demanding early payment of money the government had promised them. Hoover approved new programs for failing businesses and home owners facing foreclosure and $2 billion in public works. But his approval of a higher tariff and higher taxes hurt more than it helped. Beyond that, he felt the federal government should avoid too much direct action and encouraged private enterprise and charities to provide aid; they lacked the ability to cope, and Hoover lacked the ability to change.

A political revolution seemed in the making. In 1930 Democrats won the House of Representatives for the first time in more than a decade and seemed poised for a big victory in 1932. In New York Governor Franklin Roosevelt instituted the "Little New Deal" of work and welfare programs, and his record and political cunning enabled him to capture the Democratic nomination for president in 1932. He buried Hoover in the general election after campaigning against excessive federal spending, projecting sunny optimism, and pledging a "New Deal."

Other, more ominous, signs of change shook the world. In 1931 Japan, seeking empire due to growing militarism and its needs as an island, invaded Manchuria. China remained embroiled in a civil war between its dictatorship, allied with the United States, and Communists. In 1933 Germany's National Socialists installed their leader in power: Adolf Hitler, who pledged to annihilate Jews and other "undesirables" and wanted to rearm Germany as part of his plans for expansion and power. The Communist Party increased its US membership amid increasing doubts about the survival of the American political and economic system.

As the Depression began, Nevada seemed immune to its worst effects. Federal money promised to help, and not just from the dam project. Pittman and Oddie engineered moving the US Naval Ammunition Depot to three hundred square miles of federal land near Hawthorne; the previous dump, in New Jersey, exploded, and the navy preferred to locate its spent ammunition in a less populated area. The navy thus pumped about $5 million into the economy through construction and created a new town, Babbitt, to house workers, who spent their pay in nearby communities. But, suggesting voter displeasure with the status quo, in 1930 Republicans Balzar and Representative Samuel Arentz won reelection by closer margins than expected.

The Depression soon hit mining and ranching. In 1930 mineral production fell by half from 1929 and kept dropping. Livestock interests suffered from a combination of the need to repair parts of the Newlands Project and a drought, exacerbating conflicts with Native Americans over the water rights on reservations and unemployment among Native peoples working as agricultural laborers. But the Depression made matters worse, with Nevada's agricultural revenue plunging from more than $22 million in 1928 to just less than $6.5 million in 1932.

Given federal and state limitations, Nevada's leaders did what they could. Balzar created the Agricultural Relief Committee that fought for cuts in freight rates on feed sent to Nevada and obtained more than $12 million in wheat from the Federal Farm Board to help ranchers. Pittman and Oddie sought help for mining. Oddie's efforts on behalf of copper failed, as did Pittman's quest to lend silver to China, then the only world power on the silver standard.

Starting a Dam

The Depression had the effect of turning the Boulder Canyon Project into an enormous public works program and exciting the interest of unemployed workers who flocked to southern Nevada in search of jobs. In 1930 hundreds camped at what became known as Ragtown in Hemenway Wash, near where the Colorado entered Black Canyon. They lived in tents amid scorpions and hot sand in 120-degree summer temperatures. In Las Vegas families filled the sidewalks, the courthouse lawn, and a camp at the north end of town.

The project also created some of the leading businesses in the West and, by extension, the world. As an eventual bidder said, "Now this dam is just a dam but it's a damn big dam." Because no existing firm could do it alone, contractors formed a consortium, Six Companies, Inc.: Henry J. Kaiser and W. A. Bechtel, J. F. Shea, Utah Construction Company, Morrison-Knudsen, Pacific Bridge Company, and MacDonald & Kahn, many of whom (especially Kaiser and Bechtel) parlayed the dam into billions of dollars in government contracts. They hired veteran Bureau of Reclamation engineer Frank Crowe, and he submitted their winning bid to build Hoover Dam for $48,890,995.50, only about $25,000 more than the government estimated. Starting work on March 11, 1931, the builders would have to drill four diversion tunnels through solid rock by October 1, 1933, and the dam would have to be high enough to produce electricity by August 1, 1936, or Six Companies would pay a $3,000 daily penalty. The federal government declined to interfere in their hiring practices, except mandating that they give preference to veterans and hire no "Mongolian labor."

They would build what became known as "the eighth wonder of the world." The plans called for a dam more than 726 feet high, 660 feet wide at the base, and 45 feet wide at the crest, requiring 4.5 million cubic yards of concrete. In addition to the railroad line, it led to the building of other roads, including Boulder Highway from Las Vegas to the dam site. The dam's construction also bred a company town. In 1930 Secretary of the Interior Ray Lyman Wilbur visited Las Vegas, whose leaders wanted dam workers housed there to boost the economy and even shut down brothels and bars for the day to try to make a good impression. Despite their efforts to fool Wilbur, he announced plans for the Boulder Canyon Project Federal Reservation near the dam site. That designation meant that only federal laws applied to the land; the state of Nevada would have no authority.

Towns Going and Coming

The federal government then constructed what became known as Boulder City as a model community with homes and carefully selected businesses as well as an evening curfew. Dam workers complained about city manager Sims Ely, a federal employee who sought to keep all vice out of Boulder City and had the authority to succeed: longtime Nevada state archivist Guy Louis Rocha described it as having "elements of both the model town and the police state." But workers welcomed living in government-built homes and nearby amenities like playgrounds, parks for their children, and a mess hall serving about six thousand meals a day—and on payday they could always go to Las Vegas or the casino and brothel at Railroad Pass, just outside the reservation's limits, unless Six Companies paid them in scrip; in that case, they could spend their pay only in Boulder City.

Construction began on Boulder City within a month of work on the dam and produced Nevada's first truly planned community. Legendary Denver planner S. R. DeBoer mapped out the town, and Bureau of Reclamation officials adapted them with help from architect Gordon Kaufmann. Bureau employees moved first into modern homes. A year later workers gained access to 658 mostly two- and three-room bungalows that looked so much alike, workers coming home at night often entered the wrong one. Ely licensed a variety of businesses, from clothing stores and a hotel to a movie theater, and oversaw the city library. Ely also segregated by class (Reclamation and Six Companies families tended to occupy opposite ends of town) and race. In 1931 and 1932 the Colored Citizens Protective Association of Las Vegas (247 members in a local population below 6,000) objected to the lack of African American dam workers, who numbered 30 out of 5,000-plus workers at their peak of employment, while Ely barred them from living in Boulder City.

The dam also helped ease the Depression's effects in Las Vegas. Population expansion, and the economic opportunities the nearby project generated, led to new public works. In 1930 school superintendent Maude Frazier shepherded the opening of a high school that could accommodate 500 students, prompting complaints of waste because the town, locals said, would never grow that large. The next year a new private hospital and a new public hospital signaled the expanding town's need for medical care. In 1933 southern Nevada's first federal courthouse opened, and the federal impact on the area became apparent, with new warehouses and construction businesses opening near the tracks to serve the project on the Colorado and the Union Pacific improving its yards and terminal.

The dam's construction also eliminated one community and the remnants of another. The reservoir behind the dam would cover 247 square miles of land, or about 170,000 acres, almost all belonging to the federal government. The rest included farms and salt and gypsum mines as well as the largely Mormon farming town of St. Thomas, founded in 1865. The federal government ended up paying about $500,000 for the acreage. Just south of St. Thomas, Scrugham's friend Mark Harrington had been excavating the remains of Pueblo Grande de Nevada, which he named the Lost City. With the dam about to shift the Colorado and flood the Muddy River valley, crews continued saving important artifacts until the river's waters began rising around them.

Working on the Dam

Wilbur also returned on September 17, 1930, to drive a silver spike to complete the railroad spur and announce the name of Hoover Dam, in honor of his boss and friend, whom many of the disappointed onlookers blamed for the Depression. But jobs mattered more to them than the project's name. The dam employed as many as five thousand men at a time on everything from testing concrete samples to dynamiting, from scaling canyon walls to

The construction of Hoover Dam had the effect of a jobs project to combat the Depression and reshaped the southwestern United States, in addition to providing water to southern Nevada and boosting its increasingly tourist-driven economy. Courtesy of Special Collections, University Libraries, University of Nevada, Las Vegas.

operating a drilling jumbo, a ten-ton truck carrying three tiers of ten drills that bored holes in the rock. In the summer of 1931, they worked round-the-clock shifts, trying to move 10 million cubic yards of rock. With Crowe demanding speed, they nicknamed him "Hurry Up" Crowe.

Hurrying created danger and strife. Temperatures in the canyon topped 130 degrees, causing sixteen deaths from heatstroke and other ailments in one month. Carbon monoxide poisoning became so common, said ferry boat operator Murl Emery, "they were hauling men out of those tunnels like cord wood. They had been gassed." Doctors diagnosed pneumonia, protecting Six Companies from liability. Several workers sued, prompting attorneys to send a man undercover to Block 16 with a plaintiff who claimed to have been left impotent; the evidence proved otherwise. With Boulder City under construction, workers found little relief in the camps and barracks, nor did they receive medical help or dietary supplements. Six Companies and Crowe put deadlines and productivity ahead of safety, especially at $3.50 a day for those digging in the diversion tunnels and $6 for more skilled laborers.

Across the country, unions found organizing difficult amid high unemployment, but hoped the dam would provide an opportunity. With Las Vegas's recently established Central Labor Council accusing Six Companies of undercutting wages for skilled labor by up to 50 percent, the mostly moribund IWW announced plans to unionize dam workers and sent eleven organizers, most of whom wound up in the Las Vegas jail on vagrancy charges. On August 8, acting without the IWW, a workers committee gave Crowe a list of demands, including better pay, paid travel time, meal money, cold or iced water at the job site, and enforcement of state mining safety laws in tunnels. In response, Crowe called them radicals, locked out the fourteen-hundred-member workforce, and shut down construction. Other than the American Federation of Labor–dominated labor council in Las Vegas, the strikers found no support from Crowe, the Bureau of Reclamation, or the state. Six Companies and federal officials broke the strike in a week, although they did improve working conditions and sped up housing construction in Boulder City.

On November 13, 1932, from the perspective of the dam's supporters, the fruits of these labors became clearer. After setting off dynamite, men worked in Black Canyon to shift the Colorado into the diversion tunnels. They piled up dirt and rocks to move the river so they could erect the dam.

They did it, nearly a year before the deadline. By 1933 the dam project produced profits of $3 million a year for Six Companies and ran two years ahead of schedule.

Legalizing and Encouraging Vice?

The 1931 legislative session, meeting as dam construction began, proved to be the most important in Nevada's history. Its members passed two laws that Balzar signed on March 19 and changed Nevada's economy and society. They cut the residency requirement for divorce from three months to six weeks, effective May 1, and legalized gambling immediately. Why they passed these bills has caused considerable historical debate. Assemblyman Phil Tobin, a Humboldt County rancher who introduced the gambling bill, said that he felt it would increase state revenues and legalize what had been going on anyway. Harold Stocker, whose mother, Mayme, held the license for the Northern Club bar and casino that their family operated, claimed he sent at least one suitcase of money to the legislature. Various sources have pointed to legislators receiving bribes and contributions from organized crime interests, especially Chicago, led by Murray Humphreys, a longtime behind-the-scenes operative later tied to high-powered Southern California attorney Sidney Korshak, and Johnny Rosselli, who eventually served as the syndicate's muscle on the Las Vegas Strip.

While Tobin and Stocker presumably meant what they said, other forces had been at work as well. Lawmakers laid the groundwork in 1927 by reducing the residency limits, and neither legislature would have been likely to act without Wingfield's support. Legal gambling fitted his economic needs as a banker and hotel owner and his libertarian leanings, and he saw the potential benefits for Nevada. Although supporting legal gambling, Wingfield realized that he could be a lightning rod—in this case, for church, educational, and women's groups who had opposed gambling before. Silence would be wise, he told one ally, because "there are many other ways to skin a cat and we don't want any groups against us before the election."

Other businessmen shared Wingfield's outlook, but with a twist. As historian Eric Moody has demonstrated, another source of support for the gambling and divorce laws came from Las Vegas. Real estate developer Thomas Carroll and other local investors and officials saw that changing the law would attract visitors to Nevada. They focused less on tourism than on the goal of drawing these visitors to stay in the state and invest; if not, at least they brought income to Nevada.

Regulation and Response

Perhaps the best additional evidence for the origin of the measures comes from two factors: the regulatory system and the reactions to the laws. The legislature left licensing to cities and counties, which sent one-quarter of the fees to the state; regulating a vice mattered less than maintaining Nevada's tradition of limited state government, especially when local jurisdictions figured to lack funds for in-depth investigations. Each county would create a five-member board consisting of the three county commissioners, the sheriff, and the district attorney, with incorporated cities allowed to require licenses and fees, too.

The responses to the laws varied. The same opponents of gambling and divorce during the Progressive Era objected. Attorney Felice Cohn suggested that reducing the residency requirement for divorce would hurt economically because those who could stay for three months instead of six weeks "pay better attorney fees, and spend more money with the merchants of Reno, and the inn-keepers." Events proved her wrong: divorce quickly boosted Nevada's economy, with the number of Reno divorces doubling in the next year. The law also changed the legal profession, with more attorneys concentrating on obtaining divorces and avoiding less profitable specializations. Easy divorce encouraged the expansion of dude ranches, especially around Pyramid Lake, and the building of resorts where a divorce seeker could comfortably spend six weeks. It contributed to another, already growing, aspect of Nevada's economy: marriage. Thanks to California recently approving a waiting period between obtaining a wedding license and holding the ceremony, couples traveled to the nearest Nevada towns.

The gambling law inspired varied reactions, too. Addressing concerns about organized crime, Reno's sheriff said, "Al Capone is welcome in Reno as long as he behaves himself"—but Graham and McKay had been operating in Reno for a decade; his friend Frank Detra opened the Pair-O-Dice on Highway 91 (across from today's Wynn Las Vegas) outside Las Vegas in 1930 and reportedly contributed funds, possibly from Capone, to encourage legalization, and Capone had a history of not behaving himself. The *Las Vegas Evening Review-Journal*, published by longtime mining camp editor Frank Garside but run by his co-owner, Democratic party insider Al Cahlan, said, "People should not get overly excited over the effects of the new gambling bill—conditions will be little different than they are at the present time, except that some things will be done openly that have previously been done in secret." Whether they hoped to play down the measure's importance or expected minimal effects, Nevadans seemed less excited over legal gambling than outsiders who condemned their immorality. The *Chicago Tribune* spoke for many when a headline blared, "CANCEL NEVADA'S STATEHOOD!"

Casinos sprouted around Nevada, but Reno and Las Vegas predominated. Las Vegas's first licensees included two women, Mayme Stocker and Helen Morgan, although their role in casino operations seems to have been minor. Both cities limited casino licenses to downtown, with some exceptions. Las Vegas's first "carpet joint," the Meadows, opened on May 2 on the road to the dam, with entertainment, a hotel, and owners—the Cornero brothers—linked to the Mob in California and allegedly to Rosselli. Other than the Meadows, which later burned, and clubs like the Pair-O-Dice, most gambling occurred in Fremont Street "sawdust joints" and such spots as the Las Vegas Club and Hotel Nevada, opened in 1906, which called its casino the Sal Sagev—*Las Vegas* backwards. In 1932 the Apache, downtown Las Vegas's first "luxury" hotel-casino, opened downtown with a three-hundred-seat banquet room, the area's first elevator, a bar, and fifty thousand dollars in furnishings.

Reno also capitalized on divorce and gambling. Wingfield's holdings included hotels with gambling operations and smaller casinos, and the Bank Club and other spots that operated before legalization continued to do so. One of Wingfield's Tonopah friends, Nick Abelman, opened the Ship and Bottle Club on Wingfield property in 1932 and leased the casino inside the Riverside the next year. In 1931 local real estate investor Abe Zetooney built the seven-story El Cortez Hotel, charging six dollars a night per room—more than double the usual rate. Several casinos opened in back alleys just off the main drag, while city officials invoked a redline that allowed no casinos west of Virginia Street without hotel rooms.

Around Nevada existing properties sought to enhance profits by adding gambling or moving it into the open. Ely's six-story Hotel Nevada, the state's tallest building when it opened in 1929, ignored Prohibition and antigambling laws, but added blackjack tables and slot machines after legalization. Newt Crumley added gambling to his Commercial Hotel in Elko. Although most of these operators lacked the knowledge and capital that came later to build a bigger casino business, gambling remained just part of Nevada's economy during the Depression—a welcome part, but less significant to tourism than divorce, and seemingly less significant than mining or federal projects.

The Fall of the House of Wingfield

The Depression destroyed George Wingfield's empire. As owner of several leading mines, he felt the impact of declining ore production. As owner of major hotels, he welcomed the quest for additional visitors, but declining income and consumer spending hurt his bottom line. As owner of the leading bank in most Nevada towns, he lacked depositors—and in more prosperous Las Vegas, he had only some downtown land for a hotel he never built. Loaning significant funds to Nevada ranchers trying to survive the Depression brought a minimal return. By the June 30, 1932, annual report from the state bank examiner, four Nevada banks had failed, and Wingfield's Reno National Bank teetered on the brink. He won a loan of nearly five million dollars from the federal Reconstruction Finance Corporation but sent most of it to a San Francisco bank to pay his debts. In October, as the nation's banking system neared collapse, Balzar went to Washington to seek RFC help. Despite Wingfield's importance to Nevada and friendship with the president, who appointed the board, Balzar failed. Left with no alternative, he notified Lieutenant Governor Morley Griswold, who declared a state bank holiday on November 1.

With the savings of most of Nevada's ninety thousand residents in the balance, Nevada's banks would close for two weeks, examiners would check their assets, and those with enough cash would reopen. When examiners saw that Wingfield's banks lacked the needed capital, Balzar let bankers extend the holiday to December 18 if they felt unable to meet their obligations. But Wingfield believed his banks should live or die as a unit. Depositors in his United Nevada Bank in Reno tried to take action, but he blocked them. In hearings in February 1933, Riverside Bank cashier Roy Frisch claimed it could have stayed open. A year later, after becoming the bank's receiver, Frisch disappeared just before testifying in a trial involving Wingfield's friends Graham and McKay; the case remains unsolved.

Those hearings revealed more about Wingfield's influence. The state board of finance and bank examiner let his banks stay open despite knowing they lacked the required capital and conducted fewer examinations of his banks than state law mandated. His Nevada Surety and Bonding Company bonded state officials who knew about the worthless stock that it claimed as a major asset and failed to act quickly enough to recover more than five hundred thousand dollars in state funds held in his banks. In 1934 the *Sacramento Bee* and its reporter Arthur Waugh won a Pulitzer Prize for a series on how Pittman and other members of Nevada's congressional delegation supported federal court appointments for Wingfield allies Frank Norcross and William Woodburn, who would then have ruled on his impending bankruptcy.

That bankruptcy came in 1935. Depositors recovered a percentage of their funds, but many Nevadans never forgave him. Wingfield's political allies largely abandoned him; if they remained friends, his policy views no longer mattered. An old friend from the Tonopah-Goldfield boom, Noble Getchell, helped finance his return to mining, which restored part of his wealth, but Wingfield never again wielded power before his death in 1959. His name adorns numerous sites in Nevada, most notably a Reno park for which he donated the land to the city, and he remains perhaps the most powerful behind-the-scenes figure in Nevada's history.

The Rise of McCarran

The bank holiday occurred a week before Nevadans voted and became one of many factors helping Democrats. Roosevelt's coattails and the anger of voters whose savings sat in banks owned by the state's political boss, a Republican, figured to aid the ticket. Although the dam eased the Depression's pain in southern Nevada, many dam workers came to escape economic problems back home and had no desire to vote for the party they blamed for their woes.

The banking collapse lay in the future when state Democrats planned their campaign. Challenging Representative Samuel Arentz, James Scrugham faced the same problems he did running for reelection as governor in 1926—his big-spender image and Wingfield's opposition. Had Arentz not been allied with Wingfield, another line of attack might have presented itself: Scrugham had been governor when Cole and Malley embezzled state funds and had apparently been unaware of it; then he bought the *Nevada State Journal* from Boyle's widow and ended up publishing accounts of illegal actions that went on during his administration and Boyle's before that. Worse, Scrugham had mortgaged the paper to Wingfield.

Democrats displayed less concern about the Senate race, since Oddie seemed popular and basked in Wingfield's support. The most prominent Democrat in the primary seemed little more than a perennial candidate: McCarran. He won the right, many Nevadans assumed, to lose to Oddie. But the Depression, the GOP's resulting unpopularity, the influx of new residents, and Roosevelt combined to help him, with McCarran's ads featuring his name with the Democratic nominee's and the pledge of a "New Deal for Nevada." Coming the week before the election, the bank holiday may have sealed Oddie's fate: his most important supporter could be blamed for it, and his opponent had been one of Wingfield's leading critics.

Democrats swept Nevada in 1932, but McCarran won by the smallest margin of any statewide winner: 52–48 percent. McCarran later claimed he would have won anyway. That argument rang hollow, but he overcame a longtime enemy and joined another, Pittman, in the Senate. More important, all of the parts that would reengineer Nevada's economy, politics, culture, and society had fallen into place during the twentieth century's worst downturn. Nevada turned to a new economy based on tourism (the new gambling and divorce laws) and federal projects (highway construction, the Hawthorne depot, and, especially, Hoover Dam). A new US senator joined Pittman and fellow newcomer Scrugham to protect and expand their state, and eventually he would go well beyond them.

SUGGESTED READINGS

Arrigo, Anthony. *Imaging Hoover Dam: The Making of a Cultural Icon.* Reno: University of Nevada Press, 2014.

Dunar, Andrew, and Dennis McBride. *Building Hoover Dam: An Oral History.* Reno: University of Nevada Press, 2002.

Hiltzik, Michael. *Colossus: Hoover Dam and the Making of the American Century.* New York: Free Press, 2010.

Hundley, Norris, Jr. *The Great Thirst: Californians and Water, 1770s–1990s.* Berkeley: University of California Press, 1992.

———. *Water and the West: The Colorado River Compact and the Politics of Water in the American West.* Berkeley: University of California Press, 1975.

Kling, Dwayne. *The Rise of the Biggest Little City: An Encyclopedic History of Reno Gaming, 1931–1981.* Reno: University of Nevada Press, 2000.

McBride, Dennis. *In the Beginning: A History of Boulder City, Nevada.* Boulder City, NV: Boulder City Chamber of Commerce, 1981.

———. *Midnight on Arizona Street: The Secret Life of the Boulder Dam Hotel.* Boulder City, NV: Boulder City/Hoover Dam Museum, 1993.

Stevens, Joseph E. *Hoover Dam: An American Adventure.* Norman: University of Oklahoma Press, 1988.

Worster, Donald. *Under Western Skies: Nature and History in the American West.* New York: Oxford University Press, 1992.

11

The Federal Landscape, 1933-45

In the 1930s and 1940s, the New Deal and World War II shaped the modern American West and Nevada socially, economically, and politically by easing the region's dependence on mining and ranching and increasing its reliance on the federal government. By using the West for so many bases and projects, the federal government introduced more Americans to the West or encouraged them to migrate there, changing the population and unintentionally boosting the tourist economy westerners had been building. As historian Richard Lowitt wrote, "The New Deal offered the West an opportunity to transform itself." Nevada took advantage of it, with World War II completing the transformation.

The New Deal and Nevada

When Franklin Roosevelt took office on March 4, 1933, he declared, "This nation asks for action, and action now." As for what action, he said, "Take a method and try it. If it fails, admit it frankly, and try another. But by all means, try something." Nor did it hurt his popularity that one action pleased Nevadans and many other Americans: ending Prohibition enforcement under the Volstead Act and repealing the Eighteenth Amendment. As historian Russell Elliott said of his college days, "A number of downtown clubs in Reno began serving beer, and some university students became good customers." No other Nevada town had a university, but none lacked for customers at previously illegal establishments.

Historians point to two "New Deals," the first in 1933–34, passed mainly in the "First Hundred Days" of Roosevelt's administration, with the second, more liberal, New Deal from 1935 to 1938. During the latter, a recession struck in 1937, which liberals blamed on FDR's decision to cut government spending, while conservatives accused him of hostility to business. Whether Roosevelt spent too little or too much, the federal government and its powers grew, with New Deal programs falling into three overlapping categories: Relief, helping the unemployed and needy; Recovery, designed to restore a successful economy; and Reform, meant to avert any comparable collapse and alter the regulatory system and relationship between labor and capital that contributed to the Great Depression.

In the 1930s Nevada received more New Deal money per resident than any other state, partly from need, partly from figuring out how to obtain it. Democratic areas tended to benefit most from the New Deal, but several factors combined to help Nevada. Local leaders, especially Las Vegas mayor Ernie Cragin, sought funds for a variety of projects. More important, Nevada's congressional delegation enjoyed ample power, despite two of its members lacking seniority. Senators Key Pittman and Pat McCarran and Representative James Scrugham served on Appropriations Committees, while Pittman and McCarran sat on the Judiciary Committee. They could direct money toward their state and make deals with colleagues seeking federal dollars and help in confirming appointees as judges and marshals. When Democrats regained the Senate in 1933, Pittman became Foreign Relations Committee chair. As FDR tried to shift the nation from isolationism and toward greater interest in foreign affairs amid the rise of Nazism in Germany, fascism in Italy and Spain, and militarism in Japan, he had to please Pittman.

The Roosevelt administration's desire to please Nevada's leaders also reflected political realities and contradictions. FDR allowed states to administer many New Deal programs. State and local officials, especially in the South, bypassed African Americans in need of New Deal aid. Perhaps aware of FDR's need for support from southern Democrats who controlled Congress—and their western allies, including Pittman—African Americans became loyal Democrats, ending decades of Republican support in response to gratitude to the party of Lincoln for emancipation and support for civil rights. New Deal jobs favored men over women, especially married women, but with encouragement from First Lady Eleanor Roosevelt and appointees such as Secretary of Labor Frances Perkins, the federal government hired or gave relief to more women than ever before.

New Deal Programs

Nevada's needs varied by region. At the request of FDR aide and ally Harry Hopkins, journalist Lorena Hickok toured the West in 1933 and 1934. She deemed Nevada "a nice, quiet, simple place" and found southern Nevada booming, as well as Virginia City and its environs. Agriculture, she said, had suffered for several years, but fared better than the Great Plains, where the Dust Bowl wreaked havoc.

However it compared with elsewhere, Nevada welcomed benefits from relief programs in the New Deal's first year. In six years the Civilian Conservation Corps (CCC), created in April 1933, deployed about seven thousand Nevadans (and twenty-four thousand from out of state) ages eighteen to twenty-five in fifty-nine camps at Mount Charleston outside Las Vegas, Idlewild Park on the Truckee River, Mill Creek near Battle Mountain, and Westgate on Highway 50, among other places. Working for agencies as varied as the Bureau of Reclamation and the grazing service, they restored Fort Churchill, built roads, dug irrigation ditches, planted trees, fought soil erosion, and created trails in return for room, board, and monthly pay, which they spent in the nearest town and sent home to help their families. They worked on a resort in Lee Canyon near Las Vegas, Lake Mead National Recreation Area, and Valley of Fire, while the Panaca camp helped develop Kershaw-Ryan, Beaver Dam, and Cathedral Gorge State Parks. From November 1933 to April 1934, the Civilian Works Administration provided jobs for thousands painting schools, repairing roads, and putting up street signs and historic markers. It also enabled Las Vegas to extend sewer lines to new neighborhoods built in response to the boom the dam created.

When Congress passed the Emergency Relief Appropriation Act in 1935 to spend $5 billion in the next year, Nevadans leaped at it. The bill created the Works Progress Administration, soon the state's biggest employer. The WPA led to the hiring of artists to paint murals on public buildings and musicians to form city bands and give other performances. It employed Las Vegans to build a public golf course and a fish hatchery and provided men and material for the War Memorial Building, the closest the area had come to having a convention facility. The WPA also gave work to writers and researchers, with Nevada Historical Society founder and University of Nevada history professor Jeanne Weir supervising a WPA guide to Nevada that remains an important collection of information about the state. In addition to creating the brook and bridge in front of Reno's university at Manzanita Lake, the WPA and CCC teamed to develop Virginia Lake and its walking path and with the public health service on its Nevada Fly-Proof Privy Program, which aided rural areas by providing low-cost outhouses built to keep out insects.

The scope of New Deal projects and agencies could be staggering. Some, such as Social Security and the National Labor Relations Board, still affect the country. Road improvements led to highways long since repaved and improved. Just in 1937 the Public Works Administration (PWA) spent about $1.2 million in Nevada for street, electrical, and school projects in Las Vegas, Sparks, Ely, and Elko, Fallon's government building, and Lund's waterworks. In Nevada the New Deal built 50 bridges, 133 public buildings, and 142 miles of new roads and renovations on 900 miles more, grammar schools for Alamo and Wadsworth, and waterworks for Mina and Carlin. In 1936 PWA funding and CCC workers finished Rye Patch Dam and Reservoir, northeast of Lovelock; unfortunately, the irrigation project also flooded prehistoric sites, destroying archaeological evidence.

The Indian New Deal

Roosevelt's presidency also led to a "red new deal." After a federal report in 1928 decried conditions for Native Americans, Herbert Hoover increased funding for the Bureau of Indian Affairs. Roosevelt shared his desire for reform. Harold Ickes, his secretary of the interior, appointed Native rights advocate John Collier commissioner of Indian affairs. He largely designed the Indian Reorganization Act of 1934, which repealed the Dawes Act of 1887 and allowed tribes to organize, complete with constitutions and bylaws so that they could have more independence from the BIA. Given the choice, most Native Nevadans followed the act's provisions, with the exception of the Fallon Paiute-Shoshone; the Reno-Sparks Indian Colony had been a neighborhood that included various Nevada tribal groups until organizing under the law. In turn, participating tribes gained access to federal funds and loans to buy livestock and equipment, evaluate soil on rangelands, and learn newer farming and ranching techniques. Since the administration and Congress underfunded these programs, Collier worked with other agencies.

Although some agencies discriminated against them or favored those living on reservations, Nevada's Native Americans benefited in numerous ways. Pyramid Lake Paiutes organized and passed new rules on fishing to protect their food sources at the lake. The CCC's Indian Division set up a program to improve reservation lands, with the Duck Valley Western Shoshone building a fence to separate their cattle from herds outside the reservation and interior fences to protect soil from erosion and overgrazing. A dam built on the Owyhee River helped Duck Valley double its alfalfa output in four years. The WPA aided basket makers and other artists. The Nevada Emergency Relief Administration, the federal agency's state branch, helped Native women obtain housekeeping jobs. Another New Deal effort integrated Native Americans into local schools. The BIA failed in an effort to create a new reservation for Shoshone dispersed throughout central Nevada, although some moved to the new Reese River Reservation and formed tribal governments. The bureau also enjoyed mixed success with Southern Paiutes: those on the Moapa Reservation adopted none of the newer, more mechanized farming techniques, but a CCC project helped irrigate their croplands, and another improved the Las Vegas colony's water supply.

Yet in Nevada the Indian New Deal ran into trouble. In 1934 Collier named Alida Bowler to head the Carson Indian Agency, which oversaw reservations and colonies throughout all but northeastern Nevada. She and the bureau faced opposition from McCarran, who introduced a bill to keep Nevada's Natives from organizing. Other congressmen blocked him, as did the Pyramid Lake Tribal Council when he sought to deny them the right to counsel. Taking the side of Italian families who built an irrigation system across Pyramid Lake reservation land, failed in efforts to buy the land, and then faced eviction, McCarran accused Bowler of influencing the Paiutes. He eventually forced her transfer and her successor's removal when he obeyed a federal court decision and ejected the settlers.

Mining and the New Deal

Democratic victories in 1932 gave Pittman the clout to boost Nevada's silver industry, with help from other congressmen from mining states. Roosevelt named him one of the American representatives at the World Monetary and Economic Conference in London in 1933. Pittman's alcoholism reportedly caused problems there, but he accomplished a lot for Nevada. The eight nations present resolved to use silver coins in place of devalued paper currency, avoid actions to reduce silver prices, and stop melting coins. The

United States agreed to team with Canada, Mexico, Peru, and Australia to buy thirty-five million ounces of silver annually, with the United States responsible for more than two-thirds of that amount. Then mining state colleagues helped Pittman persuade Roosevelt to accept the deal, meaning the federal government would buy America's silver production until the end of 1937—a boon for Nevada.

Pittman's power benefited Nevada's silver industry in other ways. In June 1934 Roosevelt signed Pittman's Silver Purchase Act, mandating that the Treasury Department maintain a reserve of one ounce of silver for every three ounces of gold. To do so, Pittman navigated between the treasury secretary, who opposed the measure, and western colleagues seeking a larger spike in federal purchases. When the act's opponents sought its repeal, Pittman blocked them; when other silverites wanted more favorable legislation and tried to use a Treasury Department investigation as a bludgeon to achieve their goal, Pittman worked with Roosevelt's aides to delay the probe. When the 1934 measure ran its course, Pittman pushed through a new act in July 1939 that ensured continued subsidies of silver.

Unquestionably, the New Deal helped Nevada mining. Silver production rose 166 percent from 1933 to 1934, and unemployed miners and mill workers regained jobs in Nevada and throughout the West. Tonopah, Eureka, and Pioche never regained their old glory but enjoyed a boomlet. The National Industrial Recovery Act included a code meant to raise and stabilize copper prices and ensure better pay and conditions for miners. After the act's adoption in 1934, revenue from Ely more than doubled in the next year, and again over the next two years, pushing Nevada's mineral production in 1937 to its highest level in a decade, although the Rio Tinto mine and boomtown bloomed and faded in less than two decades. As the US economy lost steam in late 1937 and 1938, so did copper—and Nevada mining: the end of Virginia & Truckee service in 1938 attested to the Comstock's failure to rebound, and a 1939 fire shut down one of Tonopah's most productive mines. But in 1939 the Strategic Minerals Act required the US Bureau of Mines and US Geological Survey to seek new mineral sources and provide scientific information to prospectors. WPA and PWA measures helped, as would world events that, for the moment, seemed far beyond America's borders.

Agriculture and the New Deal

Just as mining rebounded in the 1930s, so did agriculture. The collapse of George Wingfield's banks resulted partly from loans to ranchers unable to repay them, and enough of them joined Wingfield in bankruptcy to create a new class of Nevada investors: eastern and California businessmen, snapping up their holdings. A drought in 1934 made matters worse, as did the time it took for New Deal programs to have an effect. Once they did, revenue doubled from 1932 to 1940. Farmers in Truckee Meadows, Wadsworth, and Fernley benefited from five hundred thousand dollars the New Deal spent pumping water from Lake Tahoe to the Truckee River, while another two million dollars went toward wells and windmills on public lands in Eureka, Esmeralda, Lander, Mineral, Nye, and White Pine Counties. Other programs bought cattle and sheep to feed other parts of the country; the Agricultural Adjustment Administration and the Soil Conservation Service also helped.

Designed to help agriculture and protect against another version of the Dust Bowl, the Taylor Grazing Act of 1934 proved unpopular with Nevada ranchers. The bill and later amendments created grazing districts for federal agencies to manage and limited grazing on federal land to protect grasses used for foraging. It set up advisory boards, which large stockmen often controlled rather than smaller ranches, and imposed fees for grazing. Ranchers objected and McCarran fought it, endearing himself to rural Nevadans and earning an exaggerated reputation as anti–New Deal. The failure to fund the grazing service enough to monitor herds eased Nevadans' pain, and in 1946 consolidating it with the General Land Office gave them a new foe: the Bureau of Land Management.

The federal expansion required the state to provide new and additional services. In 1933 the State Emergency Relief and Construction Committee, which Governor Fred Balzar created in August 1932 to seek federal aid for agriculture, became part of the new Civil Works Administration, a New Deal agency funding agricultural and other programs. The state also started the Nevada Livestock Production Credit Association to help farmers and ranchers pursuing financial help, and the University of Nevada's Cooperative Extension Service expanded its services.

Finishing the Dam

Calling the dam "the eighth wonder of the world" made perfect sense. It drew the kind of attention that fitted the description. Celebrities brought it additional notice with their visits, with tourist volume topping 265,000 in 1934 and Will Rogers writing, "It's the biggest thing that's ever been done with water since Noah made the flood look foolish." Las Vegas's economy benefited from this interest because it provided services—legal and illegal—unavailable in Boulder City.

As Roosevelt took office, Hoover Dam construction entered a new phase. New interior secretary Harold Ickes changed the name to Boulder Dam due to his dislike for Hoover and debatable claim that his role in the project had been, "at best, very casual." Ickes ordered Six Companies to stop occasionally paying dam workers in scrip—workers disliked it, and Las Vegas merchants who lost business as a result to the Six Companies store hated it even more—and sent officials to investigate potential violations of labor laws. Six Companies largely ignored his order to hire African Americans in greater numbers, and city manager Sims Ely continued to refuse to let African Americans live in Boulder City. Ely also tried to stop bars and brothels from operating outside the city's gates, but politicians knew their operator well and blocked Ely's efforts.

Another new phase shifted the emphasis from diverting the Colorado to erecting the dam. That meant pouring concrete in thirty thousand blocks up to five feet high and fifty feet square, in 230 columns. This required two plants at the site and moving a twenty-ton bucket of concrete across the canyon every seventy-eight seconds. Workers built two spillways and penstocks to move water from four intake towers to the turbines to produce hydroelectric power. Seven months after starting, on January 7, 1934, Superintendent Frank Crowe's men poured their millionth cubic yard of concrete. In February 1935 they closed the diversion tunnels, and the water rose behind the dam until it reached the intake towers.

With new jobs and new requirements came new dangers, and Six Companies claimed to want a safer workplace. One oddity helped workers: Arizona offered better workmen's compensation. When construction began, Arizona funded its program five times better than Nevada (although by completion the difference fell substantially), so workers usually claimed injuries occurred in Arizona. A federal investigation faulted Six Companies' safety record, but little changed. Then, in July 1935, a supervisor announced an earlier start to the workday so that Six Companies would no longer pay for the workers' thirty-minute lunch period. The Central Labor Council, affiliated with the more conservative American Federation of Labor, responded with a walkout; Crowe reversed the decision, but when the workers also demanded pay hikes, Six Companies broke that strike.

As the dam neared completion, Roosevelt arrived to dedicate it. Ickes saw it as the first step toward a West of small farms irrigated and powered by federal dams. Roosevelt saw more. "I came, I saw, and I was conquered . . . ," he told ten thousand onlookers and a national radio audience on September 30, 1935. "Ten years ago, the place where we are gathered was an unpeopled, forbidding desert. The transformation wrought here is a twentieth-century marvel"—a tribute to Americans, especially westerners, who adapted to, improved, and damaged the environment to suit their needs. He praised its completion two years early, pointing to the need for jobs as the reason, rather than Six Companies and "Hurry Up" Crowe. Then workers finished the site, and Six Companies handed control to the federal government on March 1, 1936, complete with the southwestern interior and art deco exterior planned by architect Gordon Kaufmann and Norwegian sculptor Oskar Hansen's bronze *Winged Figures of the Republic* statue and terrazzo star map greeting workers and visitors alike to the dam.

On September 30, 1935, President Franklin D. Roosevelt dedicated Hoover Dam and explained its historical significance to a nationwide radio audience. Courtesy of Special Collections, University Libraries, University of Nevada, Las Vegas.

The dam had intended and unintended consequences. To protect, expand, and manage the state's claim to water and dam-generated electricity, Nevada altered the Colorado River Commission, created to promote the river's development and the dam's construction. The firms constituting Six Companies—especially Kaiser and Bechtel—became major government contractors and built bigger dams in years to come. In October 1936 the first dam-generated power traveled to Los Angeles, contributing to its growth since. The lake behind the dam, later named for Reclamation commissioner Elwood Mead, became part of the first national recreation area (Pittman sought to transfer land to Nevada for a state park, but the federal government kept control). Lake Mead also shifted billions of tons of water to a new place, affecting the environment and geology as far away as Mexico, whose share of Colorado River water declined substantially. Boulder City continued to house federal workers but shrank before developing an additional role as a suburb of Las Vegas. Water from the dam later sustained Las Vegas, but it also prompted lawsuits over water allocation between Arizona and California that lasted into the 1960s. The population of the seven states that signed the compact grew exponentially, thanks to their access to water or power or both. As author Michael Hiltzik wrote, "Hoover Dam simultaneously built the West and confined it in a straitjacket": westerners depended on resources that might prove unsustainable.

State Politics and Policy

Just as federal offices went Democratic in 1932, so did state offices. Democrats enjoyed unprecedented rule: no Republican won statewide office in Nevada during Roosevelt's presidency (1933–45), and most competitive races took place in Democratic primaries. Republicans in particular suffered an important loss when Governor Fred Balzar died in 1934. Acting governor Morley Griswold sought a term of his own, but lost to Democrat Richard Kirman, a Reno banker and onetime mayor, and Elko attorney E. P. "Ted" Carville followed him into office for two terms in 1938. The lone exception, the state senate, became Republican in 1940, due partly to the "little federal plan" that gave each Nevada county one state senator; northern and rural counties leaned Republican in legislative races.

Although New Deal programs required administration, Nevadans remained committed to small government. In the late 1930s, under Kirman's leadership, Nevada began promoting itself as "One Sound State" because it had no income or inheritance taxes, enhancing its appeal to wealthy businessmen from elsewhere and emphasizing its libertarianism and independence (with a population of just over 110,000 in 1940, some Nevadans proclaimed, "One square man per one square mile"). Reno's First National Bank and the *Nevada State Journal* published a pamphlet sent to 10,000 possible migrants. It cited yeast company heir Max Fleischmann, who had already moved to Nevada, and others followed. Automaker Erret L. Cord, like Fleischmann, bought land and engaged in philanthropy and political king making. Bing Crosby bought ranches in the Elko area, mainly out of a love for land and horses. Although the campaign helped expand Nevada's population, the *San Francisco Chronicle* complained, "South Carolina achieved secession by firing on Fort Sumter. Nevada puts herself out alone by firing on Fort Taxation. . . . These people just do not belong in the United States."

Yet Nevada could be reform minded. In 1939, at state engineer Alfred Merritt Smith's behest, legislators passed a law enabling his office to regulate the pumping of underground water. With Las Vegas's dependence on aquifers, growing populace, and lack of conservation, the combination of state intervention, local measures, and federal aid helped southern Nevada use more Lake Mead water and preserve its existing supply. Making this step more important, the population and tourist influx contributed to a rapid drop in the local water table. Southern Nevadans also replaced the railroad's Las Vegas Land & Water Company with the Las Vegas Valley Water District in 1948, bringing newer, better management to bear on the problem than Union Pacific officials had displayed.

Even municipal politics became caught up in the New Deal. Las Vegas mayor Ernie Cragin lost his reelection bid for refusing to back efforts to get New Deal money to fund public power but, critics said, taking federal help to fund a political "machine." Leonard Arnett, his successor, resigned over declining support for public power, which peaked before the 1937 national economic downturn hurt the Las Vegas economy, and the local electric company and its allies mounted opposition. City government became highly controversial—at one point, after a series of squabbles, Las Vegas actually wound up with two city commissions seated and making decisions. Cragin's return in 1943 restored order, as did voters' support for hiring a city manager to operate government more professionally—a throwback to the Progressive belief in good government and management.

Pittman and McCarran

Relations between Pittman and McCarran, and their followers, roiled Nevada politics. McCarran remained a lone wolf, often uncooperative and independent minded, but he also wanted power, especially over federal patronage. Roosevelt favored the senior senator, Pittman, as would normally be the case. But McCarran won attention for opposing a few New Deal programs, and his isolationism—a far cry from Roosevelt's views—helped him back home. He also battled over appointments, most notably federal judgeships for Wingfield's old allies. McCarran won a fight over naming a US attorney; one of his supporters, Carville, received the job and gained a strong reputation for fighting corruption that helped him win the governor's race in 1938.

That year McCarran faced a potentially difficult battle for reelection. In 1937 Roosevelt had become so fed up with the US Supreme Court declaring New Deal programs unconstitutional that he proposed "the Court-packing plan": appointing a new federal judge for each jurist over age seventy, which might have expanded the court to fifteen members. Opposing the bill openly and dramatically, McCarran helped ensure its defeat and prompted FDR to seek his defeat. The national party tried to help McCarran's challenger, Albert Hilliard, and Roosevelt snubbed McCarran as he traveled across the state. For his part, knowing the president's popularity in Nevada, McCarran made it a point to criticize his advisers—not the man himself. Ultimately, Roosevelt's effort to defeat McCarran and other critics failed, and the Democratic senator cruised to a second term.

In 1940 came McCarran's long-awaited opportunity to take over the state party. Pittman sought a sixth term amid rumors that McCarran wanted Carville to challenge him in the primary; in fact, that relationship had soured, and McCarran preferred a weakened Pittman. Aging, ailing, and alcoholic, Pittman collapsed three days before the election and died five days after his reelection. Although rumors that Pittman died earlier and Democrats kept his body on ice had no foundation, few who knew him expected him to live much longer. In turn, as governor and thus responsible for naming Pittman's successor until the 1942 election, Carville faced ample pressure. Allegedly with McCarran's blessing, he chose a Mormon Democrat from Las Vegas, Berkeley Bunker, the assembly speaker, although both Key's younger brother Vail Pittman and politicians closer to McCarran had wanted the position and blamed Carville for the choice. Seeing Bunker as a threat for several reasons—his youth (age thirty-four), ties to Las Vegas and Carville (he headed the governor's southern Nevada campaign in 1938), and Mormonism, among others—McCarran determined to marginalize him.

Harold and Harrah

In the 1930s and early 1940s, Nevada's gambling industry expanded, due partly to wartime travel restrictions but, more important, to changes in California, where officials sought to clean up their state. In 1934 Californians elected Earl Warren, one of the country's most respected prosecutors, attorney general; he targeted gambling ships off the Southern California coast for closure, realizing they allowed wagering before reaching international waters, as well as card games and bingo on land. In 1938 Los Angelenos recalled a corrupt mayor and replaced him with Fletcher Bowron, who shut down illegal casinos. In both cases, many of the operators and employees headed to Las Vegas, although some went to Reno.

In the 1930s two of Reno's most significant gaming figures arrived from California and shaped the industry. In 1936 Harold Smith came from Northern California and opened a small Virginia Street casino, Harold's Club. Soon he made news with roulette played with live mice until cheating became a problem. At a time when many Americans saw gambling as something to be tolerated rather than promoted, he and his father, Raymond "Pappy" Smith, banked on publicity. They hired Thomas Wilson's advertising agency, which designed the "Harold's Club or Bust" campaign, with a covered wagon that traveled the country dispersing signs reminiscent of Gold Rush migrants; Nevadans serving in World War II took the signs around the world (Antarctica even hosts a sign, "8,452 Miles to Harold's Club"). The agency produced a series of "Pioneer Nevada" stories, later published as a book, emphasizing Old West themes. As Pulitzer Prize–winning historian Daniel Boorstin later wrote, the Smiths "aimed to produce a Woolworth's of the gambling business. Harolds Club was as different from the old gambling casino as the five-and-ten-cent store was different from the elite specialty shop."

Unlike others from Southern California, the other arrival, William Fisk Harrah, chose Reno. In 1939, joined by his father, he opened a club on Douglas Alley and soon expanded the bingo parlor to include a Virginia

The Smith family revolutionized the gaming industry and its promotion with Harold's Club in Reno. Courtesy of Special Collections, University of Nevada–Reno Library.

Street entrance and then added a casino consisting of a blackjack game, a craps table, and several slot machines. Harrah's emphasis on service and cleanliness drew a growing clientele, and his casino space expanded in turn. Also, many Reno properties at the time apparently cheated customers, but Harrah considered honesty the best policy (and knew the odds favored the house) and even encouraged stricter state gaming regulation. He embarked on such innovations as marketing studies, improved slot machines, keno, bus trips to Reno from California, and billboard advertising. Harrah and the Smiths revolutionized Reno's gaming industry, partly by promoting their clean games and family-oriented approaches to business, although older operations like the Bank Club and the Petricciani family's Palace Club still thrived.

Las Vegas: A "Frontier" Town

As Warren and Bowron shut down ships and back rooms, California's influence on Las Vegas grew until it became, as a *Los Angeles Times* columnist wrote, "the infant prodigy of our immediate hinterland." Many Southern California casino operators and employees headed for Las Vegas up Highway 91, paved and widened thanks to New Deal funding. Some had already arrived: in 1930 J. Kell Houssels Sr. invested in the Las Vegas Club and Boulder Club, among other early properties. Some took their time: Sam Boyd left his dealing job on a gambling ship for Hawaii, then arrived in 1941; Tony Cornero, operator of one of the ships after his brothers' foray into Las Vegas with the Meadows, waited until World War II before trying to open the Rex, named for his boat, inside the Apache Hotel. Others migrated more quickly, bringing professionalism to Las Vegas gambling— and, with the Chamber of Commerce, a marketing campaign to define Las Vegas thematically, decades before "theming" became popular there.

Las Vegas never promoted itself as western until the 1930s, when it issued postcards proclaiming, "Still a Frontier Town." As historian John Findlay wrote, "Las Vegas packaged the regional past and marketed it as a commodity essential to the promotion of their town to visitors." Its Chamber of Commerce named Fremont Street's casino district "Glitter Gulch," combining neon and the Old West. Carnival operator Clyde Zerby teamed with local leader James Cashman Sr. to start the Elks Helldorado western festival with rodeo and beard-growing contest, to draw tourists and unify

The annual Helldorado helped cement a sense of community in Las Vegas, served as another tourist attraction, and contributed to the town's promotion of itself as a frontier outpost. Courtesy of Special Collections, University Libraries, University of Nevada, Las Vegas.

locals (and emulate Reno, which first hosted its rodeo in 1919 and revived it as part of "Pony Express Days" in 1932). In 1939 Los Angeles vice squad captain Guy McAfee, seeing opportunity in the industries his job required him to clean up, left behind his Sunset Strip nightclub to buy the Pair-O-Dice on Highway 91. He turned it into the 91 Club in time for Las Vegas to tie itself to Hollywood. When Ria Langham Gable came to Las Vegas to establish residency to divorce her husband, Clark Gable, Las Vegas publicized her presence and gained notice as a celebrity hangout.

McAfee also joined in westernizing downtown. He opened the Frontier Club and, in 1946, teamed with other investors to build the Golden Nugget, a gambling hall with a Barbary Coast theme. His Southern California friends opened the Pioneer Club, later with neon cowboy Vegas Vic announcing, "Howdy, podner." In 1945 Wilbur Clark, another refugee from the gambling ships who had leased the Northern Club from the Stockers, renamed it the Monte Carlo, a popular name among old western bars. A few blocks away, former gambling-ship operator Marion Hicks debuted his El Cortez in November 1941 with a floor show, a western name, and ranch-style architecture. Eventually, Hicks sold the hotel-casino to another migrant from the West, Bugsy Siegel—who had engaged in a great deal of illegal activity, but not gambling, at least in California.

The Rise of the Strip and Organized Crime

The original resorts on what became known as the Las Vegas Strip fitted the western theme. In April 1941 California hotelman Thomas Hull opened the El Rancho Vegas to accompany his properties in Fresno and San Bernardino. He hired a Southern California architectural firm, McAllister & McAllister, to design a sixty-five-room low-rise with bungalows and western interiors. Once Hull expressed interest in building, James Cashman and Robert Griffith, representing the Chamber of Commerce, tried to interest him in a site closer to downtown, but Hull insisted on the highway just south of the city limits to avoid higher municipal fees and taxes. Late in 1942, a second resort joined Hull's: the Last Frontier, owned by movie theater chain owner R. E. Griffith and run by his nephew, architect William Moore. Advertising "The Old West in Modern Splendor," their property boasted wagon wheel–shaped light fixtures, cow horns on the bed frames, horseback and stagecoach rides, and the Last Frontier Village, a theme park of Old West memorabilia (now housed at the Clark County Museum).

But the evolution began just before and during World War II. Bugsy Siegel came to Hollywood in the 1930s to muscle in on movie unions and other avenues for organized crime and with the hope of becoming an actor. At some point, Siegel and Meyer Lansky agreed to invest in hotel-casinos, and they and Moe Sedway sought control of race wires. Other Mob figures joined Siegel and Sedway in Las Vegas, including Gus Greenbaum from Phoenix and Davie Berman and "Icepick Willie" Alderman from Minneapolis. Siegel tried to buy the El Rancho Vegas from Hull, who sold it, but not to him. Several mobsters wound up running the El Cortez until Houssels bought it in 1946.

As World War II wound down, Hollywood publisher and nightclub owner Billy Wilkerson began building a hotel-casino, the Flamingo, on the Strip. At some point, Siegel took over. Whether Wilkerson originated the Flamingo, as seems likely, or served as a front for Siegel and other gangsters, Siegel opened the Strip's first luxury resort on December 26, 1946. The Flamingo paled in comparison with modern resorts, costing six million dollars to build—and while wartime and postwar shortages had an effect, that price would have been lower without Siegel's managerial incompetence, which encouraged cost overruns and double billing; he or his girlfriend Virginia Hill, or both, may have stolen a million dollars themselves.

The rest of the story reached mythic proportions. The Flamingo opened before its hotel's completion, drew minimal business, closed, and reopened. As the resort began to show signs of profit, Siegel died of gunshot wounds on June 20, 1947, at Hill's Beverly Hills bungalow. Speculation has focused on various Mob hit men, sent to kill Siegel over the worsening of his violent temper, the Flamingo's failure to pay off its investors, rumors that Siegel stole money, his treatment of Hill, and his personal debts. Greenbaum, Sedway, and Berman led the group that took over operations, arriving, as Lansky biographer Robert Lacey put it, "like generals mopping up after a coup."

Beyond Siegel: Building a Resort Industry

Thanks in part to the Strip's growth, prominent entertainers began performing more often in Nevada. Newt Crumley had been the first to import big stars to Elko's Commercial Hotel, paying Ted Lewis, known for the song "Me and My Shadow," and his orchestra twelve thousand dollars for an eight-night stay, and then bringing in the Dorsey brothers, the Andrews

Sisters, and others. Other casinos featured smaller lounges, but Strip hotels opened with larger showrooms, including dancers and showgirls—one of whom, Maxine Lewis, became entertainment director at several Las Vegas properties. In 1944, at the Last Frontier, she hired a pianist who remained a fixture for four decades: Liberace. The next year the El Rancho Vegas featured the Las Vegas debut of Sammy Davis Jr., who headlined on the Strip even longer.

Expansion of the Strip and organized crime had other effects. In 1945 state officials agreed they could no longer rely on local jurisdictions to investigate and license operators. The legislature passed measures requiring all gaming license applicants to go before the Nevada Tax Commission. They also imposed a 1 percent tax on gross revenues from gaming. Governor Carville refused to sign the bill but let it become law, arguing that "the wiser course would have been to avoid this type of taxation, and obtain a just contribution from the gambling business by imposing a higher license fee"—and apparently believing that taxing casinos directly would encourage their involvement in state politics. Hired as Tax Commission secretary, Robbins Cahill essentially became a one-man regulatory system—in other words, despite his abilities, not enough to do the job.

Leaders throughout Nevada also foresaw the future possibilities of tourism and gambling. In 1944 radio station owner Maxwell Kelch became head of the Las Vegas Chamber of Commerce and established the "Live Wire Fund": each chamber member would contribute 1–5 percent of annual gross receipts, and local casino resorts pledged to provide matching funds. With eighty-four thousand dollars raised in the first year and much more to follow, Las Vegas began to market itself more thoroughly and professionally, hiring major national advertising agencies. That year Harvey Gross moved from Sacramento to Stateline, opened a small casino on Lake Tahoe's south shore, and adopted the popular western theme, calling it Harvey's Wagon Wheel—another property catering to Californians.

Trouble Overseas

While the domestic economy worried most Americans, international issues became a source of concern. Germany rearmed and Adolf Hitler expanded east into Austria and parts of Czechoslovakia. Under Benito Mussolini, Italy waged an imperial war in Africa, conquering Ethiopia, while Fascists under Generalissimo Francisco Franco defeated Communists for power in

Spain. Japan invaded China in 1937, temporarily helping to unify US ally Chiang Kai-shek, a nationalist dictator, and Mao Tse-tung, leader of the Chinese Communists. Isolationists preferred to ignore these issues, and, as Senate Foreign Relations chair until his death in 1940, Pittman emphasized Asian issues over European ones, possibly out of concern about China's role as a leading silver importer. When Hitler's forces invaded Poland, World War II began in September 1939.

European warfare affected politics and the economy nationally and in Nevada. Roosevelt backed the first peacetime military draft and the Lend-Lease program to aid England after it became the last western European bastion against Hitler. When Hitler and Joseph Stalin signed the Nazi-Soviet Pact in 1939, Americans targeted communism in the "Little Red Scare," a successor to the "Great" scare of 1919–20. McCarran won attention for trying to derail Roosevelt's appointment of American Civil Liberties Union cofounder Felix Frankfurter to the Supreme Court over his associations. The German invasion of the Soviet Union in 1941 tempered American opposition to communism for the time being.

On December 7, 1941, everything changed. That morning Japan bombed the American naval base at Pearl Harbor in Hawaii. The next day Roosevelt asked Congress to declare war on Japan. Germany followed suit on behalf of its ally, and the United States faced war in Europe and Asia. As FDR put it, he switched from "Dr. New Deal" to "Dr. Win the War." Nevada switched, too. Two years later the *San Francisco Chronicle* announced, "The second gold rush has hit the West Coast." Wartime spending just in California topped thirty-five billion dollars, as shipyards and aircraft plants became major employers. Nearly half of the fifteen million Americans who served in the military spent part of their war in the trans-Mississippi West, and some of those people and their money found their way to Nevada.

Military Bases

Long before the war, preparing for inevitable American involvement led to military bases around the state. Several Nevada towns began turning into what historian Roger Lotchin calls a "martial metropolis": cities built on and with military aid, thanks partly to surrounding federal land. In October 1940 Las Vegas offered the Army Air Corps use of its municipal airport, which belonged to Western Air Express until a federal grant helped the city buy the facility. The War Department added new runways and announced plans for a gunnery school, including a million-acre shooting range that tripled in size by the war's end. In October 1941 the Las Vegas Army Air Corps Gunnery School opened. By May 1942 it graduated classes of four thousand pilots and gunners every six weeks, and thirteen thousand men and women worked and trained there and at the nearby Indian Springs base by 1945, with several hundred more at Camp Williston, built in Boulder City at McCarran's behest to protect the dam from sabotage. They spent their payrolls on and off the base, aiding the economy in Las Vegas and the community closest to the base, North Las Vegas, which expanded rapidly. Construction and paving contractors benefited from the need to build housing and maintain runways.

Other Nevada communities benefited from military bases. Needing a facility to train flyers, the US Navy took over a Fallon airfield it later renamed for Fallon's Bruce Van Voorhis, a Congressional Medal of Honor recipient killed in action in the South Pacific. From 1942 until its

Fallon Naval Air Station opened in World War II and became an important part of that community's life. This photo shows the bomb target for a B-19. Courtesy of Special Collections, University of Nevada–Reno Library.

deactivation in 1945, the Reno Army Air Base trained signal companies and then radio operators and navigators. After the base reopened the air force named it for Croston Stead, a Reno native killed at the base on a training mission. Work on Tonopah Army Air Field resulted in 1940 from cooperation between several agencies: the Interior Department transferred the land to the War Department, and the Civil Aeronautics Administration paid for it partly with WPA funds. The base opened in 1942 to train bombers, gunners, and especially pilots (including Chuck Yeager, who later broke the sound barrier), accommodating up to sixty-five hundred military and civilian workers at a time.

The military affected Nevada in other ways. Hawthorne's naval ammunition depot and its civilian staff expanded. Military branches installed flight strips at Battle Mountain and Owyhee and a gunnery range in the Black Rock Desert, barring these lands to ranchers, miners, and Native Americans, some of whom had used them for generations. Airmen stationed at a large base in Wendover, Utah, regularly visited Elko, Ely, and other nearby Nevada towns as they trained for the mission that dropped the atomic bomb on Japan. All of these installations aided the economy of nearby towns and attracted future tourists and residents.

Basic Magnesium

Another defense project affected several areas and industries in Nevada. In the 1930s Cleveland businessman Howard Eells sent geologists to Gabbs in Nye County to look for manganese, the ore needed for magnesium, which served as an igniter. When they found deposits containing about 70 million tons, Eells bought the mineral rights and began shipments to his company, Basic Refractories. As England fought the Nazis in 1941, Eells allied with a British magnesium firm and sought a factory to refine his product closer to the manganese deposits. With support from Nevada's congressional delegation—McCarran in particular, along with Bunker and Scrugham—the federal government planned a complex southeast of Las Vegas, about 350 miles from Gabbs.

Eells's company, now called Basic Magnesium, Inc., received federal aid that boosted Nevada's economy. BMI hired thousands, peaking at 13,000 workers. The federal government improved the Las Vegas–Reno highway so that Basic could transport material more easily and built water and electrical lines from the dam to the plant. Also, the US Defense Plant

The Basic Magnesium plant in Henderson made a major contribution to the military in World War II and later provided southern Nevada's industrial base, in addition to promoting a large migration of African Americans to the area. Courtesy of Special Collections, University Libraries, University of Nevada, Las Vegas.

Corporation (DPC), a Reconstruction Finance Corporation subsidiary, reached an agreement with Eells: it would build the plant and own it, the land, and the equipment and pay employee salaries; he would generate 33.6 million pounds of magnesium annually, handle hiring and firing, and receive one dollar per ton. In just over two full years, the plant produced 166 million pounds of magnesium that it sent to factories in Southern California, another area benefiting from the defense boom the war triggered.

Eells wanted to house his workers in Boulder City and control them as Six Companies did, but the Bureau of Reclamation said no and the federal government agreed in November 1941 to build Basic Townsite. To appease Las Vegans who wanted the workers to live in their town but lacked the infrastructure to serve them, McCarran pushed the DPC into giving Las Vegas more building permits. Basic Townsite resembled Boulder City as a company town, offering community life but with fewer rules and no dictator to rival Sims Ely. The African American presence also distinguished

Basic from Boulder City. About 250,000 African Americans left the South during the war as part of a migration to seek jobs, often in western defense plants. Basic recruited hundreds of workers from the depressed mill towns of Tallulah, Louisiana, and Fordyce, Arkansas, but forced them to live in federally built Carver Park, complete with a segregated grammar school and recreation hall. Eventually, Carver Park, Victory Village, and other Basic housing and businesses formed the backbone of the city named for the RFC's chairman, a former US senator from Nevada, Charles Belknap Henderson.

The Home Front

Nevadans approached the war with unity and patriotism. In 1940, the day draft registration began, Governor Carville declared a state holiday, businesses closed, and the American Legion and Veterans of Foreign Wars sponsored parades. During the war, as their men and women joined the military, Nevadans eagerly participated in wheatless and meatless days, rationed gasoline, planted victory gardens, and formed county defense councils to save rubber and metals such as aluminum and iron.

The war's economic impact went beyond the military. Agricultural revenue doubled from 1940 to 1945; the trans-Mississippi West generated two-thirds of the nation's wheat, fruit, and vegetables and half of its grain. Nevadans benefited, from alfalfa and cantaloupe growers near Fallon to Moapa Valley farmers and ranchers from Elko to Pahrump. Aided by the federal Metals Reserve Corporation, mining production topped fifty-six million dollars in 1943, with copper, zinc, and lead outstripping gold and silver in importance and tungsten (for hardening steel and electrical purposes) in Mineral and Humboldt Counties receiving a boost; Lincoln County's mining economy revived, with investors building a mill at Caselton, near Pioche. Construction boomed, from road building to developing the Huntridge housing tract at the then south end of Las Vegas. Education benefited and contributed: after two new buildings in two decades (and the legislature spent almost twice as much on the new gymnasium as on the engineering complex), University of Nevada faculty helped train forces at a nearby base, and when the war ended the school bought army surplus buildings that it used for decades.

The war also affected gambling and prostitution. Las Vegas imposed a 2:00 A.M. curfew on casino operations amid complaints that Basic's absentee rate outstripped any other wartime plant. The military pressed municipal leaders to close red-light districts because men stationed at local bases or at nearby ones in California, Arizona, and Utah visited and then returned to camp with unpleasant medical effects. As Ronald James wrote in his history of the Comstock, "Lest Hitler's victory be hung around Virginia City's neck, its houses of ill repute closed," and Tonopah shut down its row of brothels. Reno's chief of police reported no city statute allowed him to close the Stockade, the city's red-light district, but in May 1942 the combination of federal, county, and city authorities forced the area's closure. Block 16 in downtown Las Vegas had operated as a red-light district since 1909, but during World War II the military objected to it and a real estate developer who began buying property in the area wanted to eliminate the brothels. When the city acted in 1942, Block 16 hosted a closing-night party, and then the brothels moved south of town on Boulder Highway. Meanwhile, city health officials reported a decline in the rate of sexually transmitted diseases.

Other relationships took a different course in wartime Nevada. The divorce and marriage trades, especially in Reno, mushroomed amid publicity from films like *The Women*, the popularity of Woody Guthrie's song "The Philadelphia Lawyer" ("Way out in Reno, Nevada / Where romance blooms and fades," it began), and dude ranches. Statewide, divorces tripled from 1940 to 1944, and marriages more than doubled from 1939 to 1942, climbing to eighteen thousand in 1945. Las Vegas similarly benefited from publicity about the ease with which couples could unite or disunite, travel limitations requiring Californians not to go too far, and the war bringing couples together and driving them apart. Between 1935 and 1940 marriages in Las Vegas increased 500 percent, and the county installed a license bureau in the new Union Pacific depot that opened in 1940.

The war changed male-female relations in a more significant way: women took jobs as men left home to fight. Women and Hispanics replaced unskilled workers at White Pine copper operations. Basic Magnesium hired women to drive forklifts and make asbestos gloves, among other duties, and generally paid them the same as the men, but relegated the few African American women working there to lower-paying work. Women volunteered for the Red Cross and war bond drives, and Las Vegas women continued these efforts after the war by forming the Service League, which evolved into the Junior League. Women's Army Corps units around Nevada worked in a variety of jobs, aiding the military effort, while several Nevada women entered the women's branches of the armed forces.

African Americans

The war spurred the growth of Nevada's cities and the African American populace, from 664 statewide in the 1940 census to more than 4,300 in 1950. In southern Nevada migrants unable to find work at Basic Magnesium continued to Las Vegas and sought jobs at casinos downtown and on the Strip, among other places. Despite pressure by the local National Association for the Advancement of Colored People (NAACP) and the Las Vegas Colored Progressive Club, the Cragin administration and local businesses informally zoned them into West Las Vegas through redlining—refusing to grant licenses or bank loans unless they moved west of the railroad tracks. Thus, West Las Vegas developed its own community, complete with a Jackson Street "strip" of nightclubs offering gambling, dining, and entertainment, but often without municipal services such as water lines and paved streets. With Strip and downtown casinos refusing to allow black performers to enter, entertainers had to stay in West Las Vegas motels and boardinghouses.

Other discrimination prompted action by African Americans. At Basic, amid attempts to organize with an affiliate of the left-leaning Congress of Industrial Organizations (CIO), 186 African Americans walked out in October 1943; the company fired them, and the federal War Manpower Commission denied their appeal. Black workers at the Hawthorne Naval Ammunition Depot complained of similar bias and fared better. When Katie Kelly arrived from Louisiana, her superior officer, claiming the town had no other facilities, sent her to the jail for lodgings. She complained to the Fair Employment Practices Commission, leading to a reprimand for her boss. A federal investigation found Hawthorne lacking in facilities for African Americans: a community center open to them only one night a week, the depot barbershop refusing to serve them, and businesses with "No Colored Trade Solicited" signs. A county commissioner told the navy the community wanted no black people then or later, and when naval officials promised more opportunities for African Americans, the investigation died out.

Reno's African American community also expanded. The Lake-Evans block had been a center of illegal and quasi-legal activity during

Prohibition, and black-owned businesses there, especially casinos and clubs, grew substantially in the 1930s and 1940s until the *Reno Evening Gazette* dubbed the area the "Negro resort section of Reno." The Southern Pacific's African American employees, who lived in Reno instead of the nearby railroad town of Sparks, and servicepeople at Stead frequented the block. Reno's downtown casinos also barred African American customers and required entertainers to stay elsewhere, and Chinese immigrants joined in working in and operating segregated clubs. One of those who struck a blow for civil rights in Reno, Marion Motley, became the first star black player for the university football team before going on to a Hall of Fame professional career.

Race and Racism

As historian Patricia Limerick wrote, "Long-standing Western prejudice and immediate wartime panic made a perfectly tailored fit": in February 1942, two months after Pearl Harbor, federal officials decided to relocate American-born (Nisei) and immigrant (Issei) Japanese in California, Nevada, Arizona, Oregon, and Washington to camps. They lost their property, land, and legal rights—and the US Supreme Court upheld their removal. When rumors spread that all Japanese from other western states would be moved to Nevada, Carville informed the federal government that the state would intern those already there but not Japanese from other states. Yet most Nevadans demonstrated no overt anti-Japanese sentiment: several editors around the state urged readers to be tolerant, and Carville and the American Legion commander warned against saboteurs but emphasized the number of loyal Japanese Americans.

The greatest number of Nevada's 756 Japanese worked at White Pine copper mines and suffered for their ancestry. The day after Pearl Harbor, white miners at Ruth asked the Nevada Consolidated Copper Company to keep Japanese workers off their jobs. The company soon fired most of its Japanese workers, and federal authorities transported Japanese nationals at Ruth and McGill to Salt Lake City. Two of them committed suicide. Clark County's small Japanese populace—49 in the 1940 census—had little trouble, and the sheriff championed Japanese farm families, although local residents displayed some prejudice.

The war also prompted different treatment of Mexicans. After the federal government forced many immigrant farmworkers to return to Mexico during the 1930s, the war deprived farms of their laborers just as food production expanded. In 1942 the Roosevelt administration began the Bracero Program, for Mexico to provide workers who would be guaranteed a minimum wage, room, board, and health care. Throughout Nevada Mexican farmworkers helped the agricultural industry profit during and after the war.

Wartime Politics

During World War II Nevada's political battles intensified, with McCarran at the center of them. In 1942 Bunker ran to finish Pittman's six-year term. Despite an argument over patronage that ended with Scrugham calling him "a fat four-flushing faker," McCarran backed him in the primary, hoping to eliminate Bunker and perhaps fearing a challenge from Scrugham in the 1944 Democratic primary. Bunker irked some voters by attacking the Basic plant's management, which he accused of profiteering. Scrugham won the primary and general elections, giving McCarran an aging, ailing colleague lacking in seniority and power. The rest of the ticket offered a mixed Democratic bag: Carville, whose relationship with McCarran had soured, won a second term as governor; Vail Pittman, an Ely editor, former state senator, and avowed McCarran foe, became lieutenant governor; and Alan Bible, who attended law school on McCarran's patronage, won a difficult primary and coasted to a general election victory for attorney general.

But for McCarran, a primary challenge proved unavoidable: in 1944 Pittman ran against him. Although no liberal, Pittman won support from Carville's allies and the Congress of Industrial Organizations, which critics like McCarran attacked as a communist union, although its involvement in Nevada included only the White Pine copper union and organizing efforts at BMI. For his part, McCarran stressed Pittman's CIO support and the benefits of his growing seniority: in 1944 he became chair of the powerful Judiciary Committee. More important, McCarran's emphasis on tending to constituent needs earned him considerable support—especially after he hired Eva Adams, a native of the Churchill County mining camp Wonder, as his assistant; she ran the office and handled numerous issues. With Pittman arguing that he failed to support Roosevelt and the war effort, McCarran reinvented himself from an isolationist into a strong supporter of FDR's foreign policy, including the creation of the United Nations.

Machine-style politics triumphed: McCarran survived the primary to win the general election easily. Amid predictions of a close election, one of McCarran's allies, developer Norm Biltz, said of Las Vegas, "We found a way to get the Negro vote," which Pittman expected to win despite his Mississippi heritage and lack of interest in civil rights; McCarran had expressed interest only in the plight of residents who lacked paved streets and running water. He would fight more battles to control state Democrats, who kept dominating Nevada politics, but the unanswered question remained whether their divisions resulted from success, differing ideology, McCarran's determination, or a combination of all of these. Nevada's postwar political culture would provide some possible answers.

The Cultural State, the State of Culture

In the 1940s Walter Van Tilburg Clark became Nevada's most distinguished literary figure since Mark Twain. The son of longtime university president Walter Clark (1918–38), who sought to enhance Nevada's education and society, Van Tilburg Clark earned praise for his first major book. *The Ox-Bow Incident,* published in 1940 and filmed in 1943, represented what his biographer Jackson Benson called an "attack on the popular Western, particularly the circumstances of a charismatic leader leading a mob to conscienceless violence." Clark followed in 1945 with *The City of Trembling Leaves,* an autobiographical novel emphasizing Reno's "dual nature" of "a small-town person" residing near "the ersatz jungle, where the human animals, uneasy in the light, dart from cave to cave." By contrast, the other major literary work of the era to focus on Reno's environs, Clare Boothe Luce's *The Women,* a play that became a film, examined and, ironically, promoted the divorce trade.

Nevada's art community extended beyond what its members realized at the time. The first neon sign in Nevada apparently advertised a market in Elko, but by the late 1930s neon lit up parts of Reno, Las Vegas, Ely, Elko, and Pioche. Neon lighting became an art form, especially with the gaming industry's postwar boom. Just as the dam and new schools in Reno and Hawthorne, among other buildings, represented art deco, one of the first of Paul Revere Williams's hundreds of Nevada designs brought neoclassical revival architecture to Reno through its First Church of Christ, Scientist. While S. Charles Lee created the moderne Huntridge Theatre for Las Vegas, Frederic DeLongchamps continued his decades of dominating Nevada architecture by designing an English cottage revival lodge at Lake Tahoe for George Whittell, a millionaire Gold Rush heir attracted by Nevada's "One Sound State" promotion. New Deal programs provided other artistic benefits: Adolph Gottlieb, later a leading abstract expressionist, painted a mural in Yerington's post office, while Robert Cole Caples worked on federal arts projects before a rich career depicting Virginia City and various Nevada landscapes. The Bureau of Reclamation employed Ben Glaha to photograph the dam's construction, and his art, displayed in many galleries, traced that process.

Religious groups also played an increasingly important role as Nevada's population grew. In 1931 Pope Pius XI made Nevada independent of California's and Utah's Catholic communities by creating the Diocese of Reno under Bishop Thomas Gorman. Thomas Collins, the first priest ordained in Reno, started the Catholic Welfare Program, opened USO clubs around the state to help homesick military personnel, and later served on the state welfare board. The state's Jewish populace grew, with Las Vegas's large enough to form its first synagogue, Temple Beth Sholom, in 1943, while Reno's population increase helped lead to its temple briefly dividing into two congregations.

The New West

As historian Gerald Nash said of the West, "The colonial economy of the region, heavily dependent on raw materials production before 1941, now became increasingly diversified and self-sufficient." In 1935 Bernard DeVoto had written a *Harper's* essay, "The West: A Plundered Province," but a decade later, he marveled, "The ancient Western dream of an advanced industrial economy . . . is brighter now than it has ever been." Yet this new self-sufficiency also bred a new dependence as the West hoped to continue the flow of federal help and a new desire for regional cooperation. McCarran told a meeting of eleven western governors of his "blueprint for a new frontier" that would emphasize working closely with federal agencies, conservation, development of new minerals, and more airports and roads. He also helped organize a 1944 Carson City conference on postwar planning that drew sixty delegates from five western states. Carville consulted regularly with governors of surrounding states and told the Carson City group that "the very foundation of postwar planning for the western region must be built around the conservation, development, and preservation of all our natural resources [and] the retention and development of already established war plants by private enterprise." Carville suggested to the RFC's Henderson that "it is hard for us in the West to compete with the industrial East but . . . it would be of great help to the West if these plants . . . the Government has constructed . . . could continue under private ownership after the war. We of the West are working hard to bring about a better industrial condition here and I hope in some measure the R.F.C. will be able to help us."

They envisioned a new Nevada, though not what Nevada became. Although mining remained a component of its economy, it would no longer dominate the state. Nevada's population, always predominantly urban as mining rushes created boomtowns, became centered mainly in two regions: Clark County and the Reno-Sparks–Carson City area, which grew through economic and population expansion rather than through planning and development. Urban historian Carl Abbott has cited "three fundamental changes in the national economy" as driving these changes in Nevada and the West: an increasing interest in and desire for leisure, the expansion of federal defense spending, and the growing globalization of the American economy. During the New Deal and World War II, Nevada had been at the center of these changes. After the war, it would remain so.

SUGGESTED READINGS

Benson, Jackson J. *The Ox-Bow Man: A Biography of Walter Van Tilburg Clark.* Reno: University of Nevada Press, 2006.

Brennan, John A. *Silver and the First New Deal.* Reno: University of Nevada Press, 1969.

Clark, Walter Van Tilburg. *The City of Trembling Leaves.* Reno: University of Nevada Press, 1991.

———. *The Ox-Bow Incident.* New York: Random House, 1957.

———. *The Track of the Cat.* Reno: University of Nevada Press, 1993.

———. *The Watchful Gods, and Other Stories.* Reno: University of Nevada Press, 2004.

Edwards, Jerome E. *Pat McCarran: Political Boss of Nevada.* Reno: University of Nevada Press, 1982.

Glad, Betty. *Key Pittman: The Tragedy of a Senate Insider.* New York: Columbia University Press, 1986.

Israel, Fred L. *Nevada's Key Pittman.* Lincoln: University of Nebraska Press, 1963.

Jennings, Dean S. *We Only Kill Each Other: The Life and Bad Times of Bugsy Siegel.* New York: Pocket Books, 1967.

King, R. T. *Every Light Was On: Bill Harrah and His Clubs Remembered.* Reno: University of Nevada Oral History Program, 2002.

Kling, Dwayne, and R. T. King. *A Family Affair: Harolds Club and the Smiths Remembered.* Reno: University of Nevada Oral History Program, 2003.

Kolvet, Renee Corona, and Victoria Ford. *The Civilian Conservation Corps in Nevada: From Boys to Men.* Reno: University of Nevada Press, 2006.

Laird, Charlton, ed. *Walter Van Tilburg Clark: Critiques.* Reno: University of Nevada Press, 1983.

Laxalt, Robert. *The Basque Hotel.* Reno: University of Nevada Press, 1989.

Lowitt, Richard. *The New Deal and the West.* Bloomington: Indiana University Press, 1984.

Mandel, Leon. *William Fisk Harrah: The Life and Times of a Gambling Magnate.* New York: Doubleday, 1981.

Nash, Gerald D. *The American West Transformed: The Impact of the Second World War.* Bloomington: Indiana University Press, 1985.

———. *World War II and the West: Reshaping the Economy.* Lincoln: University of Nebraska Press, 1990.

Ringhoff, Mary, and Edward J. Stoner, eds. *The River and the Railroad: An Archaeological History of Reno.* Reno: University of Nevada Press, 2010.

Ronald, Ann. *Reader of the Purple Sage: Essays on Western Writers and Environmental Literature.* Reno: University of Nevada Press, 2003.

Smith, Harold S., Sr., and John Wesley Noble. *I Want to Quit Winners.* Englewood Cliffs, NJ: Prentice Hall, 1961.

Worster, Donald W. *Dust Bowl: The Southern Plains in the 1930s.* 1979. Reprint, New York: Oxford University Press, 2004.

Ybarra, Michael. *Washington Gone Crazy: Senator Pat McCarran and the Great American Communist Hunt.* New York: Steerforth Press, 2004.

12

The Postwar Boom, 1946–58

In the fifteen years after World War II, the population of the West—
especially the Sunbelt, the nation's southern tier—nearly doubled, and
the federal government poured $150 billion into the region. Nevada bene-
fited from and symbolized these changes. As its populace rose rapidly, so
did the number of tourists visiting its resorts and casinos from within and
beyond the region, especially amid increased prosperity. Nevada and the
Sunbelt led the nation into the postindustrial society, as blue-collar jobs
gave way to white-collar, service-oriented work. Federal installations combined the characteristics of those two forms of employment as the grand
alliance that won World War II dissolved into the Cold War. The Soviet
Union forced communism on Eastern Europe, and Communist forces
finally took over China in 1949, increasing American fears about the spread
of communism and support for defense spending that helped the West
boom—at times literally.

The Strip Booms

After World War II gaming and tourism dominated Nevada's economy.
Gambling revenues more than quintupled in a decade, from $21 million
in 1945 to $110 million (and tripling in each of the two decades after that),
underscoring the change, but some Nevadans had mixed emotions. "It isn't
a very laudable position for one to have to defend gambling. One doesn't
feel very lofty when his feet are resting on the argument that gambling must
prevail in the State that he represents," Senator Pat McCarran lamented,
telling one of his patronage appointees that no Nevadan could hope for a
national office as long as their state embraced gaming. But the Las Vegas
area welcomed it and the construction boom accompanying it.

Too late to save him, Bugsy Siegel's accomplishment in building the Flamingo paid off for his Mob investors. Their success inspired further building on the highway to Los Angeles, as did reformers targeting vice in their towns, prompting casino bosses to relocate where they could practice their trade legally. Capitalism provided another motivation: economic success, increasing leisure time, and the Sunbelt's growth meant profits in catering to vacationing Americans with discretionary income. Airplane and highway improvements (the number of cars in America more than doubled in this period), and better air-conditioning in homes and cars, made the Southwest easier and more attractive to live in and visit.

Consequently, in this era, the classic Strip took shape. Built mostly by businessmen tied to organized crime, these casino resorts increased Las Vegas's reliance on tourism and created a money machine for the Mob's illegal activities elsewhere. Operators tied to Meyer Lansky and the New York syndicate continued to run the Flamingo, built the Thunderbird (1948) and Tropicana (1957), and took over the Riviera (1955) from New England's Patriarca family, although other evidence suggests the resort actually belonged to Chicago mobster Sam Giancana and lawyer and power broker Sidney Korshak. Cleveland's Mayfield Road Gang, led by Morris B. "Moe" Dalitz, built the Desert Inn (1950) and teamed with local investors on the off-Strip Showboat (1954) and Chicago mobsters on the Stardust (1958). Another New York group worked with Houston-Galveston operatives to develop the Sands (1952). Unconnected to the Mob, illegal operators from Butte, Montana, and Portland, Oregon, retooled the Club Bingo into the Sahara (1952). Detroit interests developed the Royal Nevada, bought the New Frontier from other Mob figures, and joined a St. Louis group in the Dunes (all in 1955). California motel chain owner Warren "Doc" Bayley opened the Hacienda after state regulators forced out his proposed casino manager, reputed mobster and Lansky ally Jake Kozloff. After the original owners sold the El Rancho Vegas and Hotel Last Frontier, the new regimes reportedly had Mob ties.

These resorts shared several characteristics. One concerned uncertainty about whether Italian or Jewish casino operators wielded control due to a lack of written evidence, but some of the licensed owners served as "front men" for Mob figures. As historian Eugene Moehring has noted, the Flamingo "liberated Las Vegas from the confines of its western heritage" when it "combined the sophisticated ambience of a Monte Carlo casino with the exotic luxury of a Miami Beach–Caribbean resort," complete with a waterfall in front, a tuxedoed staff, and exotic plants. Other resorts emphasized luxury over themes, although the Thunderbird's design relied on Navajo traditions and the Sahara's suggested Morocco. Content to make their profits in the casino, where the Mob-run resorts could easily skim money to send to eastern Mob interests, they offered inexpensive rooms, dining, and entertainment.

Indeed, entertainment played a key role in Nevada casinos, especially in Las Vegas. While showrooms featured a variety of performers and Broadway shows, owners judged entertainers on whether they attracted customers who gambled big money. The entertainers, too, could make big money: in 1955 Liberace opened the Riviera for fifty thousand dollars a week, and salaries escalated with success, Las Vegas's growth, and competition. The building of so many hotels in so short a period also led to experimentation:

Old and new Las Vegas meet. Big Jim Cashman, a longtime political and business leader, drives Liberace, the first act in 1955 at the new Riviera for the unheard-of salary of fifty thousand dollars a week. Courtesy of Special Collections, University Libraries, University of Nevada, Las Vegas.

nightclub alumni such as Frank Sinatra, Dean Martin and Jerry Lewis, Sammy Davis Jr., and Danny Thomas, but also unlikely headliners like English cabaret legend Noël Coward, actor-director Orson Welles, and then-actor Ronald Reagan. All of them offered lounges with lesser-known but still topflight entertainers, often from just after the midnight show until dawn, enhancing Las Vegas's reputation as a city without clocks. While hotels and the Las Vegas News Bureau marketed the Strip as an adult playground, with "cheesecake" shots of celebrities and showgirls, some resorts catered to families: the Last Frontier Village theme park and the Hacienda's go-cart track appealed to the children of baby boomers.

After World War II Americans increasingly moved from cities to suburbs, and the Strip fitted this pattern. As suburbs sprouted around the country, casino operators followed the builders of the first two resorts, the El Rancho Vegas and Hotel Last Frontier, moving south of the Las Vegas city limits. Thus, the Strip's builders actually operated in a suburb of Las Vegas and reflected suburban designs and thinking: mostly California ranch-style, low-rise properties, just off the highway for the convenience of Southern Californians reliant on automobiles, where baby boomers would feel comfortable. Reflecting national trends, Dalitz included a residential golf course and country club at the Desert Inn. After initial opposition, other owners followed suit—although Dalitz added a professional tournament with a pro-am that drew star athletes, celebrities, and favorable publicity.

Ironically, many operators wound up in gaming due to ethnic bias. Immigrants and sons of immigrants, raised in ethnic enclaves, they had trouble finding well-paying, legitimate work, so they made their living at illegal activities such as gambling and bootlegging. They also faced discrimination when they tried to join some Reno and Las Vegas organizations, sometimes kept out over Judaism or their role in gambling. In turn, they reflected the racism of their time and declined to accept African American customers or employ them in well-paying jobs, except as entertainers barred from the premises when offstage. By the mid-1950s critics called Nevada the "Mississippi of the West"—a fair statement, given its policies and attitudes, but as NAACP official Dorea Hall Pittman said in 1964, "If Arizona is the Alabama, Nevada is the Mississippi of the West, and Utah is the Georgia."

The Limits of the Strip

The Strip's building boom revealed the limits of a tourism economy. In 1955 five new hotel-casinos opened in southern Nevada—four on the Strip and one in racially segregated West Las Vegas—as the nation's economy went through a downturn. Only the New Frontier, a redesign of the old resort, escaped serious financial problems. Sands executives helped save the Dunes from bankruptcy, as did new co-owner Major Riddle, who imported the Strip's first nude show, Minsky's Follies, and built a golf course nearby. The Riviera teetered until Flamingo executives moved up the street to save it. The Royal Nevada closed, becoming part of the Stardust, while, off the Strip, the Moulin Rouge shut down.

The Strip's success highlighted another problem: access to capital. Because they associated gambling with mobsters who might choose not to repay them, few bankers would loan money for casino building or expansion. In the 1950s two new sources became available. One, the Teamsters Central States Pension Fund, at first invested off the Strip, including in a country club and a hospital. But the fund's key officials included Teamsters boss Jimmy Hoffa and his close ally Allen Dorfman, the stepson of a onetime associate of Chicago Mob boss Al Capone, and it later funded the building, expansion, or purchase of numerous casino resorts.

The other source had unusual origins. In 1955 Mormon bankers in Salt Lake City dispatched a rising star from their circle, E. Parry Thomas, to Las Vegas to help run their troubled new Bank of Las Vegas. Thomas concentrated on loans, while local investor Jerome Mack, son of pioneer Las Vegas entrepreneur Nate Mack, emphasized real estate. With Las Vegas's postwar growth, the Mormon population expanded and invested in real estate and other industries. Asked why he would loan money to casinos, Thomas replied that a banker who refused to serve his community's biggest industry probably had no business in banking. For their part, casino operators welcomed the bank and took pains to ensure its success. Within two years the bank's original $250,000 capitalization grew to $16 million in assets. Thomas and Mack went on to erect a banking and land empire, and their philanthropy contributed to the rise of the local United Way and university. But, for their trouble, they faced allegations of ties to the Mob.

Just as Thomas and Mack became involved in more than just casinos, so did casino operators, seeking legitimacy or more profits or both. In northern Nevada, reflecting his love of classic cars, Bill Harrah bought an auto dealership. Kell Houssels, who took over the Tropicana and cleared out its Mob connections, invested in a variety of enterprises, as did his son and successor. The Desert Inn's Wilbur Clark went into real estate. In the 1950s Dalitz and one of his Desert Inn partners, Allard Roen, teamed with builders Irwin Molasky and Mervin Adelson to form Paradise Development Company. Their investments and Teamster loans turned it into a colossus, responsible for hospitals, golf courses, housing tracts, and shopping malls. Eventually, Molasky and Adelson invested in Hollywood, helping to form Lorimar, which produced *The Waltons, Dallas,* and other television series and films. Most of the Strip's Jewish operators became involved in the local temple and assorted charities, winning praise and friends in the community.

Off the Strip

While casino resorts moved to the suburbs, smaller casinos opened or expanded in the urban core, often retaining ties to the Mob or those once involved in illegal gambling. In 1951 longtime Texas gambling operator Benny Binion put his stamp on the industry with his Horseshoe, the first downtown property with a carpeted casino, airport limousines, and higher betting limits. In 1956 investors tied to the Sands built downtown's first high-rise, the Fremont, and the Sahara's operators followed in 1957 with the Mint, run by Sam Boyd, a casino veteran given his first shot at management. Thanks to local growth, tourists' habits, and the Union Pacific's presence, these casinos prospered and competed with the Strip: the Fremont soon expanded, and the Mint added a tower in 1962.

New resorts extended beyond downtown, as southern Nevada's population spread through the Las Vegas Valley. In 1954 the Showboat opened at the start of Boulder Highway, seeking business from Arizona and visitors to the dam. The first "locals" casino offered the growing sport of bowling (it hosted a nationally televised tournament for more than thirty years) and country music. By contrast, the Moulin Rouge debuted in 1955 in West Las Vegas with a French theme and an integrated clientele and staff. Its revue, with African American performers, drew international attention, as did Strip entertainers like Sammy Davis Jr. and Louis Armstrong, who now could stay at a resort rather than at Westside motels and boardinghouses. Yet the resort closed within a year, a victim of mismanagement and its

Downtown Las Vegas in the mid-1950s. The Fremont had just opened as the first high-rise in Glitter Gulch. The Golden Nugget's sign includes "1905" to signify its place in the Las Vegas town site auctioned that year. Courtesy of Special Collections, University of Nevada–Reno Library.

location: too far from the Strip or downtown to attract customers and at the edge of West Las Vegas, where it proved unable to break loyalties to older clubs.

For the city of Las Vegas, the Strip posed several problems. It would inevitably triumph in competing for tourists, with its spacious resorts dwarfing downtown casinos. As cars overtook trains, hotels on Highway 91 captured drivers from California before they reached downtown. More important, the Strip lay outside the city. When Las Vegas tried to annex the area, the Strip's operators, preferring to avoid higher municipal fees, appealed to the legislature. In 1949 it passed a law creating unincorporated townships that could be annexed only by a vote of its residents. The creation of Paradise and Winchester townships ensured that land south of the Las Vegas city limits would remain in Clark County, whose government became one of Nevada's most powerful due to the Strip.

The postwar era brought southern Nevada an issue that still plagues it:

keeping up with growth, especially compared with Reno. By 1948 its children had two playgrounds to Reno's six. Reno had twice as much park land. Public works needed constant attention, but growth made what the city and county accomplished obsolete. Yet state law worked against responding to growth: by 1957 Clark and Washoe Counties generated about 87 percent of gaming revenue, but all Nevada counties equally shared the bounty. Las Vegas's municipal leadership changed in 1951, as Ernie Cragin lost his bid for a third straight term due to his ties to gaming interests and McCarran. His successor, former state senator and city surveyor C. D. Baker, supported expanding public works—including the first paved streets in segregated West Las Vegas. That won him support in the black community, which also benefited from the federally funded Marble Manor housing project in 1952. But he lost some of it by deciding the freeway planned under the Interstate Highway Act of 1956 would go through West Las Vegas, although he argued that whatever produced the best traffic flow should determine Interstate 15's location.

The Growth of Reno

Reno also reaped profits from gaming and tourism, but with a different approach. Although visitors to Las Vegas took advantage of Lake Mead— several Strip resorts kept boats there—Reno emphasized natural wonders like Lake Tahoe, where skiing and summer recreation attracted tourists and part-time residents, and Pyramid Lake. It also benefited from airport expansion and the widening of Interstate 40, but suffered due to weather: driving across the Sierra Nevada from Northern California in winter proved far more daunting than crossing the Mojave Desert from Southern California to Las Vegas, even if the highway before Interstate 15's construction could be dusty and difficult. Nor did the region lack for organized crime: famed mobster "Russian Louie" Strauss shot fellow gangster Harry Sherwood in 1948 in Lake Tahoe, and an unknown assailant shot longtime Reno casino operator Lincoln Fitzgerald in 1949.

Washoe County also refused to make available open space, as Clark County did along Highway 91, but Reno's casinos grew significantly in the 1940s and 1950s. Harold's Club swallowed other casinos and added its Roaring Camp Room with western memorabilia and a two-story mural fronting Virginia Street. George Wingfield doubled the number of rooms in the Riverside Hotel. In 1947 Charles Mapes opened his eponymous hotel; Nevada's tallest building at twelve stories, its Sky Room, with floor-to-ceiling windows for viewing the area, brought big-name entertainers to Reno for the first time. The Colony Club had just opened, the Club Cal Neva followed, and Norm Biltz's eight-story Holiday Hotel debuted along the Truckee River in 1956. Bill Harrah constantly expanded his holdings, joined Strip showrooms in emphasizing big-name entertainment, and encouraged additional tourism at Lake Tahoe with his involvement in hydroplanes.

Yet gambling became more important to Washoe County in the 1950s, and not just in downtown Reno. Ernest Primm wanted to locate his Primadonna on the west side of Virginia Street. The city council had informally decided to ban unrestricted gaming licenses there or south of Second, despite requests from the Reno Chamber of Commerce and Nevada Retail Merchants Association to make it an ordinance. Rejected, Primm sued and lost, but new council members acceded to his request in 1954, enabling him to open across from Harold's. In 1955 Dick Graves opened the Sparks Nugget; five years later general manager John Ascuaga, an Idaho-born Basque, bought it and expanded it until it had more than sixteen hundred rooms and eighty-five thousand square feet of casino space. But these clubs generally lacked the space and comforts the Strip offered its customers.

This postcard of Virginia Street at night, looking toward the famous sign, with William Harrah's club prominent on the right. Courtesy of Special Collections, University of Nevada–Reno Library.

Other factors relegated Washoe County to a secondary role in gaming tourism. As in the earlier part of the century, when libertarian-minded businessmen differed from religious and educational leaders, many Reno residents never reconciled themselves to gambling, preferring to emphasize the university and local culture. Also, Reno operators lacked unity. Photographers at the Chamber of Commerce's Las Vegas News Bureau worked closely with hotel publicists, and the resorts teamed to fund joint marketing efforts, but Reno had no such organized program. Nor did the weather help: until 1952, when Reno's city council prohibited them from doing so, some casinos closed during the winter due to the lack of visitors.

McCarran's Battles

The world war ended, but not McCarran's quest to control the Democratic Party and eliminate potential opponents. Within six years McCarran helped elect three Republicans over fellow Democrats, harming his party and eliminating potential threats to his power. In 1945, when James

During the 1948 presidential campaign in which he pulled off a shocking upset, President Harry Truman rode through Reno with fellow Democrats who had fought each other for years: Governor Vail Pittman and Senator Pat McCarran. Courtesy of Special Collections, University of Nevada–Reno Library.

Scrugham died, E. P. Carville resigned, making Lieutenant Governor Vail Pittman acting governor; he appointed Carville to the Senate. Despising Carville, McCarran encouraged a primary opponent in 1946: Berkeley Bunker, finishing his first term in the House, Carville's former ally, and once the object of McCarran's scorn. Bunker won a hard-fought primary and then lost the general election to Republican former state engineer George Malone. The national sweep that gave the GOP control of Congress helped Malone, but so did the refusal of Carville supporters to back Bunker. Charles Russell, a Republican editor from Ely, won Nevada's lone House seat, meaning McCarran belonged to the political minority but, with two rookie colleagues, dominated the state's politics and its congressional delegation.

McCarran involved himself in the 1950 governor's race, even as he ran for his fourth Senate term. Pittman sought a second full term as governor, and McCarran saw an opportunity to avenge earlier battles and exert his control. After Russell lost his reelection bid for the House in 1948 to Democrat Walter Baring, a frequent McCarran critic, the senator helped Russell obtain a job with the Marshall Plan, a US program to rebuild wartorn Western Europe. Russell returned home and ran for governor, aided by McCarran's financial backers, including Republicans Norm Biltz, a Reno and Lake Tahoe developer, and Bonanza Airlines executive Ed Converse. After beating Pittman, Russell angered McCarran and his allies by refusing to accede to their demands for special treatment.

McCarran then thrust himself into the 1952 Senate election. His protégé, former state attorney general Alan Bible, announced his candidacy against Malone. His Democratic primary opponent, Thomas Mechling, the husband of a Wells native, blasted Bible as a tool of McCarran. Between Democrats angry at the senator's interference, Bible taking the primary for granted, and new residents without old loyalties, Mechling nipped Bible by 475 votes out of more than 31,000 cast. After that, instead of concentrating on Malone, Mechling attacked McCarran, whose friend Biltz caught Mechling on tape offering to stop his criticism in return for financial help. That soured some Mechling supporters, and McCarran announced his refusal to endorse the Democrat. Dwight Eisenhower's success in the presidential race helped Malone win a second Senate term by only 2,722 votes, and Republican House candidate Cliff Young beat Baring, temporarily eliminating another thorn in McCarran's side. None of this affected Nevada's influence nationally: as long as McCarran remained in the Senate, the state had power.

McCarran fought other dubious battles. He tried to obtain water rights for Italian families squatting on twenty-one hundred acres of Pyramid Lake Reservation (see chapter 11). In 1944 the Ninth Circuit Court of Appeals upheld the Northern Paiutes, but McCarran kept trying to take the land from them. They eventually hired their own attorney, Carville, the former governor who had fought McCarran politically. By the early 1950s, as A. J. Liebling put it in the *New Yorker*, "The Indians still had the waterless land and the squatters the landless water." Malone aided McCarran, but to no avail, although some of the squatters ultimately received federal money.

In northern Nevada a thirty-year fight culminated in 1944 in the Orr Ditch Decree, designed to settle a dispute over how much Truckee River water belonged to the Pyramid Lake Reservation. Residents of Truckee Meadows and Lake Tahoe, utility companies, Newlands project users near Fallon, utilities, and ranchers all wanted their percentage. But growth posed a problem: the available water and the desired amount differed. The problems in determining the distribution of the Carson, Truckee, and Walker Rivers and Lake Tahoe led to the two affected states creating the California-Nevada Interstate Compact Commission, with Fred Settelmeyer, from one of Douglas County's oldest ranching families, playing a key role, especially in fighting on behalf of those depending on the Carson River.

McCarthyism, McCarranism, and Greenspun

When not interfering in Nevada, McCarran concentrated on fighting communism: Soviet domination of Eastern Europe, China's fall to Mao Tse-tung's forces, the Korean War, and concerns about domestic spying. President Harry Truman instituted a loyalty oath for federal employees, and many states acted similarly; Nevada passed a law allowing employers to refuse to hire Communists. House Un-American Activities Committee investigations brought fame to young California politician Richard Nixon. The entertainment industry began a blacklist to keep Communists—real or rumored—from performing or working behind the scenes (originating in the *Hollywood Reporter*, owned by Billy Wilkerson, the Flamingo's original builder). At a GOP dinner in West Virginia on February 9, 1950, Joseph McCarthy claimed to hold a list of Communists working for the federal government and repeated the charges the next day in Reno. The senator from Wisconsin became a national sensation, holding Senate hearings and becoming a sought-after speaker whose endorsement swayed voters, although whether he believed what he said remains debatable.

A true believer, McCarran had long warned about Communist infiltrators. As chair of the Senate Judiciary Committee and its Internal Security Subcommittee, he questioned and harassed dozens of citizens he suspected of Communist sympathies, aided by committee counsel Julien Sourwine, an attorney from Reno. He worked closely with "my friend the director," as he called the FBI's J. Edgar Hoover, who targeted those he considered Communists, with or without evidence.

McCarran also pushed through two major anti-Communist laws. The McCarran Internal Security Act of 1950 set up a board to investigate those suspected of supporting communism or fascism, required Communist groups to register with the US attorney general, authorized federal officials to detain anyone accused of such activities or suspected of espionage, barred those involved from becoming citizens, and made picketing a federal courthouse a felony. Truman vetoed the bill as an assault on the First Amendment, but Congress easily overrode him. Truman also vetoed the McCarran-Walter Immigration and Nationality Act of 1952, which ended racial quotas from the last immigration reform in 1924 but kept them for nationalities and regions, targeting Eastern Europeans suspected of being Communist infiltrators. Truman argued that immigrants from that region sought to escape communism, not spread it, but Congress again overrode him.

McCarthy and McCarran faced one of their fiercest critics in Nevada. Hank Greenspun reflected postwar trends as a World War II veteran migrating from New York City to Las Vegas in 1946 for better weather and more interesting activities than practicing law. He found them, publishing an entertainment weekly, working as the Flamingo's publicist, investing in a radio station and the Desert Inn, and spending more than a year away from home running guns to the fledgling nation of Israel, then at war to preserve its existence. A national hero in Israel as a result, Greenspun wound up pleading guilty to violating the federal Neutrality Act—news he published in the *Las Vegas Sun*, which he bought in 1950. Typesetters locked out of the *Review-Journal* had founded a triweekly, which they sold to Greenspun, who changed its name, expanded it to a daily, and added a front-page column, "Where I Stand."

Greenspun targeted McCarran over the senator's machine-style politics and anti-Semitism, although success required him to distinguish himself from the pro-McCarran *Review-Journal* and appeal to other newcomers who resented longtime Nevadans. He strongly backed Mechling and blistered McCarran as corrupt. The senator retaliated: one morning in 1952 almost every local casino canceled its *Sun* advertising, prompting Greenspun to sue him and the casino owners in federal court for conspiracy. When Greenspun found key evidence, his opponents settled and restored the ads, in a courtroom presided over by District Judge Roger T. Foley, who owed his appointment to the senator and conducted the trial fairly. Greenspun also developed close friendships with Houssels and Binion, who disagreed with the boycott and supported him.

Greenspun also took on McCarthy. When the senator campaigned in Las Vegas in 1952, Greenspun attacked him in a front-page column; McCarthy replied before a large crowd, calling him "an admitted ex-communist" publishing the "local *Daily Worker,*" a Communist paper. Greenspun said, "I knew his tongue must have slipped. . . . He meant to say 'convict.'" Since McCarthy slandered him, Greenspun had more freedom than many journalists and took advantage of it with reports accusing him of being a secret Communist, wartime Nazi sympathizer, and homosexual (considered an insult then and a charge that McCarthy used against his victims). In 1954, citing the number of lives McCarthy had ruined, Greenspun predicted his violent death: "Really, I'm against Joe getting his head blown off, not because I do not believe in capital punishment or because he does not have it coming, but I would hate to see some simpleton get the chair for such a public service as getting rid of McCarthy." The Republican administration then indicted the publisher for inciting assassination. A federal jury acquitted Greenspun, who had been exercising his First Amendment rights.

Atomic Testing

During World War II scientists working for the Manhattan Project developed an atomic bomb. After a successful test in New Mexico, the United States dropped bombs on two cities, Hiroshima and Nagasaki, prompting Japan's unconditional surrender to end the war in August 1945. After testing bombs in the South Pacific, the Atomic Energy Commission (AEC) wanted a domestic area with ample space, a temperate climate, and an urban area and transportation close enough to convey people and material, but far enough away to maintain security. In December 1950, reportedly at McCarran's behest, President Truman designated part of the Nellis Bombing and Gunnery Range as the nation's atomic proving ground, the Nevada Test Site. The first mushroom cloud rose at Frenchman Flat on January 27, 1951, and Governor Charles Russell proclaimed the desert would bloom with atoms.

By 1963 the AEC tested one hundred atomic bombs aboveground, except for a three-year moratorium (1957–59), before President John Kennedy and Soviet premier Nikita Khrushchev agreed to a ban. Testing then continued underground until 1992, with at least eight hundred announced detonations and an unknown number of secret blasts. While the tests flattened, cratered, and radiated large parts of Nevada, they also brought thousands of residents and visitors to the state to work on the blasts and research their effects, and well over one hundred million dollars of the test site's payroll entered Nevada's economy. The AEC built a town, Mercury, to house test-site workers, who developed their own community.

Atomic testing also became a tourist attraction. Hotels and motels set

A postcard of Las Vegas icons from the 1950s: the neon lights of downtown Glitter Gulch; cowboy Vegas Vic announcing, "Howdy, podner"; and a mushroom cloud from the Nevada Test Site, which Las Vegas turned into a tourist attraction. Courtesy of Special Collections, University Libraries, University of Nevada, Las Vegas.

up parties or places to watch the blasts. A beauty contest produced a Miss Atomic Blast. In Las Vegas salons offered the Atomic Hairdo (for seventy-five dollars, a stylist pulled a woman's hair over a mushroom cloud–shaped wire and sprinkled on silver glitter), and saloons served the Atomic Cocktail—brandy, vodka, champagne, and a little sherry. From the official Clark County seal to Las Vegas High School's yearbook, and in postcards and photos, the mushroom cloud became the area's symbol.

It also symbolized much worse. The federal government denied the dangers of atomic testing, despite the evidence from the bombs dropped on Japan, with one AEC pamphlet claiming "only one known instance in which testing resulted in accidental injury to anyone": "Startled by the blast from a nuclear detonation while shaving," a Hiko man "reacted so sharply that he strained his neck." Changes in the wind diverted clouds from Operation Upshot-Knothole, a series of tests in 1953, over southeastern Nevada and southern Utah, leading to the death and illness of hundreds of sheep and the spread of cancer among the cast and crew of *The Conqueror,* a movie filmed in the area. Federal officials imperiled lives and contributed to an ongoing attitude in Nevada that distrusted the government.

Labor and Economics

As they did after World War I, unions that accepted wage limits during World War II sought raises when the war ended. Again, they faced trouble. When Republicans took back Congress in 1947, they responded to the militancy of mostly Democratic unions by passing the Taft-Hartley Act, including Section 14(b), barring closed shops for unions, which Nevada had enacted in 1911. Long a union supporter, McCarran opposed the Taft-Hartley law, but on July 4, 1949, Reno's culinary and bartender unions walked out, demanding better pay on one of the biggest tourist days of the year, in the midst of the popular Reno rodeo. Angry local hotel and bar owners responded by locking them out and holding a downtown picnic where they distributed free or low-cost food and beverages. Harrah persuaded his employees to decertify the union but made it a point to maintain salaries and benefits high enough to discourage the Culinary's return.

Other businesspeople went further. Numerous casino owners and other employers formed the Nevada Citizens Committee, which developed a right-to-work initiative. They submitted it to the 1951 legislature, advertised it across the state, and worked for bipartisan support. In 1952 the initiative passed by about a thousand votes, prompting southern Nevada labor leaders, eventually joined by their northern counterparts, to back an initiative repealing it. In 1956 and 1958 Nevadans rejected them by increasingly larger margins, retaining right-to-work.

Like the right-to-work law, the Freeport Law of 1949 reflected Nevadans' desire to please business. Due to the lack of storage space for war matériel, a federal administrator bought land near Reno—a transportation crossroads—and proposed a bill to eliminate taxes on goods stored in Nevada, which would make it only the third place in the United States, after Wisconsin and Washington, DC, to do so. Attorney General Bible wrote the legislation, the Reno press and Chamber of Commerce publicized it, and the legislature easily passed it. A revision expanded the definition of warehousing, as long as the products remained "in transit." With the Freeport Law generating $750 million in shipping in the next quarter century, warehouse construction boomed near Reno and Sparks, and more than half of the states followed Nevada's lead. Nor did these developments hurt efforts to improve transportation: the Interstate Highway Act of 1956 helped the trucking industry and made it easier for tourists to reach Nevada and led to better Nevada highways, particularly Interstate 40, which finally grew to four lanes.

Nevada also emphasized economic diversification, with mixed results. After the war, at McCarran's urging (his seat on the Appropriations Committee gave him power over its budget), the General Services Administration offered to sell the Basic Magnesium plant to the state, which bought it for $1 down and $24 million payable later from rental income. In 1952 the state's Colorado River Commission sold the property to the tenants, consisting of chemical companies making potash, sodium chlorate, and chlorine and processing titanium metals—some of which proved important to national defense. The resulting profits and surrounding population growth led to Henderson's incorporation as a city in 1953 and fueled creation of the Southern Nevada Industrial Foundation to promote a business-friendly climate in 1957; it later became the Nevada Development Authority and now the Las Vegas Global Economic Alliance.

The legislature also tried to merge tourism with industry. In 1955 it passed a law to let counties set up fair and recreation boards to build convention facilities, and Reno and Las Vegas took advantage of it. Las Vegas struck first, although good fortune helped: a horse-racing track failed, and

casino owner Joe W. Brown agreed to buy the bankrupt complex and transfer 480 acres of land to the city. Clark County wound up controlling the
acreage, but local governments reached an agreement and voters supported
a bond issue. In April 1959 the Las Vegas Convention Center opened just
east of the Strip with the World Congress of Flight.

The Midcentury Mining Boom

Although less of a defining moment than the Comstock or the early-
twentieth-century boom, mining boosted Nevada's economy in the 1950s.
The Cold War, including the fighting in Korea, aided mining, just as World
Wars I and II had, with revenues setting a new state record of $57 million
in 1951. Despite cheap foreign competition, copper prices and production
rose, benefiting Kennecott's White Pine operations, including an open-pit
mine in Ruth, a mill in McGill, and the railroad in East Ely. Near Yerington
the Anaconda company's new open-pit mine and nearby Weed Heights, a
company town, aided the local economy. Other ores brought jobs to Lincoln County and Nye County's Round Mountain. Lead and zinc mining
made their presence felt, as did iron in Douglas County, oil and gas in Railroad Valley, a uranium rush near Austin, lime at Basic and Sloan in Clark
County, and gypsum in Blue Diamond. Humboldt County's Cordero Mine
generated one-quarter of the nation's mercury supply, and Nevada topped
the nation in tungsten, producing $77.4 million in three years, mainly from
Humboldt, Mineral, and Nye Counties, due partly to a federal purchasing
agreement. California's building boom and increasing suburbanization
across the country powered another part of Nevada's mining industry: per-
lite from southern Nevada mines helped make wallboard.

Nevada leaders also maintained their commitment to mining. Congress passed laws encouraging mineral, gas, and oil exploration; McCarran,
Malone, Baring, and Young all lobbied their colleagues for support. But
in 1957, after a state production record of more than $126 million the year
before, the stockpiling program ended, world prices declined, and mines
closed. The resulting job losses—about a thousand—reflected a trend.
From 15 percent of the state's workers in 1940, mining's numbers fell to just
over 5 percent by 1950 and 3 percent by 1958, as technology rendered many
of their jobs obsolete.

While other mining camps benefited, revived, or sprang up in response
to the 1950s boom, the Virginia City area remained quiet—in terms of

mining. In 1950 the shutdown of the Virginia & Truckee, which had gradually scaled back service, seemed to signify the old Comstock's decline. But tourism revived Virginia City. Authors Lucius Beebe and Charles Clegg moved there from New York City in the late 1940s and revived the *Territorial Enterprise* as a weekly. They persuaded literary friends to write for it, attracting attention to their publication and tourists to the town. They also drew a bohemian community of fellow would-be westerners, mostly wealthy easterners looking for adventure or, like Beebe and Clegg, a place to be left alone: the two writers' homosexuality might have made them unpopular locally if not for the economic benefits they inspired.

The Post-McCarran Political World

By 1954, despite health problems, McCarran planned to seek a fifth Senate term at age eighty in 1956. After supporting a candidate against Pittman in the Democratic governor's primary, he campaigned for the ticket, hoping for a united party. On September 28, 1954, he collapsed and died of a heart attack in Hawthorne. What happened to his machine echoed the aftermath of Wingfield's empire: their allies would go wherever they could have power and influence. In McCarran's case, the dozens of attorneys he put through law school went on to major roles in Nevada political and legal life. The personal and ideological divisions he created among Democrats survived him, but with less open warfare. More immediately, Russell named his successor, Republican Ernest Brown, but Democrats won a state supreme court ruling that because McCarran died long enough before the November election, Brown would have to appear on the ballot. Two years after his surprising loss to Mechling, Bible defeated Brown.

At the time, with Malone in the minority and Bible a freshman, Nevada had less clout in the Senate than it had had in decades. In 1956, tired of Washington and missing Nevada, Bible declined to seek reelection. When GOP representative Cliff Young announced his candidacy, Democrats feared the loss of the seat could cost them their narrow control of the Senate. Majority Leader Lyndon Johnson of Texas pressured Bible to run again, and the Nevadan agreed. Bible won a close, hard-fought race, while Walter Baring regained the House seat he had lost to Young. Two years later Bible parlayed his willingness to keep serving and his relationship with Johnson into the seat on the powerful Appropriations Committee that Nevada had lost with McCarran's death.

Bible's rise reflected another way that McCarran influenced the state. He had been the first "McCarran boy," one of about fifty Nevadans who went to law school in the Washington, DC, area on the senator's patronage and then returned home to practice law. They often became involved in local or state politics, and their loyalty provided McCarran with a built-in support network that he preferred not to consider a machine. Their number included Bible; Grant Sawyer, who rose from Elko County district attorney to university regent to governor; Jon Collins, a White Pine judge and state supreme court justice; Clark County commissioner Ralph Denton; and Joe and Bob McDonald, sons of the *Nevada State Journal*'s editor and behind-the-scenes operatives. Decades after McCarran's death, his influence continued through his "boys" and the federal projects he brought to Nevada.

Land and Water: The Federal Spigot

McCarran's death and Bible's ascent affected Nevada in other ways, especially on land and water issues. The Eisenhower administration had supported handing millions of acres of public lands to the states, which would be free to do largely as they wished. Although McCarran hounded federal officials overseeing grazing, Bible proved less wedded to livestock interests and unfettered development. He backed the Upper Colorado Storage Act, which took effect in 1956; although Nevada belonged to the Lower Colorado group of states, the bill included provisions for Nevada to receive electricity from Utah's Glen Canyon Dam.

Republicans preferred privately developed dams and other reclamation projects, but Bible, a Democrat raised in Fallon in the Newlands Project's shadow, wanted federal control. Bible worked with other western congressmen and tried to balance development and the environment. In 1955 he secured sixty-six thousand dollars for the Bureau of Reclamation to study whether and how to pump Lake Mead water to Las Vegas—the seeds of a future project. Soon afterward, he and Malone introduced a bill for the Washoe Reclamation Project. With the Truckee having just flooded Reno and Sparks, the new measure, for an expected fifty-two million dollars, would regulate the river's flow, set up two storage facilities (at Stampede Dam in California and at Watasheamu on the Carson River's east fork) with power plants nearby, and build the Prosser Dam and Reservoir. Later, the Washoe Project's Marble Bluff Dam and Pyramid Lake Fishway made it easier for fish to reach the Truckee.

Nevada's major cities faced water issues. A 1964 study by the University of Nevada's Mackay School of Mines and US Geological Survey made the telling point that until World War I, Nevada communities developed and grew around mining discoveries, but after that they grew around water sources. After World War II, Nevada's urban growth in Reno and Las Vegas highlighted this change. The Washoe Project helped Reno, as did senators from Nevada and California winning passage of legislation to allow their two states to negotiate a compact to regulate the waters of Lake Tahoe and the Carson, Truckee, and Walker Rivers.

Southern Nevada's water problems involved access and availability. Replacing the Las Vegas Land and Water Company, a Union Pacific subsidiary, with the Las Vegas Valley Water District in 1948 improved management, but as the population rose, the water table fell. In 1952 the district and the Basic plant made a deal: once it built a connecting line and improved distribution, Basic would pump up to thirteen million gallons from Lake Mead to Las Vegas daily. Three years later Las Vegas obtained its first Colorado River water. Meanwhile, with Bible arguing the case and working with state engineer Hugh Shamberger to determine water needs, the US Supreme Court ensured Nevada's access by letting it intervene in the dispute between Arizona and California over Colorado River water.

Southern Nevada exemplified historian Gerald Nash's description of the modern West as largely "the creature of the federal government." To prosper as a tourist destination, Las Vegas needed good transportation. Since opening in 1941, the gunnery school shared space with the municipal airport. The army scaled back the base as the war ended, but McCarran pressured Pentagon officials to reopen it. The Cold War defense buildup and McCarran's power persuaded them, but their conditions included the city moving its airfield. Clark County approved a bond issue to finance a new airport, bought Alamo Airport on Highway 91, expanded the old field, opened it in 1948, and named it for McCarran.

Meanwhile, Nevada's military bases opened during World War II benefited from federal largesse. The newly created air force took over the gunnery school and expanded it, renaming it in 1950 for Lieutenant William Nellis, a Searchlight native killed on his seventieth mission over Europe during the war. The continuing Cold War and the Korean War inspired the base's growth: by 1953 fifty-two hundred employees earned a payroll of fifty million dollars a year and prompted home-building projects near

Nellis; in 1958 it became the home of the Tactical Air Command. What Dwight Eisenhower later called "the military-industrial complex" benefited Nevada as it did other western states, although less so than elsewhere in higher education. Nevada enjoyed the fruits of population and income growth, improved roads, and tourism from surrounding areas, but colleges and universities elsewhere became more involved in research contracts.

The Limits of Nevada Women's World

"Rosie the Riveter" and her Basic plant equivalent, "Magnesium Maggie," symbolized wartime opportunities for women. After the war most women returned to the home, but more of them began to question why they should. In Nevada women occupied an anomalous position. With resorts and showrooms expanding, female performers found opportunity—and African Americans such as Lena Horne and Dorothy Dandridge encountered racism. Some women found work as dancers in what *Life* magazine called a "showgirl Shangri-La," although they received treatment that varied from paternalistic to harsh. Maxine Lewis rose from showgirl to entertainment director on the Strip, but proved the exception rather than the rule. Showgirls faced criticism from outside as promiscuous, but the reality proved far different; also, they made a living outside the home at a time when many women found that avenue closed to them.

Journalism provided opportunities for Nevada women that might not have existed elsewhere. Yerington native Ruthe Deskin became Hank Greenspun's assistant and vital to the *Sun*'s survival. Avery Stitser took over the *Humboldt Star* on her husband's death in 1939 and owned it until 1960, becoming the State Press Association's first woman president in 1955. Florence Lee Jones Cahlan spent several decades at the *Las Vegas Review-Journal* as a reporter and chronicler of the area's history. Boulder City teacher Gene Segerblom wrote freelance articles, often about the community, with photography by her artist husband, Cliff. Flo Burge started writing for the *Reno Evening Gazette* and wound up the award-winning editor of its women's pages. Alice Key became an editor for the West Las Vegas *Voice* and cohosted a local television show with fellow civil rights activist Bob Bailey, breaking both the color line and the glass ceiling.

More women had an impact in politics. McCarran's top aide, Eva Adams, wielded great power on Capitol Hill and in Nevada; after his death she worked for his successors until her appointment in 1961 as director of the

United States Mint. Social worker and accountant Flora Dungan became active in local politics. Former educators Maude Frazier of Clark County and Hazel Denton of Lincoln County won assembly seats and fought for civil rights and to improve Nevada schools. Reno lawyer Nada Novakovich, who worked for Carville in his brief Senate tenure, became one of the first women to seek federal office, losing a House bid in 1956. After three terms as the only woman elected state superintendent of education before the office became appointive, Mildred Bray served as the governor's secretary. Sallie Springmeyer, the wife of a progressive political activist, spent three terms on the state board of health and played key roles in the Nevada Society for Crippled Children and the League of Women Voters. Emilie Wanderer, one of southern Nevada's first women lawyers, represented the NAACP and worked to help establish family courts—not in office, but as an active citizen. Mary Fulstone made a mark on the Lyon County and state boards of education, but even more as a physician, serving Native Americans in the surrounding area and leading an effort to build a new hospital in Yerington.

Steps Toward Reform

The 1950s marked a turning point in the development of education in Nevada. Primary and secondary education reached a crisis, thanks partly to growth (the Las Vegas school population shot up 25 percent just from 1952 to 1953) and long-term underfunding that forced many double sessions. Worse, with no state standards for school districts, about two hundred of them existed—fourteen just in Clark County. Lawmakers increased funding in 1953 without a tax hike, but Frazier failed in an effort to revamp state support and administration. Reno parents formed a citizens group to seek reforms, joined by various Parent-Teacher Association groups, while Las Vegas's superintendent warned of initiative petitions if the legislature did nothing about funding.

The legislature did something. In 1954, at a special session, lawmakers set aside twenty-five thousand dollars for a School Survey Committee, which hired the George Peabody College for Teachers in Tennessee. The Peabody Report urged consolidating jurisdictions into county-wide districts and improving and standardizing teacher salaries and school facilities. Legislators accepted the recommendations at the 1955 session and passed a 2 percent statewide sales tax for education. The next year voters endorsed the tax in a referendum, despite an antitaxation group's attempt to stop it, and lawmakers approved a graduated tax on gross gaming revenue, requiring a higher tax rate of more profitable casinos, though not just to fund schools. The legislature also asked voters to approve changing the state's superintendent of public instruction to an appointed position from an elected one. But some aspects of the problem persisted: Clark and Washoe County residents complained that they generated more than 80 percent of the sales tax revenues, but a larger percentage of the money went to rural counties.

Higher education also expanded significantly. In the late 1940s the University of Southern California and Brigham Young University discussed opening satellite campuses in Las Vegas, where a growing populace lacked access to college and teachers resented having to go to Reno for classes required for certification. The state felt the pressure and acted. In 1951 the University of Nevada opened a southern regional division administered by English professor James Dickinson, who recruited instructors and found space at Las Vegas High School. Las Vegans wanted a campus, but the rural-dominated legislature agreed to fund it only with community contributions. Las Vegans raised the money and obtained the land. In 1957 Frazier Hall opened, named for the legislature's most ardent advocate of higher education in southern Nevada, on what became the UNLV campus.

Yet higher education suffered another, different, crisis. In 1952 new university president Minard Stout, a veteran of secondary education and its different form of governance than universities, sought to impose new policies, lowered entrance requirements, and objected when professors expressed opinions. When biology professor Frank Richardson distributed a *Scientific Monthly* article criticizing "professional educators" and "quackery in the schools," Stout called him a "buttinsky"—in the McCarthy era, no minor insult. As Richardson's lawyer, Bruce Thompson, said in response to a pro-Stout editorial, "Those who speak of communism and academic freedom in one breath understand neither." After legislative hearings, possibly on orders from the Board of Regents, Stout fired five faculty who testified, three from English and two from biology, all well regarded on campus, tenured, and thus supposedly immune from firing, for exercising First Amendment rights. He charged them with "engaging in 'disturbing activities,'" and several proadministration professors received pay raises. Negotiations and investigations dragged on, with Nevada's leading author, Walter Van Tilburg Clark, resigning from the English Department in protest, students hanging Stout in effigy, and most of the professors returning; one of them, Robert Gorrell, the author of a widely used English textbook, later became a dean and academic vice president. Harassed after his reinstatement, Richardson left and had a distinguished career at the University of Washington.

The 1955 legislature reacted to the controversy by naming a group to investigate. The McHenry Report credited Stout with bettering salaries, the library budget, and fund-raising, but criticized his leadership style as "quasi-military." It recommended expanding the Board of Regents and making it appointed rather than elected. The legislature went halfway, expanding the board from five to nine. In 1957 the new members, including younger and more liberal politicians like Thompson and Elko County district attorney Grant Sawyer, joined with several members to fire Stout and work to heal the wounds.

In addition to its educational system, Nevada's social policies prompted a great deal of criticism. In 1955 crusading journalist Albert Deutsch headlined an article in *Collier's*, a national magazine, "The Sorry State of Nevada." After noting its low taxes and the nation's third-highest per capita income, he pointed out Nevada had the nation's highest crime and suicide rates, among the highest infant mortality and tuberculosis death rates, overcrowded prisons and orphanages, and welfare services "below those of many of the poorest states." The Peabody study had revealed a low rate of public school spending per student and wealth disparities and a heavy reliance on federal funding for local programs. A 1954 article in *Ebony* proclaimed, "Negroes can't win in Las Vegas," and could have said the same of the rest of the state.

Yet Nevada also made progress in several areas. In 1945, under Dr. Sidney Tillim's leadership, the state mental hospital hired its first psychologist and began both an occupational therapy program and a clinic that traveled throughout rural Nevada. Governor Charles Russell pushed through changes to the welfare system and an Aid to Dependent Children program. He also reorganized the state parks commission, which won its battle for funds to renovate existing parks and add others, including Fort Churchill, Ward Charcoal Ovens, and Cathedral Gorge.

The Civil Rights Revolution

In World War II African Americans fought for "Double V for Victory" against fascism abroad and for equal rights at home. Their efforts bore fruit: when he joined the Brooklyn Dodgers in 1947, Jackie Robinson desegregated Major League Baseball, in 1948 President Harry Truman ordered the military integrated over objections from many top officers, and the NAACP pursued a legal strategy of demanding truly "separate but equal" facilities, requiring states to spend large sums to provide professional and graduate education for black people or to allow them to enter previously all-white schools. Dominated by southerners and other conservative Democrats, Congress expressed no interest in legislating equal rights.

Nevada's leaders proved similar. After earlier efforts failed in the 1939, 1947, and 1949 legislative sessions, Assemblyman George Rudiak, a Las Vegas attorney, introduced a bill in 1953 to criminalize discrimination on the basis of race, creed, or color. Despite support from a few other legislators, their colleagues blocked it, and Rudiak lost his next election. Also in 1953 the NAACP urged Las Vegas to enact a civil rights ordinance. City attorney Howard Cannon responded that the city charter's silence on the issue made it a matter for the legislature. In Las Vegas political and business leaders continued to confine African Americans, joined by a few whites

African Americans and other minorities migrating to southern Nevada wound up segregated in West Las Vegas. The corner of D and Jefferson, shown here in 1943, suggests the growth and lack of such services as paved streets and sidewalks. Courtesy of Special Collections, University Libraries, University of Nevada, Las Vegas.

and Hispanics, west of the railroad tracks, and similar practices flourished in Reno.

Early in the twentieth century, scholar and activist W. E. B. DuBois argued for the creation of a "talented tenth," a professional class that would deprive whites of money they made serving the black community's needs and lead the fight for civil rights. The growth of Las Vegas's black population attracted the needed group. Doctor Charles West, dentist James McMillan, entertainer Bob Bailey, and journalist Alice Key joined nurse Lubertha Johnson; teacher Mabel Hoggard and her husband, David; businessman Woodrow Wilson; and ministers such as Donald Clark. In 1951 Wilson opened the Westside Federal Credit Union so that African Americans would have their own banking institution. They started community newspapers that informed and exhorted African Americans, organized boycotts of businesses that refused to hire them, and worked for pro–civil rights candidates. In Reno the NAACP chapter continued to grow, and Black Springs north of Reno grew and expanded, in many ways resembling earlier West Las Vegas, with its lack of streetlights and pavement and mostly African American population.

Ethnicity and Awareness

After the war Congress cut funding to the Bureau of Indian Affairs as part of a new policy of "termination"—removing itself from Native American affairs. In 1946 the Indian Claims Commission (ICC) Act permitted lawsuits against the federal government for compensation for past mistreatment. The Western Shoshone split between "traditionals" seeking acknowledgment that they retained landownership under the 1863 Treaty of Ruby Valley and those who hoped for federal economic support. In 1950, amid these divisions, Shoshone groups from Nevada, Idaho, and Utah met and agreed to pursue financial redress. The process proved long and divisive. The federal government also tried to defeat cases brought by Northern and Southern Paiutes by claiming that neither legally constituted a unique tribe.

Nevada's Native people benefited and suffered from federal interest. The Interstate Highway Act reduced isolation among reservations. The BIA's "Long Range Program" helped ease the transition to termination. The Elko colony received funds to hook into the town's sewage system, and the Duck Valley group received funds to help with its cattle and alfalfa. While McCarran proved unable to obtain funds for the Battle Mountain colony,

Malone failed with a bill designed to repeal the Indian Reorganization Act of 1934 and essentially gut the BIA. In 1955 the BIA contracted with the University of Nevada's extension service, which helped several tribes improve agricultural production.

At other times, though, the federal government showed less interest in Native Americans' problems. In 1947 the BIA's Indian Education Division became part of Nevada's Department of Education, and by 1956 Indian day schools became public schools. Southern Paiutes received no aid from the Long Range Program, despite a BIA report describing the Moapa and Las Vegas groups as "ready" to run their own affairs. With the BIA overseeing all twenty-eight Nevada reservations from Carson City, distant tribes received less help: in the mid-1950s the Moapa band lived too far from schools to compete educationally; the Las Vegas colony lacked electricity and air-conditioning, and the one well went dry each summer as the water table dropped; and at the Owyhee reservation on the Idaho-Nevada line, with little BIA support, most Western Shoshone women obtained domestic work.

Robert Laxalt (*right*), produced a shelf of fiction and nonfiction classics, most notably *Sweet Promised Land,* about the return of his father, Dominique (*left*), to the Pyrenees after years of sheepherding in Nevada. Photo by Bill Belknap. Courtesy of the Basque Studies Library.

Although smaller, another ethnic group gained more prominence: Basques. The Taylor Grazing Act of 1934 drove out "tramp sheepmen" grazing their stock for free on government land. More important, Carson City reporter Robert Laxalt published magazine articles and, in 1957, *Sweet Promised Land,* which began, "My father was a sheepherder, and his home was the hills," and introduced millions to Basque culture. "Conditioned by years of discrimination, Basques had learned to keep a low profile and to assert their ethnicity only in the privacy of their homes," wrote literary scholar Cheryll Glotfelty, but Laxalt "helped Basques to be openly proud of their ethnic identity." He wrote dozens of books and articles, directed the University of Nevada Press, taught at the university, and helped start its Basque studies program and the national Basque festival in Sparks.

In this era Nevada's Hispanic populace remained small. The Bracero Program, begun to attract Mexicans to make up for the wartime manpower shortage, drew some Latinos, especially to Moapa Valley, where about fifteen hundred to two thousand spent a few months on the spring harvest, and Pahrump Valley in Nye County. But in 1955 the State Employment Service refused to certify them as farmworkers, prompting many of the migrants to work in Arizona instead. Hispanics also encountered some of the same discrimination as African Americans, limited to menial casino jobs and unable to obtain bank loans to buy homes in traditionally white areas.

Image Problems: Good and Bad Government

As governor, Russell sought to modernize and streamline state government. The legislature dissolved some regulatory boards, but he backed several social programs and an economic development office to attract industry. Russell sought reforms in civil service requirements and the purchasing department, costing himself potential supporters who resented losing patronage and contracts. Russell also led an effort to eliminate the election of the surveyor general after learning that the last two winners—a Democrat and a Republican—pocketed significant sums selling state lands, prompting state grand jury and legislative investigations.

Political corruption affected all levels of government. In 1954 a county grand jury indicted the mayor of North Las Vegas and three councilmen for taking kickbacks from a sewer contractor. All four resigned, leaving the council member they declined to include in their activities: Dorothy

Porter, a former showgirl who became Nevada's first female mayor. In 1957 the city's first mayor, Horace Tucker, barely escaped a manslaughter conviction after shooting and killing a fellow political operative in his home—but when Tucker killed another man six years later, he went to prison, although for less than two years.

After the city of Las Vegas shut down its Block 16 in 1942, doctors and school officials cited a decline in the local venereal disease rate as proof of their success. But operators moved south into Clark County on Boulder Highway, opening brothels four miles away in—appropriately—Formyle. Chamber of Commerce, gaming, and law enforcement officials all condemned prostitution, as did local religious leaders. Despite these opponents and laws against them, the brothels somehow stayed open. South of town in Searchlight, the brothel flourished under the same owner as the local casino and airport.

Nevada also needed to address the legal standing of brothels, since no state law barred them. In 1948 Washoe County commissioners targeted a new brothel on Commercial Row, but the owner ignored them. When the district attorney ordered it closed as a public nuisance, she sued. The next year the Nevada Supreme Court upheld the county in the absence of any statute. The legislature responded with a bill allowing brothels and barring the use of the public nuisance law. Governor Vail Pittman vetoed the bill, and local jurisdictions acted. Reno and Las Vegas banned prostitution within city limits by holding it to be a public nuisance. Smaller counties often looked the other way: in 1958, running for the Democratic nomination for governor, Clark County attorney George Franklin accused Elko's district attorney, Grant Sawyer, of allowing five brothels near the local elementary school. Sawyer responded that Franklin erred, and eight brothels functioned there; Sawyer said, "Everybody laughed, and the whole thing just went away."

Trouble in Gaming Regulation

Russell's support for enhanced gaming regulation came from a desire for better government, but also due to a brothel-related scandal and public pressure. After the 1945 law directly taxed gaming revenues and gave licensing authority to the Tax Commission, Nevada did little to police gaming. The commission handled a variety of other matters, and secretary Robbins Cahill had few staffers to help him. Worse, as the state increased its taxes on the industry from the original 1 percent in 1945, state employees collecting them knew little about the business. Attorney General Alan Bible wrote an opinion upholding the Tax Commission's primacy over local regulators and its right to deny an applicant a license due to "just cause, unsavory reputation, or other reasons of public interest," and the legislature joined in strengthening the commission.

The problems with Nevada's regulatory system gained attention when Senator Estes Kefauver of Tennessee held hearings on organized crime (1950–51). Hoping to break ties between Democratic machines and the Mob, Kefauver toured the United States and became one of the first television stars. Kefauver declared, "As a case history of legal gambling, Nevada speaks eloquently in the negative," citing Lieutenant Governor Cliff Jones, a part-owner of the Thunderbird and Pioneer Club, and William J. Moore, a member of the Tax Commission who also owned the Last Frontier and El Cortez. While similar connections existed almost everywhere, the hearings, including a one-day stop in Las Vegas, did nothing for Nevada's reputation—although the reforms they prompted in other states drove casino owners and employees to Nevada. Kefauver's supporters introduced a bill to tax gaming receipts, but McCarran blocked it, warning that if it passed, "Virginia Street would be in mourning, and the gleaming gulch of Las Vegas would be a glowing symbol of funereal distress" (in 1955, after McCarran's death, another attempt to tax Nevada gambling winnings and profits failed in the Senate).

Yet Kefauver mattered less to the development of gaming regulation than a *Las Vegas Sun* exposé just before the 1954 election. Greenspun accused Clark County sheriff Glen Jones of taking bribes to allow brothels to operate at Formyle. When Jones countered with a one-million-dollar libel suit, the *Sun*'s source, as the publisher put it, "developed memory loss." Greenspun, his staff, and the Clark County district attorney's office set up a sting operation. They hired a private detective to pose as a mysterious hoodlum, newly arrived in Las Vegas, with large investment plans and secretly recorded his meetings with local officials.

The *Sun*'s publication of its transcripts had explosive effects. According to the *Sun*, Cliff Jones (no relation to the sheriff, but linked through marriage to the *Review-Journal*'s management) told the hoodlum that Pittman's return as governor would lead to the destruction of the Tax Commission's power and Cahill's ouster. Jones resigned as Democratic national committeeman and never again sought office. The sheriff dropped his lawsuit, and a county commissioner resigned. Russell's reelection had appeared doomed, but when Pittman defended his Democratic allies and attacked the reports as a "cheap, scurrilous political trick," he raised doubts among voters. Russell benefited and eked out a victory.

More crucially, the exposé prompted action at the 1955 legislature. According to the *Sun*, Cliff Jones claimed Meyer and Jake Lansky owned a hidden interest in the Thunderbird, demonstrating the state's failure to regulate its major industry. Russell won creation of a Gaming Control Board of three gubernatorial appointees with expertise in accounting and investigations who would investigate applicants and make recommendations for final action to the Tax Commission. The Tax Commission revoked the Thunderbird's gaming license over the allegation about the Lanskys and a loan from another gangland figure, George Sadlo. The resort's owners sued in response, and the case wended its way to the state's high court.

Casino operators also pressured legislators. They overwhelmingly passed Senate Bill (SB) 92 in 1957 to strip the state of most of its power by involving the courts in any license revocation. Gaming executives hoped to force the state to produce evidence that would stand up in court, as opposed to the lower standards required by a state agency. After the governor vetoed the bill, one state senator, Republican Ralph Lattin of Churchill County, switched his vote to defeat the bill and uphold Russell, who described him as "a nervous wreck over the thing." Nevada almost gutted the process designed to ensure the honesty of its leading industry, except for what historian James Hulse, who covered the events as a reporter, called "a singular act of courage without parallel in the history of the legislature."

But the lawsuit loomed. In 1957 just after SB 92's defeat, in *Tax Commission v. Hicks*, Nevada's three high court justices held the commission wrongly revoked the Thunderbird's license. Justice Charles Merrill, who later spent two decades on the US Ninth Circuit Court of Appeals, rebuked the commission for acting "without substantial evidentiary support." Otherwise, he gave the state what it wanted and needed. "Nevada gambling, if it is to succeed as a lawful enterprise, must be free from the criminal and corruptive taint acquired by gambling beyond our borders," he wrote. "If this is to be accomplished not only must the operation of gambling be carefully controlled, but the character and background of those who would engage in gambling in this state must be carefully scrutinized." The state won the power to regulate its casinos, and Merrill's opinion strengthened it.

The Revolution of 1958

Nationally, the 1958 midterms led to a more liberal Democratic US Senate, but Nevada had its own minirevolution. At the deadline for filing for office, three rising young Nevada Democrats had yet to state their plans. Then Grant Sawyer, thirty-nine, announced for governor; Howard Cannon, forty-five, the Las Vegas city attorney and a former House candidate, for the Senate; and Roger D. Foley, forty, the federal judge's son and former Clark County district attorney, for attorney general. Cannon faced a primary against Fred Anderson, a Reno doctor and friend of Bible's, while Sawyer—also close to Anderson—would have to overcome Clark County attorney George Franklin and Attorney General Harvey Dickerson, an ally of the McCarran machine's remnants and the son of a governor.

McCarran's legacy shaped the race. Bible avoided his habit of meddling, and Cannon won and then cruised past Malone in the general election—a sign of the southern Nevada growth that McCarran's support for federal projects and gaming helped foster. Sure of his rural support, Sawyer concentrated on winning enough votes in Clark County. Although Sawyer attended law school on McCarran's patronage, most of the old machine backed Dickerson; Sawyer attacked those connections, including E. L. Cord, a wealthy car manufacturer living in Nevada. Sawyer won and then beat Russell in November, and Foley had a comparatively easy race. The elections, Greenspun wrote in the *Sun*, "shattered the sphere of influence over Nevada politics enjoyed these many years by a bipartisan group." Greenspun spoke too soon, but the winners would change Nevada in significant ways.

Yet Nevada had already changed. By the end of the 1950s, three-quarters of the state's residents lived in its most urban counties, Clark and Washoe, with Las Vegas having replaced Reno as Nevada's largest city. In some ways, Nevada exemplified the affluence of the postwar baby boom—but also the discrimination and poverty that would bubble to the surface during the 1960s.

SUGGESTED READINGS

Bailey, William H. "Bob." *Looking Up! Finding My Voice in Las Vegas.* Las Vegas: Stephens Press, 2009.

Balboni, Alan. *Beyond the Mafia: Italian Americans and the Development of Las Vegas.* 1996. Reprint, Reno: University of Nevada Press, 2006.

Ball, Howard. *Justice Downwind: America's Atomic Testing Program in the 1950s.* New York: Oxford University Press, 1986.

Barber, Phyllis. *How I Got Cultured: A Nevada Memoir.* Athens: University of Georgia Press, 1992.

————. *Raw Edges: A Memoir.* Reno: University of Nevada Press, 2010.

Berman, Susan. *Easy Street.* New York: Dial Press, 1981.

Blachley, Annie. *Pestilence, Politics, and Pizzazz: The Story of Public Health in Las Vegas.* Reno: Greasewood Press, 2002.

Boulard, Gary. *Louis Prima.* Urbana: University of Illinois Press, 2002.

Bracey, Earnest N. *The Moulin Rouge and Black Rights in Las Vegas: A History of the First Racially Integrated Hotel-Casino.* Jefferson, NC: McFarland, 2009.

Clavin, Tom. *That Old Black Magic: Louis Prima, Keely Smith and the Golden Age of Las Vegas.* Chicago: Chicago Review Press, 2010.

Davies, Richard O., ed. *The Maverick Spirit: Building the New Nevada.* Reno: University of Nevada Press, 1998.

Davis, Sammy, Jr., Jane Boyar, and Burt Boyar. *Yes I Can.* New York: Farrar, Straus, and Giroux, 1990.

Douglass, Jack, and William A. Douglass. *Tap Dancing on Ice: The Life and Times of a Nevada Gaming Pioneer.* Reno: University of Nevada Oral History Program, 1996.

Fradkin, Philip L. *Fallout: An American Nuclear Tragedy.* Tucson: University of Arizona Press, 1989.

Geran, Trish. *Beyond the Glimmering Lights: The Pride and Perseverance of African Americans in Las Vegas.* Las Vegas: Stephens Press, 2006.

Hevly, Bruce, and John M. Findlay, eds. *The Atomic West.* Seattle: University of Washington Press, 1998.

Kefauver, Estes. *Crime in America.* Garden City, NY: Doubleday, 1951.

Kille, J. Dee. *Academic Freedom Imperilled: The McCarthy Era at the University of Nevada.* Reno: University of Nevada Press, 2004.

Lacey, Robert. *Little Man: Meyer Lansky and the Gangster Life.* Boston: Little, Brown, 1991.

Land, Barbara, and Myrick Land. *A Short History of Las Vegas.* Reno: University of Nevada Press, 2004.

Laxalt, Robert. *Sweet Promised Land.* 1957. Reprint, New York: Harper & Row, 1974.

Lewis, Marvin. *Martha and the Doctor: A Frontier Family in Central Nevada.* Reno: University of Nevada Press, 1977.

Liebling, A. J. *A Reporter at Large: Dateline—Pyramid Lake, Nevada.* Reno: University of Nevada Press, 2000.

McMillan, James B., Gary E. Elliott, and R. T. King. *Fighting Back: A Life in the Struggle for Civil Rights.* Reno: University of Nevada Oral History Program, 1997.

McNamara, Elaine Cali. *In the Midst of Cowboys, Crooners, and Gangsters: Recollections of the Las Vegas Glamour Era*. Las Vegas: Stephens Press, 2011.

Moehring, Eugene P. *Resort City in the Sunbelt: Las Vegas, 1930–2000*. Reno: University of Nevada Press, 2000.

———. *UNLV: The University of Nevada, Las Vegas: A History*. Reno: University of Nevada Press, 2007.

Moehring, Eugene P., and Michael S. Green. *Las Vegas: A Centennial History*. Reno: University of Nevada Press, 2005.

Moody, Eric N. *Southern Gentleman of Nevada Politics: Vail M. Pittman*. Reno: University of Nevada Press, 1974.

Moore, William Howard. *The Kefauver Committee and the Politics of Crime, 1950–1952*. Columbia: University of Missouri Press, 1974.

Murchie, Archie, and R. T. King. *The Free Life of a Ranger*. Reno: University of Nevada Oral History Program, 2002.

Nelson, Warren. *Always Bet on the Butcher: Warren Nelson and Casino Gaming*. Reno: University of Nevada Oral History Program, 1994.

Odessky, Dick. *Fly on the Wall: Recollections of Las Vegas' Good Old, Bad Old Days*. Las Vegas: Huntington Press, 1999.

Paris, Beltran, and William A. Douglass. *Beltran, Basque Sheepman of the American West*. Reno: University of Nevada Press, 1979.

Ronald, Ann. *Friendly Fallout, 1953*. Reno: University of Nevada Press, 2010.

Russo, Gus. *Supermob: How Sidney Korshak and His Criminal Associates Became America's Hidden Powerbrokers*. New York: Bloomsbury, 2006.

Schwartz, David G. *Suburban Xanadu: The Casino Resort on the Las Vegas Strip and Beyond, 1945–1978*. New York: Routledge, 2003.

Sheehan, Jack E., ed. *The Players: The Men Who Made Las Vegas*. Reno: University of Nevada Press, 1997.

———. *Quiet Kingmaker of Las Vegas: E. Parry Thomas*. Las Vegas: Stephens Press, 2009.

Sheehan, Jack, and Brian Hurlburt. *City of Champions: The History of Professional Golf in Las Vegas*. Las Vegas: Stephens Press, 2012.

Szasz, Ferenc Morton. *Atomic Comics: Cartoonists Confront the Nuclear World*. Reno: University of Nevada Press, 2012.

Titus, A. Costandina. *Bombs in the Backyard: Atomic Testing and American Politics*. Reno: University of Nevada Press, 2001.

Zook, Lynn M., Allen Sandquist, and Carey Burke. *Las Vegas, 1905–1965*. Charleston, SC: Arcadia, 2009.

13

Reshaping Nevada, 1958–70

America reinvented itself in the 1960s, expanding the social safety net through John Kennedy's New Frontier and Lyndon Johnson's Great Society while inviting robust debate and enduring violence. The decade produced a "rights revolution" among African Americans, women, Latinos, Native Americans, and the young, often encouraged by the most liberal Supreme Court in US history and by foreign events: the long involvement in Vietnam led to fifty-eight thousand American deaths (and those of up to two million Southeast Asian people), inspired protests, and increased questioning of authority at all levels. The Sunbelt's growth went on: by the early 1960s California passed New York as the most populous state, and its prosperity and proximity made tourism an even bigger bonanza for Nevada. About one-third of Nevadans had moved to the state in the previous five years, more than half of them from California or the Southwest. These changes and others unique to the state altered Nevada's political, economic, social, and cultural life.

Hanging Tough

Taking office as governor in 1959, Grant Sawyer saw gaming regulation as crucial to protecting the industry and economy. He sought to separate regulation from politics and the Tax Commission, which decided on gaming licenses. While the governor served on the commission, and could be susceptible to pressure, he would simply appoint the five members of the new Gaming Commission and have nothing to do with its deliberations. The legislature approved these proposals and in 1961 Sawyer's call for an appointed advisory Gaming Policy Board. Sawyer told his regulators, "Hang tough and you will be doing a great service to me, to the industry, and to the state." But that also meant offending casino owners who felt that regulators treated them unfairly, and Attorney General Roger D. Foley, a civil libertarian, condemned some of the regulators' actions.

Sawyer took other controversial steps. Regulators proposed a "List of Excluded Persons," known as the "Black Book" for the binder containing the names, barring some criminals or suspected criminals from entering a casino. The first class consisted of a dozen, all of Italian background, all reputed mobsters. Sawyer said, "I didn't see how we could put somebody's name on a list and say, 'You can't go into a public accommodation,'" but "I was in favor of doing anything within the law to keep those people out of Nevada." One of them, Marshall Caifano, also known as Johnny Marshall, sued in a federal court, which upheld Nevada's actions.

The Black Book embroiled Sawyer in another fight. In 1963 Chicago mobster Sam Giancana, an original entrant, ignored it and visited Lake Tahoe's Cal-Neva Lodge as a guest of licensed owner Frank Sinatra, leader of the entertainment "Rat Pack" (with no connection to Reno's Cal-Neva, owned by a group that included Tonopah native Jack Douglass, a onetime slot route operator in central Nevada mining camps, and longtime Reno

Elected president in 1960, John F. Kennedy enjoyed support from a variety of Nevadans, including Grant Sawyer (with wife Bette on the right), who pushed for civil rights and improved gaming regulation during his two terms as governor. Courtesy of Special Collections, University of Nevada–Reno Library.

gaming executive Warren Nelson). Amid rumors that Sinatra served as Giancana's front man, Gaming Control Board chair Ed Olsen spoke with representatives for Sinatra, who called Olsen, swore at him, and seemed to threaten him. That discussion remained secret, but Sinatra surrendered his license. A few weeks later Sawyer went to Las Vegas to greet Kennedy, speaking at the Convention Center. After pleasantries, Kennedy asked, "What are you guys doing to my friend Frank Sinatra?" Sawyer replied, "Mr. President, I'll try to take care of things here in Nevada, and I wish you luck on the national level."

Despite being Kennedy's leading Nevada supporter in 1960 (Senators Alan Bible and Howard Cannon backed Senate majority leader Lyndon Johnson for the nomination), Sawyer increasingly saw the federal government as more enemy than friend. Kennedy's brother Robert had been part of a Senate probe of the Teamsters and their pension fund and targeted them as attorney general, despite Mob interests helping the Kennedy campaign. He backed the Wire Act of 1961 to ban using telephone and telegraph lines for sending information about gambling, taking aim at the Mob's illegal bookmaking operations. The Department of Justice asked Foley—another Kennedy backer in 1960—to deputize sixty-five federal agents as part of the Gaming Control Board to raid Nevada's casinos. Sawyer and Foley went to visit Bobby Kennedy, who treated the governor "as someone who had just stepped out from behind a crap table; and he seemed to imply that I was connected with the mob, which really burned me up." From there they went to the White House, where Sawyer warned of dire consequences in case of a raid, although he later admitted to being unsure of what those consequences might be. Whatever Sawyer and Foley told John Kennedy, his brother's proposed raid never happened.

Yet problems persisted with federal officials. After seeking to cooperate with J. Edgar Hoover, Sawyer accused the FBI of taking information the state supplied, claiming it as its own discoveries, and providing no help in return. Sawyer learned the FBI and Justice Department illegally wiretapped Nevada casino executives and then leaked their findings, which no court would have admitted, to favored news reporters. The governor saw these acts as violations of the Bill of Rights. He called for Hoover's resignation, suggested prosecuting FBI agents who violated Nevada laws against wiretapping, and attacked the FBI director's "Nazi tactics."

Nevada: The Entertainment Capital

Since Elko's Commercial Hotel started hosting headliners in 1941, Nevada had been known for big-name entertainment. Elko still drew stars, as did Harrah's in Reno and Lake Tahoe and a few other properties, but Las Vegas gained the biggest reputation for headliners. In the 1950s and 1960s, as the proliferation of hotels tapped the talent pool, Strip resort owners both copied one another and innovated. In 1958 the Stardust opened with Lido de Paris, a French revue. The Tropicana followed with the Folies Bergère and the Dunes with Casino de Paris. A few hotels imported Broadway productions. Some moved away from variety in the showroom to emphasizing one headliner, with one opening act. Lounge performances gained importance, as the Sahara brought in comedian Don Rickles and legendary jazz and swing musician Louis Prima with his wife, singer Keely Smith, and Sam Butera and the Witnesses. Joining the Mary Kaye Trio, a popular Strip act, they turned the lounges into important attractions in their own right.

No performers demonstrated the impact of entertainment more than the Rat Pack. Filming *Oceans 11* in Las Vegas early in 1960, Sinatra, Dean Martin, Sammy Davis Jr., Joey Bishop, and Peter Lawford appeared for several weeks in the Copa Room at the Sands. Their shows drew Hollywood visitors who joined them onstage and then candidate John Kennedy, whose sister Patricia had married Lawford (on the trip Kennedy received a substantial sum from casino owners for his campaign and began an affair with Judith Campbell, also Giancana's mistress). The Rat Pack's behavior onstage and offstage symbolized Las Vegas: a "cool" place where people could misbehave or do what seemed scandalous back home.

The Rat Pack also fitted into Nevada's evolving image and the promotion of it. Emphasizing the Strip and downtown offered tourists carefree fun, *Oceans 11* reflected the Rat Pack's free-spirited ways, while *Viva Las Vegas* (1964) with Elvis Presley and Ann-Margret highlighted youth and love—all emotions that Las Vegas marketers encouraged. *Bonanza,* one of America's most popular television shows, depicted a Hollywood version of early ranching and Comstock life. The era's most prominent movie about northern Nevada, *The Misfits,* based on a story by playwright Arthur Miller, stressed western themes, much as the nearest large city, Reno, did—and just as Reno modernized its approach, the film depicted conflicts between the older West and the new. Finally following in Las Vegas's footsteps, Reno casino owners pooled their resources to better market the city and its attractions and moved away from the mythic western approach and divorce and toward the year-round recreational opportunities locally and at nearby Lake Tahoe.

Reno proved more ambivalent than Las Vegas about gaming. "The Biggest Little City" could make its own claim to the Rat Pack: it boasted many stars, but Sammy Davis Jr. performed there from 1930 at the Club Fortune until 1988 at Harrah's, which named its showroom for him. But in 1961, when Ernest Primm tried to extend the city's redline to include his new club, city officials blocked him, and Mayor Bud Baker said Reno could do without gaming. At the same time, while southern Nevada's gaming executives often worked together on issues, those in Reno and Lake Tahoe proved less willing to cooperate with one another, and their lack of unity reduced their chances of expansion.

Building a Tourism Infrastructure

After the Stardust opened in 1958, fewer new hotels appeared on the Strip until the mid-1960s, but existing ones added rooms and attractions. Several factors kept Las Vegas booming: owners plowing profits back into the operation, Bank of Las Vegas and Teamsters loans, and the Las Vegas Convention Center's opening in 1959. Demonstrating how world events could affect Las Vegas, Fidel Castro's takeover in Cuba in 1959 led to the Havana casino district's closure; a significant number of its employees moved to southern Nevada, and its owners, mobsters and otherwise, had Nevada connections and redoubled their efforts where gambling remained legal (the previous year Nevada regulators barred state gaming license holders from operating in Cuba, too). The expansions took various forms, with the Hacienda developing a thirty-plane fleet, complete with bar and piano, to fly in customers, and the Stardust adding a grand prix raceway and a twenty-seven-foot-high neon sign and joining the Dunes in building golf courses. High-rise towers went up at the Sands, Dunes, and Fremont. Del Webb added a hotel tower and forty-four-thousand-square-foot convention facility to the Sahara and built the Sahara Tahoe. In 1969 Harrah's added a tower to its Reno property.

Reno and Las Vegas expanded their transportation systems to suit their tourism economy. By 1959 Clark County's McCarran Field served a million passengers a year, but required a bond issue to turn it into an international airport with runways long enough for jet aircraft. In 1963 McCarran's new jetport terminal opened, funded partly by one million dollars in federal aid obtained by Bible and Cannon. Cannon's service on committees affecting airlines enabled him to press the Civil Aeronautics Board for more routes to and from Las Vegas and Reno and to win approval of a bill using the tax on airline tickets to pay for airport improvements, ultimately bringing more than seventy-five million dollars to Nevada during the 1970s.

Reno's airport services also improved in this period. In 1959 the airport's new terminal opened to serve those expected to arrive for the 1960 Winter Olympics in nearby Squaw Valley, California, which drew about 250,000 tourists to the region. When Stead Air Force Base closed in 1964 amid federal budget cuts, Reno lost some of its military population, but Cannon pushed through legislation to transfer Stead to the city of Reno, which it served as a municipal airport.

Other factors boosted tourism to Nevada's two largest cities and, in some cases, the hinterland. Cannon and Bible sought funds to improve highways. Reno and Las Vegas had to wait for the completion of interstates, but I-80 made it through Reno in 1974 while I-15 reached downtown Las Vegas in 1970, four years after its dedication. Both cities also took advantage of the 1955 state law permitting the creation of county fair and recreation boards. In 1959, as the Las Vegas Convention Center opened, Reno created its board. Over the next few years, political and business leaders debated where to locate the Pioneer Center, finally settling on downtown, but it proved too small to attract larger meetings.

Mining: A Boom Waiting to Happen

The 1950s mining boom petered out. After lead and zinc production fell from $8.4 million a year to $320,000 in a decade, Bible and Cannon helped pass higher tariffs on imports to subsidize production and protect domestic mines. When the Kennedy administration repealed the Pittman Silver Purchase Act of 1934, the Nevadans pushed the minting of silver dollars known as cartwheels, but to no avail. The Bureau of Mines tried to consolidate Nevada operations in Reno by closing its Boulder City office and titanium research program, but Bible blocked the bureau's efforts. He also helped pass a measure in 1970 to task the federal government with promoting mining research and development.

Just as the Korean War prompted a mining boom, American involvement in Vietnam helped the industry and promoted exploration. The federal government encouraged mining with investment and brains: US government geologists led by Ralph Roberts examined north-central Nevada's geology, and what they found and reported inspired Newmont Mining Company to explore the area. Newmont opened the largest gold mine up to that point in the twentieth century, and the first open-pit gold mine in the United States, near Carlin in 1965, with a second one in 1969 in the Cortez mining district, sixty miles to the southwest.

One of the more significant mining developments of the time bore fruit later. In 1968 Newmont Gold invented large-scale heap leaching, which uses cyanide to remove gold from rock, reducing the cost of eliminating trace metals from low-quality ore, for the Carlin Trend west of Elko. More than forty miles long and five miles wide, it became one of the world's best veins, and the world's gold output almost doubled in the next four decades, due in part to leaching. Consequently, economic prosperity and environmental issues continued for Nevada mining.

Changing Nevada Governments

With rapid population growth came changes in local governments. Carson City's population nearly doubled during the 1960s and strained local services. The community added a new hospital, library, park, and post office and finally paved its side streets. After two decades of debate, approval by two legislative sessions, and two statewide votes, Carson City absorbed Ormsby County in 1969 to end duplication. Other jurisdictions discussed similar actions, but Reno and Sparks voters rejected a consolidation proposal in 1967, while the effort never went that far in Clark County, despite efforts by a few city and county officials.

Other local governments changed significantly. Reno voters approved a new charter allowing a strong city manager (originally Joseph Latimore, who stayed for fifteen years) with considerable independence from elected officials. Like Las Vegans a decade before, Reno residents supported reform candidates with fewer ties to gaming. Yet the effect of these changes proved limited. The city council finally voted in 1970 to end the ordinance redlining gaming licenses and let any hotel with at least one hundred rooms have an unrestricted license. Meanwhile, voters rejected a tax hike for Project RENOvation, intended to beautify the area near the Truckee and possibly turn part of Virginia Street into a pedestrian mall.

Las Vegas entered a long period of stability when Oran Gragson won the first of four terms as mayor in 1959. A New Mexico native who came west to work on the dam, he stayed and opened a furniture store. Upset that law enforcement failed to stop a rash of burglaries, he hid at his business one night and caught policemen breaking in, inspiring his candidacy and establishment of a police training academy soon after his election. Concentrating on expanding services and promoting development while streamlining government, he and other officials confronted a major growth spurt in the 1960s. Not only did Clark County's population more than double, but, demonstrating the construction industry's importance and how much the area drove the state's growth, five of every seven new Nevada housing units went up in Clark County. With suburbanization, downtown redevelopment became a significant issue. Government operations grew more important to the area with the opening of newer and larger buildings—a county courthouse in 1960, a new federal building in 1967, and a city hall in place of the old War Memorial Auditorium in 1971—as did Interstate 15's construction through the city.

New leadership reshaped North Las Vegas. After a near recall of its mayor in 1960, voters elected an almost entirely new council. Mayor William Taylor pushed to hire former Henderson city manager Clay Lynch, who floated bond issues to revitalize public works and began annexing land in all directions, expanding the city's footprint and tax base. A new civic center included a city hall and a public library, while Lynch planned an industrial park, housing projects, and more local parks. North Las Vegas benefited from expansion on Las Vegas Boulevard North in 1964, as Dunes owner Major Riddle opened the Silver Nugget and Jerry Stamis and Jerry Lodge built the smaller but profitable Jerry's Nugget.

The Battle of 1962

Most Democrats, including Bible and Sawyer, coasted to victories in the 1962 general election. But that year marked a significant moment in Nevada politics. Although the Great Society and civil rights measures of the 1960s, and important changes in Nevada, lay ahead, the state showed signs of moving toward the conservatism the rest of the country adopted in the 1970s and beyond.

Walter Baring exemplified the trend. The onetime New Deal liberal had won five terms in the House. With Kennedy proposing social programs and civil rights, Baring, an ally of right-leaning Harold's Club owner Raymond Smith, broke with his party. Declaring himself a Jeffersonian states' rights Democrat, he attacked Kennedy and his allies as liberals and possible Communists. Starting in 1962, a more liberal Clark County Democrat (district attorney John Mendoza, county commissioner Ralph Denton, former Sawyer aide Dick Ham, and county health officer Otto Ravenholt) challenged Baring in the primary, often with backing from party leaders. All fell short, unable to overcome Baring's rural and conservative support, buttressed by his devotion to mining and ranching interests; his record of constituent service; and Republicans crossing over in the primary to vote for a conservative and offering mostly token opposition in the general elections.

In 1962 Republicans made a significant gain, but not as they expected. Sawyer anticipated a tough campaign against two-term lieutenant governor and former cowboy actor Rex Bell. But Bell died, and Republicans lacked a strong replacement. A primary pitted Gragson against *Las Vegas Sun* publisher Hank Greenspun. When Greenspun accused resort owners of spending a then-lavish $250,000 to defeat him, Moe Dalitz reportedly said, "Hah, it cost almost twice that, but we got results!"—not the first or last time that casino owners tipped the scales. Gragson easily beat Greenspun, but Strip and downtown casino bosses saw he had no chance and threw their support to Sawyer, who coasted to victory.

The big GOP gain came in the lieutenant governor's office. Seeking Mormon support, Sawyer urged former senator and representative Berkeley Bunker to run. Republicans had high hopes for former Ormsby County district attorney Paul Laxalt, part of the Basque family in *Sweet Promised Land* and the son-in-law of John Ross, a longtime Republican and federal judge. Laxalt campaigned tirelessly, became one of the first statewide candidates to air television commercials, and benefited from conservative northern Nevada gaming interests like fellow Basque John Ascuaga of the Sparks Nugget and Lake Tahoe casino owner Harvey Gross. Some Democrats refused to forgive Bunker's involvement in the political controversies of the 1940s. A few of Cannon's allies feared a Democratic lieutenant governor would free Sawyer to challenge the senator's reelection in 1964 and worked behind the scenes for Laxalt, who won.

Rights, and Righting Wrongs

Early in 1960 African American students in the South began holding sit-ins. The NAACP urged local chapters to respond, and, on March 16, Las Vegas chapter president Dr. James McMillan wrote to Oran Gragson, seeking a meeting on access to public facilities and threatening a protest march if hotels and casinos failed to desegregate within ten days. After the *Las Vegas Sun* reported on the letter, McMillan received death threats. The mayor and city commissioner Reed Whipple, a banker, reportedly offered to work to ease redlining of mortgages and loans if McMillan called off the protest, but he stood firm. Finally, the casino owners agreed to integrate the Strip and downtown. Both sides, joined by Sawyer, Gragson, and Greenspun, met at the Moulin Rouge on March 25, 1960, and agreed to the terms. The local NAACP sent groups of men and women to test the new policy. Two local casinos refused to go along but eventually capitulated.

The meeting that settled the Moulin Rouge Agreement, allowing African Americans to patronize Las Vegas Strip and downtown casinos. *From left:* Woodrow Wilson, Lubertha Johnson, Bob Bailey, county commissioner Clesse Turner, Sheriff W. E. "Butch" Leypoldt, Hank Greenspun, Dr. James McMillan, Oran Gragson, Dr. Charles West, police chief Ray Sheffer, county commissioner Art Olsen, possibly David Hoggard, and Rev. Donald Clark. Courtesy of Special Collections, University Libraries, University of Nevada, Las Vegas.

While Las Vegas gained more notice, similar issues roiled northern Nevada. NAACP Reno-Sparks branch cofounder Alice Smith noted signs in restaurants saying, "No Indians, dogs or Negroes Allowed." Local reporter Ruth Giles Jones started the monthly *Sentinel* to report on the black community. The local NAACP demonstrated in connection with the 1960 Winter Olympics at Squaw Valley and held sit-ins that June at Arch Drug and other downtown businesses, while Eddie Scott lobbied legislators with enough dedication to become known as "Bulldog Eddie." In the late 1960s the new Reno Race Relations Center worked with the American Civil Liberties Union (ACLU) to publicize police brutality, and the Westbrooks and other Black Springs residents fought for civic improvements. But in 1962 Reno's city council declared it had no power to revoke gaming licenses over treatment of African Americans, and local casinos resisted integration and fair employment until federal legislation in 1964 and Nevada's counterpart in 1965 forced their acceptance. The Las Vegas and Reno chapters lobbied and picketed together on behalf of these measures.

A more rural chapter joined them. In 1960 Manuel Gray, a veteran Hawthorne Naval Ammunition depot employee, organized a local NAACP. Many African Americans who worked at the depot had no choice but to live in a segregated section of Babbitt, a government housing facility finally abandoned in 1987. They encountered no official segregation in local schools, but from the naval officers at the depot and from private businesses in Mineral County, especially motels and restaurants (most notably the El Capitan, operated by brothers Lindsay and Gordon Smith). Only after federal and state civil rights legislation took effect did these establishments agree to serve African Americans.

While access to previously segregated businesses pleased African Americans, they also sought better jobs. In 1963 the Las Vegas NAACP threatened to march on the Strip at the time of a heavyweight championship fight. Sawyer, Greenspun, Gragson, and the state Equal Rights Commission then helped negotiate an agreement that led to a few jobs, but not enough. Gragson also found the city had a fund to help depressed areas and made sure most of it went into West Las Vegas. In Reno a poor people's march called attention to poverty-stricken minorities. Unfortunately, both Las Vegas and Reno civil rights leaders complained that historically black areas lacked capital investment and customers, as African Americans increasingly patronized businesses and areas once off-limits to them.

Sawyer and Civil Rights

As the civil rights law defeated in the 1953 legislature showed, Nevada leaders usually had minimal interest in civil rights. Several of them had been southerners, while others campaigned in segregated areas as elections neared. Officials such as Bible and Cannon lacked the prejudice of earlier eras, but protecting Nevada's interests required them to work closely with southern Democrats who dominated Senate committees and opposed civil rights. Those connections enabled them to aid mining and defense and fight taxes that might hurt tourism. That industry's importance reduced its vulnerability to pressure, and change came slowly: in 1966 the first African American dealer began working on the Strip; the first African American female dealer started in 1970.

Sawyer had reasons to tread lightly. Just after Sawyer's election, Elko district judge Taylor Wines issued a controversial order permitting labor leader Harry Bridges to marry a Japanese woman, contrary to a state law against interracial marriages—a decade before a similar US Supreme Court ruling and an indication that change might be difficult. When Sawyer ran in 1958, he said nothing publicly about civil rights to avoid "political suicide," as he put it; the 1960 census showed eleven thousand African Americans in Clark County and two thousand in Washoe County, not enough to overcome opponents of civil rights. But Sawyer campaigned among black voters as no major candidate had before and attacked discrimination. As governor he faced an obstacle: the mostly rural legislature blocked civil rights legislation. The "little federal plan" provided each county a state senator and at least one assembly seat; due partly to this system, the GOP controlled the state senate from 1941 to 1965, and conservative Democrats ruled the assembly. They defeated fair employment bills that Sawyer supported in 1961 and 1963.

But Sawyer, the NAACP, and sympathetic lawmakers made progress. The governor signed Maude Frazier's bill ending discrimination in state employment. In 1961, after sit-ins at several Reno businesses, legislators heeded his call for an Equal Rights Commission, but approved minimal funding and no subpoena power; Sawyer irked civil rights leaders by naming Reno lawyer Bert Goldwater to chair it (his African American successor, Bob Bailey, pleased advocates more). When commissioners investigated job discrimination in Las Vegas casinos, owners who showed up to testify claimed to lack qualified applicants, while others refused to appear; the commission also survived a repeal effort by Storey County state senator James Slattery, who contended that "the colored people in this state have never been so well off." In 1964 the commission subpoenaed Hawthorne hotel owner Lindsay Smith about denying accommodations to African Americans. Smith countered by suing the commission and its members, denying their legal authority to enforce the subpoena and claiming harassment. A Reno judge approved the injunction he sought, but the Nevada Supreme Court, in an opinion written by Justice Gordon Thompson, upheld the commission's powers.

Sawyer also worked behind the scenes. A Hawthorne motel refused to serve an African diplomat headed to the 1960 Winter Olympics near Lake Tahoe; Sawyer persuaded the owner to change his mind. He tried to threaten gaming licenses over discrimination, but Attorneys General Foley and Harvey Dickerson held that he and gaming regulators lacked such power. In 1965, when protests and riots broke out in Watts, the segregated section of Los Angeles, Sawyer went to the homes of West Las Vegans in a successful effort to urge them not to follow suit. A Sawyer appointee in Clark County district court, John Mowbray, obtained grant money to set up a public defender system that helped the poor, indigent, and minorities.

Despite their disagreements, Sawyer also enjoyed Foley's support. Foley urged civil rights leaders to pressure gaming regulators and politicians. As Foley put it, the "only answer to the lack of civil rights in Nevada will come when the state legislature has enough guts to pass an effective law." In 1962 Foley became a federal judge, and the legislature acted only when it had to: after the federal Civil Rights Act of 1964. Introduced by Mel Close, a Las Vegas Democrat, Assembly Bill 404 passed after pressure from Sawyer, support from Bishop Robert Dwyer of the Roman Catholic diocese, threats from Bailey of mass demonstrations in Carson City, and cajoling by Laxalt, who felt that Republicans needed to build bridges to African Americans. Nevada reflected broader trends: the national civil rights movement owed much of its success to black and white advocates who marched, often at risk of physical violence and arrest, and generated white support that helped politicians enact needed reforms.

Political Battles and the Press

As competing young politicians with strong ideologies and great skills, Sawyer and Laxalt had a frosty relationship. When Sawyer left Nevada on business, Laxalt made appointments and once convened a grand jury. Finally, the governor filed a lawsuit to determine the extent of the lieutenant governor's powers. *Sawyer v. District Court* (1963) held that the lieutenant governor could act only in an emergency, leaving Laxalt to preside over the state senate, disagree with Sawyer's policies, and concentrate on building up the Republican Party.

In 1964 Laxalt ran for the Senate; Cannon loyalists who backed him in 1962 to avert a primary challenge from Sawyer had miscalculated. Nationally, Lyndon Johnson won a landslide over conservative senator Barry Goldwater of Arizona, and Nevada joined the trend, electing a Democratic state senate for the first time since 1938. But Laxalt ran a strong campaign, while Cannon faced questions about ties to reputed Mob figures and Washington lobbyists. Further, while tight with his party's leaders during his first term, he operated mostly behind the scenes. As a Las Vegan, he found it hard to win support in northern and rural counties. Laxalt benefited from support from the *Las Vegas Review-Journal*, the state's largest daily, which emphasized the allegations against Cannon and heavily promoted the Republican. But Johnson reportedly called *Review-Journal* and *Carson City Appeal* publisher Donald Reynolds and threatened the Federal Communications Commission licenses of his Reno and Las Vegas television stations. The *R-J's* editor, Robert Brown, resigned (he then joined Laxalt's campaign), and the scandal and Laxalt vanished from its pages. Laxalt's difficulties in Las Vegas combined with Cannon receiving enough support in West Las Vegas to reelect him by 48 votes out of 125,000 cast; Cannon voted for ending the southern-led filibuster on the Civil Rights Act of 1964, which helped him in the African American community. A recount increased Cannon's margin to 84, and, now ensconced, he would have little trouble winning two more terms.

The 1966 governor's race marked another turning point. Sawyer faced Laxalt, running for the third time in as many elections. The incumbent won a primary against Charles Springer, who briefly served as his attorney general and attacked him from the left, and Clark County district attorney Ted Marshall, who assailed him from the right. But during two controversial terms, Sawyer had taken stands bound to offend voters. When he backed granting early release to some prisoners, his opponents capitalized on growing concerns about crime. Beyond his own ample talents, and Republicans recording gains nationally in the midterm elections, Laxalt benefited when he publicly apologized to J. Edgar Hoover for Sawyer's criticisms; Hoover sent a letter to the *Las Vegas Sun* calling for Sawyer's defeat. Yet the gaming executives the FBI targeted proved no help to him: Dalitz and the Desert Inn, resenting efforts to include two of their allies in the Black Book, helped fund Laxalt. That combination helped elect Laxalt by 5,000 votes.

These elections highlighted the impact of journalists in Nevada politics. In Las Vegas Greenspun feuded with the *R-J,* and by the early 1960s the *Sun* neared the *R-J* in circulation and may have surpassed it in impact. But the *R-J* improved the paper, and a fire destroyed the *Sun's* building in 1963, setting it back, although Greenspun remained powerful. Greenspun's former editor Adam Yacenda made his *North Las Vegas Valley Times* a player in that city. Although the same company owned Reno's dailies, the *Nevada State Journal* backed Democrats and the *Evening Gazette* remained Republican. The Steninger family's *Elko Daily Free Press* continued as an influential voice, while the weekly *Elko Independent's* Warren "Snowy" Monroe also had an impact as a longtime state senator. Republicans Jack McCloskey of the *Mineral County Independent* and Walter Cox of the *Mason Valley News,* known as "the only newspaper in the world that gives a damn about Yerington," influenced rural voters and supported McCarran and later Bible, believing they served Nevada well. Reflecting the importance of television, Reynolds and Greenspun owned stations, while Morry Zenoff, who published the Henderson and Boulder City newspapers, started a third station in Las Vegas.

The Supreme Court and Its Impact

As California attorney general, Earl Warren changed Nevada with his antigambling policies; as chief justice of the US Supreme Court, he did far more. In 1954 Warren wrote the opinion in *Brown v. Board of Education,* holding segregated schools unconstitutional. The Warren Court remained consistent on civil rights, but in the 1960s it moved toward "incorporating" the Bill of Rights, applying its protections to the states. The Court redefined First Amendment libel law, barred unreasonable search and seizure, guaranteed the right to counsel in court cases, and required the police to read suspects their rights in the "Miranda warning."

But Warren later called the reapportionment decisions the most important of his tenure, and they reshaped Nevada. In *Baker v. Carr* in 1962, the Court asserted the right to decide the fairness of the redistricting after each census. In *Reynolds v. Sims* in 1964, it held that states failed to comply with the US Constitution and ordered legislative redistricting on the principle of "one man, one vote." This applied to the congressional-style "little federal plan." Soon, Assemblywoman Flora Dungan and Clare Woodbury, a longtime Las Vegas doctor and school board member, filed a successful lawsuit against state officials, demanding redistricting.

Thus, Nevada legislators met in 1965, knowing that if they failed to act by April 15, a three-judge US District Court panel would do the job for them. When the legislature proved unable to agree, the judges ordered a special session that met on October 30; if lawmakers did nothing within three weeks, the judges would step in. Both houses agreed to expand by three seats with representation by population, ending the little federal plan and each county having a state senator. Clark County, with 40 percent of Nevada's population, would have that percentage of the legislature. Reapportionment reduced the influence of rural Nevadans—not only legislators, but also newspaper editors. One rural legislator feared a takeover by southern Nevada's "hippies, beatniks, and communists," but the more urban districts led to the elections of the first woman state senator, Helen Herr, and African American assemblyman, Woodrow Wilson.

Another Supreme Court decision affected Nevada's future. In 1963, in *Arizona v. California,* the justices upheld the allocation in the Colorado River Compact and the Boulder Canyon Project Act: California would receive 4.4 million acre-feet a year, Arizona 2.8 million, and Nevada 300,000. Although the state tried to obtain more, Nevadans found that agreeable, but disliked other parts of the ruling. The Court gave the secretary of the interior the power to divvy the waters during shortages or surpluses, ensuring, as historian Gary Elliott wrote, that "the federal government reigned supreme in western water law." Worse, the opinion also upheld the *Winters* reserved rights doctrine of 1908, making Native American water rights superior to non-Native claimants.

Federal Projects: Nevada's Mixed Emotions

As chair of the Senate Interior and Insular Affairs Committee's Parks and Recreation Subcommittee, Bible played an important role in environmental policy. From Rachel Carson's *Silent Spring* on pesticides to the Sierra Club's warnings of dangers to giant redwoods, advocacy propelled the movement's growth. Johnson's Great Society continued "Mission 66," a ten-year, one-billion-dollar project that National Park Service director Conrad Wirth began in 1957 to make parks better known and more commercial—including nearly one million dollars to improve Lake Mead, which Bible later helped turn into a national recreation area. With George Hartzog's appointment to run the park service in 1964, environmental protection and recreation for their own sake outweighed commercial considerations.

As subcommittee chair, Bible influenced parks legislation but made a rule: a state's entire congressional delegation must support a park before he would move it forward, and affected groups would have to agree. Thus, Bible proved unable to win a park for his own state. In 1957 interested parties formed the Great Basin Range National Park Association to seek protection for Wheeler Peak, Lehman Caves, and nearby Bristlecone Pines. Bible asked the Interior Department to study the possibility and joined Baring in introducing legislation for a 147,000-acre facility. At hearings late in 1959, despite the area's lack of mineral production, the American Mining Congress and Kennecott Copper opposed it due to the potential loss of future revenue. Ranchers argued even more strongly that they would be unable to graze their stock.

Bible and his colleagues tried to accommodate every concern. Bible, Cannon, and other westerners had already aided ranchers by blocking a 50 percent hike in grazing fees in 1962. New legislation allowed grazing on park lands for twenty-five years, reduced the park's size to permit beryllium exploration, and allowed existing operations within the park's acreage to continue. When the Forest Service tried to limit grazing along the Snake Range due to years of overuse, Bible and Cannon strained to protect the parks bill. But, in 1962, without telling his colleagues, Baring proposed cutting the park's size by more than half and allowing virtually unlimited hunting, fishing, grazing, and mining, and both bills wound up in limbo. When Bible tried again in 1965, Baring joined mining and ranching interests to fight the park. Secretary of the Interior Stewart Udall rejected Baring's plan, killing a park for White Pine County—for a while.

Land use remained controversial in other ways. In 1964, seeking new ideas for the federal domain, Congress created the Public Land Law Review Commission, including Bible, Baring, Battle Mountain rancher John Marvel, and American Mining Congress Public Lands Committee head W. Howard Gray. Six years later their report recommended placing mineral exploration above other uses of public lands and rules to enable the United States to "receive full value for the use of the public lands and their resources," less red tape, and better environmental protection. Nevadans neglected to notice the federal government staked a claim to far more authority over public lands. Worse, from the perspective of the Nevada Cattlemen's Association, grazing fees increased by nearly half.

Federal Aid for Southern Nevada

While this period brought Nevada no new defense projects, existing ones grew. Nellis Air Force Base expanded with the arrival of new F-111 jet fighters, training programs for modern weapons, and a new tactical center. The number stationed there more than doubled, and the cost of base operations tripled. Once the 1963 test ban treaty moved blasts underground, new Atomic Energy Commission programs increasing funding at the Nevada Test Site and expanded to Fallon to determine how earthquake zones reacted to nuclear tests. The federal government widened the highway to Mercury, known as "the widow-maker," to four lanes, encouraging workers to commute from Las Vegas and saving lives.

In the early 1960s Senators Bible and Cannon began seeking ways to bring more water to southern Nevada. They used their friendships with Johnson and the Democratic majority and the area's growing role in national defense, exemplified by the test site and Nellis Air Force Base. In 1965, after four years of laying groundwork, Bible introduced the Southern Nevada Water Project to fund water mains to carry 132,000 acre-feet a year from Lake Mead to Las Vegas with a $7 million grant. Despite his and Cannon's efforts, the project ran into trouble. Secretary of the Interior Udall preferred a unified western plan, not individual state projects, but went along with the Nevadans. The Nevada plan became caught in the continuing battles between Arizona and California, but Bible persuaded their congressional delegations that Nevada needed to be separate from whatever they did. President Johnson and the House almost balked due to Baring's opposition to the Great Society and civil rights laws, but Johnson's connections to Bible and Cannon, and Nevada's status as a Democratic state, overcame any opposition.

Johnson signed the law in 1965. It would create thirty-one miles of pipelines, a four-mile tunnel, and six pumping plants, making 132,200 acre-feet of water flow upon the project's completion in 1971. Funding it proved harder, as the Vietnam War consumed more of the budget, but Bible's service on the Appropriations Committee helped him keep money coming. A $120 million federal loan and $460 million in state bonds paid for the next phase, completed in April 1982. Without the project Nevada would have lacked access to its share of Colorado River water, and the growth of the Las Vegas metropolitan area, which topped two million residents in the 2010 census, would have been impossible.

Lawsuits and Anger

While civil rights legislation helped, discrimination and segregation continued. In 1967 Laxalt and NAACP leader and attorney Charles Kellar held a conference on civil rights to focus on these issues, and Kellar filed a complaint with the National Labor Relations Board against eighteen southern Nevada hotels and casinos and the local Culinary and Teamsters Unions. Kellar threatened a march down the Strip, which led to shots being fired into his home. He accused Culinary leader Al Bramlet, who made the union a force despite the right-to-work law, of failing to aid black workers, although Bramlet worked closely with Sarah Hughes, an African American organizer; Ruby Duncan, a longtime civil rights advocate, said, "African American women built that union." After Kellar accused the hotels of "unfair labor practices," a Nevada League of Women Voters report echoed his criticism of the hotels' failure to hire and promote African American workers. In 1970, urged on by executive director Robbins Cahill, once the state's top gaming regulator, the Nevada Resort Association proposed an eight-point minority hiring plan, including funding for the NAACP and more training and education.

The pace of change proved no faster for West Las Vegans. They welcomed the 1965 creation of the Economic Opportunity Board, which set up such antipoverty programs as Head Start. But by 1970 their average annual income remained less than half of white southern Nevadans, while four in five West Las Vegans never finished high school. A 1966 US Human Relations Commission report criticized local police for brutality against minorities, but the lack of a response irked African American residents. Early in 1969 students and law enforcement fought at several high schools amid claims that news coverage worsened the tension. That October, assaults on West Las Vegas streets led to twenty-three injuries, hundreds of police pouring into the area, ministers and civil rights leaders trying to tamp down the anger, police erecting a blockade and using tear gas on demonstrators, a curfew, and looting. The next spring, amid more protests and as fights broke out at schools, the school district agreed to hire thirty more African American teachers.

Residential segregation may have contributed to the violence: children attended neighborhood schools until high school, reducing exposure to peoples of color, and four of every five African American teachers in southern Nevada taught in West Las Vegas. In May 1968 fourteen years after the *Brown* decision, Kellar sued to force Clark County schools to integrate. When US district judge Bruce Thompson agreed, an antibusing group proposed voluntary busing, and the local League of Women Voters offered a plan for thorough integration. The school district proposed testing integration at a West Las Vegas school, and Thompson permitted it for two years. Kellar returned to court in December 1970 to demand action, and Thompson ordered mandatory integration in the next school year.

Native Americans

Native Americans joined the rights movement of the 1960s. Starting with the Great Society and continuing through the 1970s, the African American civil rights movement encouraged Native Americans to become more organized and vocal. In 1960 a group of college students founded the National Indian Youth Council, which organized events to promote "Red Power" under the leadership of its first president, Mel Thom, a native of the Walker River Northern Paiute Reservation in Schurz. By 1970 the group grew to five thousand members and continued to protest and lobby for more educational opportunities and political influence. But some old issues refused to die: in 1962 the Indian Claims Commission ruled "gradual encroachment" meant the Western Shoshone had lost the land they never surrendered in the 1863 Treaty of Ruby Valley.

The Red Power movement and government reforms brought changes to the lives of Nevada's Native peoples. Some of their actions celebrated Native culture: the Western Shoshone revived their fandango events and expanded the teaching of their language, and Nevada's four major tribes worked on producing tribal histories. In 1964 Native Nevadans founded the Inter-Tribal Council of Nevada, which held its first conference at the university in Reno, and started publishing the monthly *Native Nevadan* newspaper, which continued until 1992. This cooperation also mirrored controversy within Nevada society: with the council's office located in Reno, other tribes complained that it favored the nearby Northern Paiutes and Washoe rather than the Southern Paiutes and Shoshone.

The New Frontier and Great Society, and the ideology behind them, influenced Native life in the 1960s. Elaine Walbroek's work led to a home health service and efforts to eradicate tuberculosis from Fort McDermitt Indian Reservation; she later helped start the Inter-Tribal Council and ran Clark County's Economic Opportunity Board. The Department of Housing and Urban Development and the Bureau of Indian Affairs teamed on the Mutual Help Homeowners Program, enabling residents of several Nevada reservations and colonies over the next two decades to build new homes and pay them off with a small monthly fee to the federal government. The BIA's Housing Improvement Program helped renovate older homes. The Area Redevelopment Administration and Economic Development Ad-ministration included offices that aided tribes in developing long-range goals, including—in Nevada—new homes and community centers. These programs did everything from build corrals at the Sheep Creek Reservoir on the Duck Valley Reservation to help Western Shoshone teens find jobs in the Elko area. In 1962 the city of Las Vegas finally extended water service to the downtown Paiute colony, which wrote its own constitution in 1970.

The Young and the Counterculture

Nationally, Students for a Democratic Society and the Student Non-Violent Coordinating Committee engaged in political action, but Nevada's young responded, too. At Nevada Southern University, now UNLV, Students to Remove Upstate Domination promoted the newly independent school (as of 1968), protested, and petitioned for more funding. But student activism ultimately went in directions similar to those around the country, including protests and teach-ins against the Vietnam War. When Governor Laxalt suggested that he would be unable to increase funding to Nevada Southern University, students hanged him in effigy, while African American students objected to the school being called the Rebels and to its Confederate mascot.

One of the largest protests could have been violent. On May 5, 1970, UNR hosted its annual Governor's Day to honor the governor and the school's ROTC, but students and some faculty demonstrated in response to the killing the day before of four students at a protest over the Vietnam War at Ohio's Kent State University. Marchers reached the stadium, went inside, and, by agreement, circled the track before some sat in the stands and chanted. Although one commander yelled, "Kill! Kill!" to his drill team, no

In 1968, a year of national turmoil, UNLV students became part of the protest movements, picketing on a variety of issues, including state funding of their institution. Courtesy of Special Collections, University Libraries, University of Nevada, Las Vegas.

injuries resulted, although regents voted to fire one of the professors, Paul Adamian, who actually discouraged violence.

Given their recent and large growth, Nevada's larger cities probably lacked the community to produce as vibrant and controversial a youth culture as elsewhere, but a smaller area provided an outlet for the national counterculture. The Red Dog Saloon in Virginia City attracted various San Franciscans in pursuit of seclusion and libertarian freedom. Janis Joplin performed there, *One Flew over the Cuckoo's Nest* author Ken Kesey and his Merry Pranksters amused themselves, and artists produced psychedelic posters. It provided a contrast to *Bonanza*.

The Problem with No Name

In 1963 Betty Friedan's *The Feminine Mystique* addressed "the problem with no name"—the feeling among women that caring for families provided too little intellectual and personal fulfillment. Civil rights legislation included women, but gender discrimination proved hard to end, and many Nevadans had no desire to end it. As Molly Flagg Knudtsen put it, "Women's lib has not reached the ranches of Nevada"—although, she noted, numerous Basque women in rural Nevada took over ranch operations when their husbands or fathers died.

Women pursued political and social change. Kitty Rodman ran a major Las Vegas construction company and became a leading philanthropist. Nancy Gomes, a social worker and legislator, started a foster-grandparent program and sought reforms in juvenile justice, child welfare, and adoptions. Hazel Erskine of Reno pioneered polling and surveys in Nevada for Sawyer's election and research for the university, and civil rights leader Lubertha Johnson helped begin Clark County's Head Start and Manpower programs. Knudtsen, a historian and Lander County rancher, became the first woman regent in 1960 and an advocate of community colleges for her rural constituents. In 1962 Sawyer named Maude Frazier to finish Rex Bell's term, making her Nevada's first woman lieutenant governor. The legislature's expansion after federally mandated redistricting also opened doors for women in politics.

The gaming industry varied in its treatment of women. In the Reno-Tahoe area, women dealers long had been common. In Las Vegas dealer claims that casinos hired women to undercut their salaries led to a city ordinance in 1958 that recommended against hiring them. North Las

Vegas followed in 1959 with a ban on women bartenders. Both cities repealed these measures under pressure from local and national groups by 1970. Yet Claudine Williams, who ran the Silver Slipper with her husband, Shelby, learned to deal cards from Benny Binion; after they sold the Slipper to Howard Hughes, it hired a female dealer. Other women moved into the executive ranks: Kay Goodwill as an accountant and later as the first woman comptroller of a Strip resort, the Tropicana, and Jo Harris as a designer for such hotels as Caesars Palace and Circus Circus. After her husband's death, Judy Bayley became the Hacienda's president and the first woman to own and operate a Nevada hotel-casino—and gained wide respect for her managerial skills. Service industries also may have offered women more opportunities to work than in other industries: about half of the women of legal working age in 1960 and 1970 in Las Vegas had jobs, above the national average.

An Activist Conservative

An important figure in the modern conservative movement, Laxalt shared Sawyer's desire to influence legislation and change how the state functioned, and a willingness to adapt. Laxalt pushed through creation of the Nevada State Council on the Arts to obtain money from the National Endowment for the Arts—a Great Society program of the sort that Laxalt disliked at the national level, but he saw that it could help Nevada. In 1968, when inmates at the state prison went on strike to protest conditions—a problem that Sawyer also had tried to resolve—Laxalt met alone with the prisoners and tried to improve their situation. Under Laxalt, Clark County Health District director Otto Ravenholt added duties as state director of health and welfare and improved conditions in mental hospitals. Laxalt backed the Equal Rights Commission's requests for more staff and funding but originally opposed a law to eliminate racial bias in housing. Then, after a fact-finding committee found "overwhelming evidence" of discrimination, Laxalt backed a fair housing law, which went down to defeat amid divisions between its advocates.

Laxalt also proved willing to raise taxes. In 1965 the legislature approved a casino tax on food, drinks, and charges related to entertainment, and Congress repealed a similar federal tax. At a 1966 special session, Cyril Bastian of Caliente and Ray Knisley of Lovelock redid the tax formula. The next year, in part to fund educational programs, Laxalt proposed hiking

gaming taxes by a quarter and sales taxes by a half and then smoothed relations with other Republicans who opposed his plans by lobbying them and
calling for smaller increases. Longtime GOP state senator Carl Dodge of
Fallon worked with his Democratic colleague from southern Nevada James
Gibson Sr. to develop the Nevada School Support Tax, a 1 percent sales
levy. Their actions continued a trend: by 1960 Nevada ranked ninth nationally in spending per public school pupil, Sawyer maintained that level, and
Laxalt sought to do the same. But growth remained a problem, with many
K–12 schools in Reno and Las Vegas still on double sessions.

Higher education expanded significantly, despite a growing north-south
divide that limited southern Nevada's access to needed funding. The Desert Research Institute (DRI, founded in 1959) brought plaudits and grants,
Nevada Southern University (UNLV as of 1969) won autonomy, and lawmakers created a community college branch in 1967. The Reno campus
developed new doctoral programs, and the University of Nevada Press
opened in 1961 to publish scholars from Nevada and elsewhere. Private
funding remained crucial—the Fleischmann Foundation paid many of
DRI's expenses for a decade, and Howard Hughes provided seed money for
a medical school—but the lack of research at UNLV, and to a lesser extent
at the older UNR, kept Nevada from devising technology and science
programs that would have drawn Cold War defense contracts like those
in other states. But the Nevada Resort Association and individual casino
operators supported UNLV's effort to create a hotel management program,
which began in 1967 and eventually ranked as one of the nation's top two
such colleges. Laxalt named a study committee to devise a plan to fund
higher education, and it came back with an enrollment-based formula that
would benefit the largest campuses.

With funding in place, Laxalt also overcame opposition from the Reno
campus and its alumni to setting up community colleges. At the time
Nevada had been the only state without one. An effort in Carson City to
create a college failed for lack of support. In 1967 Elko leaders acquired
funds and land, hired an administrator, and started a college with twenty-
five classes and three hundred students. When a special session the next
year tried to block Laxalt's request for state funds, Hughes funded a study
that recommended the creation of community colleges.

A Building Boom

The return of resort construction in the late 1960s reshaped the Strip. Jay Sarno dreamed of a place where anyone could be an emperor for a day, and thus the lack of an apostrophe in its name: all would be Caesar. Jo Harris, designing the resort for Sarno and his partners, believed evoking Rome required consistency, meaning tons of Italian marble and stone, a frieze of the battle of the Etruscan Hills near the Noshorium Coffee Shop (*nosh* being a Yiddish term for "snack"), the Circus Maximus Theatre designed to resemble the Coliseum, the gourmet Bacchanal Room, and eighteen fountains along a 135-foot driveway leading into a 680-room hotel. Caesars Palace opened on August 5, 1966, with the largest bill ever for caviar and champagne.

Caesars set standards in more ways than one. It combined luxury and excess like no previous Las Vegas hotel, marked the return of themed resorts to the Strip, and influenced future projects. While other hotels hosted big events like heavyweight fights and golf tournaments, Sarno and his partners let daredevil Evel Knievel try to jump over the hotel's fountains in 1967, bringing Caesars and the motorcyclist worldwide attention (Knievel failed, suffered major injuries, and lay in a coma for nearly a month). But some of Caesars Palace's effects proved less pleasant. Although several properties expanded under Teamsters auspices, Caesars marked the pension fund's first loan for a new hotel. Whether that linked Caesars to mobsters remained open to question, but charges that its financial manager had ties to New York and New England Mob interests helped prompt Sarno and his partners to sell Caesars to a restaurant chain operated in Miami by brothers Clifford and Stuart Perlman, who later faced similar accusations.

Meanwhile, Sarno achieved another longtime dream: of owning a circus. He and his investors opened Circus Circus in 1968. It began as an adults-only casino; Sarno greeted opening-night arrivals in a ringmaster's outfit, with trapeze acts above the casino inside a structure shaped like a circus tent. Soon, the owners installed a net, stopped charging admission, let children attend, and obtained a Teamsters loan to add a hotel. Although Circus Circus never made substantial profits under Sarno's control, it continued the trend of themed hotels. It also seemed to exemplify Las Vegas's excess and kitsch: Hunter Thompson wrote in *Fear and Loathing in Las*

A gathering of the Las Vegas elite at the Stardust in the 1960s. *Back row, from left:* hotel builder Jay Sarno, Toni Clark (widow of Wilbur of the Desert Inn), Hank Greenspun, and Kirk Kerkorian. *Front row, from left:* Jean Kerkorian, Charlie Harrison, Joyce Sarno, Theda Harrison, Harold Ambler, and Barbara Greenspun. Courtesy of Special Collections, University Libraries, University of Nevada, Las Vegas.

Vegas, "The Circus Circus is what the whole hep world would be doing on Saturday night if the Nazis had won the war."

Another themed resort debuted in 1966. Former Sahara owner Milton Prell renovated the Tally-Ho into the Aladdin with a fifteen-story neon sign, a par-three golf course, and three different shows nightly in the main theater. The Aladdin also won worldwide attention when Elvis Presley and Priscilla Beaulieu married there. But Prell's ill health forced him to sell to Parvin-Dohrmann; Albert Parvin had owned the Flamingo and by then controlled the Stardust and Fremont—and demonstrated the extent of Las Vegas's reputation. Parvin, who started out furnishing Strip hotels, created a center to promote democracy and paid US Supreme Court justice William O. Douglas to run it—and, given his gaming operation, prompted rumors that the justice might be tied to organized crime. Although unfounded, the charges became part of an effort to impeach Douglas.

Other hotel-casinos contributed to the building boom. In 1966 long-time casino executive Ben Goffstein opened the downtown Four Queens (named for his wife and daughters). In 1967 the New Frontier's owners renovated their resort, and the Bonanza Hotel opened at Flamingo and the Strip—with Lorne Greene, *Bonanza*'s star, in the showroom. After financial issues and a land dispute with Ernest Lied, owner of a nearby motel and later the namesake of UNLV's library, the hotel went under in 1970, but Kirk Kerkorian bought more of the land around it, leased the casino, and began planning a new hotel.

The Hughes Era

Howard Hughes had been a legend long before moving to Las Vegas in November 1966. Born in Houston in 1905, he inherited millions from his father's tool business. A talented engineer who founded Hughes Aviation, he moved to Hollywood and entered the film industry. His love of airplanes inspired him to flying records and innovations—and led to a plane crash in 1947 that left him in pain and drove him to a drug addiction. His connections to Las Vegas included obtaining thirty thousand acres of land northwest of town in a deal that Senator Pat McCarran helped engineer for him with the Bureau of Land Management and using then city attorney Howard Cannon to help him with legal matters related to his marriage in Tonopah in 1957.

But Hughes's public appearances dwindled as his phobias about germs and privacy worsened. By the late 1950s he communicated with the world mainly through Robert Maheu, a former FBI and Central Intelligence Agency agent who handled security issues for him. In 1966, after selling his interest in Trans World Airlines for more than five hundred million dollars, Hughes wanted to invest some of his money to avoid capital gains taxes and relocate from Southern California to an area where he could guarantee his privacy. A wide network helped ease his move to Las Vegas: Maheu, Greenspun, mobster Johnny Rosselli, and Edward Morgan, a Washington, DC, attorney tied to the Teamsters who had represented the publisher during the McCarthy era. Hughes arrived and took over the Desert Inn's top two floors.

A short visit turned into a historic event. Hughes wished to remain, but owner Moe Dalitz wanted him out to make room for the high-rollers who usually occupy hotel penthouses. Pressure from Teamsters boss Jimmy

Hoffa, whose union's pension fund loaned money to Dalitz, bought Hughes more time. What followed remains murky: Hughes may have decided to buy the hotel in response, but Maheu had already been negotiating through Morgan and Greenspun. Not only did Hughes now want to own a hotel-casino, but Dalitz and his partners had tired of increased federal pressure on anyone with ties, alleged and otherwise, to organized crime: Doc Stacher pleaded guilty to tax evasion, two owners of the Flamingo soon would do so, and Meyer Lansky and Sam Giancana faced indictments. Finally, in April 1967, Hughes bought the Desert Inn for more than thirteen million dollars, although Dalitz and his partners remained to consult and as owners of the land itself. Excited that a legitimate billionaire investor would replace owners reputed to be part of organized crime, Laxalt helped Hughes through the licensing process.

Hughes had only just begun. Within months he bought the Sands, reportedly tied to eastern Mob interests, and the Frontier, linked to organized crime in Detroit; the Castaways and Silver Slipper, the latter allegedly

In the late 1960s, Howard Hughes ended up owning six Las Vegas hotel-casinos, including the Landmark (*left*) and the Frontier (*right*), while living in the Desert Inn (*toward the center*). The results contributed to a change in Nevada's reputation. Courtesy of the Howard Hughes Collection at Special Collections, University Libraries, University of Nevada, Las Vegas.

because the neon-lit slipper atop its sign shone into his penthouse; and the unfinished Landmark Hotel, which he completed. He expanded to Reno and bought Harold's Club and picked up mining claims around the state. Continuing his interest in aviation, Hughes also purchased North Las Vegas's airport (its owner, Ralph Engelstad, used the money to start his own casino empire), Alamo Airways, and the original McCarran Field, which became the Hughes Air Terminal. He bought Air West, which included what had been Bonanza Airlines. Unhappy with no movies to watch during the night, the insomniac acquired KLAS-TV, a local television station, from Greenspun and his partners and began airing movies he wanted to see.

Some of Hughes's efforts failed or made poor business sense. He offered half of his acreage to Boeing if it would move its aircraft plant to Las Vegas, but to no avail. He ended the Desert Inn's sponsorship of a professional golf tournament and an Easter egg hunt out of a fear of germs. He tried to buy the Stardust, but the US Justice Department, concerned about a monopoly, thwarted him. His attempts to buy out Bill Harrah failed. He made substantial political donations, including a reported one hundred thousand dollars each to two presidential candidates in 1968, hoping they would stop nuclear tests; Hughes worried about how they shook the hotel tower and the effects of radiation. He also made clear his opposition to racial equality, telling Maheu that "the Negroes have already made enough progress to last the next 100 years, and there is such a thing as overdoing it."

Corporations and Kerkorian

Hughes's arrival marked a turning point. The Mob still prospered: Hughes eliminated ownership but not executives or staff who kept skimming without his knowledge, and those surrounding him lacked the background in gaming to do much about it. But at least Hughes's background differed from that of the men he bought out, and Laxalt and other state leaders found that Nevada became more respectable around the country. Hughes seemed like an antidote to books like *The Green Felt Jungle* (1963), in which reporters Ed Reid and Ovid DeMaris attacked gaming in Las Vegas as a Mob enterprise; *Gamblers' Money* (1965), in which *New York Times* reporter Wallace Turner reached similar conclusions; and Gilman Ostrander's *Nevada: The Great Rotten Borough* (1964), a political history that assailed the state's corruption and outsized national influence.

Laxalt sought other ways to remove Nevada's Mob stigma and found one: changing gaming licensing requirements to enable corporations to invest. Nevada required each stockholder to be licensed, making it impossible for a publicly traded corporation to own a property; after building several hotel-casinos, Del Webb bought the Sahara, Mint, and Thunderbird in the early 1960s, but skirted the rule by creating a special company, separate from his corporation. Laxalt proposed licensing only key stockholders and executives. As governor, Sawyer had opposed the changes, predicting the Mob would find a way around the new rules. Laxalt reasoned that corporate money ultimately would drive out organized crime, even if it took a while, and support from Harrah in the North and banker Parry Thomas in the South helped him win over the legislature. Harrah's went on to become the first Nevada gaming company to be listed on the New York Stock Exchange.

Laxalt's efforts also benefited from Kirk Kerkorian. A high-stakes craps player who operated flights for Las Vegas high-rollers, Kerkorian bought the Flamingo in 1967 after its previous owners went to prison on charges

From the late 1960s, soon before Kirk Kerkorian bought the Flamingo and ended Mob influence there. Al Martino played a singer allegedly modeled on Frank Sinatra in *The Godfather;* the Mills Brothers and other African American entertainers once had had to get lodgings in West Las Vegas but, by then, could stay where they played. Courtesy of Special Collections, University of Nevada–Reno Library.

linked to skimming. Under Kerkorian the hotel showed more profits than ever and trained staff for a bigger property his corporation built and owned: the International, east of the Strip on Paradise Road. The world's largest hotel-casino, with fifteen hundred rooms and a thirty-thousand-square-foot casino, it opened in 1969 with two showrooms, one with Barbra Streisand, the other with the Broadway hit *Hair,* and rock stars Ike and Tina Turner in the lounge. Elvis Presley signed an exclusive pact and sold out 837 straight shows at the hotel before his death in 1977. Kerkorian banked on business from the Convention Center next door and catered to families with a youth hostel and activities for children. In a sign of the corporate gaming law's impact, a conflict between Kerkorian and the US Securities and Exchange Commission prompted him to sell the Flamingo and International to another corporation, Hilton.

Western Waters and the Reagan-Laxalt Connection

In the wake of the Washoe project, and after a decade of discussions, California and Nevada negotiated several agreements to divide the waters they shared. They agreed that California would receive just over two-thirds of the thirty-four thousand acre-feet of Lake Tahoe's flow with a similar percentage from the Walker River for Nevada, and they worked out deals on the Truckee and Carson. After overcoming opposition due to concerns about Native American water rights, and federal assurances to Pyramid Lake Paiutes of another sixty thousand acre-feet a year from the Truckee, the two state legislatures ratified the California-Nevada Compact by 1971. No bill passed Congress, but the two states agreed to abide by the compact.

The compact's effects went beyond water to the environment and, ultimately, American history. In 1958 the Fleischmann Foundation helped start the Lake Tahoe Area Council, which issued studies of water and air pollution, including their potential impact on the Reno-Sparks water supply, that encouraged interest in protecting the lake and its environs. The growing environmental movement added to the pressure on Nevada leaders to act. Although neither seemed influenced by environmentalists, and they shared a dislike for each other's politics, Sawyer and Laxalt wanted to protect Lake Tahoe. Doing so required them to work with California's governor. Sawyer developed a friendship with Democrat Edmund "Pat" Brown, and they teamed on issues of mutual interest, supporting Bible's unsuccessful plan to turn part of the lake into a national park.

The Thunderbird Lodge at Lake Tahoe, amid the pristine surroundings that California and Nevada have both fought with each other and united to protect. Courtesy of Special Collections, University of Nevada–Reno Library.

With the Republican Party making gains nationwide, Brown and Sawyer lost their third-term bids in 1966 to conservative, telegenic opponents who expanded the gubernatorial friendship and the effort to clean up the lake. Laxalt had closer personal ties than Sawyer to Lake Tahoe—his father herded sheep near there, and the Laxalt family owned a camp above it at Marlette Lake—but developed stronger ties to California's governor. A sportscaster and an actor before entering politics, Ronald Reagan had been campaigning for Barry Goldwater when he met Laxalt, then running for the Senate, in 1964. Both faced pressures on Lake Tahoe—from owners and developers to environmentalists and residents.

When they met, Reagan and Laxalt produced two important results. One, with support from environmentalists concerned about growth and development in the area, they agreed to create the Tahoe Regional Planning Agency, consisting of officials from California and Nevada and set up to deal with environmental and other issues; the bill creating it became law in 1969. But the TRPA proved willing to accommodate developers more than some residents and politicians wanted, and the lake lost a quarter of its clarity from 1960 to 1974, thanks largely to increases in population and tourism occasioned by the opening of Harvey's Wagon Wheel Hotel in 1961 and Del Webb's Sahara Tahoe in 1965. Bible introduced legislation to expand Toiyabe National Forest, limiting development, and President Richard Nixon signed it in 1970. In the other important outcome of the meeting, the governors became close friends. That friendship would have profound effects.

Changing the Landscape, Politically and Otherwise

No year in American history compared with 1968, with the assassinations of Martin Luther King and Robert Kennedy, the Vietnam War and the debate over it, urban uprisings, violence at the Democratic convention in Chicago, and a divided presidential election in which Nixon defeated Democrat Hubert Humphrey, with a third-party challenge from segregationist George Wallace, as a rebuke to Lyndon Johnson and liberalism. Nevadans protested the war and varied in their support for civil rights and remained as divided politically as ever. The state easily gave its electoral votes to Nixon, a native of neighboring California whose wife came from White Pine County. When Bible sought a fourth Senate term, Lieutenant Governor Ed Fike, his Republican opponent, figured to benefit from Nixon's support, being from southern Nevada, and Bible's close relationship with Johnson. After Fike attacked Bible as an LBJ supporter and Washington insider, Bible reminded Nevadans of the benefit of his long service and barely acknowledged Johnson's existence—and cruised to reelection, thanks mainly to Clark County, which demonstrated the area's growth and its appreciation for the water project.

Two years later, Laxalt surprised the state by announcing his departure from politics. The national GOP had hoped that he would challenge Cannon again, or at least seek reelection. With Laxalt out, Washoe County district attorney Bill Raggio hoped to run for governor but, under White House pressure, challenged Cannon. He lost and felt the Nixon administration did too little to help him. The governor's race proved even less pleasant for the GOP. Fike sought to move up. In the Democratic primary Mike O'Callaghan, a party official, civil rights advocate, and former teacher who had worked for the Sawyer administration and later ran a Great Society Job Corps office, upset Hank Thornley, a Las Vegas newscaster and city commissioner. O'Callaghan outworked his favored opponents and benefited when the *Las Vegas Sun* reported just before the election on Fike's role in a questionable land deal. The news reports, Cannon's coattails, and a united party helped carry O'Callaghan to victory, along with his candidate for lieutenant governor, an assemblyman who had been one of his students: Harry Reid.

By the late 1960s Nevada had changed in significant ways. Other harbingers made themselves clear or loomed, from the Great Society's naturalization law easing Hispanic immigration to changes in gaming: Hughes's arrival and the new corporate gaming law portended a different economy, in 1967 Si Redd founded a company that revolutionized slot machines, and in 1970 a four-day Culinary and bartenders strike in Las Vegas closed casinos and cost millions of dollars, foreshadowing other labor problems, and the Binions began a tournament called the World Series of Poker that attracted little notice at the time. While muckraking of its Mob ties continued to attract attention, so did other analyses. Tom Wolfe's commentary on Las Vegas's architecture, design, and appearance—"Las Vegas (What?). Las Vegas (Can't Hear You! Too Noisy.) Las Vegas !!!"—first in *Esquire* and then in a book; the 1968 article that evolved into the Robert Venturi, Denise Scott Brown, and Steven Izenour book *Learning from Las Vegas: The Forgotten Symbolism of Architectural Form;* and the writings of French sociologist Jean Baudrillard suggested that Nevada's biggest city, and thus the state itself, could be taken seriously as a topic for legitimate study. Legitimacy thus took many forms, but achieving it would prove difficult.

SUGGESTED READINGS

Barlett, Donald L., and James B. Steele. *Empire: The Life, Legend, and Madness of Howard Hughes.* New York: W. W. Norton, 1979.

Barnes, H. Lee. *The Lucky.* Reno: University of Nevada Press, 2003.

Brill, Steven. *The Teamsters.* New York: Simon and Schuster, 1978.

Bunch, Betty. *High Heels and Headdresses: Memoirs of a Vintage Vegas Showgirl.* Las Vegas: Stephens Press, 2011.

Bushnell, Eleanore, ed. *Sagebrush & Neon: Studies in Nevada Politics.* Reno: University of Nevada, Reno, Bureau of Governmental Research, 1973.

Denton, Ralph L., and Michael S. Green. *A Liberal Conscience: Ralph Denton, Nevadan.* Reno: University of Oral History Program, 2001.

Denton, Sally, and Roger Morris. *The Money and the Power: The Making of Las Vegas and Its Hold on America, 1947–2000.* New York: Alfred A. Knopf, 2001.

Drosnin, Michael. *Citizen Hughes.* New York: Holt, Rinehart, and Winston, 1985.

Elliott, Gary E. *Senator Alan Bible and the Politics of the New West.* Reno: University of Nevada Press, 1994.

Faiss, Robert D., Dwayne Kling, and R. T. King. *Gaming Regulation and Gaming Law in Nevada.* Reno: University of Nevada Oral History Program, 2009.

Goodwin, Joanne L. *Changing the Game: Women at Work in Las Vegas, 1940–1990.* Reno: University of Nevada Press, 2014.

Knepp, Donn. *Las Vegas: The Entertainment Capital.* Menlo Park, CA: Sunset Books, 1992.

Knudtsen, Molly Flagg. *Under the Mountain.* Reno: University of Nevada Press, 1982.

Laxalt, Paul. *Nevada's Paul Laxalt: A Memoir.* Reno: Jack Bacon, 2000.

Laxalt, Robert. *The Governor's Mansion.* Reno: University of Nevada Press, 1994.

——. *In a Hundred Graves: A Basque Portrait.* Reno: University of Nevada Press, 1972.

Levy, Shawn. *Rat Pack Confidential: Frank, Dean, Sammy, Peter, Joey, and the Last Great Showbiz Party.* New York: Anchor Books, 1998.

Lucas, Brad. *Governor's Day, 1970: A Retrospective View.* Reno: University of Nevada Oral History Program, 2005.

Maheu, Robert, and Richard Hack. *Next to Hughes: Behind the Power and Tragic Downfall of Howard Hughes by His Closest Advisor.* New York: HarperCollins, 1992.

Makley, Michael J. *Saving Lake Tahoe: An Environmental History of a National Treasure.* Reno: University of Nevada Press, 2014.

Moehring, Eugene P. *Reno, Las Vegas, and the Strip: A Tale of Three Cities.* Reno: University of Nevada Press, 2014.

Rappleye, Charles, and Ed Becker. *All-American Mafioso: The Johnny Rosselli Story.* New York: Doubleday, 1991.

Reid, Ed, and Ovid Demaris. *The Green Felt Jungle.* Garden City, NY: Doubleday, 1963.

Sawyer, Grant, Gary E. Elliott, and R. T. King. *Hang Tough! Grant Sawyer, an Activist in the Governor's Mansion.* Reno: University of Nevada Oral History Program, 1993.

Schumacher, Geoff. *Howard Hughes: Power, Paranoia, and Palace Intrigue.* Las Vegas: Stephens Press, 2008.

Schwartz, David G. *Grandissimo: The First Emperor of Las Vegas; How Jay Sarno Won a Casino Empire, Lost It, and Inspired Modern Las Vegas.* Las Vegas: Winchester Books, 2013.

Smith, Art. *Let's Get Going!* Reno: University of Nevada Oral History Program, 1996.

Thompson, Hunter S. *Fear and Loathing in Las Vegas: A Savage Journey to the Heart of the American Dream.* New York: Random House, 1971.

Turner, Wallace. *Gamblers' Money: The New Force in American Life.* Boston: Houghton Mifflin, 1965.

Urza, Monique Laxalt. *The Deep Blue Memory.* Reno: University of Nevada Press, 1993.

Weatherford, Mike. *Cult Vegas: The Weirdest! The Wildest! The Swingin'est Town on Earth.* Las Vegas: Huntington Press, 2001.

14

Conservative Nevada,
Changing Nevada, 1971–89

After recession, the energy crisis, and Watergate and other scandals in the 1970s, the 1980s brought similar problems, but also Ronald Reagan's election as president, a rising conservative tide, and the Berlin Wall's fall in 1989, signaling the Cold War's demise. Reagan's ascent from governor of California to president also symbolized the West's growth: from 1970 to 1974, 93 percent of the nation's urban growth had been in the Sunbelt. Nevada's rapid growth continued, with tourism and federal projects dominating the economy, and rising fuel costs and inflation combined with gaming expanding into other states to increase the state's reliance on western tourists—and its sense that it needed to change.

Government: Nevada's Friend and Enemy

Nevada has a tradition of supporting limited government while craving federal dollars to fund infrastructure and generate jobs. From 1963 to 1983, with western states raking in Cold War funds, Nevada's annual defense payroll jumped from $52 million to $242 million. Senator Howard Cannon also continued to work on behalf of the tourism industry. An annual $250 federal tax on every slot machine had long vexed casino operators. Assemblyman William Swackhamer of Battle Mountain hatched a plan in 1965 for the government to rebate $200 of each $250 to Nevada. After much lobbying, Cannon and Bible won agreement from their colleagues in 1971. Cannon gained a cut in another federal tax—on the gross revenues of sports betting operators—from 10 to 2 percent. The number of Nevada race and sports books septupled by 2000, and the combination of earnings and state revenues spiked accordingly.

Cannon also shaped tourism and travel beyond Nevada. Viewing the

Civil Aeronautics Board as too bureaucratic and unwilling to support lower rates and newer carriers, Cannon designed a bill and drove it to passage. The Airline Deregulation Act of 1978 phased out domestic fare regulations by 1983, eased standards for new airlines, and required the CAB to prove a route should not be approved. Cannon's measure led to lower fares and more passengers per flight, since airlines could more easily change routes and aircraft. The number of new carriers at Reno's airport tripled, while in the three years after deregulation nonstop flights to Las Vegas shot up 200 percent.

But as cynicism about government grew, especially amid lies about Vietnam and the Watergate scandal, and as Great Society programs reduced but failed to eradicate poverty, Nevadans shared these views and sometimes wound up at the forefront of them. Watergate involved Nevada, thanks to Howard Hughes, who donated heavily to candidates as well as lending money to President Richard Nixon's brother and hired national Democratic chair Lawrence O'Brien as a lobbyist in 1972, when Nixon ran for reelection. By then Hughes had fired his right-hand man, Robert Maheu, who sued him and provided copies of Hughes's handwritten memos to *Sun* publisher Hank Greenspun. The men who broke into the Watergate complex in Washington, DC, to wiretap O'Brien also tried to blow up Greenspun's office safe to obtain the documents. Greenspun believed Hughes had been central to the scandal that led to Nixon's resignation as president.

Doubts about government took forms unrelated to scandal. In 1978 Californians passed Proposition 13, cutting property taxes and requiring a two-thirds legislative majority for tax hikes. Nevadans approved the similar Question 6, which needed to pass again in 1980 to take effect. Fearing the initiative would cripple state government, political and business leaders campaigned against it by vowing to change the tax structure. Voters went along, and, in 1981, with Governor Robert List promoting their cause, lawmakers cut property taxes by more than a quarter, increased Nevada's reliance on sales taxes, and rejiggered how counties provided revenue to the state. As Washoe gained and Clark lost money, critics complained of the "tax shaft," and Clark County legislators demanded their area's "fair share" of state revenue, worsening the north-south rivalry.

Gaming found additional reason to be suspicious of the federal government. In the early 1980s the Internal Revenue Service began taxing dealers' income from tips or "tokes." Nevada's congressional delegation fought the effort, heading off an IRS plan to tax all tip earners equally, and the IRS reached an agreement with the industry on how and what to tax. Casinos and their employees had to report earnings, some of which historically had been individual rather than pooled.

At times state officials encouraged anger at government. In 1989 legislators passed a bill increasing state pensions. Although most of the measure made sense, one section applicable to senior lawmakers became known as the "300 Percent" increase. Veterans pressured junior colleagues to go along. Governor Bob Miller vetoed it, and the legislature overrode him and then reversed itself in a special session. Nevada voters exacted revenge: thirteen lawmakers lost in the next election, reminiscent of those who created the state police force after the Goldfield strike of 1907 and hiked taxes after the Cole-Malley scandal in 1927.

The Return of Laxalt

In the 1974 midterms, Nevada demonstrated electoral independence. Nixon's resignation due to Watergate and his pardon by Gerald Ford ensured GOP losses. The victims included Nevada's lone congressman, David Towell, elected in 1972 due to Nixon's landslide reelection and Walter Baring's defeat in the Democratic primary; Baring's supporters switched to Towell rather than back Las Vegan Jim Bilbray. This time Towell fell to Las Vegas Democrat Jim Santini, who established himself as a key player in mining and environmental matters.

Despite national gains, Democrats endured two nail-biting races. Mike O'Callaghan won reelection with 67 percent, the largest margin ever in a governor's race, but for the first time since the 1910s, a third party created havoc. Promising riches to voters through his silver business, Independent American candidate James Ray Houston gained support. Then the *Las Vegas Sun* reported that he ran a Ponzi scheme and had little of the silver he claimed to own. After his defeat Houston continued his career in scam artistry until dying in prison in 2012.

Nevada's other big election turned out unexpectedly. In 1973 Senator Alan Bible notified O'Callaghan and former governor Grant Sawyer of his retirement plans. With neither interested, Lieutenant Governor Harry Reid beat Reno activist Maya Miller in the primary. In the general election against Paul Laxalt, who sought a political comeback, Reid made the mistake of attacking Laxalt's family, which received a loan from the Teamsters pension fund to buy Carson City's Ormsby House casino. While Reid cost himself support in northern Nevada, Laxalt's base, some of Reid's fellow Mormons preferred the Republican, who won by 611 votes—the only Senate seat the GOP gained that year. Putting state above party, Bible retired early so that O'Callaghan could name Laxalt to the Senate, where he gained seniority and seats on the coveted Judiciary and Appropriations Committees.

1978: Collision of Cultures

The 1978 election highlighted southern Nevada's power and the Mob's impact. Myron Leavitt, of a pioneer Mormon family, became lieutenant governor; Richard Bryan, a veteran legislator raised in Las Vegas, attorney general; and Stan Colton, descended from Searchlight pioneers, state treasurer. Reflecting the nation's growing social and fiscal conservatism, Nevadans rejected a referendum on the Equal Rights Amendment and backed Question 6.

Nevadans also reiterated that they voted for individuals over party. Amid these and other Democratic victories, Republicans gained nine assembly and two state senate seats. In the governor's race, two-term attorney general Robert List easily won the GOP primary. The Democratic race pitted Lieutenant Governor Bob Rose, a former Washoe County prosecutor from the party's liberal wing, against conservative Clark County state senators John Foley and Jack Schofield. Rose won, but Foley refused to endorse him. Democrats, reliving the McCarran era, entered the general election divided. List won handily.

Then came the controversy. List received endorsements from almost every newspaper except the *Valley Times,* a North Las Vegas–based daily published by Republican Bob Brown. After the election the *Las Vegas Sun* reported Brown tried to extort List: in return for a story not being printed, List would back a gaming license for Frank Rosenthal, the Mob-connected executive running several Las Vegas casinos. Then the *Times* ran its story: List took "comps" of about three thousand dollars in food, rooms, and entertainment at the Stardust and then billed the state for his per diem. List defended himself: "Certainly if a public official were going to sell out, he would not do it for the price of a room and a meal." Investigations settled nothing, but several political leaders asked Rosenthal to use his influence to dissuade Brown from publishing the story, suggesting the Mob's power.

State Government, Society, and Economics

O'Callaghan and the legislature shared a desire for better government. In the 1970s they eliminated dozens of state commissions but added others, including a parole board to decide whether prisoners should reenter society. O'Callaghan also fought to replicate the Great Society–style programs he served in the 1960s. In 1971 he set up an environmental task force, and lawmakers approved the agency that became the Nevada State Environmental Commission, which rural legislators did their best to control. It oversees another O'Callaghan favorite, the Division of Environmental Protection, which concentrates on air and water quality. Despite economic issues, O'Callaghan also won bigger budgets and services for the mentally ill. Some of these programs suffered in the late 1970s and early 1980s amid economic troubles and the more conservative List's administration.

Nevada's economy recovered slowly in the 1980s. List faced a variety of problems, especially the national recession and its impact on the state, competition for tourists due to newly legalized gambling in New Jersey, a brief burst of increased mining followed by a longer decline, and a stream of trials, hearings, and bad publicity related to efforts to root out the Mob in Las Vegas. The Republican governor both reflected and encouraged the conservative tide that discouraged government spending and action.

Elected in 1982, Governor Richard Bryan stressed diversification, with some success. In the 1970s and 1980s, Deere & Company's credit arm moved to Reno, and new economic development groups formed in the region. Southern Nevada's development authority and other groups helped attract Ocean Spray Cranberries, Bally's Manufacturing, Ethel M Chocolates, Ford Aerospace (which left a decade later), and, in a homecoming, Levi Strauss: Reno tailor Jacob Davis helped design its original jeans in the 1870s. But Las Vegas lagged behind other southwestern cities in trucking and warehousing, despite the Freeport Law, and Nye County cotton production did little to boost any nearby textile industry.

Bryan shared O'Callaghan's concerns about social issues. In 1984, amid high rates of alcoholism, violent crime, divorce, and suicide, Bryan named a Health Care Cost Containment Committee that suggested a rate-setting commission, but the legislature balked. With the nation's highest per-patient daily charge and hospital profits, Bryan countered, "The question is no longer whether the state needs to take direct action to control health care costs but rather which action will be most effective." He and the legislature compromised on requiring hospitals to charge a set amount, and his successor, Miller, negotiated a deal with the state's five largest hospitals to freeze charges for a year and then limit increases.

With a biennial citizen legislature, lobbyists exerted power during sessions and otherwise as political consultants. Mining and railroad representatives dominated the state capital in the nineteenth century, and John Mueller, working with George Wingfield and then Pat McCarran, continued the tradition. Lobbyists may have achieved their heyday in the 1970s and 1980s, although the passage of term limits in the 1990s enhanced their influence. In 1973 legislators required lobbyists to register for the first time; by century's end their number had nearly tripled. Las Vegas advertising executive Jim Joyce led a group that worked on campaigns and legislation. Joyce's many achievements included overcoming opposition from medical groups to make Chinese medicine legal and working with Washoe County state senator Sue Wagner in 1981 to pass a five-dollar fee on marriage licenses to help fund shelters for abused women. Joyce also lobbied pro bono for numerous causes.

Along with governors and lobbyists, several legislators dominated Carson City. Elected to the senate in 1972, Bill Raggio joined a GOP minority of four but became a force through preparation, knowledge of procedure, and an ability to compromise. Indeed, the legislature then lacked the partisan nastiness that later characterized it, because both parties inclined to be moderate to conservative. Raggio worked closely with Floyd Lamb and Jim Gibson, often similarly minded conservative southern Nevada Democrats who dominated the Finance Committee.

When Republicans won the senate in 1987, Raggio became majority leader, but little else changed: former majority leader Gibson and new Democratic assembly speaker Joe Dini tended to be conservative. A moderate Democratic governor, Bryan, and a divided legislature approved increased taxes on cigarettes, gasoline, and mining and new programs to aid seniors in need of medical treatment. In 1989, with moderately conservative governor Bob Miller and liberal minority leader Joe Neal, legislators hiked mining, cigarette, and insurance premium taxes.

The Sagebrush Rebellion

Nevadans and the West chafed at expanding federal power and easterners viewing their region as a colony to exploit. In 1975 Nevada legislators created a commission to seek more control of public lands, and Congress egged on the revolt with the Federal Land Policy and Management Act of 1976, reemphasizing federal control. After the Bureau of Land Management recommended reserving millions of acres of Nevada for wilderness, the 1979 legislature passed Elko County rancher and assemblyman Dean Rhoads's bill demanding nearly fifty million acres of federal land; four states passed similar laws. Rhoads and his allies saw the Nevada Constitution's provision to "forever disclaim all right and title to the unappropriated public lands" as extortion in return for statehood and argued that the federal guarantee of "equal footing"—equality for states regardless of size or order of entry into the Union—had been impossible for Nevada because the federal government owned more than 86 percent of the state's land and up to 97 percent in some counties. Lawmakers agreed to spend up to $250,000 to prove their point in court and began what became known as the Sagebrush Rebellion.

Reactions to the rebellion varied. Some yawned that the West had made such demands before. Philip Fradkin spoke for many environmentalists when he called Nevada and Arizona "the two most overgrazed states in the West" and noted "more illegal grazing on public lands, politely termed trespassing, in Nevada than any other state." Laxalt and other conservatives backed the Sagebrush Rebels; Santini introduced a bill to hand public lands to the state. But Cliff Young, the former GOP congressman serving in the state senate, disagreed and attacked the "combination of demagoguery, avarice, and animosity." Also, the US Constitution's bar on the federal government being sued without its consent figured to derail the rebellion.

The Sagebrush Rebels made some gains with Reagan's election in 1980 and his naming a like-minded interior secretary, James Watt. But Watt proposed to sell public lands, possibly destroying ranchers' ability to graze livestock. Between their concerns, his antienvironmental views, and controversies over his public statements, Watt left office in 1983 without achieving his goals, and Reagan's dislike for BLM regulations appeased ranchers. Also, in 1979, new BLM state director Edward Spang made it a policy to meet with ranchers and pushed his staff to act similarly; giving the agency a human face eased some of the tension.

The MX

In 1979, after the Soviet Union tested nuclear missiles that reportedly could reach any part of the United States, President Jimmy Carter revealed plans for a new weapon system in southern Nevada and southern Utah: Missile-Experimental (MX), with forty-six hundred sites for launching missiles and two hundred nuclear weapons moved around by railroad. In case of attack, federal officials reasoned, the Soviets would expend their firepower by having to target both fake and real missiles. Federal officials tried to sell Nevadans on the plan with a twenty-four-million-dollar public relations effort and assurances of no damage to the environment. At first, Nevadans welcomed the prospect of the jobs that would result, especially in Clark and Lincoln Counties. Land speculators began buying up property.

Then opposition grew. Scientists and academics questioned the MX's usefulness. Native Americans objected to its impact on their lands and way of life. Mormon leaders voiced concerns. Environmentalists worried about the vast amounts of water and power it would require. About four hundred Nevadans came together to rebut the air force's nineteen-hundred-page Draft Environmental Impact Statement with their own twelve-hundred-page study. Politicians varied in their responses: List switched from neutral to anti, and Santini opposed it early. Cannon, an air force reserve general, backed it and likened its potential economic impact to Hoover Dam.

Finally, the tide turned. In 1980 voters overwhelmingly opposed the MX in advisory questions. Laxalt agreed but claimed not to have used his friendship with Reagan, who rejected the MX "racetrack plan" because it provided no guarantee of safety against attack. With the MX dead in Nevada, historian and Pioche native James Hulse, one of its opponents, wrote, "Here, not among the cattlemen of the north or the politicians of Carson City, was the genuine sagebrush rebellion, a grass-roots reaction to a military mentality gone insane." He suggested Cannon's support for the MX came back to haunt him politically.

Nevada and the Reagan Revolution

Ronald Reagan performed at the Hotel Last Frontier in Las Vegas in 1954, but his links to Nevada came from his election as California's governor in 1966 and friendship with Laxalt, who chaired his three presidential campaigns. They also played key roles in the rise of modern conservatism. Laxalt led an unsuccessful Senate fight against a treaty to give up American control of the Panama Canal, but won national attention and rallied conservatives to the cause and to Reagan, who also opposed it. Laxalt introduced the Family Protection Act of 1979 to deny federally funded legal services for abortion rights and school desegregation and opposed "gay rights quotas in employment, and . . . government funds to advocate homosexuality." Social issues, economic stagnation, Carter's inability to free American hostages in Iran, and Reagan's political skills helped him cruise to the

One of the most important political partnerships in recent American history: Paul Laxalt (*center*) with his friend Ronald Reagan (*right*), introducing him to Clark County commissioner Dick Ronzone. Laxalt managed Reagan's presidential campaigns. Courtesy of Special Collections, University Libraries, University of Nevada, Las Vegas.

presidency in 1980, while Laxalt easily defeated Mary Gojack, a former assemblywoman from Reno.

These elections had a ripple effect in Nevada. Declining conservative pleas to seek the Senate GOP leadership, Laxalt became a major figure as Reagan's adviser and spokesman. By obtaining key posts for Nevadans—including Reno lawyer Frank Fahrenkopf as national party chair and Las Vegas advertising executive Sig Rogich as a GOP adviser—Laxalt gave more credibility to a state with an image linked to the Mob and gambling. Also, in 1982, Nevada gained a second House seat, one for Clark County (won by Harry Reid), the other for the rest of the state. Gojack lost to longtime Laxalt aide Barbara Vucanovich, who campaigned as a "tough grandmother" and served seven terms, entering the GOP leadership when Republicans took over the House in 1994 for the first time in forty years; a breast cancer survivor, she strongly supported research and treatment. Her daughter, attorney Patricia Cafferata, followed her into politics as a GOP legislator and became state treasurer the year her mother entered the House.

Reagan had long coattails. When he carried Nevada in 1984 by a two-to-one margin, Republicans took the assembly (several Democrats later switched their affiliation as the Republican Party gained popularity). Assembly Republicans vexed Bryan by joining in approving a retroactive pay raise for state employees but trying to block one for pro-Democratic teachers and stopping his effort to increase special education funding. They pleased the gaming industry by cutting fees, rejecting tax hikes, and passing a law to limit picketing, angering unions. But the Republican base resented their support for several small tax hikes. In 1986, without Reagan on the ballot, Democrats poised to gain in the midterm voting, and labor determined to make them pay, the assembly majority swung from 25–17 Republican to 29–13 Democratic, and Bryan sailed to reelection.

In 1982 Chic Hecht's defeat of Cannon highlighted Reagan's impact and the state's changing political culture. National conservative groups aided Hecht's campaign, funding the same kind of negative advertising they used against other Democratic senators defeated in the Reagan wave two years before. Hecht, a Las Vegas businessman and former state senator, concentrated on attack ads and promised to support Reagan, who stumped for him. Unprepossessing and with a speech impediment, Hecht rarely showed up on television. Nevada's tradition of objecting to outside involvement in

Some of Nevada's political leaders of the early 1980s. *From left:* Richard Bryan, a governor and US senator; Senator Chic Hecht; Representative Barbara Vucanovich; Representative Jim Santini; and Senator Paul Laxalt. Courtesy of the Barbara F. Vucanovich Collection.

campaigns, voting for individuals over the party, and respecting the value of Senate seniority seemed to be dying.

Cannon proved weaker than expected for a four-term incumbent. Despite moderate voting and a strong record on defense (he even test-flew planes before deciding on budget requests for them), his vote for the canal treaty and national profile made him seem more liberal. A federal grand jury indicted Chicago mobsters and the Teamsters president for conspiring to attempt to bribe him, and he had to testify just before the election. Reminiscent of earlier intraparty fights, Santini challenged him in the primary. Although Cannon won, party unity suffered when some Santini supporters sat out the general election or backed Hecht, who beat Cannon by more than five thousand votes statewide.

The governor's office also switched parties. In 1982 Bryan beat Leavitt and Colton in an all-southern Nevadan primary to face List. With Democrats united and a bad economy plaguing List, Bryan won easily. But in his first year, Nevada literally ran out of money: to meet payroll Bryan changed how the state collected gaming revenues. Some legislators who opposed Bryan in the primary cooperated less than he would have liked, and Lieutenant Governor Bob Cashell, a Reno-area casino owner, fought him on several issues and switched to the GOP.

A Nuclear Dumping Ground?

In the 1950s and 1960s, Nevadans accepted nuclear tests and promises of their safety, but their attitudes evolved. In 1970 the Baneberry test exposed hundreds of test-site workers to fallout. When the widows of two employees sued, federal officials called the test a "discretionary function" related to national security and not open to challenge. US district judge Roger D. Foley disagreed and held the government negligent, but ruled the widows failed to prove that radiation killed their husbands. Other lawsuits raised similar issues, and Congress passed the Radiation Exposure Compensation Act, with two hundred million dollars set aside and Cannon pushing to include test-site workers. In response to these revelations, protests became more frequent. In 1975 Citizen Alert, financed partly by northern Nevada philanthropist Maya Miller, broadcast information about nuclear policy in Nevada. Religious groups demonstrated at the test site at Christmas and as part of the Lenten Desert Experience, led by, among others, Sister Rosemary Lynch.

Amid doubts about the tests' safety, another issue caused controversy. A California-based firm opened Beatty's low-level nuclear waste dump in 1962. By the late 1970s, seven states accounted for almost three-quarters of the waste there, and lax safety standards led to spills along the highway near Las Vegas. In July 1979, after the meltdown at Pennsylvania's Three Mile Island nuclear plant, List ordered the Beatty dump closed. It reopened in two weeks, but he demanded that it shut down again after the discovery of radioactive waste outside the site.

In 1982 the federal Nuclear Waste Policy Act directed the Energy Department to find a site for high-level waste disposal. Congress and the Department of Energy stressed safety: the waste would be buried in special containers in rock formations to last ten thousand years and protect against leaks. The DOE chose three sites to study: Hanford, Washington; Deaf Smith County, Texas; and Yucca Mountain on the Nevada Test Site. All three states sued in response. In 1987 Congress, hoping to overcome delays and opponents, approved the Nuclear Waste Amendments Act, settling on one potential site: Yucca Mountain. The measure by Senator Bennett Johnston, a Louisiana Democrat, became known as the "Screw Nevada" bill.

Nevada reacted angrily. The state rejected DOE permits for research at the site and filed lawsuits; although Nevada kept losing, it slowed the process. With Bryan taking the lead, in 1985 the legislature created the Agency for Nuclear Projects, joined by the Commission on Nuclear Projects. Under Robert Loux it tracked the DOE and the nuclear industry. In 1987 the legislature created Bullfrog County at the site in hopes of obstructing plans or driving up fees, but since the county had no population, the courts rejected it. Nevada also declined financial incentives to accept waste and promises of consideration for federal scientific projects.

Yet most Nevadans supported the test site and federal projects. Thanks to the Reagan administration's defense spending, the test site peaked at eleven thousand workers in 1988 and Nellis at fourteen thousand in 1985. With new programs in supersonic aircraft and combat training, Fallon Naval Air Station trained twenty thousand pilots a year into the late 1980s, with payroll topping twenty million dollars in 1985. As in the 1950s, federal activities promoted tourism: Test Site Area 51, at Groom Lake, reportedly tested stealth fighters and other vehicles designed to be kept secret, but federal denials that anything interesting went on there stoked reports that Area 51 housed extraterrestrials and their crafts. Highway 375 became known as "The ET Highway," and nearby Rachel, founded in connection with a Union Carbide mine at Mount Tempiute, became a center for visitors.

Race, Education, and Activism

In the 1970s the national debate about school integration continued to roil Nevada. After the Clark County School District (CCSD) experimented with a voluntary plan and US district judge Bruce Thompson ordered integration, trustees agreed to send sixth grade students to West Las Vegas schools, whose first through fifth graders would attend white schools. The NAACP opposed the plan as a burden on African American families. A "Bus-Out" group kept seventeen thousand white children home for a day in May 1971, and Thompson waited as the district appealed his ruling. A new law (supported by Nevada's congressional delegation) allowing school districts with appeals pending to delay busing led to more waiting. Finally, in August 1972, after a League of Women Voters suit, Thompson ordered integration.

A federal-state standoff followed. Bus-Out asked Clark County district judge Carl Christensen for an injunction. He issued it the day classes began, delaying school for elementary students. When neither judge budged, Nevada's Supreme Court scheduled a hearing but ordered schools opened under Thompson's plan. Bus-Out and Parents for Neighborhood Schools set up schools for sixth graders until CCSD trustees and superintendent (and future governor) Kenny Guinn refused to accept their grades. Finally, with help from sympathetic leaders, the NAACP and Kellar integrated Clark County schools. Guinn went on to appoint an African American deputy who succeeded him and hired black counselors.

African Americans fought for and won integration and influence in other areas. In 1971 Black Student Union members occupied UNR's student union and picketed the president in a quest for office space and received aid from the local African American community and UNLV's black students. Redistricting and growth opened other opportunities. Joe Neal became the first African American state senator in 1972, serving eight terms, including one as Democratic leader. West Las Vegas usually had two assembly seats with African Americans—almost always Democrats—elected to the county commission and school board, the state Board of Regents, and the Las Vegas and North Las Vegas City Councils.

Ending housing segregation, which might have sped school integration, proved difficult. The 1965 state civil rights law did nothing about it. In 1969 Woodrow Wilson, the first African American legislator, introduced a fair housing bill that died when two assemblywomen, Las Vegas Democrat Eileen Brookman and Reno Republican Mary Frazzini, added *sex* to his bill, which would have barred discrimination on the basis of "race, religion or national origins." Two years later Wilson's law passed amid O'Callaghan's backing, compromises, and threats of federal action. Wealth might segregate minorities, but not restrictive covenants like the one African American casino operator Sarann Knight Preddy saw in a Las Vegas neighborhood: "No niggers, no Chinese, and no goats."

The issue of minority hiring at Las Vegas casinos also proved hard to resolve. After years of complaints from the NAACP's Kellar, US Attorney Bart Schouweiler sued several casinos and unions in 1971, accusing them of violating Title VII of the Civil Rights Act of 1964, barring racial bias in hiring. Foley oversaw a consent decree. The casinos agreed to fund training and hire African Americans into twenty-two job categories until their numbers approximated their percentage of the population. The Equal Employment Opportunity Commission tracked the hotels, which cooperated minimally. While a 1981 decree for women workers met its goals by 1986, the hotels fell short for African Americans. The decree stayed in effect in the early 2000s, but few paid attention—including the EEOC.

Local leaders concentrated on job issues. In 1971 civil rights advocate Bob Bailey began running Manpower Services, providing job training; he later set up the Nevada Economic Development Corporation to aid minority businesses. In 1971 and 1972, as leader of the National Welfare Rights Organization's Nevada branch, Ruby Duncan, a onetime hotel maid fired for trying to organize other workers, protested state government cuts in

In the late 1960s and early 1970s, Ruby Duncan led a campaign for welfare rights and then developed programs to help women and children in southern Nevada. Used by permission of the North Las Vegas Library District.

welfare payments and insistence on conducting home checks at any hour. She led marches on the Las Vegas Strip, joined by national figures. The welfare office agreed to several NWRO demands.

Duncan and the other so-called welfare mothers sought to reshape West Las Vegas life. Duncan formed Operation Life, which set up preschools and job training for poor Las Vegans, especially single and working mothers; helped build a library and child care center; and began food programs. In addition to working with Duncan, Ethel Pearson led successful protests to include an interchange for the area during construction of Interstate 15.

Native Americans

"Red Power" efforts by groups like the American Indian Movement produced resistance and lobbying. After the Native Education Act of 1972 and Indian Self-Determination and Education Act of 1975 encouraged tribes to set up schools, the Duckwater Shoshone did so, removing their children from Nye County schools. Although the US Supreme Court denied their claims for more water in 1983, Pyramid Lake Paiutes lobbied and teamed with environmentalists to help block congressional ratification of an agreement to regulate the Truckee River.

Nevada's tribes sought economic independence. Working with Mormon allies, the Las Vegas Paiute colony obtained electric and water lines. The colony ratified a constitution in 1971 that continued to ensure women a voice in tribal affairs and, in 1983, opened a "smoke shop" that sold cigarettes and turned into a gold mine since only the tribe could collect taxes— none of the revenue went to the state. Pyramid Lake Paiutes built two hatcheries, enhancing breeding and fishing.

The Western Shoshone fought for the Ruby Valley land. As early as 1951, the Newe claimed nearly forty thousand square miles covered in the treaty of 1863. In 1973 the Indian Claims Commission decided they should divide twenty-six million dollars for the land, but many Shoshone said no. In 1974 the BLM accused Mary and Carrie Dann, ranching sisters near Beowawe, of illegally grazing cattle on public land. Claiming they owned the land, they sued the federal government with aid from the Western Shoshone Sacred Lands Association. Finally, in 1985 the US Supreme Court ruled the tribe lost its rights to the land (not in the treaty, but when the ICC put the money aside for them in 1979) but could sue for "original aboriginal rights." In 1986 Judge Thompson ruled the Danns had such rights and could graze their cattle, but lacked ownership of the land. Despite support from Native American and environmental activists, the battle had largely ended.

Women's Rights

When Congress passed the Equal Rights Amendment and sent it to the states for ratification, its prospects in Nevada seemed debatable. Nevada Democrats tended to be more conservative than their national party; Mormon influence and cowboy culture seemed likely to doom the ERA. But in 1975, with women's groups lobbying, the assembly strongly supported it; the state senate, which Democrats controlled 17–3, rejected it under pressure from Mormon women's groups in Clark County. Since the amendment still enjoyed ample support, pro- and anti-ERA groups stepped up their efforts, and ERA backers gained two senate seats. In 1977 the state senate voted ten to eight against passage. Lieutenant Governor Bob Rose said the state constitution empowered him to cast the two absent members' votes, making it ten to ten—a tie he broke as presiding officer, pushing the ERA through the senate. The assembly reversed itself, opposing ratification, but lawmakers agreed to an advisory question on the ballot in 1978. Nevadans opposed it, killing the ERA in their state—and defeating Rose, for whom the ERA became an issue, for governor.

Despite obstacles, women advanced in gaming. When the Union Plaza opened in Las Vegas in 1971, co-owner Sam Boyd broke a local barrier by hiring women dealers. In 1973 Claudine and Shelby Williams and other investors opened the Strip's Holiday Casino. After he died she became Nevada's first female casino board chair (after selling to Holiday Inn, which took over Harrah's) and, in 1981, when she and her partners created the American Bank of Commerce, the first to chair a bank board. Jeanne Hood, the only other woman running a Las Vegas casino, took over the Four Queens after her husband died and advanced to president of Elsinore, the Hyatt subsidiary that owned the property; later, she served as an investment company director. After marrying their owner, Paul Lowden, television anchor Sue Lowden held executive posts at Las Vegas resorts.

Women expanded their influence in politics and government. As governor, O'Callaghan nearly doubled the percentage of women in state administrative jobs; one of his successors, Richard Bryan, named Marlene Lockard his chief of staff as governor and then as a US senator. In 1986 Democrat Frankie Sue Del Papa became the first woman elected to major statewide office (secretary of state) and later won three terms as attorney general. Among other actions, she backed a measure enabling voters to register when obtaining driver's licenses.

After volunteering for Pat Hardy Lewis, Reno's first city councilwoman, Republican Sue Wagner won an assembly seat in 1974. She teamed with Reno Democrat Mary Gojack and Las Vegas Republican Jean Ford, who became a Democrat after a long career promoting libraries and environmental issues. Ford pushed through bills for equal pay and hours for women and equal rights for men in child custody cases. A foster care and campaign finance reform advocate, Wagner bucked her party by being pro-choice and pro-ERA. In 1980 she moved up to the state senate, introduced the measure that led to the creation of family courts, and joined Ford to fight a bill requiring women to obtain their husbands' permission for an abortion. They triumphed after proposing that men obtain approval from their wives before getting a vasectomy.

Journalism continued to provide opportunities. After Reno's *Journal* and *Gazette* merged in 1983, Sue Clark-Jackson became publisher and Barbara Henry editor. In Las Vegas Mary Hausch served as *Review-Journal* managing editor; executives Barbara Greenspun and Ruthe Deskin and managing editor Sandra Thompson played key roles at the *Sun*. Women published weeklies in Sparks, Pioche, Lovelock, and Battle Mountain and a daily in Fallon. Newspapers and local television stations employed increasing numbers of women; they often covered women's issues, but also established themselves as anchors and reporters.

The Most Peculiar Institution?

Nevada retained its notoriety for permitting prostitution. In 1970 Storey County legalized brothels by establishing licensing fees (twenty-five thousand dollars a year, since increased to six figures). Four rural counties followed suit. But in 1971, amid rumors that Mustang Ranch owner Joe Conforte planned a brothel near the Strip, Clark County officials backed a law barring prostitution in counties with a population of more than two hundred thousand. The legislature since doubled that limit, encompassing Clark and Washoe, and banned prostitution in Carson City. Lincoln and White Pine Counties made it illegal, but the other twelve counties allow it.

Prostitutes faced unusual treatment. Some towns barred them from associating with local residents. A federal lawsuit forced an end to restrictions, but local police and brothel owners still try to limit their move-ments. Prostitutes usually work as independent contractors rather than official employees, with a percentage of their income going to cab drivers who bring customers to the brothels, which state law bars from advertising. Nevada mandates monthly tests to protect against sexually transmitted dis-eases and makes owners liable for damages for anyone contracting HIV at their brothels. Only Storey and Lyon Counties let eighteen-year-olds work as prostitutes; the other counties set the limit at twenty-one.

Empowering Minorities

The 1970s marked Nevada's first major Latino influx. The Hispanic percent-age of southern Nevada's population tripled from 1970 to 1990 and again in the next two decades, often in older areas, as more whites moved to suburban developments and tourism-related jobs attracted immigrants. Hispanic numbers grew in Washoe County, mainly in central Sparks and northeast Reno. Hispanics set up the Nevada Association of Latin Ameri-cans in Las Vegas in 1968 and in Reno in 1971, when the federally funded Service, Employment, and Redevelopment Agency opened and provided job training for southern Nevada Latinos until 1984. With population growth in the two major cities, social and cultural groups expanded.

Just as African Americans differed on issues, Hispanics split over goals, class, politics, and ethnicity. As M. L. Miranda noted in his study, among the twenty-two Latino groups then in southern Nevada, "class-conscious" middle- and upper-class Cuban refugees from gaming or Fidel Castro's repression looked down on poorer Mexicans and Puerto Ricans who par-ticipated in the Chicano Rights movement led by Cesar Chavez in the 1960s. But Hispanics gradually unified. A mostly Cuban group started the Latin Chamber of Commerce in 1976 in Las Vegas and opened a short-lived office in Reno; it developed Hispanics in Politics, or HIP, and pro-vided services to all Hispanic groups. Three Mexican groups began Washoe County's Centro de Información Latino Americano to provide referrals, information, and translation. Yet with a few exceptions, Hispanics held few elective offices or business leadership positions.

While ethnic communities grew, Nevada's LGBTQ (lesbian, gay, bisexual, transgender, and questioning) population made its presence felt. Riots at New York City's Stonewall Inn in 1969 marked a turning point in the gay rights movement, and Nevada's gay residents sought wider acceptance.

In the 1970s efforts to repeal Nevada's sodomy law led to amendments to make it more antigay and harsh, and lawmakers tried to bar gay teachers and sex education. Much like Socialists in Nevada City, some gay Nevadans tried but failed to start a separate community, Stonewall Park, at Silver Springs near Fallon, Rhyolite in Nye County, and Thunder Mountain in Pershing County, near a large sculpture tribute to Native Americans. In 1975 the Reno gay rodeo began; by 1979 it drew two thousand spectators but inspired attacks, including one from Lieutenant Governor Leavitt. The rodeo ended in 1987 when organizers found city officials and businesspeople unwilling to allow it to proceed, but it returned in 2004.

Nevadans also made progress on dealing with Acquired Immune Deficiency Syndrome. In 1987 legislators began requiring AIDS education in public schools, thanks to Las Vegas assemblyman Marvin Sedway, but amendments let conservative local school boards control it. That year, Las Vegas gained its first AIDS ward, now an outpatient clinic. AFAN—Aid for AIDS in Nevada—held events to build awareness, often with other groups serving the gay population. Longtime Las Vegas performer and resident Liberace denied suffering from AIDS but died from complications of it in 1987, bringing more attention to the issue.

Higher and Higher Education

Higher education grew with Nevada's population and suffered from regional and political rivalries. In 1982 northern regents and a new chancellor pushed rewriting the system code to order faculty to have psychiatric evaluations as part of an effort to reduce or eliminate tenure. Historian James Hulse called the fight "weirdly reminiscent of the oppressive years of the Stout regime" in Reno in the 1950s, and it prompted similar attention, lawsuits, and distrust. The regents backed off on the psychiatric portion amid national criticism, including a *Los Angeles Times* editorial alluding to George Orwell's novel about "Big Brother": "In Nevada, It's 1984."

North-south rivalries stoked budget issues. O'Callaghan pushed funding higher education based on enrollment, but cuts began after he left office; by the late 1980s, Nevada ranked thirty-ninth in tax revenue per college student. The medical school remained underfunded, a victim of regionalism that doctors and community members tried to bridge. After UNLV passed UNR in enrollment in 1977, sniping intensified, with Las Vegans complaining their per-student funding lagged behind northern schools. UNR enjoyed stability under the leadership of Joseph Crowley, a political science professor promoted to president in 1978. His twenty-two-year tenure surpassed Joseph Stubbs (1894–1914) and Walter Clark (1918–38). Crowley built strong relations with regents and legislators, especially Raggio, and remained a lobbyist and an adviser after retiring in 2000. Meanwhile, Robert Maxson's appointment as UNLV's president in 1984 brought that school a hard-charging fund-raiser and advocate, and the campus and donations grew accordingly.

Community colleges also spread. After Elko's success, Clark County Community College (now the College of Southern Nevada) opened in 1971, moved to a North Las Vegas campus, and expanded to the western valley, Henderson (offering its first classes in priest Caesar Caviglia's parish), and satellite locations. Western Nevada Community College (now Western Nevada College) opened in Carson City with help from local government, merged with a technical institute at the old Stead air base, included the Washoe County School District's adult education program, and added branches in Fallon, Hawthorne, Incline Village, Yerington, and Zephyr Cove. By 1980, after WNC spun off its Reno branch into Truckee Meadows Community College, Nevada's community colleges—combined—boasted more enrollment than either of the two universities.

A New Environmental Awareness

In the 1970s the Environmental Protection Agency (EPA), Endangered Species Act, and Earth Day reflected the environmental movement's success, stoked the antigovernment sentiment that helped inspire the Sagebrush Rebellion, and did much for awareness of Nevada's natural wonders. Bible introduced legislation in 1971 that led to the Alaska National Interest Lands Conservation Act of 1980, setting aside more than one hundred million acres as public land. He also cosponsored the Wild and Free-Roaming Horses and Burros Act of 1971 to ban capturing or hurting wild horses and burros and to provide forage for them. This bill resulted largely from the advocacy of Velma "Wild Horse Annie" Johnston, a Washoe County rancher who had fought for federal and state legislation.

Environmentalism heightened concerns about Lake Tahoe. The local populace more than tripled from 1960 to 1975, with about twenty million tourists annually, requiring steps to protect the lake. In 1980 the Tahoe Regional Planning Agency and federal officials devised a plan to limit growth and development. Committed to Tahoe's preservation, Bible found Interior Department funding to buy most of George Whittell's ten-thousand-acre estate from Crystal Bay in the north to Zephyr Cove in the south. Representative Jim Santini helped: the Santini-Burton Act of 1979 promoted land exchanges, expanding northern Nevada ranches and allow-ing the BLM to sell land in southern Nevada, aiding development there, with the Forest Service to use the revenue to buy land around Lake Tahoe. It also prompted arguments over whether the swaps involved equal value and boosted land prices.

Miners and ranchers kept battling environmentalists and federal offi-cials. In 1976 Foley barred ranchers from pumping water near Ash Mead-ows in Nye County because lowering the Devil's Hole water level would threaten the desert pupfish, a minnow found only there; a rural Nevada bumper sticker declared, "Kill the pupfish and Foley too!" Representa-tive Harry Reid revived Bible's effort to create Great Basin National Park in White Pine County. Reid battled Vucanovich, who sought a park about

The Great Basin National Park, with its bristlecone pines, Wheeler Peak, and Lehman Cave, became the state's first national park in 1986 after a fight that had begun three decades before. Copyright iStockPhoto/Dave Rock.

two-thirds smaller, and mining and ranching interests. But the park, dedicated in 1987, drew visitors to the region to see Lehman Caves, ancient bristlecone pines, and Wheeler Peak and its glacier.

Two events bookending this era showed that mining retained its political power. In 1971 Bible introduced the Mineral Development Act to amend the 1872 mining law. Bible wanted royalties to go to the federal government and limits on how long miners could explore on public lands before finding anything, but lobbyists for the American Mining Congress killed the bill. At the state level, in 1989 mining representatives backed a state constitutional amendment to limit taxes to 2 percent of net proceeds. When gaming and resort owners objected, Governor Bob Miller proposed a mining tax of 5 percent on net profits. Sedway sought a 6 percent tax on gross proceeds, but Miller's plan prevailed.

Yet in the 1970s and 1980s, Nevada mining slumped. While the Vietnam War's end reduced demand, some in the industry blamed environmentalists and new federal regulations. As "deindustrialization," which brought high joblessness to the Rust Belt and exported jobs overseas, reduced domestic markets, White Pine's copper industry declined: Kennecott closed Ruth in 1978 and, in 1983, McGill's ore reduction plant and the Northern Nevada Railway (preserved in the Ely Railroad Museum), leaving the BLM with the county's largest payroll, although a maximum security prison opened in 1985 made up some of the loss. Attempts to mine the Comstock cost too much, and Lyon County's Weed Heights mine and mill closed in 1978. Yet the Carlin trend kept producing, new owners at Round Mountain would generate ten million ounces of gold, and White Pine's Silver King Mines dedicated a one-thousand-ton-a-day gold and silver mill at Ruth.

Urban Development and Developments

Urban growth affected other environmental issues. After deadly floods in 1976 and 1984, Clark County commissioner Bruce Woodbury sought a sales tax hike to fund better flood control, and the county created a regional district to prepare a thirty-year plan. In northern Nevada, with Truckee flooding still a concern, the EPA opposed federal funding to expand the Reno-Sparks sewage treatment plant until the cities devised an air pollution plan. In 1976 a judge barred further city building permits because they overloaded the treatment plant, prompting the county to raise fees on builders of new construction projects to fund the expansion.

Boulder City also confronted growth issues. It became a city, free from federal ownership, in 1960. A federal enclave and bedroom suburb of Las Vegas, it still banned gambling (Nevada's only other town to do so, Panaca, had been a Mormon settlement; while Mormons wielded political power in Boulder City, including Bob Broadbent's election as its first mayor and later a county commissioner, the desire to maintain its way of life dictated that policy). In the 1970s Boulder City finally allowed liquor sales but reduced growth by limiting housing construction.

Scandals rocked North Las Vegas politics in the 1970s. In 1975, after fifteen years of expanding borders and infrastructure, city manager Clay Lynch resigned amid allegations of substance abuse and using public money for private purposes. In 1976, angered at the city council over budget and pay decisions, the North Las Vegas police department led a recall of the three councilmen who formed the majority; the new members joined with the remaining ones to approve a pay hike.

Howard Hughes played a key role in urban growth—posthumously. Melvin Dummar once picked up a bedraggled man near a rural brothel and drove him to Las Vegas; the man claimed to be Hughes. After Hughes died in 1976, Dummar produced a will designating him, the Mormon Church, and several charities as heirs. When a trial before Clark County district judge Keith Hayes dismissed the "Mormon Will" as a forgery, Hughes's cousins, led by William Lummis, inherited and sold the resorts, turning to developing Summerlin, a planned community in northwestern Las Vegas; in the late 1980s, southern Nevada's first private secular prep school, the Meadows, opened near there, and Del Webb began developing Sun City. Hughes's Summa Corporation opened the Fashion Show Mall in 1981 and Wet 'n Wild theme park in 1985, previewing changes on the Strip.

Gaming Expansion

In the 1970s and 1980s, Las Vegas sought to redevelop downtown. The Union Plaza opened in 1971 at the old railroad depot site, followed by the California in 1974 and the Sundance's (now the D's) tower in 1980. The Golden Nugget grew into a resort under Steve Wynn, but Jackie Gaughan dominated the area, owning or co-owning the Las Vegas Club, El Cortez, and Plaza. Between downtown and the Strip, Bob Stupak's Vegas World stressed mail promotions and unusual games, much as Harold's Club had done. Stupak also entered politics, almost winning election as mayor of

Las Vegas in 1987 and later backing his children and other candidates. His companion, Janet Moncrief, later won a Las Vegas City Council seat and became its first member recalled from office.

With forty-six thousand hotel rooms by 1980, Las Vegas competed with larger eastern cities as a major convention destination. In a decade the number of conventions nearly doubled, delegates more than doubled, and the money they pumped into the local economy more than tripled. The most significant addition to the Strip debuted in 1973. MGM owner Kirk Kerkorian decided to adapt one of the studio's films, opening the MGM Grand Hotel on December 5, 1973. The $107 million resort included a movie theater that showed classic films, jai alai (a Basque sport), two show-rooms, and twenty-one hundred rooms—the world's largest hotel-casino.

After the MGM and Holiday Casino openings, new resort development on the Strip slowed. Several resorts expanded, but most stood pat. The smaller Marina Hotel opened in 1975 with a nautical theme; Kerkorian bought it in 1989, changed it to the MGM Marina, and planned a bigger property. In 1977 the Maxim opened east of the Strip, followed in 1979 by the Barbary Coast, built by Gaughan's son Michael and his partners, and the Imperial Palace. Over the next decade its owner, Ralph Engelstad, added four towers and an auto collection.

Although he built there, Gaughan became part of the evolution of gaming beyond the Strip. The first time-share, the Jockey Club, opened in 1974 south of the Dunes, and Hilton added condos behind the Flamingo. Neighborhood casinos gained importance, as former Riviera operator Ross Miller and Strip executive Frank Fertitta Jr. opened the Bingo Palace, later Palace Station and the core of the Fertittas' gaming empire, in 1976. The Showboat sat alone on Boulder Highway until Sam and Bill Boyd opened the western-themed Sam's Town in 1979. Gaughan added the Gold Coast in 1986. The Beckers, veteran southern Nevada home builders, debuted Arizona Charlie's.

Other changes on the Strip portended gaming's future. In 1974 Circus Circus owners Jay Sarno and Stanley Mallin leased (and later sold) the casino to former Del Webb casino official William Bennett and business-man William Pennington. They forced out Mob-connected managers and boosted profits with a buffet, a child-friendly circus operation, and more slot machines. They sought to draw not high-rollers but middle-class baby boomers and their families, enhancing that market throughout Nevada when they expanded into Reno and Laughlin.

Reno: Gaming and Growth

While Strip growth tapered off during the 1970s and 1980s, Reno's industry mushroomed. In 1973 the Eldorado became the first gaming resort north of the railroad tracks. Reno veteran Lincoln Fitzgerald bought several lots, leveled four buildings, and opened a sixteen-story resort to the south. In 1978 Del Webb's Sahara Reno and Circus Circus Reno debuted the same day, and soon the MGM Grand Reno doubled local convention capacity. Then came the Onslow, Sundowner, Comstock (launched by owners of the Cal-Neva, which finished its expansion in 1980), Riverboat, Virginian, and Reno Ramada. West of downtown the Sands Regency opened as an expansion of a motor inn begun in 1964 by Greek immigrant Pete Cladianos. The Peppermill and Mapes Money Tree expanded, while Harrah's added a tower and a new owner: in 1980, two years after Bill Harrah died, the company merged with Holiday Inn. Others headed south—the Peppermill opened in 1981 in Mesquite, and Harrah's bought Las Vegas's Holiday Casino—while Kerkorian sold to Bally's and Hilton bought out Webb.

Construction also caused growth issues. With an estimated $1 billion in resort building in 1978 and a 1.6 million–square-foot J. C. Penney warehouse, Reno faced overcrowded schools and limited housing. After decades concentrated on Virginia Street, Reno's hotel-casinos began branching out into suburban areas. The growth diluted Reno's version of a "strip"—and created a construction boom and a housing crisis when casino growth led to a lack of available rental units.

Reno's 4–5 percent annual growth rate in the 1970s prompted discussions about whether to limit new arrivals and building. Many Reno residents and visitors saw it as "a city, whereas Las Vegas is a resort." As historian Alicia Barber has noted, "Reno did not experience the onset of widespread blight, entire neighborhoods of slums, white flight, or urban riots as did many larger cities," but east of downtown, brothels, homeless, and minorities populated the red-light district, the Stockade. Washoe County even created a panel that produced a ten-volume report in 1974; it found most citizens favored limiting growth and touched off a debate between advocates of that approach and those seeking economic expansion.

Area residents also supported streamlining government and growth. In 1971 Reno, Sparks, and the county created the Washoe Council of Governments to map out unified responses to issues and discuss consolidation, but with little success. In 1979 Reno mayor Bruno Menicucci failed in efforts to consolidate the two cities with the county (unincorporated townships rejected similar plans in Clark County). After Menicucci approved hotels that planning commissioners opposed, he lost his reelection bid to Barbara Bennett, who backed planned growth; two councilmen allied with Menicucci also lost. Voters continued the trend when, in 1983, they chose as Bennett's successor Pete Sferrazza, a slow-growth advocate, over long-time Chamber of Commerce official Jud Allen, who sought the opposite.

Struggling with Growth: Las Vegas

Although Las Vegas's decision to end redlining of casinos produced none of the leapfrog growth plaguing Reno, downtown redevelopment ran into trouble. The proposed Minami Tower on Las Vegas Boulevard South remained a hole in the ground until the city gave the land to the federal government for a federal building named for longtime judge Lloyd George. With city support Bob Snow, developer of Church Street Station in Orlando, Florida, bought an older downtown hotel and turned it into the Victorian-themed Main Street Station. But it failed until Boyd Gaming took it over in 1993 and linked it to the company's other downtown properties, the California and Fremont.

Growth issues proved problematic for Las Vegas. In 1973 Clark County and Las Vegas police consolidated, but in 1975 county voters rejected a merger with the city, despite support from Bill Briare, a longtime county commissioner who succeeded Oran Gragson as mayor that year. Meanwhile, development continued to spread. In the 1970s business and residential building pushed west of Decatur, once the edge of town, toward the mountains, leading to another unincorporated township, Spring Valley, and, in the 1980s, suburban developments such as the Lakes, Desert Shores, Peccole Ranch, and Spanish Trail.

Just as Las Vegas lacked revenue from the county-based Strip, Henderson faced a similar irony: the Basic plant, which spawned the city, sat on county land, costing the city property taxes. Henderson became known as a blue-collar town in a white-collar, service-oriented region and for the industrial plant's gray-green cloud above the city. But in the early 1970s,

Sun publisher Hank Greenspun and his family began developing Green Valley. With Greenspun's funds limited (the family later amassed more wealth from the local cable television franchise), his then-son-in-law, Mark Fine, sold acreage to developers, commissioned public art to enhance the landscape, and stressed family-related activities. By the late 1980s, Green Valley blossomed into a suburban area, altering Henderson's image and geography. So did an explosion: on May 4, 1988, the PEPCON plant blew up, killing two. The blast from an ammonium chlorate leak registered 3.5 on the Richter scale and rattled buildings across the valley. Damage and law-suits led to a seventy-one-million-dollar settlement, and the company relo-cated its facility to southern Utah, while Henderson residents demanded the expulsion of other chemical companies.

Small Towns to Small Cities

Gambling helped smaller Nevada towns prosper. In the North Harvey Gross and his wife went from running a small diner in the late 1940s to building their Wagon Wheel in Stateline at Lake Tahoe; four more casi-nos followed in the area. In the South, after owning clubs in Las Vegas and North Las Vegas, Don Laughlin bought a motel on the Colorado River by the Arizona line in 1966. Expecting Arizonans and Californians to frequent the nearest casino, he expanded the Riverside Hotel to fourteen hundred rooms, catered to water sports fans and recreational vehicle drivers, and built a bridge across the river to supplant the dangerous road around Davis Dam. Laughlin's success inspired other casino operators, including Steve Wynn and Circus Circus, to build in his town.

Mesquite's success story resembled Laughlin's. Mesquite outpaced Bun-kerville after Interstate 15's completion. Its population hovered around 800 until Si Redd bought a truck stop in 1976 and expanded it into the Oasis. When the larger Virgin River property, including a golf course and conven-tion center, followed, Redd countered with a five-thousand-acre mixed-use development. His company later sold most of its Mesquite property to the Virgin River's owners.

Although not a tourist town, Pahrump's growth during the 1970s and 1980s reflected gaming's expansion. Inhabited first by Southern Paiutes, long led in the valley by Chief Tecopa, and then ranchers, it drew water from artesian wells that supported farming (especially of cotton) and vine-yards for wine. Road building in the 1950s and 1960s made Pahrump more accessible to Las Vegas and the Nevada Test Site. From a few dozen, the population grew to 2,000 by 1980 and more than 35,000 by 2010, as Pahrump developed into a commuter town or exurb for Las Vegans seeking distance from urbanization. It grew without noticeable zoning, mixing casinos with homes and promoting limited government.

Another pocket of gambling sprouted in Jackpot on the Idaho line and West Wendover on the Utah border. From 1970 to 1990, Elko County's population rose from 14,000 to 34,000, but these two towns nearly quadrupled with casino building, prompting West Wendover's incorporation in 1991. Gamblers from nearby states limited their driving to more distant resort areas in the wake of the 1970s energy crisis, boosting tourism in Elko County.

Disaster and Death

Within a six-month period, tragedy or near tragedy affected three Nevada resorts. A bomb containing one thousand pounds of dynamite prompted the evacuation of Harvey's Resort Hotel in Stateline on August 26, 1980. Attempts to disarm it failed, causing an explosion the next day that destroyed much of the casino and the building's north side and broke some of the windows at the nearby Harrah's Lake Tahoe. But no one suffered injuries, and authorities arrested the perpetrators.

On November 21, 1980, the MGM Grand Hotel fire in Las Vegas killed 85 and injured 700 of the estimated 4,000–5,000 people in the building. The fire department responded with 550 personnel. In the hotel deli, a wire sparked until the fire came through the wall at about 7:00 A.M. and spread quickly. Guests lost an estimated $270 million worth of personal possessions, and first responders reported nightmares and memories of dead bodies for decades to come. Two months later 8 people died when an arsonist started a fire in the Las Vegas Hilton.

The MGM and Hilton fires reshaped several aspects of Nevada life. Lawsuits resulting from the MGM blaze brought more specialized attorneys to Las Vegas. Governor Robert List appointed a commission chaired by future governor Kenny Guinn that recommended changes in building codes, many of them adopted in other states. Nevada evolved from having few safety rules for high-rises to mandating sprinkler systems in new hotels and retrofitting in older ones. Building codes led to changes in stairways and the pressurizing of elevators to keep out smoke, easing evacuation, and improvements in doors to keep fire out. More modern alarm and communications systems also made hotels safer. The MGM overcame its $50 million in damage and reopened on July 30, 1981. Two weeks later a minor fire from a welder's touch proved its new $5 million fire safety system worked. The changes also reflected the realities of politics and publicity: national media in Las Vegas for a Gaming Control Board hearing (Frank Sinatra won approval to become a consultant at Caesars Palace) covered the Hilton fire, and Nevada leaders realized the physical and economic dangers of failing to do enough to avert another disaster.

The Runnin' Rebels

"For nearly twenty years Jerry Tarkanian was Nevada's most famous resident," historian Richard Davies has observed. In 1973, hoping to increase UNLV's name recognition, officials and boosters sought out Tarkanian, then at Long Beach State, to coach basketball. By his departure in 1992, he took twelve teams to the National Collegiate Athletic Association tournament, four to the Final Four, and UNLV won the 1990 title. NCAA games had been low scoring, but the "Runnin' Rebels" revolutionized the sport with a "run-and-gun" offense. Tarkanian reversed his defensive-minded coaching style in midcareer and influenced generations of coaches and players. Few would dispute his success: in 1984 the Rebels moved from the seven-thousand-seat Convention Center rotunda to an eighteen-thousand-seat campus arena, which they regularly filled.

Tarkanian invited scrutiny and criticism. His popularity drew fans, but also questionable figures to "Gucci Row," the arena's best seats. Some of his recruits had troubled pasts. He signed Lloyd Daniels, a barely literate New York City athlete one of his assistants adopted and provided with a car. Arrested for trying to buy crack cocaine from an undercover officer, Daniels never played for UNLV.

But Tarkanian considered the NCAA hypocritical and said so. In response, the NCAA investigated and disciplined Long Beach State and reopened an earlier probe into UNLV a week after he took that job. In 1976 the NCAA announced ten major violations, limited UNLV's postseason play and scholarships, and made an unprecedented demand: that UNLV suspend him for two years. Tarkanian sued the university and won back his job in a friendly Nevada court. Appeals crawled through state and federal courts until the US Supreme Court turned him down by a 5–4 vote in 1988.

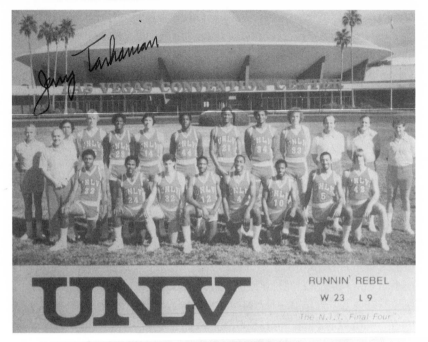

RUNNIN' REBEL

W 23   L 9

Jerry Tarkanian (*second from left*) led the UNLV Runnin' Rebels to a new style of basketball, national fame, and, in 1979, a 23-9 record and the National Invitational Tournament semifinals. In 1990 they won the NCAA championship. Courtesy of Special Collections, University Libraries, University of Nevada, Las Vegas.

Finally, UNLV and the NCAA reached a settlement, making the team ineligible for postseason for a year.

The Sporting Life

The Rebels helped make the 1970s and 1980s a high-water mark for sports in Nevada. Bond issues underwrote UNLV's Thomas & Mack Center and UNR's Lawlor Events Center, which hosted sports and assorted events. UNLV's football team featured future National Football League (NFL) stars like quarterback Randall Cunningham. Under UNLV pioneer "Chub" Drakulich and later Dwaine Knight, the golf team won a national title, and Fred Dallimore's baseball teams became a powerhouse with such players as future Major League star Matt Williams. In 1976 UNR named alumnus Chris Ault its football coach. He coached for twenty-eight years, went to ten bowl games, created the widely imitated "Pistol" offense, and sent UNR graduate Colin Kaepernick to a successful NFL career.

Other athletes from Nevada gained national attention. David Humm became an All-America quarterback at Nebraska and in the NFL. Greg Maddux set pitching records with the Chicago Cubs and Atlanta Braves. Andre Agassi began winning professional tennis championships in his teens, starred through the 1990s, and later turned his attention to philanthropy in southern Nevada. Reno prosecutor and later judge Mills Lane became one of boxing's most recognized referees.

Sports also meant tourism. Las Vegas regularly hosted boxing matches, gaining national attention, significant revenue, and prominent visitors, as did comedian Alan King's procelebrity tennis tournament at Caesars Palace. The Reno and Las Vegas Minor League Baseball teams had Major League affiliations. In 1985 the National Finals Rodeo moved from Oklahoma City to Las Vegas. Veteran publicist Herb McDonald, who cofounded and ran Las Vegas Events, pitched the idea to local leaders and

The National Finals Rodeo has brought more than one billion dollars into southern Nevada and returns Las Vegas to its "frontier town" image each December. Courtesy of L. E. Baskow and the *Las Vegas Sun.*

then the rodeo group, and Horseshoe owner Benny Binion provided funds to increase the prize money. By 2012 the rodeo's purse had tripled, and the annual event had pumped more than one billion dollars into the economy.

Fighting the Mob

By 1975 statewide gaming revenues annually topped one billion dollars, nearly three-quarters from southern Nevada. The continued success of corporations (by 1977 its two Las Vegas hotels provided 40 percent of the revenues for the 185 Hilton hotels in the United States) filled Nevada leaders with hopes for driving out the Mob, and regulators remained vigilant. But many investors still saw gaming as illegitimate, limiting Wall Street's role. Worse, mobsters formed corporations with front men and women who proved to be easily manipulated or secretly in the Mob.

Federal efforts to eliminate the Mob from casinos expanded in the 1970s and 1980s. The Racketeer Influenced and Corrupt Organizations (RICO) Act, part of the Organized Crime Control Act of 1970, toughened penalties and made it easier to prosecute a boss or "capo" for crimes committed on his orders. The Justice Department's Organized Crime Strike Force expanded, targeted Las Vegas, and assigned more agents and prosecutors. In the early 1980s, they successfully prosecuted skimming classes involving mobsters and Teamsters union leaders.

Nevada joined the effort. In 1976 the US Commission on the Review of the National Policy Toward Gambling praised its regulators as "capable of maintaining the integrity of the gaming industry at an acceptable level." But doing so proved difficult and controversial. After Harry Reid's defeat for the Senate in 1974 and loss in a Las Vegas mayoral election, Governor Mike O'Callaghan named him Gaming Commission chair in 1977. Reid and other commissioners expanded the Black Book, denied licenses to Mob-connected applicants, and even ordered one casino's closure. Other officials, elected and appointed, raised questions. Reporting by Ned Day and his colleagues at the *Valley Times,* a southern Nevada daily newspaper, revealed Mob activities and prompted further media scrutiny, and federal and state investigations engaged public attention.

Lefty, the Ant, and the Stardust

In 1975 Teamsters leader Jimmy Hoffa disappeared, but Allen Dorfman still ran the pension fund, dispersing money in Nevada. In the early 1970s,

In the 1970s and early 1980s, Tony Spilotro (*right*) represented the Chicago Mob in Las Vegas. Oscar Goodman (*left*) represented Spilotro and a variety of other figures as an attorney. Later, he became a popular three-term mayor. Used by permission of the North Las Vegas Library District.

Detroit and St. Louis investors tied to the fund bought the Aladdin and Dunes, and San Diego investor Allen Glick bought the Stardust, Fremont, and Hacienda; formed Argent Corporation with $62.7 million in loans; and claimed to know of no strings attached. But the strings formed a web: Chicago, Kansas City, and Milwaukee mobsters had hidden interests, received skim money, and sent Frank Rosenthal to run the casinos. An oddsmaker who went to jail for trying to fix a college basketball game and took the Fifth Amendment 138 times before a congressional committee, he held titles in public relations and entertainment, hoping to avoid licensing. He sued the state to stop its efforts to force licensing and won a favorable ruling by a friendly judge. The Nevada Supreme Court overturned the decision, and gaming commissioners rejected Rosenthal in 1979.

Skimming and arrogance caused Rosenthal's undoing. Despite concerns about taking on Argent, state gaming agents raided the Stardust in 1976 to seek evidence of skimming. After struggling with notoriety when dealing with Prohibition and illegal casinos, earlier mobsters tried to avoid attention, but Rosenthal wrote newspaper columns and hosted a weekly television show from the Stardust race and sports book, which he made a major profit center. He involved local businessmen in skimming, using an advertising agency and the *Valley Times*. When the Gaming Commission denied him a license, he accused Reid of seeking favors from him, attacking regulators as though he had been simply a businessman who expected them to do his bidding.

One of Rosenthal's friends further demonstrated how modern mobsters differed from earlier ones. Accused of felonies, including murder, in Chicago, Tony "the Ant" Spilotro had never been convicted; witnesses disappeared or lost their memory. In 1971 he took over the Circus Circus gift shop: the Teamsters financed Sarno, and Dorfman requested help for Spilotro. After Spilotro shifted to the Dunes, owned by Hoffa's lawyer, regulators put him in the Black Book. Spilotro also moved into prostitution and loan-sharking and formed a burglary ring with Chicago friends and an ex–police detective, belying popular claims that the Mob kept Las Vegas safer.

The Collapse of a House of Cards

Other examples of the Mob's hubris sped its downfall. Chemical heiress Mitzi Stauffer Briggs owned the Tropicana with investor Deil Gustafson, but Kansas City mobsters tied to him took advantage of her naïveté about gaming. A veteran of the Mob skim at the Stardust and Circus Circus, Carl Thomas worked at the Tropicana with Joe Agosto, its supposed entertainment director. FBI wiretaps caught them discussing the skim, Dorfman and Thomas bragging of ties to Clark County district attorney Bob Miller (casino owner Ross Miller's son), and Agosto claiming influence with a politician he called "Cleanface": Reid. Federal officials found no corroboration for the claims about Reid or Miller. But with ample evidence of skimming at Argent and the Tropicana, and Glick, Agosto, and Thomas testifying, the midwestern bosses went to prison. The FBI's "Operation Pendorf" targeted Teamsters officials with union official Jackie Presser as an informant, telling the FBI of Dorfman's ties to Las Vegas's Culinary Union and politicians. After Dorfman's conviction, he died of gunshot wounds.

Nor did the violence end there. In 1981 Reid found a bomb attached to his car, although he suspected an unhappy licensing applicant. In 1982 a car bombing, possibly the work of a Milwaukee boss or Spilotro to warn him against testifying, injured Rosenthal. In 1986 mobsters he challenged for control in Chicago beat Spilotro to death along with his brother. In 1987 Day, the reporter who dug into the Mob's activities in Las Vegas, died on vacation in Hawaii of a heart attack; the belief persisted, after an earlier bombing of his car, that the Mob killed him.

The hotel-casinos changed hands, with mixed results. Ramada Inns bought the Tropicana, creating the corporate ownership the state welcomed. Entertainer Wayne Newton and casino executive Ed Torres bought the Aladdin after state regulators forced out its owners; they later sold to Japan's Ginji Yasuda, the first foreign businessman to own a resort. Japanese investor Masao Nangaku bought the bankrupt Dunes. Argent sold the Stardust to investors from whom Glick had bought it, but state regulators found the skimming continuing, fined the Stardust a record $3.5 million, and forced its sale. Sam and Bill Boyd, their family free from Mob taint, agreed to run it after the state stepped in and then bought it in 1985.

The Mob's elimination from casinos fitted into a broader quest for respectability. The arrival of Hughes and corporate gaming marked crucial steps in that process. But so did two federal studies, the review commission of the mid-1970s and the Presidential Commission on Organized Crime in the mid-1980s. In keeping with national trends away from big government, the first group concluded that states should handle regulation; the Mob exorcism to come and Laxalt's declaration that organized crime had cleared out while he served as governor had no effect. The organized crime study, as historian David Schwartz has noted, reflected Ronald Reagan's willingness to expand government for needed purposes and looked on the Mob, not gambling or its burgeoning industry, as evil. In another sign of its growing respectability, gaming became a subject for academic study and training: UNR economist William Eadington developed research and conferences, while UNLV's hotel college, under Dean Jerome Vallen, emphasized training in all fields of hospitality, including gaming management.

Labor, Laboring, and Striking

The Las Vegas Culinary had long been Nevada's most powerful union. As secretary-treasurer—the key operating post—Al Bramlet led walkouts in

1967 and 1970, the latter leading to a 31.5 percent benefit hike over three years for more than thirteen thousand workers and wages that at least equaled those paid in New York and Chicago. But Strip operators, seeking a united front, had organized the Nevada Resort Association. In 1976 the Culinary joined musicians and stagehands in a fifteen-day strike over several issues, including honoring other picket lines; the unions agreed to some limits, but the strike cost hotels an estimated $26 million in revenue.

Meanwhile, Bramlet grew more controversial. Politically connected, wealthy from dubious investments, he ignored orders from the union international and allegedly approved bombings of restaurants that refused to accept his contract offers. In 1977 Bramlet died, shot by Tom and Gramby Hanley, whom he refused to pay for bombs that never detonated; Spilotro may have ordered the killing. Tom Hanley had a violent record and a history in labor: he organized sheet-metal workers and failed in an effort to do the same with casino dealers.

Bramlet's death changed little about the union. His successor, Ben Schmoutey, negotiated a contract so promanagement that members rejected it and ousted him; he later went to jail for joining racketeer Joey Cusumano to get kickbacks from the union's health insurance company. In 1984 a two-month strike cost the Culinary political support and six resorts whose workers decertified the union; arrests led to a court order barring picketers from blocking driveways at local resorts. The final pact gave management the lower costs and power it wanted. But the Culinary began regaining ground as the national and local purged their Mob ties and the local gained new leadership, organizers, and political skills.

Targeting Nevada

Federal moves against the Mob extended into the broader community. In 1979 came the arrival of new chief FBI agent Joseph Yablonsky, known as "the King of Sting." In 1982 he showed why: after "Abscam" caught members of Congress, the FBI unveiled the results of a Nevada operation, "Yobo," named for Yablonsky. An FBI agent posed as the operator of a weight-loss center and bribed Floyd Lamb, the state senate Finance Committee's powerful chair and leader of a prominent southern Nevada family, and another legislator, two Clark County commissioners, and a Reno city councilman. All of them went to prison.

But Yablonsky enjoyed less success beyond that. While some Las Vegans saw him as an interloper, the agent offended others by declaring his plan to "plant the American flag in Nevada" and bring down prominent Nevadans, including Laxalt and federal judges Foley and Harry Claiborne. To no avail, Laxalt complained to Reagan administration allies and reportedly had said of one target, "For a Nevada politician to refuse a contribution from Moe Dalitz would be like running for office in Michigan and turning down a contribution from General Motors." Foley blasted Yablonsky and the Strike Force office, which featured a dartboard with his picture on it. Yablonsky feuded with Greenspun, whose *Las Vegas Sun* attacked him.

Claiborne's role at the center of the storm symbolized Nevada's struggle with change. A legendary defense attorney, Claiborne represented casino executives accused of Mob ties, including the Horseshoe's Binion. In 1977, impressed with his work on several cases, Cannon named Claiborne to the bench. Claiborne saw himself as proprosecution, but also issued rulings unfavorable to federal agents and criticized their actions.

The Strike Force and Yablonsky targeted Claiborne. Mustang Ranch owner Joe Conforte claimed to have bribed him. Conforte had long been suspect, with the *Nevada State Journal* and *Reno Evening Gazette* winning a Pulitzer Prize for editorial writing in 1977 for their criticism of him. But Conforte, then a fugitive living in Brazil, received immunity to testify, and a grand jury indicted the judge. Claiborne's lawyers—Oscar Goodman, another famed defense attorney, and Bill Raggio, whom Conforte once tried to blackmail—destroyed the brothel owner's credibility. But the Strike Force kept after Claiborne and won a conviction on tax fraud in 1984. In 1986 the US House impeached him and the Senate convicted him.

The proceedings divided Nevadans. The *Sun* defended Claiborne and attacked the government; Greenspun said, "A federal judge is being hanged by a pimp. It's outrageous." When Yablonsky reached mandatory retirement in 1983, he accused Greenspun of blackballing him from the usual casino security job that awaited former FBI agents. After his release, Claiborne applied to practice law, despite his felony. In 1988 the Nevada Supreme Court ruled in his favor in an unusually long 125-page opinion that criticized federal prosecutors.

New Order in the Courts

In the 1970s and 1980s, with the district court appointments of former Washoe County School Board member Edward Reed, veteran Las Vegas bankruptcy judge Lloyd George, and former magistrate Philip Pro, the federal bench became calmer. But the Nevada Supreme Court remained a hotbed of infighting, with justices often feuding with one another publicly and involving themselves in judicial elections. Usually, even in rulings that outlawed school segregation in 1872 and sodomy in 1914, the court avoided the spotlight. The Nevada Constitution set membership at three, with the chief justiceship rotating and usually one justice from the Reno area, one from the South, and one from rural Nevada. But more residents and cases prompted voters to approve adding two justices to the court in 1967. Ideology mattered less than personalities—justices who attacked one another sometimes voted together—but the controversy split the legal community and opened the nonpartisan judges to charges of being too political.

Nevadans ignored some of these problems and acted on others. Voters kept most incumbents and rejected the "Missouri Plan," which allows the governor to appoint judges who then face a yes-or-no popular vote on their retention. But they also tried to reform the judiciary. In 1976 they approved two constitutional amendments the legislature proposed. One created a Commission on Judicial Selection with judges, lawyers, and laypeople to recommend three finalists for vacancies; the governor chose one, instead of the old system in which he acted alone. The other set up a similarly chosen Commission on Judicial Discipline whose members investigated judges and removed them if found guilty of "willful misconduct, willful or persistent failure to perform the duties of his office or habitual intemperance." Legislators also changed and expanded judicial districts and added family courts to improve handling of custodial and marital issues.

The Evolving World of Gaming

Controversy over gaming continued—not over the Mob, but what author Jeff Burbank called "one of the most infamous political embarrassments for Nevada and its casino industry." Imperial Palace owner Ralph Engelstad amassed antique cars (the world's third-largest such collection) and World War II memorabilia that led to reports of Nazi-themed parties. Engelstad and his friends attacked the stories and defended plans to display his relics, but regulators fined him three million dollars, part of which funded a Holocaust education program. Engelstad also became a leading philanthropist, aiding the handicapped, education, and health care.

While the state's emphasis evolved from the Mob to other problems, regulators adapted to changes elsewhere. In the 1970s the spread of corporations affected policy toward gaming. State officials wanted to limit licensees to Nevada, but after New Jersey approved gambling in Atlantic City in 1976, Nevada casino owners expanded there, with eleven casinos drawing thirty million visitors a year by 1985. A key figure in this process, Robert Faiss, the Gaming Commission's first assistant executive secretary, wrote the original manual of procedures in 1959; as a top aide to Grant Sawyer, then as his law partner, Faiss and his colleagues in the new field of gaming law worked with lawmakers and regulators on licensing rules for domestic and international firms. In 1977 legislators repealed the rule barring Nevada operators from owning out-of-state casinos, but empowered regulators to limit them if their actions threatened Nevada. In 1993 the legislature eliminated that authority, enabling Nevada gaming executives and companies to invest freely.

Nevadans also confronted the spread of gaming to sites beyond Atlantic City. Mississippi riverboats cut into tourism and revenues from the nation's midsection. In 1984 California's state lottery began diverting visitors from Nevada's closest market. In 1987 the US Supreme Court upheld gambling on reservations. Congress responded with the Indian Gaming Regulatory Act, which Nevada officials and gaming firms welcomed and Native groups attacked. States saw it as a way to limit the spread of casinos, but Nevada companies made agreements to operate casinos, expanding their profits, enriching Native Americans with no experience in the field, and finding revenue outside of Nevada, for good and ill.

Gambling itself changed significantly. In 1967 jukebox and amusement-game distributor Si Redd moved to Nevada, took over Bally Distributing, and emphasized slot machines. After selling Bally in 1978, he started Sircoma, later International Game Technology (IGT). Redd wanted to enter the video-poker market. Slot machines traditionally mattered less than the "pit" and its card and craps tables. But computers revolutionized gaming, moving the slot machine beyond 7s, cherries, and lemons. The casino floor changed dramatically, and IGT became the world's largest gaming-machine maker, producing about two-thirds of all casino slot machines, and adding the Megabucks progressive machine.

Exit Laxalt, Enter Democrats

In 1986, despite pressure from Reagan and other Republicans, Laxalt decided not to seek reelection. Laxalt explored a campaign for president and chose not to run, but not before a controversy. In 1983 the *Sacramento Bee* reported that federal agents suspected Mob skimming at the Ormsby House, which Laxalt and his family bought with a Teamsters loan. Laxalt sued for libel, seeking $250 million. In 1987 they reached a settlement, with the *Bee* admitting no skim had occurred but denying the libel claim because it never accused Laxalt of involvement in it; a panel awarded Laxalt legal fees, implicitly rebuking the *Bee*.

Laxalt's retirement would change Nevada's representation in Washington. After two terms in the House, Reid declared his candidacy. Representative Barbara Vucanovich wanted to run, but Laxalt backed Jim Santini, the former Democratic congressman who had switched to the GOP. Between questions about contributions to Santini's previous campaign and midterm elections going against the party in power, Reid, the Democrat, won with 53 percent of the vote.

In 1988 Governor Richard Bryan opposed Senator Chic Hecht. The GOP tried to make an issue of Lieutenant Governor Bob Miller, the son of a Mob casino operator, succeeding Bryan if he won, while Hecht ran effective ads against Bryan. But Hecht's gaffes, early support for a nuclear waste dump, and Bryan's popularity proved too much. Bryan won, but only 51–47; while Democrats questioned Hecht's ability as a senator, he had more political talent than they realized. Reid and Bryan had entered the legislature together in 1969, and their friendship meant they would be a unified force for Nevada. Their elections suggested a slowing of the Reagan revolution in Nevada, although George H. W. Bush won the state in 1988 and may have hurt Bryan's vote total. In a sign of Nevada's move from libertarianism toward social conservatism, Republicans who supported evangelist Pat Robertson took over the state party leadership.

Cultural Growth

Critics often lamented Nevada's lack of high culture and historical perspective. But this period brought giant strides. Reno and Las Vegas leveled many historic buildings, but Nevada expanded the state library and archives and created a historic preservation office that helped rehabilitate Virginia City's Fourth Ward School. Founded in 1972, Nevada Humanities supported a variety of programs, including Chautauquas and book festivals. Public broadcasting began with KUNR radio on the Reno campus in 1963 and KLVX, a television station in Las Vegas, in 1968, and spread with KNPR radio in Las Vegas in 1980 (split into two stations in 2003) and Reno's KNPB-TV in 1983 as well as translators to broadcast into rural areas.

With population growth the state's cultural community mushroomed. In 1972 classical dancers Vasili Sulich and Nancy Houssels played key roles in the Nevada Ballet Theatre, joining nationally renowned performances by Marta Becket at the Amargosa Opera House, just across the California line. Besides programs at local universities and colleges, Las Vegas and Reno developed symphonies and opera companies. The Rainbow Company, a Las Vegas children's theater group, won national honors. In 1975 impresario Charles Vanda arrived to run UNLV's performing arts center and attracted major figures in classical music, while also selecting prominent speakers for a lecture series endowed by Marjorie Barrick, a noted philanthropist and the widow of former casino executive Edward Barrick.

Southern Nevada developed a large and respected library system. North Las Vegas's library won recognition, and in 1971 Charles Hunsberger became Clark County Library District director, remaining when it merged with Las Vegas's district. Several bond issues in the mid-1980s led to new and bigger libraries with space for galleries, theaters, and computer facilities. Hunsberger's prescient planning caused controversy and, with complaints about his spending practices, eventually led to his resignation in 1993. The resulting rancor continued to create problems within the library district and with the general public.

Perhaps Nevada's most significant cultural contributions in this era involved literature. The Lake Tahoe Shakespeare Festival began in 1972. In 1985 Elko began hosting the annual National Cowboy Poetry Gathering, produced by the Western Folklife Center, in late January and early February. It grew into a weeklong attraction that built on more than a century of the genre, drew thousands of visitors, and pumped an estimated seven million dollars into the economy. Robert Laxalt continued to produce a remarkable oeuvre, often on Basque themes. Gaming and urban life spawned a variety of fiction and nonfiction, and sometimes a mixture.

Hunter S. Thompson's *Fear and Loathing in Las Vegas* addressed society as a whole in the context of his coverage of the Mint 400 desert auto race, but also attacked various aspects of Las Vegas. Award-winning films focused on different parts of the Nevada experience, with the *Godfather* movies depicting the Mob and *Rainman* the possibilities that gambling offered.

Harbingers

Historian Eric Foner once wrote, "Events only become inevitable after they happen." Yet signs of change appeared in the late 1980s. Reflecting Reno's reduced reliance on gaming and declining downtown, the Riverside and Mapes closed. In November 1988 a Price Waterhouse study found Nevada's tax system regressive, limited, unpredictable, and conducive to business but not social services. It found Nevada underfunded education, public welfare, and hospitals at the expense of police and prisons and ranked near the bottom in spending on public welfare, hospitals, health, and higher education—and other Sunbelt states, growing almost as fast as Nevada, ranked similarly. The study predicted shortfalls without broadening the tax base—and events proved that to be true.

The deaths of three longtime southern Nevadans suggested a changing of the guard. Binion, Greenspun, and Dalitz—all contributors to Las Vegas's evolution and development since the 1950s—died in 1989. The year before they died, Sheldon Adelson, the owner of the enormous and enormously profitable COMDEX computer convention, bought the Sands. Months after their deaths, the Mirage opened, the brainchild of Steve Wynn, the day before Thanksgiving 1989—and provided Las Vegans more reason to give thanks. After nearly two decades of ups and downs, prosperity turned out to be just around the corner.

SUGGESTED READINGS

Agassi, Andre. *Open: An Autobiography.* New York: Alfred A. Knopf, 2009.

Albert, Alexa. *Brothel: Mustang Ranch and Its Women.* New York: Random House, 2001.

Alverson, J. Bruce. *Flamboyant Lawyer in a Maverick Western Town: Las Vegas Through the Eyes of Harry Claiborne.* Las Vegas: Alverson, Taylor, Mortensen, and Sanders, 2011.

Amaral, Anthony A. *Mustang: Life and Legends of Nevada's Wild Horses.* Reno: University of Nevada Press, 1977.

Archer, Michael. *A Man of His Word: The Life & Times of Nevada's Senator William J. Raggio.* Ashland, OR: Hellgate Press, 2011.

Barber, Alicia, ed. *We Were All Athletes: Women's Athletics and Title IX at the University of Nevada*. Reno: University of Nevada Oral History Program, 2011.

Barlett, Donald L., and James B. Steele. *Forevermore: Nuclear Waste in America*. New York: W. W. Norton, 1985.

Barnes, H. Lee. *Dummy Up and Deal: Inside the Culture of Casino Dealing*. Reno: University of Nevada Press, 2002.

Becket, Marta. *To Dance on Sands: The Life and Art of Death Valley's Marta Becket*. Las Vegas: Stephens Press, 2009.

Carp, Steve. *Runnin': UNLV Rebels, a Basketball Legacy*. Las Vegas: Stephens Press, 2005.

Cawley, R. McGreggor. *Federal Land, Western Anger: The Sagebrush Rebellion and Environmental Politics*. Lawrence: University Press of Kansas, 1993.

Davies, Richard O., and Richard G. Abram. *Betting the Line: Sports Wagering in American Life*. Columbus: Ohio State University Press, 2001.

Dixon, Mead. *Playing the Cards That Are Dealt: Mead Dixon, the Law, and Casino Gaming*. Reno: University of Nevada Oral History Program, 1992.

Dombrink, John, and William N. Thompson. *The Last Resort: Success and Failure in Campaigns for Casinos*. Reno: University of Nevada Press, 1991.

Goodman, Oscar, with George Anastasia. *Being Oscar: From Mob Lawyer to Mayor of Las Vegas—Only in America*. New York: Weinstein Books, 2013.

Griffin, Dennis N., and Frank Cullotta. *Cullotta: The Life of a Chicago Criminal, Las Vegas Mobster, and Government Witness*. Las Vegas: Huntington Press, 2007.

Hadley, C. J. *Trappings of the Great Basin Buckaroo*. Reno: University of Nevada Press, 1993.

Harpster, Jack. *King of the Slots: William "Si" Redd*. Santa Barbara, CA: Praeger, 2010.

Hulse, James W., Leonard E. Goodall, and Jackie Allen. *Reinventing the System: Higher Education in Nevada, 1968–2000*. Reno: University of Nevada Press, 2002.

Jacobsen, Annie. *Area 51: An Uncensored History of America's Top Secret Military Base*. New York: Little, Brown, 2011.

Kania, Alan J. *Wild Horse Annie: Velma Johnston and Her Fight to Save the Mustang*. Reno: University of Nevada Press, 2012.

Kasindorf, Jeanie. *The Nye County Brothel Wars: A Tale of the New West*. New York: Linden Press / Simon and Schuster, 1985.

Knudtsen, Molly Flagg. *Here Is Our Valley*. Reno: University of Nevada College of Agriculture, 1985.

Kraft, James P. *Vegas at Odds: Labor Conflict in a Leisure Economy, 1960–1985*. Baltimore: Johns Hopkins University Press, 2009.

Lamm, Richard D., and Michael McCarthy. *The Angry West: A Vulnerable Land and Its Future*. Boston: Houghton Mifflin, 1982.

Laxalt, Robert. *A Cup of Tea in Pamplona*. Reno: University of Nevada Press, 1985.

———. *A Man in the Wheatfield*. Reno: University of Nevada Press, 1987.

Lowitt, Richard, ed. *Politics in the Postwar American West*. Norman: University of Oklahoma Press, 1995.

Mackedon, Michon. *Bombast: Spinning Atoms in the Desert*. Reno: Black Rock Institute Press, 2010.

Manteris, Art, and Rick Talley. *SuperBookie: Inside Las Vegas Sports Gambling*. Chicago: Contemporary Books, 1991.

Melton, Rollan. *Sonny's Story: A Journalist's Memoir*. Reno: University of Nevada Oral History Program, 1999.

Merrill, Karen R. *Public Lands and Political Meaning: Ranchers, the Government, and the Property Between Them*. Berkeley: University of California Press, 2002.

Morin, Paula. *Honest Horses: Wild Horses in the Great Basin*. Reno: University of Nevada Press, 2006.

Newton, Wayne, and Dick Maurice. *Once Before I Go*. New York: Morrow, 1989.

Nie, Martin. *The Governance of Western Public Lands: Mapping Its Present and Future*. Lawrence: University Press of Kansas, 2009.

Orleck, Annelise. *Storming Caesars Palace: How Black Mothers Fought Their Own War on Poverty*. Boston: Beacon Press, 2005.

Pileggi, Nicholas. *Casino: Love and Honor in Las Vegas*. New York: Simon and Schuster, 1995.

Plaskon, Kyril D. *Silent Heroes of the Cold War Declassified: The Mysterious Military Plane Crash on a Nevada Mountain Peak and the Families Who Endured an Abyss of Silence for a Generation*. Las Vegas: Stephens Press, 2009.

Pryon, Darden Asbury. *Liberace: An American Boy*. Chicago: University of Chicago Press, 2000.

Rinella, Heidi Knapp. *The Stardust of Yesterday: Reflections on a Las Vegas Legend*. Las Vegas: Stephens Press, 2006.

Rowley, William D. *Reno: Hub of the Washoe Country*. Woodland Hills, CA: Windsor, 1984.

Rusco, Elmer R., and R. T. King. *Not Like a River: The Memoir of an Activist Academic*. Reno: University of Nevada Oral History Program, 2004.

Russo, Gus. *The Outfit: The Role of Chicago's Underworld in the Shaping of Modern America*. New York: Bloomsbury, 2001.

Schoenmann, Joe, and Wendy Mazaros. *Vegas Rag Doll: A True Story of Terror and Survival as a Mob Hitman's Wife*. Las Vegas: Stephens Press, 2011.

Sheehan, Jack. *Forgotten Man: How Circus Circus' Bill Bennett Brought Middle America to Las Vegas*. Las Vegas: Stephens Press, 2010.

Skillen, James R. *The Nation's Largest Landlord: The Bureau of Land Management in the West*. Lawrence: University Press of Kansas, 2009.

Smith, John L. *Of Rats and Men: Oscar Goodman's Life from Mob Mouthpiece to Mayor of Las Vegas*. Las Vegas: Huntington Press, 2003.

Tarkanian, Jerry, and Terry Pluto. *Tark: College Basketball's Winningest Coach*. New York: McGraw-Hill, 1988.

Venturi, Robert, Denise Scott Brown, and Steven Izenour. *Learning from Las Vegas: The Forgotten Symbolism of Architectural Form*. Cambridge, MA: MIT Press, 1977.

Vernetti, Michael. *Lies Within Lies: The Betrayal of Nevada Judge Harry Claiborne*. Las Vegas: Stephens Press, 2010.

———. *Senator Howard Cannon of Nevada: A Biography*. Reno: University of Nevada Press, 2008.

Vucanovich, Barbara F., and Patricia D. Cafferata. *Barbara Vucanovich: From Nevada to Congress, and Back Again.* Reno: University of Nevada Press, 2005.

Wagner, Sue, and Victoria Ford. *Through the Glass Ceiling: A Life in Nevada Politics.* Reno: University of Nevada Oral History Program, 2006.

Walker, J. Samuel. *The Road to Yucca Mountain: The Development of Radioactive Waste Policy in the United States.* Berkeley: University of California Press, 2009.

Ward, Kenric F. *Saints in Babylon: Mormons and Las Vegas.* Miami: 1st Books, 2002.

15

A Troubled Boom, 1989–2001

In 1985, in *Amusing Ourselves to Death,* cultural commentator Neil Postman called Las Vegas "a metaphor of our national character and aspiration" because it "proclaims the spirit of a culture in which all public discourse increasingly takes the form of entertainment." By 1994, as casinos and large-scale entertainment spread, *Time* said, "Las Vegas has become Americanized, and, even more, America has become Las Vegasized." The boom that began in 1989 reinvented Las Vegas through a complex process that demonstrated continuities for itself and the rest of the state.

Steve Wynn and the Mirage

Steve Wynn epitomized the boom. He first came to Las Vegas in 1952 at age ten with his father. As Wynn graduated from the University of Pennsylvania, his father died, leaving his son with his bingo hall and debts and friends who helped him obtain an interest in the Frontier Hotel, just before its sale to Howard Hughes. Viewing Wynn as ideal for leading Las Vegas away from its Mob image, banker Parry Thomas helped him buy land that Caesars Palace needed for expansion, making Wynn a large profit that he put into the downtown Golden Nugget in 1973. He expanded it and then built a resort in Atlantic City, but he tired of battles with New Jersey gaming regulators who criticized his associates over encounters with Mob figures. Bally's corporation offered him an opportunity when it needed to fend off a takeover and paid Wynn well for his property in 1986.

The timing proved to be perfect. That year a study found about one-third of Nevada's casinos losing money. With no major Strip resort opening in a decade, Wynn declared, "They don't need another casino in Las Vegas, but they sure as hell could use a major attraction." He bought land and obtained financing from junk bond king Michael Milken, a college friend who had helped him invest in New Jersey. Milken became an architect of the 1990s megaresort boom, also aiding Circus Circus on a public stock offering and recommending the hiring of Glenn Schaeffer, a key player in that company's expansion and at age thirty the youngest chief financial officer at a company traded on the New York Stock Exchange.

On November 22, 1989, Wynn opened the $630 million Mirage with more than three thousand rooms, a ninety-five-thousand-square-foot casino, a rain forest, a twenty-thousand-gallon aquarium behind the front desk, illusionists Siegfried and Roy in the showroom, their white tigers on display, and a volcano in front of the property. Revenues averaged $2 million a day the first year. By the late 1990s, more than half of the Mirage's (technically, *The* Mirage's) revenues came from outside of the casino. With its design and ability to cater to gambler and nongambler alike, it created a template for the modern Las Vegas megaresort.

Beginnings of the Megaresort Boom

Wynn devised a new kind of resort and propelled the boom, but not alone. Almost concurrently, William Bennett and William Pennington of Circus Circus saw that bigger, attractive new hotels could pull in more tourists. If they succeeded, others would follow—and a $12 billion construction boom ensued in the next decade. From 1990 to 1997, convention attendees doubled, bringing in an estimated $4.4 billion at thirty-seven hundred conventions, while the number of Las Vegas tourists in the 1990s shot from 20.9 to 33.8 million, passing Orlando as the nation's top destination.

Circus Circus had bought a mile of land at the Strip's south end. In 1990, less than a year after the Mirage opened, the Excalibur debuted with a Camelot theme. Whereas Wynn targeted the upper and upper-middle class, the Excalibur aimed at baby boomers with more income than the clientele at Circus Circus. In 1993, hoping to compete with the Mirage, the company added the Luxor, a thirty-story pyramid-shaped hotel with "King Tut's Tomb," a ten-story sphinx, and a waterway meant to simulate Cleopatra riding down the Nile River.

Two other large resorts soon followed the Luxor, but without the economic trouble that ensued when five major resorts debuted in Las Vegas in 1955. Wynn opened the Treasure Island next to the Mirage, with nearly 2,900 rooms and suites, a pirate theme, and a moat in front with a regular battle between a pirate ship and British warship. Shortly thereafter, Kirk Kerkorian dwarfed them all with the world's largest hotel-casino for the third time: the new MGM Grand with 5,000-plus rooms, a 171,000-square-foot casino, a 33-acre theme park, a 15,000-seat arena, and an "Oz" theme, including a yellow brick road. In 1997 the MGM required more construction: the 88-foot-high lion's head entryway from the Strip drove away Asian customers who considered the lion bad luck, leading to a $40 million renovation with a smaller lion on a pedestal.

Older hotels also created trends. Caesars pioneered a new approach with the Forum Shops in April 1992. The mall's 600,000-plus square feet included moving Roman statuary and, later, an attraction based on Atlantis. They also featured Spago, a restaurant built by Wolfgang Puck, whose success inspired numerous other celebrity chefs to bring their wares to almost every newer hotel. Thus, Las Vegas became a culinary destination, contributing to higher prices for dining and shifting the image of the Strip's food from cheap buffets to gourmet offerings.

The Boom, the Baby Boom, and Blasts

These attractions reflected Las Vegas marketing itself as a family destination. Emphasizing more diverse entertainment, resorts boasted such features as the MGM Grand's virtual reality arcades and day-care center and the Mirage's white tiger and dolphin habitats. Circus Circus added thrill rides in a glass-covered park. Some of these provided revenue while operators pondered how to make more money: the MGM replaced its theme park with a conference center. Hilton opened its Grand Vacation Club behind Flamingo and added another on Paradise Road before erecting a high-rise in 2004 near Circus Circus. Alluding to the Mirage's volcano, journalist Marc Cooper warned that the town might be "swept away by a lava flow of respectability and Family Values."

Other factors inspired this approach. Baby boomers had children to take on vacations, and Strip image makers sought to attract them and their money. Just as Nevada proclaimed itself "One Sound State" in the 1930s, Las Vegas marketed its attractions: amid a patriotic rebirth and Ronald Reagan's presidency in the 1980s, Las Vegas became "The American Way to Play." In the early 1990s, "family values" gained political currency, especially among Republicans. More corporate and always seeking respectability, Las Vegas did itself no harm by adapting family values to tourism. After a few years, Las Vegas changed its emphasis again, partly over concerns about exposing children to gambling—especially after a five-year-old girl's rape and murder in Primm in 1997.

Las Vegas devised another marketing idea during the 1990s: implosions as attractions, giving new meaning to economist Joseph Schumpeter's point, "Creative destruction is the essential fact about capitalism." In 1993 Wynn imploded the Dunes, the future site of his Bellagio, with two hundred thousand chanting "Blow it up!" on a national telecast. The Landmark, now a Convention Center parking complex, came down two years later in a scene in the film *Mars Attacks!* Late in 1996, the Sands (the Venetian) and Hacienda (Mandalay Bay) became rubble; a street party celebrated the latter. In 1998 with some of the twenty thousand spectators paying $250 for VIP tickets, the Aladdin gave way for the new Aladdin, later Planet Hollywood. The El Rancho, originally the Thunderbird, fell in 2000, but its replacement remains unbuilt. In 2001 Wynn completed the cycle by leveling the Desert Inn, to be replaced by his Wynn Las Vegas.

The Modern Boom: Continuity and Change

In the next round of expansion, Las Vegas catered to families and twentysomethings with discretionary money, reflecting author Pete Earley's description of "a new class of casino—the so-called entertainment superstores, commonly called 'super casinos.'" The MGM adjusted its theme to a "city of entertainment," with a Studio 54 nightclub, and pursued highrollers with "the Mansion," private suites and villas up to 14,000 square feet, some with indoor pools and classic art. The Hilton added the $70 million "Star Trek: The Experience." Circus Circus Enterprises designed Mandalay Bay to appeal to wealthier customers with a Four Seasons Hotel and gourmet restaurants, younger ones with the "House of Blues" and nightspots, and families with the "Shark Reef." Off the Strip, the Hard Rock Hotel's opening in 1995 reached a hipper clientele with concerts and memorabilia.

Las Vegas also continued to stress themes and luxury. From 1997 to 2000, the Strip went through another burst. First came New York–New York, with its roller coaster, 150-foot Statue of Liberty, and replicas of skyscrapers. In 1998 Wynn added the Bellagio at a then-record $1.6 billion with the highest-end shopping yet found in Las Vegas, more than 3,000 luxurious rooms, a plant conservatory, and $300 million in art on display in its gallery. The 3,700-room, $950 million Mandalay Bay and nearly 3,000-room,

$785 million Paris with its replicas of the Eiffel Tower and the Paris Opera House followed. After opening the locally oriented Rio west of the Strip in 1990, builder Anthony Marnell entered on major expansions—a new tower in 1993 and Masquerade Village, reminiscent of a Brazilian carnival, in 1997, before its sale to Harrah's. In 2000 the new Aladdin opened with 2,500 rooms and a London Club high-roller casino.

The Venetian's opening in 1999 also marked a turning point. Sheldon Adelson sold his Computer Dealers Association show, COMDEX, which, along with the Consumer Electronics Show, brought millions of dollars to Las Vegas annually as attendees paid triple the usual room rates. In 1989 he bought the Sands and built a convention hall. With the Sands unable to compete with newer resorts, Adelson replaced it with the $1.5 billion Venetian, including replicas of the Doge's Palace, a 113,000-square-foot casino, gondolas traversing a high-end mall with 500,000 square feet of retail space, and later a Guggenheim-Hermitage art museum designed by architect Rem Koolhaas. Adelson's emphasis on conventions paid off for him and the Strip. By the year's end, the number of hotel rooms in southern Nevada reached 120,000, eighteen of the nation's twenty largest hotels towered over Las Vegas, and worldwide gaming revenue reached $1 trillion.

Corporate Las Vegas: Merger Mania and Entertainment

With its success enhancing Las Vegas's appeal to Wall Street (in 1997 *Fortune* ranked Mirage Resorts among the nation's best companies to work for), Nevada joined the international trend of corporate partnerships, mergers, and takeovers. MGM teamed with Primadonna Resorts on New York–New York and then bought out co-owner Gary Primm and his three resorts on the California-Nevada line along Interstate 15. Wynn and Circus Circus Resorts partnered on the Monte Carlo on old Dunes land. When Bennett tried to oust other executives and a takeover attempt loomed, his board forced him out; he then bought the Sahara for $193 million and renovated it.

Harrah's, Nevada's first publicly traded gaming company, adapted to corporate culture and new technology. Harrah's pioneered mathematical calculations and computer programs to research its customer base. Under Reno lawyer Phil Satre's leadership, it bought the Rio Hotel for $880 million, the Showboat company for more than $1 billion, and Harvey's at Lake

Tahoe for $675 million. Several maneuvers affected Caesars Palace, a future Harrah's property: ITT Corporation, which owned the Desert Inn and Sheraton Hotels, took over Caesars World in 1995 for $1.7 billion. Starwood Hotels bought the company in 1998 and sold Caesars and other gaming properties for $3 billion to Park Place, which had been part of the Hilton chain and outbid Wynn for them.

The most notable takeover involved Wynn. Building the Bellagio increased his company's debt, and investors worried about Wynn's spending on his home, private planes, salaries, bonuses, and art displayed as an attraction at the Bellagio. Wynn became a takeover target for Kerkorian, whose MGM bought Mirage resorts for $6.7 billion early in 2000. Wynn received $550,000, half of which he used to buy the Desert Inn. Wynn began planning a new resort to replace it.

The new boom also changed entertainment. In 1989 Wynn's Mirage charged $125 a ticket to see Siegfried and Roy, veterans of several Strip production shows. They broke all Las Vegas records, selling out their shows for thirteen years until an onstage incident involving one of their tigers in 2003 nearly killed Roy Horn and forced their retirement. Their success, and the desire to diversify the Strip's attractions and entertainment, prompted Wynn to import a production show when he opened Treasure Island. Mystere marked the first American residency for Cirque du Soleil ("Circus of the Sun"), a Canadian production headed by Belgian-Italian theatrical director Franco Dragone. Its success led to several such shows on the Strip, both original and based on the music of such performers as the Beatles and Michael Jackson. Other production shows combined music, special effects, and entertainers not normally considered Las Vegas superstars, such as the MGM Grand's EFX show with headliners from Broadway and popular music.

Cirque du Soleil's success reflected and affected changes in entertainment. The hotels broke the musicians union in 1989 in an effort to reduce the number and cost of orchestra players and use recorded music in production shows. Variety shows with showgirls continued on the Strip, but rising ticket prices and new arenas led to fewer performers appearing for a week at a time in a showroom. Veterans often moved to neighborhood casinos or emulated Las Vegas icon Wayne Newton, who worked out the first "headliner-in-residence" deal at the Stardust, where he performed for forty weeks a year. Symbolizing the transition of Las Vegas entertainment, the heart of the "Rat Pack" died in the 1990s: Sammy Davis Jr., Dean Martin, and Frank Sinatra.

Expansion in Reno

As Alicia Barber has noted, "a complete role reversal" since 1960 changed Las Vegas "from Reno's primary competition to an international tourist destination in a class all its own." In 1990 Clark County drew 24.2 million tourists with Strip revenues of $3.9 billion; 4.9 million tourists in Reno-Sparks contributed about $1.16 billion. Construction in Reno's gaming and tourism industry also trailed Las Vegas. The Peppermill expanded, as did Bally's Reno after its sale to Hilton. In 1995 the Eldorado's operator, Reno attorney Donald Carano, and Circus Circus teamed on the Silver Legacy, which linked their hotels with two towers and more than 1,700 rooms and suites, an Old West and Victorian theme, a 21-story dome, and a 127-foot mining rig. The Silver Legacy enabled visitors to patronize the three resorts without going outside—a benefit during the winter, but discouraging movement between resorts, unlike the Strip's moving walkways.

The Atlantis provided another success story for Reno. The Farahi family bought a 142-room motel in 1972 and added a 12-story tower in 1991. They decided to begin trading on the New York Stock Exchange two years later, raising capital for an expansion. They added an 18-story tower, changed the hotel's name to the Atlantis, and planned a 27-story addition that included a terrace over South Virginia Street and hourly light shows when completed in 1999.

These successes seemed limited in comparison with the effects of losing Bay Area tourists to Indian gaming and other competitors. By 1999 thirty-six downtown Reno businesses had been shuttered; between 1995 to 2000, the Colonial, Holiday, Comstock, Horseshoe, Riverside, Speakeasy, Virginian, and Pioneer casinos closed. After Harold's Club closed, supposedly for a remodeling to become an Australian-themed resort, Harrah's bought it and the Nevada Club and razed both. In 1996 the city bought the Mapes for $4 million in hopes of revitalizing it. The National Trust for Historic Preservation placed it on its list of Eleven Most Endangered Historic Places in America. But when redevelopment efforts fell through, the city council voted to level it. The Mapes went down on January 30, 2000, with its location eventually housing a public plaza.

The Growth of Gambling

The expansion of gaming resorts began physically in southern Nevada with movement away from the Strip and downtown. The Palace Station became the base for the Fertitta family's neighborhood casino empire, stretching to Boulder Highway, northwestern Las Vegas, North Las Vegas, Green Valley, and Summerlin. They concentrated on locals and keeping the Culinary from organizing their staff. Other operators added neighborhood properties, while Bob Stupak replaced Vegas World between downtown and the Strip with the 108-story, 1,141-foot-tall Stratosphere Tower, with amusement rides at the top. But Stupak went bankrupt building it and had to surrender control to outside investors, eventually led by Carl Icahn, a Wall Street operator who later took over the Arizona Charlie's properties.

These local changes reflected outside developments. In 1999 Portugal gave China control of Macau, and its expansion reshaped the world market. Michigan, South Dakota, Iowa, and Illinois permitted gambling, while Louisiana, Mississippi, Missouri, and Indiana allowed riverboats. From 1989 to 1997, Nevada's share of domestic gambling revenue fell substantially—from more than 60 percent to under 40. Several other attractions—entertainment, rooms, shopping, and dining—matched and even exceeded gambling revenue in Las Vegas.

Indian gaming also had significant effects. Its expansion in California hurt Reno, but similar expectations for Laughlin proved wrong. Instead, in 1995 the Fort Mojave Reservation opened Laughlin's $60 million Avi, with nearly 500 rooms and a 25,000-square-foot casino. Indian gaming left bigger footprints elsewhere: in Connecticut the Pequots' Foxwoods and the Mohegans' Mohegan Sun cut into Atlantic City's business. By the late 1990s, more than 180 tribes with 276 gambling operations produced $7 billion a year. Since their inexperience prompted many of the tribes to bring in gaming management teams from Nevada, historian Hal Rothman noted that "the colony became the colonizer."

With Nevada retaining its monopoly on legal sports betting, that part of the industry also grew. Kirk Kerkorian and Frank Rosenthal had dedicated ample space to race and sports books in their casinos, and oddmakers like Jimmy "the Greek" Snyder and Bob Martin attracted attention to betting and point spreads. The growing popularity of the NFL's Super Bowl and the NCAA's "March Madness" attracted more bettors to Las Vegas in late winter and early spring. More professional sports books also helped law enforcement: by reporting unusual betting patterns on college football and basketball games, operators helped authorities target would-be game fixers and point shavers.

This growth drew federal attention. In 1994 the Clinton administration suggested up to a 4 percent federal gaming tax; the Culinary Union and gaming interests helped defeat it. In response to the threat, gaming officials created their first trade group, the American Gaming Association, run by Nevadan and former GOP chair Frank Fahrenkopf. The AGA created the international Global Gaming Expo, lobbied Congress, and supported programs to deal with problem gambling.

The AGA also faced challenges from Republicans. After the GOP took over the House in 1994, Christian conservatives in particular pushed for the National Gambling Impact Study Commission. But other party leaders, conscious of the industry's campaign contributions, weakened the board by denying it subpoena power. Nevadans took heart that its members would include Terry Lanni, a top MGM Resorts executive; John Wilhelm, who ran the Culinary's parent, the Hotel Employees and Restaurant Employees International Union; and Gaming Control Board chair Bill Bible. The commission expressed concern about addiction, the availability of gambling in places like grocery stores, and automatic teller and credit card machines. It opposed betting on college sports, but as Senate Democratic whip, Harry Reid helped block legislation that would have hurt the state's sports books. The commission's June 1999 report suggested more oversight of Indian casinos but created few concerns for Nevada.

Governing amid the Boom

With Richard Bryan's election to the US Senate, Lieutenant Governor Bob Miller succeeded him in 1989 and won easily in 1990. The boom required Nevada to improve services and education, especially in areas related to the entertainment industry and the needs of baby boomers and older migrants. Despite the South's population and economic growth, the more conservative North kept power in Carson City: Republican Bill Raggio of Reno dominated the state senate and Democratic speaker Joe Dini of Yerington the assembly. Gaming made its presence felt as Wynn set up a political arm that included many of the services provided by consultants and parties. Yet the legislature also became more liberal, due to women

(Nevada ranked second among states in its percentage of female lawmakers by 1999, although the women winning statewide office in 1990 included two Republicans, Lieutenant Governor Sue Wagner and Secretary of State Cheryl Lau), the Culinary's growing activism and power, and lobbying groups such as the newly formed Progressive Leadership Alliance of Nevada (PLAN).

These groups and ideologies converged on a national controversy. In 1991 the Tailhook Association of former naval officers held its annual meeting at the Las Vegas Hilton. Some forced an attendee, former navy pilot Paula Coughlin, and other women in hallways to run a "gauntlet" of drunken officers who groped and fondled them. Hilton security officers saw this but did nothing. Coughlin sued the Hilton and won a $5.2 million judgment. In 1995 the legislature passed a tort reform bill to make it harder to win jury awards from businesses for their employees' actions. Under pressure from Miller, lawmakers eliminated a provision to make the rule retroactive, which would have negated Coughlin's victory.

Miller had an impact in other ways. He stressed reducing class size in elementary schools, aiming for 1 teacher per 16 students in first and second grades. At the time, Clark County sought to hire at least 1,200 new teachers a year and opened a new public school each month, adding to the need to hire teachers; eventually, Miller won reductions for third grade. He also sought to redesign the executive branch, including consolidating numerous agencies and boards; the legislature went along partway, but not when his authority would have increased.

But other issues dogged the state. A recession in 1991–92 led to lower revenues than projected, prompting Miller to lay off 266 state workers and cut $174 million; in 1993 he ordered 10 percent cuts. While lawmakers added five cents to the fuel tax for road building, the State of Nevada Education Association planned an initiative to tax corporate income and create a corporate license fee. Miller persuaded the union instead to accept an alternative business tax, leading to the SNEA opposing its own initiative. The legislature approved a payroll tax levied per employee and capped at $100,000 per quarter in response to gaming industry concerns. The teachers and gaming industry pronounced themselves satisfied.

Miller and the legislature made other important changes. In 1991 southern Nevadans united to pass a "Fair Share" bill to redo state formulas and keep more of Clark County's revenue. Washoe County lost nearly $20 million in sales tax funds in the next three years and reimbursed Clark County for $6 million received in error, but Raggio managed to halve the payment. Legislators approved greater disclosure from lobbyists but made it easier to donate to campaigns, prompting an initiative limiting contributions and stricter laws on reporting those funds. In 1993 Raggio introduced a bill to create the Nevada Economic Forum, composed of political appointees and banking and finance representatives, to estimate state revenue; it often underestimated the amount available, prompting passage of leaner budgets than necessary. In the same year, after a lengthy battle that crossed party lines, the legislature finally repealed the state's law against sodomy.

In 1994, when Miller sought a second full term, Las Vegas mayor Jan Jones challenged him. She attacked his stand on abortion: a Catholic, Miller opposed choice but backed a 1990 referendum in which 63 percent of Nevadans endorsed abortion rights. More important, she questioned whether Miller could run. A state constitutional amendment passed in 1970 barred a governor from serving more than ten years. Because Miller finished Bryan's term and would serve ten years and four days, Jones argued the law made him ineligible. The SNEA, supporting Jones due to Miller's veto of a bill that would have enabled state workers to engage in collective bargaining, sued to stop his candidacy. The Nevada Supreme Court ruled for Miller, and he easily defeated Jones in the primary and Assemblyman Jim Gibbons in the general election and served as governor for ten years and three days. In the same election, the assembly wound up in a twenty-one to twenty-one tie, leading to cospeakers, cochairs of all committees, considerable negotiation, and, according to some participants, better cooperation than before or since.

Redeveloping Reno

Reno concentrated on redeveloping its core, with some success. In 1989 the National Automobile Museum opened near the Truckee River. A little more than two decades and two million visitors later, it included vehicles that had belonged to celebrities like Elvis Presley, Frank Sinatra, and James Dean and others featured in movies. It opened just before the Mirage, highlighting the differences between the two areas and their approaches to tourism development. At one point Steve Wynn suggested to Reno, "You need Bill Harrah to come back," and, in the auto museum, he did: most of its collection consisted of his cars, donated by Holiday Inns, which had bought out his company.

Like the auto museum, other attractions targeted locals and tourists. In 1991 the $7.8 million Raymond I. Smith Truckee Riverwalk introduced public art, paved trails, fountains, and the Wingfield Park Amphitheater to encourage activity by the river and downtown. In 1993 the Reno-Sparks Convention and Visitors Authority (RSCVA) borrowed $6.7 million in city redevelopment funds to help build the $50.2 million National Bowling Stadium, one block east of Virginia Street's casinos, and the American Bowling Congress and Women's International Bowling Congress championships kept downtown busy for months at a time. In 1999 a new plaza, complete with a skating rink, added to Reno's offerings, as did the Sierra Arts Foundation and Artspace teaming to create artists' lofts in the old Riverside Hotel, while the Comstock became a condominium complex.

Northern Nevadans also took a page from the past by emphasizing the area and its natural attractions. In 1992 Carson City unveiled the thirty-one-thousand-square-foot Pony Express Pavilion in Mills Park for community events, including auto shows and farmers markets. In 1994, relegating

The Truckee Riverwalk, named for Raymond I. "Pappy" Smith of Harold's Club fame, has been a key part of Reno's downtown redevelopment, combining old and new buildings with shopping and dining. Copyright iStockPhoto/alacatr.

the former senator to the terminal, Washoe County's airport authority renamed its facility from Cannon to Reno-Tahoe International Airport. In 2001 Reno and Sparks hotels and several agencies led by the RSCVA and Incline Village/Crystal Bay Visitors Bureau formed a Regional Marketing Committee to promote the "Reno-Tahoe area." They began efforts to attract the winter Olympics and stressed year-round recreation.

Black Rock and Burning Man

Another natural tourist attraction won attention for different reasons. The 400-square-mile Black Rock Desert, more than 100 miles north of Reno, drew those thirsting for speed. Drivers of rocket cars, designed to set speed records, sought out salt flats, with a 19-mile course and the Bureau of Land Management requiring permits and environmental studies. In 1983 Richard Noble set a new land speed record there of more than 633 miles per hour, prompting numerous other attempts. In 1997, driving a car that Noble owned, Great Britain's Andy Green broke the speed of sound, reaching 763 miles per hour. Land sailers and rocket drivers joined them, setting records in the northern Nevada desert.

In 1991 the annual Burning Man Festival moved from the Bay Area, where it began in 1986, to the Black Rock Desert. Held for one week through Labor Day, it takes its name from the effigy that participants burn on the gathering's Saturday evening. Dedicated to community, art, and intellectual and personal independence, Burning Man takes place in a C-shaped area, with medical services, broadcast stations, publications, and cars licensed by the "Department of Mutant Vehicles." By 1997 its growth prompted organizers to form Black Rock City, LLC, and move it from Pershing County into Washoe's portion of Black Rock, now part of a 380,000-acre national conservation area. The festival's operators added a 7-mile-long plastic fence and various rules involving driving. Growth bred growth: ticket prices reached $420 in 2012, with attendance reaching seventy thousand in 2014. Temporarily, Black Rock City became Nevada's seventh largest community.

Burning Man consists of varied "camps" with certain rules, including participation and no commercial sales except for ice and coffee. Those coming to Burning Man must bring their equipment and materials and take everything when they go; as organizers say, "We clean up after ourselves and endeavor, whenever possible, to leave such places in a better

The Burning Man Festival in the Black Rock Desert has become not only a social and cultural phenomenon, but also a major event for northern Nevada. Copyright iStock-Photo/Owens Imaging.

state than when we found them." A different annual theme guides the art displayed, as well as camps and costumes. Organizers also burn a specially constructed, themed temple at each festival.

Redeveloping Southern Nevada

In 1991, in the wake of criticism of city officials over questionable business and land deals, Las Vegas voters elected a new mayor: Jan Jones, a Stanford alumna known to locals for her commercials for her family's market and car dealership. Jones supported several downtown redevelopment efforts. The most noteworthy, the $70 million Fremont Street Experience, a canopy 90 feet above "Glitter Gulch" with 2.2 million bulbs flashing an hourly music and light show, increased revenue and traffic downtown. The $100 million Neonopolis theater, shopping, and dining complex also helped—but less than hoped. In 1998 the city designated an eighteen-block area the Las Vegas Arts District, attracting lofts, galleries, and bistros.

When Jones chose not to seek a third term in 1999, a city councilman and a developer entered the race, followed by Oscar Goodman. An attorney known for representing mobsters like Lefty Rosenthal and Tony Spilotro, Goodman had become bored with his law practice. Critics said his wife, Carolyn, the founder of Summerlin's prep school, should have run and that his election would set back city efforts to shed its Mob past. Goodman banked on Las Vegans feeling nostalgic for that past and wanting another colorful, media-savvy mayor to follow Jones. The voters proved him right, easily electing him. Goodman began seeking a major league sports franchise and executed a land swap with Lehman Brothers to obtain sixty-one acres of downtown land the Union Pacific left vacant.

Las Vegas and its leaders also benefited from Summerlin generating revenue and construction on city land. In the 1980s, amid discussions about the future of its land northwest of town, the Hughes company pleased environmentalists with a land swap with the Bureau of Land Management to protect Red Rock Canyon from development (and would make another trade in 2002). The city set up a Special Improvement District to help with needed public improvements. In 1990 housing construction began, and by the time the master-planned community reached eighteen thousand homes in 2001, it included a library and performing arts center, miles of parks and trails, and Summerlin Parkway, a ten-mile extension of Interstate 15.

Suburban Growth in Southern Nevada

The resort boom fed construction and population growth in southern Nevada—but so did other factors. An estimated 2.5–4.5 jobs resulted from each new hotel room—besides other local employment opportunities. According to one estimate, Southern Californians bought more than 60 percent of the homes sold in Las Vegas in 1989 and 1990 as they sought new opportunities, as the Cold War's end hurt their defense economy, smaller communities or less government and regulation. As the 1980s ended, Nevada's population had grown by nearly half, more than double the percentage growth of California and Texas combined. Nevada led the nation as the fastest-growing state each year from 1986 to 1999, with Las Vegas the fastest-growing metropolitan area of the 1990s. By 1990 Nevada's population had risen 650 percent since 1950, with Arizona the distant runner-up at less than 400 percent.

Henderson's population shot from 67,000 to 186,000 in the 1990s. In 1997 the mayoral election of Jim Gibson, son of a legendary legislator from Henderson, helped ensure a balance between the older town center and newer developments. Henderson welcomed Nevada State College and passed three parks-and-recreation bond issues in a decade. In 1996 the first residents of Lake Las Vegas moved into homes near a Jack Nicklaus–designed golf course, luxury hotels, and numerous amenities. In 2001, with

Green Valley Ranch hotel-casino opening in partnership with the Fertittas, the Greenspuns invested in the District, a mixed-use development with pedestrian-friendly shopping and a residential district. Within about a year, a shopping mall, an auto mall, and Sunset Station opened, and new planned communities, including two senior areas, added to Green Valley's cachet.

North Las Vegas also evolved from a blue-collar town, showing how suburban growth shaped landscapes and images. Once derided, even by some residents, as a slum they called "Northtown," the city took bids in 1988 for the new Eldorado master-planned community on one thousand acres of federal land it acquired at its northern end. The 2001 sale of more than nineteen hundred acres to the Greenspun family's company and Del Webb led to construction of the Aliante master-planned community. But local politics remained split, with traditional powers like the Mormon Church, the police union, and African Americans gaining more competition from the growing Hispanic community, whose members settled mainly in the older part of town.

The Problems of Growth

These developments prompted criticism that southern Nevada wanted growth at any cost. Decrying "the fanatical persistence of an environmentally and socially bankrupt system of human settlement," urbanist Mike Davis likened Las Vegas to "a hyperbolic Los Angeles, the land of sunshine on fast forward." Some sought to slow the movement. In the late 1990s, high-rise condos joined the skyline, fostering hopes for "Manhattanization" or better use of space, but much of the development appealed to wealthy visitors seeking a second home. In 1997 Democratic state senator Dina Titus tried to pass a law similar to that controlling growth in Portland, Oregon—a "ring around the valley" to fill in undeveloped land. Trying to protect their turf, city and county officials managed to defeat it. The 1999 legislature set up the Southern Nevada Regional Planning Coalition, uniting the county, its cities, and the school district to aid natural resources, population forecasting, public facilities, air quality, transportation, and land use.

By 1990 about 90 percent of westerners lived in towns of twenty-five hundred or more, and Nevada fitted that mold as one of the nation's most urbanized states—with many related problems. It had among the nation's worst rates of suicide, high school to college, dropouts, bankruptcy, smokers, teen pregnancy, voting, home ownership, domestic violence, Medicaid participation, immunization, and drinking. Pollution became a bigger issue. From 1975 to 1995, Nevada's rate of incarceration rose 325 percent, with the number of prisoners well above national averages. Mental health treatment suffered each time Nevada cut its budget.

Having the nation's fastest-growing fifty-five-plus population created other issues. By 1998 more than one-third of Las Vegans exceeded that age. As sociologists Mark Gottdiener, Claudia Collins, and David Dickens pointed out, this community split into two groups: wealthier migrants and locals, often from the tourism industry, who had limited means. But the former's lack of community ties and the latter's lack of finances tended to make them conservative on tax and bond issues. Thus, in 1994 Clark County voters took the unusual—for them—step of defeating part of a school bond issue, due partly to the question of whether older neighborhoods would pay to build schools in newer ones. Support from Summerlin's builders led to passage of part of that school bond and another in 1996 to help the school district keep up with the area's growth.

Southern Nevadans also focused on transportation. In 1990 voters approved Question 10, a "Fair Share Funding Program for the Master Transportation Plan." The county began a two-billion-dollar, fifty-three-mile beltway named for county commissioner Bruce Woodbury, a native southern Nevadan and the driving force behind it. Mass transit also reached a turning point, more than a decade after Reno modernized its bus system. In 1979 the area's 19 buses fell nearly 100 short of what consultants recommended. Question 10 enabled Clark County's Regional Transportation Commission to make improvements. Citizens Area Transit debuted in 1992 with 128 buses; that number nearly tripled in two decades, with almost fifty-five million riders a year, making it the nation's eighteenth-largest bus system.

Growth and a Growing Culture

Population expansion fostered a corresponding growth in Nevada's culture. While universities and libraries offered programs, local groups like Reno's Sierra Arts Foundation and Las Vegas's Allied Arts Council provided support—although Las Vegas's symphony closed due to lack of funds and the loss of musicians due to a strike and despite the renown of its conductor, Ukrainian-born pianist-composer Virko Baley. Founded in 1931, the Nevada Museum of Art in Reno, the state's only nationally accredited art museum, outgrew the fifteen-thousand-square-foot building it had occupied since 1988 and began raising money for the four-story, sixty-thousand-square-foot building that debuted in 2003. Reno also began its monthlong Artown arts festival in 1996. In the next two years, the Las Vegas Art Museum moved into a thirty-thousand-square-foot space and Las Vegas created a downtown arts district.

Nevada's artistic community tended to attract iconoclasts, perhaps because the state often paid so little attention to cultural institutions, perhaps as a reflection of its history. Poets like Gary Short and Shaun Griffin reflected Nevada influences, while Griffin edited anthologies and translated the poetry of Latina activist Emma Sepulveda. Dave Hickey, then a UNLV professor, received a MacArthur Genius Grant in 2001 after writing on everything from Andy Warhol to women wrestlers. After creating *Double Negative* by cutting ramps into Moapa Valley's Mormon Mesa, Michael Heizer obtained land in Lincoln County and worked on *City*, a multiacre complex of structures. Near Rhyolite the Goldwell Open Air Museum,

Wendover, at the border between Nevada and Utah, has long served travelers along Highway 50, in addition to being part of the film *Independence Day*. Air-conditioning used to be a major selling point. Courtesy of Special Collections, University of Nevada–Reno Library.

begun in 1984 with a sculpture, expanded in the 1990s under the leadership of Charles Morgan and Suzanne Hackett, with Belgian artists adding six pieces. In 1993, after living in other parts of Nevada for two decades, Wally Cuchine moved to Eureka to run the Opera House and Eureka Sentinel Museum and developed a collection of Great Basin artists and a roster of cultural programs, partly with support from Nevada Humanities. The facilities attracted tourists traveling the "Loneliest Road in America," sometimes just to see his museums.

Although Hollywood long paid attention to Nevada, movies began examining it more analytically. Superb films mythologized gangsters: Warren Beatty's *Bugsy* overstated Siegel's role in Las Vegas history, and Martin Scorsese's *Casino* overemphasized a love triangle's role in the Mob's collapse. Other films bowed to how ingrained Las Vegas had become in popular culture: Wayne Newton played a key role in *Vegas Vacation;* *Honeymoon in Vegas* inspired groups of Flying Elvis impersonators; an *Ocean's Eleven* remake starred a modern Rat Pack, including George Clooney and Brad Pitt; and *Honey, I Blew Up the Kid* built on neon's popularity. *Leaving Las Vegas* and *Showgirls* depicted the area's seamier side, and *Independence Day* used Wendover and the nearby desert to simulate other locales. *Pink Cadillac, Sister Act,* and *Kingpin* included Reno scenes, but—appropriately, given northern Nevada's economic approach—with less emphasis on gambling.

Growth and Controversy in Higher Education

The battles at UNLV over basketball came to a sad conclusion. In 1990 Jerry Tarkanian's "Runnin' Rebels" won the NCAA championship, routing Duke in the most lopsided men's final ever. In 1991, weeks after they lost their title defense, the *Las Vegas Review-Journal* ran a picture of Richard "the Fixer" Perry, once convicted of bribing players to fix college basketball games, in an arena seat from Tarkanian's allotment and photos of several team members at his home. The coach said he knew nothing about the photos or Perry's past. Soon, after meetings with UNLV officials, Tarkanian announced his resignation after the next season.

Many southern Nevadans blamed not Tarkanian or his players, but UNLV president Robert Maxson. His contributions to UNLV's growth, fundraising prowess, and faculty support failed to overcome the bad publicity surrounding the Tarkanian controversy. Allegations about fund-raising practices and contracts under Maxson further hurt his reputation. In 1994 he left UNLV to be president of Long Beach State (ironically, where Tarkanian had been before UNLV). Tarkanian went on to Fresno State, which the NCAA sanctioned, but the coach won another victory—not on the court, but in court. In an unprecedented move, the NCAA paid him $2.5 million to settle his lawsuit accusing the organization of creating evidence and harassing him. In 2013 the National Basketball Hall of Fame finally inducted him, long after honoring less accomplished coaches.

Nevada's accomplishments in higher education sometimes seemed lost amid the controversy. With Joe Crowley as president, UNR enjoyed growth and stability: a five-year campaign begun in 1990 raised nearly $125 million for various programs. In 1995 the arrival of Nevada's first woman university president, Carol Harter, reduced the uproar at UNLV. She diversified the administration, promoted new degrees, and tried to rebuild the athletic program, which wound up on probation again. She obtained seed money for the William S. Boyd School of Law, which, between donors (including its namesake) and founding dean Richard Morgan, quickly won accreditation and a growing reputation. In 2001, three years after the law school opened, UNLV added the new Lied Library and a dental school.

By then the rest of the higher education system changed markedly. Northern Nevada Community College—renamed Great Basin College as it added four-year degrees—expanded its physical plant and fund-raising; its student body grew to three thousand in Elko and fifteen other locations. Western Nevada College's population neared five thousand but suffered from budget cuts and operating in UNR's shadow as it spread to a half-dozen counties. Truckee Meadows grew faster, but administrative battles inspired its faculty to become the first in Nevada to endorse collective bargaining. Enrollment at the Community College of Southern Nevada, now CSN, almost doubled from the early 1980s to the mid-1990s. Richard Moore's arrival as president in 1994 led to better marketing, another doubling of enrollment, expansion, and controversy over his spending and relations with others in the system. In 1999 Nevada State College's debut added a state college to the system's community colleges, universities, and Desert Research Institute.

Yet problems remained. Nevada State survived and grew, but regents and Henderson leaders pushed through its creation with money earmarked to study the need for it; Basic Magnesium's LandWell Corporation donated four hundred acres of land that proved too contaminated to be used; and with other institutions fighting for funding, adding another to the mix caused divisions. By 1995 only Nevada and four other states still had an elected board governing higher education, and regents often created political storms. By the late 1990s, UNR received $3,000 per student more than UNLV, and the state funded CSN students at a lower rate than any other school in the system, despite redistricting and population growth favoring the South. UNR officials and their northern Nevada supporters cited the school's older buildings and land-grant status as requiring the greater moneys.

African Americans

Hard-fought civil rights victories had yet to produce the investment and jobs that Nevada's African Americans wanted. Civil rights leader Bob Bailey helped as director of the US Commerce Department's Minority Business Development Agency. But in 1990 the Las Vegas Alliance for Fair Banking reported four local home mortgage lenders made only fifty-nine out of more than ten thousand of their loans in West Las Vegas, with African Americans turned down twice as often as whites. In 1994 protests that the new West Las Vegas library would lack the facilities of other local libraries prompted the addition of a theater. Until 1998 the area had no middle school, despite more school-age children per capita than any other part of Clark County. After local activist Marzette Lewis's Westside Action Alliance Korp-Uplifting People (WAAK UP) complained to the US Justice Department, the school district turned the area's sixth grade centers, created to foster integration in the early 1970s, into elementary and magnet schools and built a middle school.

But other action followed violence with a national connection. On April 29, 1992, after a jury acquitted four white Los Angeles police officers who had beaten an African American, Rodney King, violence began in West Las Vegas, where relations with the police had long been spiky. The police cordoned off large parts of the area, especially after learning that rioters had designs on moving toward downtown. Miller sent in the National Guard but, hoping to avoid confrontations, provided ammunition only to officers. After $6 million in damage and sixty-five arrests (compared with $800 million in damage and fifty-two deaths in Southern California), business and government funded a new community center, supermarket, and theater in West Las Vegas. Nevada's other large African American community in Reno avoided violence: the white police chief and an African American woman led six hundred residents in a parade and multicultural events.

West Las Vegas also benefited and suffered from increased political power. In 1992 African Americans organized a boycott that prompted the Clark County School District to end busing to sixth grade centers in favor of neighborhood schools. In the wake of organizing by the NAACP in the 1950s and 1960s and then by Ruby Duncan and welfare mothers in the 1970s, African Americans served on local city councils and the Clark County Commission. Perhaps the most powerful, Las Vegas city councilman Frank Hawkins, a former NFL star, grew up in West Las Vegas and graduated from Western High School and UNR. Hawkins wielded considerable influence, including helping to ease the appointment of another African American councilman. But his political career derailed over ethics issues. He lost his reelection bid in 1995 and later became president of the local NAACP.

Other African American politicians enjoyed success. In 1995 State Senators Bernice Mathews of Reno and Maurice Washington of Sparks, and Assemblyman Thomas Batten of Reno became the first African American lawmakers outside Clark County, the latter two as Republicans. Winning a term on the Las Vegas City Council representing the new Summerlin area, Lynette Boggs McDonald became the first African American in southern Nevada elected to an office outside of a traditionally minority area, except in a judicial election.

The Hispanic Wave

By 1990 Latinos surpassed African Americans as Nevada's largest minority. The state ranked eighth nationally in the Hispanic percentage of its population, with nearly 125,000, up 131 percent from 1980, due to the boom, California's economic woes, and such Latin American issues as Guatemala's civil war and Mexico's economic problems. Yet unemployment spiked higher for Hispanics than for whites, and the percentage of minority workers in government ran behind the population. Miller ordered the state to increase minority hiring in 1990, but cuts the next year and a downturn negated the effects. Hispanics objected to their absence from city and county elective bodies; none served on the city council in Las Vegas until 2011, in Reno until 2012, or in North Las Vegas until 2013.

Education reflected the change. Latino students constituted one-third of Clark County's kindergarten and first grade classes, and the number of students went from 13 percent in 1991 to 23 percent in 1997. From 1982 to 1994, Hispanic school enrollment increased nearly 300 percent, but more than 30 percent in Clark County dropped out before graduating. Another factor may have been that many Hispanics settled in historically lower-income, underserved areas, but those able to do so followed a national trend by relocating to newer suburbs—which fostered resentment among some Hispanics, much as similar developments sometimes did in the African American community.

With population growth came more prominence in politics and business. Miller named longtime judge John Mendoza to chair the Public Service Commission and Hispanic in Politics leader Fernando Romero to head the Equal Employment Opportunity office. Longtime county commissioner Manny Cortez moved over to run the Las Vegas Convention and Visitors Authority. Bob Coffin served in the legislature for nearly three decades. Assemblymen Dario Herrera and Brian Sandoval gave hope for Hispanics: Herrera won election to the Clark County Commission in 1998, while Sandoval resigned his Washoe County seat to join the Gaming Commission and, in 1999, at age thirty-five, became its youngest chair. Cuban émigré Antonio "Tony" Alamo came to Circus Circus with the new management in 1974 and left to oversee the MGM's construction in 1993 before returning to Circus Circus Enterprises as an executive and a major stockholder. Eddie Escobedo rose from Sahara Hotel bartender to developer and publisher.

Religion and Ethnicity

Hispanic growth affected Nevada society in other ways. The Catholic Church grew more rapidly in Nevada than in most states, prompting the Vatican to divide it into two dioceses in 1995 with Daniel Walsh as bishop of Las Vegas, succeeded by Joseph Pepe, and Phillip Straling as bishop of Reno, followed by Randolph Calvo. The southern diocese, which extended into Lincoln, Esmeralda, Nye, and White Pine Counties, included ninety priests, twenty-nine parishes, and a Catholic population of more than 640,000, reflecting the Hispanic influx, while the Diocese of Reno, covering about two-thirds of the state, reported fifty-one priests in 2013.

By 2000 Mormons numbered about 80,000 in southern Nevada, second only to the Catholic Church as the area's largest religious group, and nearly 25,000 in the Reno area. The church dedicated a temple in Las Vegas in 1989 and in Reno in 2000, underscoring its statewide growth. Mormons wielded ample power through such members as Senator Harry Reid, Clark County commissioner Bruce Woodbury, Henderson mayor Jim Gibson, Nevada Assembly leader Richard Perkins, and McCarran International Airport director Bob Broadbent and his successor, Randy Walker. Mormons had majorities on the Henderson and North Las Vegas councils, and later the county commission, and often dominated the school board. By 2014 the church reported more than 180,000 members in Nevada's thirty-seven stakes.

Other religious groups felt the effects of population growth. Religion united many otherwise disparate communities, such as Muslims from Europe, the Middle East, and Asia; Buddhists from Asia and the Indian subcontinent; and Hispanics from different Latin American states, for example. In 1998 Central Christian Church, founded in 1962, moved to a twenty-three-million-dollar Henderson complex seating thirty-two

The Chinatown Mall, built by developers in a neighborhood where many Asian residents settled, represented Las Vegas's take on ethnic neighborhoods turned tourist attractions in cities like New York and San Francisco. Courtesy of Greenspun Media Group.

hundred. The number of southern Nevada synagogues grew from two in 1975 to at least fifteen by 2000, Lake Tahoe's Jewish population grew enough to support two congregations, and Reno's Temple Sinai expanded rapidly during a quarter of a century under Myra Soifer, one of the first female rabbis in Reform Judaism.

In the 1990s, while southern Nevada's populace grew 83.5 percent, the Asian and Hispanic populations each grew by 260 percent. In the late 1990s, the Asian and Pacific Islander population reflected general trends and the importance of gaming. Las Vegas and Reno (by the early 2000s the first and eighth most popular US destinations for Asian travelers) included marketing, programs, and events that also involved residents. In 1995 Las Vegas welcomed a Chinatown west of the Strip—a spin on the history of ethnic neighborhoods that featured a plaza with dining and shopping. Despite its name, it reflected the presence of the broader Asian population, especially Filipinos, the largest ethnic group from Asia.

The Rise of Labor

With membership down significantly since the 1950s, unions saw Las Vegas as ripe for organizing in the 1990s. AFL-CIO leader John Sweeney, calling it America's "fastest growing union city," predicted that "as surely as New York set the standards for the past 100 years, Las Vegas will be setting them for the next 100 years." The musician union's defeat in 1989 contradicted that, but public employee unions numbered about eight thousand members and, like similar groups nationally, faced accusations of creating budget issues through funding pensions and health care. Electrical workers and the Teamsters wielded influence through sheer numbers, but organized labor preferred to point to food workers and the Culinary. Although the union grew in Reno, it enjoyed less success there, perhaps due to the less tourist-driven economy. With the MGM Grand hiring seventy-five hundred and the Bellagio about eight thousand, competition demanded trained employees. The Culinary helped resorts manage their workers, including large numbers of Hispanics who learned their jobs and improved their English through union training programs.

New Culinary leaders played a key role. John Wilhelm became the parent union's head and worked with federal officials to purge it of Mob ties. In Las Vegas Jim Arnold became secretary-treasurer in 1987, joined in 1990 by president Hattie Canty, an African American who became a housekeeper

The Culinary Union's seven-year strike against the Frontier
Hotel on the Las Vegas Strip became America's longest such
labor action and ended with the owners selling the hotel. Courtesy of the *Las Vegas Sun* Archives.

when her husband's death left her to raise ten children. Arnold requested
aid in expanding the local, and organizers D. Taylor and Glen Arnodo
arrived to help build the union's political muscle. They succeeded partly
through cooperation and picking their battles, not concentrating on organizing neighborhood casinos and doing little to encourage—indeed, discouraging—increases in gaming taxes.

The Culinary first demonstrated its power under its new leaders in 1990. Weeks after patriarch Benny Binion's death, Horseshoe management fired union organizers, prompting a lengthy strike that cost the hotel-casino an estimated $16 million in business before the two sides settled. Soon, the Culinary negotiated a pact with the Boyd Group, which had avoided unionization at its Las Vegas properties for more than a decade. The MGM Grand opened without unions in 1993, but the Culinary fought a prolonged battle and finally won a contract late in 1994.

The Culinary showed its power in other ways. After the Elardi family, who had been successful in downtown Las Vegas and Laughlin, bought the Frontier, they opposed organizing at the Strip resort. More than five hundred employees walked out, and the Culinary maintained a picket line outside the hotel for nearly seven years; William Bennett of Circus Circus even served picketers meals and donated $1 million to help them, while Governor Bob Miller tried numerous times to settle the dispute before the Elardis, their revenues down 40 percent, finally sold to hotelman Phil Ruffin in 1997 after the longest strike in American history.

The Culinary also lost battles and faced criticism. At the Strip's Venetian, Adelson refused to negotiate, barred picketers from the property, and accused the union of anti-Semitism when someone wrote obscenities in his cabana. In return for avoiding difficult and drawn-out elections, the union used a "card-check" system, becoming the agent for the employees once 51 percent of them signed cards asking to be represented. The hotels extracted a guarantee that they could reclassify and dismiss employees as needed. Several companies stipulated against "sympathy strikes," enabling them to shut out other unions.

Mining: Expansion and the Environment

The end of the century brought renewed success to mining. Nevada ranked third in gold production behind South Africa and Australia, generating $3.1 billion in mining revenue in 1998. In 1994 Nevada produced three-fifths of the nation's gold and one-fifth of its silver. Round Mountain enjoyed a small boom, as it generated as much as $75 million in gold in 1990. The Carlin Trend continued to produce millions for Nevada and the owners of its mines and encouraged further development: in 2000, having expanded beyond Carlin into the Battle Mountain area, Newmont Gold bought the

Battle Mountain Gold Company and expanded its exploration to several continents.

But the mining industry faced what it saw as obstacles and its critics considered improvement. In 1992 Senator Dale Bumpers, an Arkansas Democrat, tried to reform the Mining Law of 1872. At the time, mining companies paid only $5 for each acre of land they patented and no royalties. Bumpers wanted the federal government to invest the $200 million his reforms would raise on cleaning up old mines and creating tougher standards. The House passed the measure, but a Senate filibuster, led by Reid and others from western mining states, killed it.

Environmental issues and concerns also continued to affect mining. In the late 1990s, the EPA found four northern Nevada gold operations releasing too much mercury into the air. The companies agreed to reductions, but environmentalists questioned whether they would go far enough. Another issue involved the Humboldt River basin's underground water and the impact of open-pit mining on it. Mining companies could profitably dig for disseminated gold, despite its tiny size, but that meant deeper pits and possibly interfering with the aquifer. The federal and state governments and Barrick Goldstrike agreed to study the effects.

Pyramid Lake's Waters

After decades of effort, politicians, businesspeople, and the Pyramid Lake Paiutes finally agreed on dividing northern Nevada waters. In 1990 Congress approved the Truckee-Carson–Pyramid Lake Water Rights Settlement Act. After Paul Laxalt's effort fell short, the Pyramid Lake tribe and Sierra Pacific Power persuaded his successor, Reid, to try it. He sought to involve all parties in the talks, although the Fallon Western Shoshone stayed out amid their own negotiations with federal officials and Truckee-Carson Irrigation District representatives opposed the agreement. Once everyone came to terms, Reid worked with the interior secretary to ensure support from federal agencies, while Barbara Vucanovich protected against opposition in the House. They faced political issues: amid TCID-led efforts to kill the bill, a Senate committee added measures to demand more efficiency from the agency and provide water to additional users who might then divert some of it from the Fallon-area farmers tied to the TCID.

The legislation appeared dead until Reid attached the Pyramid Lake settlement to another, less controversial, bill that determined water allotment to the Fallon Paiutes. It passed, ensuring the Fallon tribe a settlement fund of forty-three million dollars to be used for economic development and improvements to their reservation's irrigation system. The Pyramid Lake Paiutes received sixty-five million dollars for economic improvements and to help protect endangered fish. Disputes and litigation would continue, but the act effectively settled the distribution of the region's water.

Reid benefited and suffered for his efforts. Those near Fallon felt he added the amendment to punish them for opposing a settlement and, among other things, hanged him in effigy. They joined other rural Nevadans who objected to his efforts on behalf of Great Basin National Park, which inspired the *Elko Daily Free Press* to nickname him "Sierra Harry," as in Sierra Club environmentalists. But Vucanovich's support for the bill helped ease some of the criticism, and the final agreement restored the Lahontan Valley's wetlands and fisheries for both of the fish on the endangered species list, the cui-ui and the Lahontan cutthroat trout.

The Judiciary: Growth and Controversy

Already known for personal conflicts, the Nevada Supreme Court grew more controversial. In 1992 the Judicial Discipline Commission investigated Washoe County district judge Jerry Whitehead on charges of inappropriate talks with attorneys involved in cases he heard and improper behavior toward lawyers who wanted other judges to hear their cases. Two justices criticized the commission and its defenders and supported intervening in the probe; their colleagues responded, making the court look unjudicial at best. Eventually, Whitehead resigned as part of an agreement with federal officials who dropped any plans to prosecute him.

Other controversies besides Whitehead inspired discussions of the wisdom of electing judges. In 1992, in one of several nasty elections, Clark County district judge Miriam Shearing defeated her colleague Charles Thompson and became the first woman on the Nevada Supreme Court, but the Judicial Discipline Commission rebuked them for the "tone and conduct" of their campaign, which fell largely along partisan lines. Two years later Justice Bob Rose won reelection against Myron Leavitt in a rematch of a previous race between former Democratic lieutenant governors; on both occasions they attacked each other vociferously.

But changes loomed for the judiciary. The legislature increased the number of justices to seven, with two new members elected in 1998 (including Leavitt), to handle the increasing workload caused by population growth. Justices began sitting in three-member panels in Carson City and Las Vegas, with the chief justice administering the court and hearing cases only as a substitute. Lawmakers added judges, especially in Clark County, until by 2013 thirty-two judges heard civil and criminal cases, with another twenty in family court, while Washoe County's bench included nine civil and criminal judges and six for family matters.

Nuclear Issues

The Soviet Union's collapse in 1991 changed the nation's defense policies and needs. With the Cold War ending, the Defense Department dumped obsolete weapons in the Great Basin. More important, in 1992 Congress passed and President George H. W. Bush signed the Nuclear Test Moratorium Act. President Bill Clinton continued it, effectively changing the test site's role after about a thousand aboveground and underground nuclear tests. It continued as a research facility, and thus brought researchers and contractors to the region, aiding its economy.

Nevadans objected to one potential use for the test site: the proposed waste repository. In 1991 the American Nuclear Energy Council launched a three-year, $8.7 million effort to sell Nevadans on the dump, but most Nevadans resented the effort and the legislature buried a bill to consider at least finding out what the Department of Energy would offer to accept the repository. In 1992 an earthquake measuring 5.6 on the Richter scale twelve miles from Yucca Mountain caused $1 million in damage to DOE structures and affected groundwater. The National Academy of Sciences and the federal General Accounting Office criticized DOE research and spending, and utilities sued the federal government for failing to meet contractual obligations to start accepting waste. In April 2000 Reid and Bryan used their clout with the White House to persuade Clinton to veto a bill to speed the process of sending waste to Yucca Mountain. During the 2000 presidential campaign, under political pressure, Nevada Republicans supporting candidate George W. Bush produced a statement from him, promising to let "sound science" decide the dump's location.

The Yucca Mountain fight became inseparable from other issues. As a senator, Bryan worked to raise Corporate Average Fuel Economy (CAFE) rules on cars to improve gas mileage and ultimately help automakers financially. His efforts irked Michigan's delegation, and powerful senior members of Congress from that state blocked him. Senator Bennett Johnston, who introduced the "Screw Nevada" bill and represented oil-rich Louisiana, suggested that he would accommodate Nevada on nuclear waste if Bryan would back off on CAFE standards, which neither mattered nor proved true. Meanwhile, Reid began rising in his party's leadership as head of the Democratic policy committee and then as assistant leader. In those positions he negated some of the support for the waste dump.

Fighting the Feds

The Sagebrush Rebellion faded, but the issues and attitudes that gave rise to it remained. The number of cattle in Nevada fell to a fifty-year low in 1996, down about 30 percent from the peak in 1982, and the million sheep roaming Nevada in the 1930s dwindled to about fifty thousand. Ranchers, especially in Nye County, the nation's third-largest county and 90 percent federally owned, complained loudly. Nye County commissioner Dick Carver of the Great Smoky Valley advocated county supremacy, an idea rooted in the Articles of Confederation, which ceased to operate when the US Constitution took effect in 1788. In 1994, angry that the US Forest Service closed an access road in Toiyabe National Forest's Jefferson Canyon, Carver bulldozed the road as neighbors cheered. His Nevada Plan for Public Land contended the state controlled land the federal government claimed—much as state legislators did in the late 1970s. He took his argument to court, where US district judge Lloyd George ruled against him.

Ranchers found other causes for complaint. They resented the growing herds of federally protected wild horses, but the Bureau of Land Management and Forest Service countered that such efforts guarded against the ill effects of overgrazing and drought. Another Nye County rancher, Wayne Hage, sued the United States for twenty-eight million dollars over ownership of federal lands after the Forest Service confiscated some of his cattle and billed him for the cost of the auction. Like miners, Hage argued that ranchers could claim authority over grazing and water through prior range rights before the government took surrounding land for a national forest. His family continued Hage's fight after his death, but to no avail.

Relations between the Forest Service and Elko County proved far worse. When a Jarbidge River flood washed out South Canyon Road in 1995, the Forest Service planned to rebuild it. After an environmental group challenged its assessment of the effect on the river's trout, the Forest Service proposed a walking trail, angering many around Elko who disliked federal control and conservationists; as the issue grew more political, the Forest Service's supervisor resigned. A federal report responding to her accusations found Forest Service and BLM employees felt threatened by local citizens. Federal and county officials reached a settlement that would have led to a new road, with the federal government paying for it and the county in charge of it, but other local leaders opposed even that. On July 4, 2000, the three-hundred-member Shovel Brigade moved a boulder blocking the road. They followed through on a proposal by a supporter, Assemblyman John Carpenter, to build a thirty-foot statue of a shovel on the county courthouse lawn.

Other controversies showed Nevada's troubled relations with the federal government. When Forest Service officials ordered the removal of a pipe a local rancher installed to carry water from the Humboldt-Toiyabe National Forest, five hundred people fenced in the spring and claim it as state land. Before the rancher obtained a permit, Elko County spent almost five hundred thousand dollars defending him in court. After the 1995 bombing of a Forest Service building in Carson City and the discovery of a pipe bomb at a campground near Elko, both sides sought to restore calm. Veteran legislator and Sagebrush Rebellion founder Dean Rhoads called the Jarbidge brigade "more a right-wing group. . . . They're not willing to cooperate and compromise." In 1997 new state BLM director Bob Abbey improved communication between the federal agency and those it regulated, easing tensions.

Environmental Issues

Nevada also found ways to profit from federal largesse. In 1998 Bryan and Representative John Ensign introduced the Southern Nevada Public Lands Management Act. When the BLM auctioned land in the Las Vegas Valley, the resulting funds would stay in Nevada, with most of it buying endangered lands and improving public land, with 15 percent for education and the Southern Nevada Water Authority. The auctions aided local development, especially the land sale that led to the Aliante master-planned community. By 2014 the auctions had netted more than three billion dollars.

Other environmental issues caused tensions and attracted attention. The Forest Service authorized and underwrote the Sierra Nevada Ecosystem

Project to study forests and environmental effects on them. In 1996 the SNEP report called for attention to climate change and population growth, better fire suppression and air pollution policies, and restoration of damaged areas. But between changing political administrations and partisanship, the expenditures to promote these policies and the commitment to various aspects of them varied.

Yet Republicans and Democrats could agree—or, as one, disagree—on some actions. In 1990 President George Bush signed a bill creating the 83,100-acre Red Rock Canyon National Conservation Area, protecting its sandstone mountains. In 1994 legislation doubled the conservation area's size, and a 1998 bill added more until it topped 195,000 acres. Bill Clinton signed a 1993 bill creating the 316,000-acre Spring Mountain National Recreation Area, part of America's largest national forest, the Humboldt-Toiyabe, and including Mount Charleston. The next year the California Desert Protection Act turned Joshua Tree and Death Valley Monuments into national parks and created the 1.6 million–acre Mojave National Preserve, although many residents opposed it and blamed environmentalists for it.

Some environmental issues proved harder to solve. In 1999 lightning caused at least one hundred wildfires in northern Nevada, costing thirty-eight million dollars to put out and burning about 1.6 million acres, more than in all range fires in the past forty years. In the previous seasons, cheatgrass, which develops compactly and spreads fires easily, grew rapidly. Just as the 1964 fires that burned 300,000 acres in Elko County led to the first federal plan to restore areas burned in wildfires, the new blazes renewed awareness of their destruction. By ordering no grazing in a burned area for two years, the BLM let cheatgrass expand, making wildfires likelier. Congress increased funding for firefighting, dealing with the effect but not the cause.

Growth also heightened environmental concerns. Southern Nevada grew faster than services kept up: its 1.4 acres of parkland per thousand residents fell well below the national recommended 10-acre minimum. Between 1991 and 1995, Las Vegas passed New York City as the American city with the fifth dirtiest air, and the city ranked eighth out of 238 metropolitan areas for deaths related to air pollution. In 1994 a protozoan hastened or caused the deaths of thirty-seven people, mostly with AIDS, from Lake Mead tap water. Although Howard Hughes protested the dumping of sewage into the lake in the late 1960s, not until the 1990s did southern

Nevadans take serious action to stop it. A film of algae had appeared on the lake, and in 1996 the US Geological Survey reported male Lake Mead carp had begun to turn into females. The Environmental Protection Agency followed with the Lake Mead Water Quality Forum to try to rectify the problem.

Pat Mulroy and Water Policy

During earlier booms Las Vegas simply used up and then sought more water, but conservation became a goal and necessity in the 1990s. Las Vegans averaged more than 350 gallons of water per person daily, almost as much as Los Angeles and Tucson combined, and Nevada used more water per capita than any other western state. The problem lay less with the hotels than with local residents watering lawns and washing cars: as late as 2000, residents accounted for two-thirds of southern Nevada's water use, with the Strip taking less than 10 percent.

No one since the Las Vegas Land and Water Company, the railroad subsidiary that ran early Las Vegas, exerted more influence on local water policy than Pat Mulroy. After several years in county jobs, she joined the Las Vegas Valley Water District in 1985 and helped set up a regional agency, the Southern Nevada Water Authority, which she ran from 1991 until retiring in 2014. The SNWA began offering rebates to customers who replaced lawns with xeriscape. Although rates stayed low, the tiered system rewarded those who used the least. She pushed Strip resorts to use "graywater," or recycled wastewater, for such popular attractions as the Mirage's volcanoes, the Bellagio's fountains, and the Venetian's canals.

Mulroy and other leaders encouraged conservation, but set out to obtain more water than the 300,000 acre-feet the Colorado River Compact allotted. In 1989 the water district claimed 805,000 acre-feet of water in twenty-six valleys up to 250 miles away. In the 1990s the state authorized the Colorado River Commission to make agreements on water transfers and expanded the CRC to four members named by the governor and three by the SNWA. The CRC ceded control of water issues to the SNWA while concentrating on the lower Colorado's wildlife. When the SNWA asked lawmakers to approve a quarter-cent sales-tax hike for a "second straw" from Lake Mead into the valley, and the gaming industry warned that not doing so could eliminate five to six billion dollars in new casino projects, state officials punted to Clark County commissioners. They put it on the ballot rather than take a stand on taxes, and voters overwhelmingly approved it. The state began using its entire Colorado River allotment, banking any extra underground, and, thanks to a policy approved by Secretary of the Interior Bruce Babbitt (1993–2001), storing water elsewhere. Under an agreement that Babbitt signed, California received surplus water but agreed to conservation, and southern Nevada could store up to 1.2 million acre-feet in Arizona and 500,000 acre-feet in Nevada.

Antigovernment but Proincumbent?

Although Nevada joined the majority in casting electoral votes for Clinton in 1992, its tendency to distrust government still flourished. Texas billionaire Ross Perot's third-party race and antigovernment rhetoric resonated with Nevadans who had joined the "Reagan Revolution." Perot won 26 percent in the state, one of his best showings nationally, while Clinton carried 37 percent and Bush 35. Perot supporter Charles Woods notched more than one-third of the vote challenging Reid in the Democratic Senate primary. But Reid easily won the general election against Elko rancher Demar Dahl, suggesting that with urban growth, rural candidates would have little chance statewide.

The 1994 elections marked a significant change, as Republicans took over the House of Representatives for the first time in forty years. In southern Nevada's district, veterinarian John Ensign, the son of a gaming executive, beat four-term Democratic representative Jim Bilbray by about 1,500 votes out of 150,000 cast. With Republicans controlling the House, Vucanovich became conference secretary and the first Nevadan to hold a leadership post in the House, where the state's small delegation limited its influence. Ensign's victory over Bilbray and so many changes in membership propelled him onto the Ways and Means Committee, where new members rarely served due to its importance to tax issues.

That year and in 1996, Nevadans approved two constitutional amendments that reflected the Republican view of government as more of a problem than a solution. One backed by GOP consultant Sig Rogich set term limits of twelve years in each legislative chamber, as of the next election; anyone elected in 1998 or after faced restrictions. Another amendment backed by Jim Gibbons, a Republican running for governor in 1994, required a two-thirds vote of the legislature in favor of any tax hike. Both changes would have significant effects later.

Yet Nevadans demonstrated independence or inconsistency by reelecting two longtime Democrats. In 1994, despite GOP strength and his ballot initiative, Gibbons lost his bid for governor to Miller. After a quarter century as an assemblyman, state senator, attorney general, governor, and now senator, Richard Bryan won reelection over lobbyist Hal Furman. With the GOP running against government, Bryan's campaign painted Furman as part of the problem while emphasizing the incumbent's desire to straighten out Washington.

The 1998 Election: Transition and Continuity

After winning in 1994 and 1996, Ensign challenged Reid's quest for his third Senate term in 1998. Ensign benefited from a better television presence—an increasingly crucial part of campaigns everywhere. More than half of its voters moving to Nevada or coming of age since Reid's last election in 1992 reduced the benefits of incumbency, much as growth hurt McCarran's prospects in southern Nevada in the 1950s and Cannon's around the state in 1982. Helping Reid, women constituted the rest of the Democratic ticket for major offices, aiding turnout in an off-year election. Reid won Clark and Mineral Counties and came close to Ensign in Washoe for a 401-vote victory. Amid reports of irregularities in Washoe, Ensign challenged the results, but the recount added slightly to Reid's lead, and he won by 428 votes. Having already held leadership positions, Reid became his party's whip, making him the Senate's second-ranking Democrat.

The governor's race proved less contested than the Senate race, but unusual for what political analyst Jon Ralston called "the anointed one." Raised in central California, Kenny Guinn came to Las Vegas in 1964, at age twenty-eight, to work for the school district and rose to superintendent by 1969. A decade later he went on to a business career with Nevada Savings and Loan and Southwest Gas, and a year as UNLV's interim president. Long courted by fellow Republicans for higher office, and friendly with many Democrats, he declared for governor early and scared away most competitors with prodigious fund-raising.

In the general election, women demonstrated their growing political presence. Las Vegas mayor Jan Jones easily won the Democratic primary but lost to Guinn. Nevadans elected their second woman lieutenant governor—Republican Lorraine Hunt, a Clark County commissioner and longtime entertainer, over the first African American to seek that office in the general election, businesswoman and former government official Rose McKinney-James. Democrat Frankie Sue Del Papa won a third term as attorney general, and the number of women on the ballot aided Reid's narrow win.

Politics and Gaming

As with Guinn's election, the other prominent woman on the ballot reflected the power of gaming. Democrat Shelley Berkley, a regent and former assemblywoman, won the Clark County house seat that Ensign vacated against Don Chairez, a former judge who switched to the GOP. Serving seven terms, Berkley stressed constituent service and her interests in foreign policy and veterans' affairs. In her next elections, she overcame Republican state senator Jon Porter and Las Vegas councilwoman Lynette Boggs McDonald. Her campaigns reflected a different political activism that accompanied the rise of corporations. Both Steve Wynn and Sheldon Adelson backed her opponents: Wynn supported UNLV president Robert Maxson, whose policies Berkley had questioned as a regent; Adelson fired her as a vice president of his hotel and criticized her as prounion, and Berkley charged that he wanted her to switch to the GOP.

Yet Wynn and Adelson usually approached politics differently. Wynn backed some candidates more than others for personal reasons—most notably pro-Maxson regents—but pioneered more scientific political involvement for gaming through in-house polling and calling to help candidates. Much like earlier owners, he tried to remain friendly with both sides. In the mid-1990s, he associated with Clinton, but gaming industry support for his 1996 opponent, Senator Robert Dole of Kansas, led critics to call him "Vegas Bob." Wynn donated to both sides, with $7 million from Las Vegas going to races around the country that year.

By contrast, Adelson supported Republicans even in losing causes. In 1998 he also funded three GOP candidates for the county commission, although they ran in Democratic districts and lost handily. He helped underwrite a recall effort against Clark County commissioner Yvonne Atkinson-Gates, who faced corruption allegations. Adelson backed the Paycheck Protection Initiative, designed to ban using union dues on political campaigns without written approval from the members. The effort failed, with a predictable split mostly along party lines.

Guinn as Governor: Continuity and Change

Like Miller, Guinn dealt with a legislature that varied between more liberal and conservative views. Guinn signed a bill by David Parks, Nevada's first openly gay state legislator, to bar workplace discrimination against gay Nevadans. Led by Raggio, lawmakers backed a constitutional amendment limiting their sessions to 120 days, and voters overwhelmingly agreed—leading to more special sessions so the legislature could complete its work. Guinn faced challenges on taxes: in 1999 State Senator Joe Neal proposed raising gaming taxes by 2 percent to 8.25 percent to raise more than $110 million. MGM chair Terrence Lanni countered that most casinos made only a 5 percent profit and thus could barely afford higher taxes, if at all. Neal tried to put an initiative on the ballot to amend the Nevada Constitution to raise the gaming tax to 10 percent, while teachers sought an initiative to tax the net profits of businesses. Guinn asked teachers and other voters to wait for legislators to act, but both measures fell short of the needed signatures for the ballot, with the teachers' efforts struck down by the state supreme court.

Guinn also introduced one of Nevada's most innovative educational programs. When Nevada received money from the federal settlement with tobacco companies over their products' impact on health, the state spent some of it on services for older citizens, but with the nation's lowest high school–to–college rate and well under half of students completing bachelor's degrees in six years, Guinn proposed putting 40 percent of it toward what he called "Millennium Scholarships." All Nevada high school graduates with a B average would receive $1,000 a year toward their college tuition. The idea bred concerns about grade inflation, whether colleges could keep up with enrollment hikes and the program would recognize financial need, the growing number of recipients who still required remedial classes, and the possibility that students enrolled at magnet schools and more affluent schools would benefit disproportionately. But the Millennium Scholarships proved successful, helping more students go to college and enhancing enrollments.

Yet while the 1990s boom revitalized Nevada's economy, it left problems in its wake. The employee turnover rate at some casino properties reportedly neared 50 percent a year. Pawn shops remained open twenty-four hours a day to help gamblers who had lost their savings (the state began dealing with gambling addiction, but slowly). Schools remained over-crowded in urban areas, with Clark County unable to keep up with growth and transience: from 1990 to 2010, data from address changes on income tax returns showed that for every 2 people who moved to Clark County, 1.3 people left. An estimated one hundred street gangs numbering up to 4,000 members formed, many of them criminals from Southern California, contributing to rising crime rates. And on September 11, 2001, Nevadans and the world learned a sad lesson about the fragility of their economy, and of life.

SUGGESTED READINGS

Burbank, Jeff. *License to Steal: Nevada's Gaming Control System in the Megaresort Era.* Reno: University of Nevada Press, 2006.

Cladianos, Pete, Jr. *My Father's Son: A Gaming Memoir.* Reno: University of Nevada Oral History Program, 2002.

Cooper, Marc. *The Last Honest Place in America: Paradise and Perdition in the New Las Vegas.* New York: Nation Books, 2004.

Dufurrena, Linda, and Carolyn Dufurrena. *Fifty Miles from Home: Riding the Long Circle on a Nevada Family Ranch.* Reno: University of Nevada Press, 2002.

Dufurrena, Carolyn, Linda Hussa, and Sophie Sheppard. *Sharing Fencelines: Three Friends Write from Nevada's Sagebrush Corner.* Salt Lake City: University of Utah Press, 2002.

Earley, Pete. *Super Casino: Inside the "New" Las Vegas.* New York: Bantam Books, 2001.

Fischbacher, Siegfried, and Roy Horn. *Mastering the Impossible.* New York: Morrow, 1992.

Fox, William L. *In the Desert of Desire: Las Vegas and the Culture of Spectacle.* Reno: University of Nevada Press, 2005.

Fox, William L., and Jeff Kelley. *Mapping the Empty: Eight Artists and Nevada.* Reno: University of Nevada Press, 1999.

Gilmore, Lee, and Mark Van Proyen, eds. *AfterBurn: Reflections on Burning Man.* Albuquerque: University of New Mexico Press, 2005.

Gottdiener, Mark, Claudia C. Collins, and David R. Dickens. *Las Vegas: The Social Production of an All-American City.* Malden, MA: Wiley-Blackwell, 2000.

Hadley, C. J., ed. *Grit, Guts, and Glory: Portrait of the West, the Lives, Work, and Pleasures of Cowboys and Sheepherders.* Carson City, NV: Purple Coyote, 2004.

Herzik, Eric, Dennis Soden, and Royse Smith, eds. *Nevada in the New Millennium.* Dubuque, IA: Kendall-Hunt, 2001.

Hess, Alan. *Viva Las Vegas: After Hours Architecture.* San Francisco: Chronicle Books, 1993.

Lane, Mills, and Jedwin Smith. *Let's Get It On: Tough Talk from Boxing's Top Ref and Nevada's Most Outspoken Judge.* New York: Crown, 1998.

Laxalt, Robert. *Child of the Holy Ghost.* Reno: University of Nevada Press, 1992.

——. *Dust Devils*. Reno: University of Nevada Press, 1997.

——. *The Land of My Fathers: A Son's Return to the Basque Country*. Reno: University of Nevada Press, 2000.

——. *A Lean Year, and Other Stories*. Reno: University of Nevada Press, 1994.

——. *Travels with My Royal: A Memoir of the Writing Life*. Reno: University of Nevada Press, 2001.

Lerude, Warren. *Robert Laxalt: The Story of a Storyteller*. Reno: University of Nevada, Reno, Center for Basque Studies, 2013.

Logsdon, Richard, Todd Moffett, and Tina D. Eliopulos, eds. *In the Shadow of the Strip: Las Vegas Stories*. Reno: University of Nevada Press, 2003.

Martin, Gregory. *Mountain City*. New York: North Point Press, 2000.

Miller, Bob. *Son of a Gambling Man: My Journey from a Casino Family to the Governor's Mansion*. New York: Thomas Dunne Books, 2013.

Millman, Chad. *The Odds: One Season, Three Gamblers, and the Death of Their Las Vegas*. New York: PublicAffairs, 2001.

O'Brien, Timothy L. *Bad Bet: The Inside Story of the Glamour, Glitz, and Danger of America's Gambling Industry*. New York: Times Business, 1998.

Ralston, Jon. *The Anointed One: An Inside Look at Nevada Politics*. Las Vegas: Huntington Press, 2000.

Rothman, Hal K., and Mike Davis, eds. *The Grit Beneath the Glitter: Tales from the Real Las Vegas*. Berkeley: University of California Press, 2002.

Smith, John L. *Bluegrass Days, Neon Nights: High Rolling with Happy Chandler's Wayward Son, Dan*. Las Vegas: Stephens Press, 2010.

——. *No Limit: The Rise and Fall of Bob Stupak and Las Vegas' Stratosphere Tower*. Las Vegas: Huntington Press, 1997.

——. *Running Scared: The Life and Treacherous Times of Las Vegas Casino King Steve Wynn*. New York: Barricade Books, 1995.

Thomson, David. *In Nevada: The Land, the People, God, and Chance*. New York: Alfred A. Knopf, 1999.

Tronnes, Mike, ed. *Literary Las Vegas: The Best Writing About America's Most Fabulous City*. New York: Henry Holt, 1995.

Vinegar, Aron, and Michael J. Golec, eds. *Relearning from Las Vegas*. Minneapolis: University of Minnesota Press, 2009.

Wilds, Leah J. *Water Politics in Northern Nevada: A Century of Struggle*. 2nd ed. Reno: University of Nevada Press, 2014.

Yaeger, Don. *Shark Attack: Jerry Tarkanian and His Battle with the NCAA and UNLV*. New York: HarperCollins, 2002.

16

Nevada in the Twenty-First Century

On September 11, 2001, two planes flew into New York City's World Trade Center, causing the twin towers to collapse. Another aircraft crashed into the Pentagon, and a fourth, headed for the Capitol, went down in Pennsylvania. The United States had begun a new era that included wars in Iraq and Afghanistan, new security measures, laws that reduced individual privacy, and terrorist "watch lists." For Nevada, whether it marked a long-term change remained to be seen.

Changes After September 11: Tourism and Nuclear Waste

The victims included a Las Vegas teacher and relatives and coworkers of several Nevadans; others died in the wars that followed, and Nevada's more than ten thousand Muslims reported more bigoted comments and difficulties traveling. Tourists and locals created a memorial by leaving T-shirts and notes at the Strip's New York–New York. With so many choosing not to travel in the attack's aftermath, revenue at the state's 342 casinos fell nearly 4 percent and Las Vegas casinos dismissed about fifteen thousand employees. Federal officials stopped traffic across Hoover Dam and restricted dam tours. The Reno Hilton closed six weeks after the attacks, and the Aladdin went bankrupt.

Other projects went forward, to Nevadans' pleasure and displeasure, as it turned out. George Maloof opened his $270 million Palms, hiring more than six hundred recently laid-off workers as part of its two-thousand-member staff; Green Valley Ranch followed, adding another two thousand jobs. Local, state, and federal authorities expanded training programs to protect Nevada's cities against terrorism. In 2002 Secretary of Energy Spencer Abraham recommended opening the federal repository at Yucca

Mountain, noting the need to protect nuclear waste against terrorists, and President George W. Bush agreed. As permitted in the original bill, Governor Kenny Guinn vetoed the decision—the only time Congress has given a state that right. But Congress could override the veto, and did.

Nevada tried to slow the dump by suing, delaying licensing, and publicizing questions about safety and scientific studies. In 2004 an appeals court tossed out federal standards to protect against radiation. In 2008 the Department of Energy issued a report predicting the dump would open in the next decade, with a $2.5 billion railroad from Caliente through Goldfield to transport the waste. Many Nevadans criticized this news, but some rural Nevadans and businesspeople wanted federal funds from the dump, for jobs or to buy the state's acquiescence.

By the 2010s the dump's foes seemed triumphant. With Barack Obama's election in 2008 and Nevadan Harry Reid as Senate majority leader, the new president had no desire to antagonize the member of Congress most crucial to his legislative agenda. In 2009 new energy secretary Steven Chu described the repository as "off the table." The project's office closed. In 2012 the Blue Ribbon Commission on America's Nuclear Future recommended a "consent-based" strategy to seek a state that wanted the waste. Its budget correspondingly declined, and planning began on what to do instead with nuclear waste.

Yet the dump refused to die. Two states sued to restart the process, and a federal appeals court ruled in their favor. Managers of the Nevada National Security Site's landfill altered rules to bury waste five times more radioactive than before, and the DOE planned to send 403 canisters of uranium waste to the site. While Nye County commissioners said they would accept it if safe, Governor Brian Sandoval attacked the DOE, and former senator Richard Bryan, chair of Nevada's Commission on Nuclear Projects, said that "we should raise hell."

Federal Projects

Although wary of federal projects, Nevadans welcomed defense spending. Nellis Air Force Base and the National Security Site, the renamed test site, remained economically vital. Christened in 2005, Creech Air Force Base in Indian Springs served as the nation's hub for training and operation of the Predator and other remotely piloted aircraft used extensively in Iraq and Afghanistan. Late in 2012 North Las Vegas–based Bigelow Aerospace became southern Nevada's first winner of a lead contract with the National Aeronautics and Space Administration, thanks to a $17.8 million deal to put a module at the International Space Station. Speculation also continued about what went on at Area 51, and tourists continued visiting nearby Rachel, hoping to find out.

Improving transportation remained a priority. A bullet train, Las Vegas mayor Bill Briare's goal in the late 1970s, gave way to the Desert XPress to Victorville, California. Officials discussed a public-private partnership to complete a $1 billion project to ease traffic flow in southern Nevada. Nevada and Arizona teamed in hopes of linking Las Vegas and Phoenix with a new Interstate 11 from Canada to Mexico, affecting a number of towns along its route. The $114 million Hoover Dam bypass bridge, named for Governor Mike O'Callaghan and Arizona Cardinals linebacker turned Green Beret Pat Tillman, opened in 2010, eliminating the two-lane drive across the dam.

Federal funds also boosted northern Nevada. In 2012 an expensive new highway opened between Reno and Carson City. The Fallon Naval Air Station's fighter weapons school remained important to navy operations and the local economy. In 2005 a federal commission recommended closing Hawthorne's army ammunition depot, which had been transferred from the navy in 1994. Since one-third of the county's residents owed their jobs to the depot, they welcomed the Pentagon's decision to spare it because it could provide training facilities.

Las Vegas: Return to Boom

In Las Vegas the post-9/11 downturn receded in an unprecedented boom. By 2007 thirty-nine million tourists arrived annually, causing 90 percent hotel occupancy. As land values skyrocketed, a construction boom spread beyond the Strip. In the 1940s and 1950s, home building lagged behind local population growth, but in the 1990s and 2000s it became a major industry. By late 2005 more than one hundred thousand in Clark County worked in construction, and the cost of living soared past that of Phoenix, Salt Lake City, and Denver. By 2007 McCarran International Airport became the nation's sixth busiest airport and fifteenth in the world; officials even planned another airport at Ivanpah, south of Las Vegas, to relieve traffic.

Earlier hotel-casino corporate mergers had been substantial, but newer ones proved larger. In 2004, after teaming with MGM on Atlantic City's $1.1

billion Borgata, Boyd Gaming bought Michael Gaughan's Coast Casinos for $1.3 billion. That year, enticed by Mandalay Resorts' success and convention facilities, MGM acquired it for $7.9 billion. When Phil Satre retired from Harrah's in 2005, he chose as his successor Harvard business professor Gary Loveman, who completed a $9.4 billion takeover of Caesars Entertainment.

In the early 2000s, existing resorts expanded rapidly, often emphasizing convention space. Caesars Palace added more than 1,500 rooms and a 240,000-square-foot convention area. The Bellagio's new 925-room tower added 60,000 square feet of convention space. Mandalay Bay built a 1.8 million–square-foot convention complex. In 2004, THE hotel at Mandalay Bay opened, a 1,118-room tower with high-tech suites, a 1.4 million–square-foot conference center, and art by Andy Warhol. While the Hard Rock added 875 rooms, Planet Hollywood renamed the Aladdin and teamed with Westgate Resorts on a $750 million time-share with two fifty-story towers. Off the Strip, Aliante Station and Red Rock Station at Summerlin opened, as did the Cannery hotel-casinos in Las Vegas and North Las Vegas, and the Orleans added an arena and a tower.

As the Strip's north end remained quiet, resorts moved south of town. Boyd opened the $500 million South Coast, but Gaughan sold his stock to Boyd in return for the new resort, renamed it SouthPoint, and added a third tower with 2,100-plus rooms and 160,000 square feet of convention space. Further south, Anthony Marnell III, the son of a hotel-casino builder, finished the $1 billion M Resort, with 390 rooms and a 92,000-square-foot casino. In the megaresort era, those statistics defined it as "boutique," despite being larger than the original Strip resorts.

The other major resort building occurred at one Strip intersection. Steve Wynn imploded the Desert Inn for the $2.7 billion Wynn Las Vegas, which opened in April 2005 with 2,700-plus rooms, high-end shopping and restaurants, a Ferrari-Maserati dealership, and a waterfall behind a mountain. Although luxurious and highly rated, the Wynn did run into problems: the design changed due to Wynn's inability to buy out all of the owners on the adjacent Desert Inn Country Club, he and investor Kazuo Okada had a falling-out that led to lawsuits, and Wynn's divorce from his wife, Elaine, another major stockholder, prompted a court case.

Across the street, Sheldon Adelson added to the Venetian with the Palazzo in December 2007. Larger than the Wynn, the Palazzo's nearly

7 million square feet made it the largest single building in the United States. Besides luxury retail and a nightclub with celebrity hosts and guests, the Palazzo boasted a Lamborghini dealership and combined with the Venetian and the Sands Expo Center to provide more convention space than in the entire city of San Francisco.

For an encore, Wynn built the Encore, a hotel linked to the Wynn by a shopping area. Roger Thomas, his longtime designer and the son of banker Parry Thomas, emphasized luxury and more natural light than most casinos employ. It opened just before Christmas 2008, amid the Great Recession. Besides offering nightclubs, art, and a beach club, in addition to suites and restaurants, Wynn lured singer Garth Brooks out of retirement to perform acoustical shows in the theater. Wynn and Adelson competed for the designation of tallest resort and for attention; in the process they boosted the local economy with jobs and new standards for Strip luxury—and eventually found common ground in seeking to expand their companies into Macau and in support for Republican politicians.

Entertainment and Tourism

In keeping with advances in technology and competition from other tourist areas, Nevada's approach to entertainment tourism changed early in the twenty-first century. While Reno and Las Vegas hotel-casinos continued their tradition of showroom and lounge performers and revues, some old attractions won increased interest. Harrah's bought the World Series of Poker and moved it from Binion's to the Rio; it grew to more than sixty kinds of poker, topped six thousand entrants, and offered a $10 million first prize in 2014. The National Finals Rodeo filled Las Vegas's Thomas and Mack every day early in each December, pumping about $1.3 billion into the economy since moving to Las Vegas in 1985.

In Las Vegas entertainment moved in new directions. Many "name" acts eschewed showrooms for arenas, and prices and attendance rose accordingly. Cirque du Soleil expanded to several resorts. Caesars Palace built the four-thousand-seat Colosseum for Celine Dion, one of many "residencies" that included Penn and Teller at the Rio and Blue Man Group, which played three Las Vegas resorts. With the Tropicana closing the Folies Bergère just before its fiftieth anniversary, Jubilee at Bally's presented the last of the classic showgirl revues. Las Vegas also exported entertainers: rock groups like the Killers won fans, local native Matthew Gray Gubler costarred in the series *Criminal Minds,* and onetime resident Jimmy Kimmel became a popular comedian and television host.

Some resorts catered to Millennials and "Gen Xers" (born after the 1946–64 baby boom). The Wynn's $100 million Club xs joined six other Las Vegas venues among the nation's ten most profitable dance clubs and drove Strip beverage departments to $1 billion in earnings in 2011. As extreme sports and ESPN's "X Games" grew, the Rio planned VooDoo Skyline, a seventy-second ride four hundred feet up, going up to thirty-three miles per hour, and South Lake Tahoe's Heavenly Mountain Resort added zip lines and rope courses. Amid Nevada's golf, skiing, and water sports, shooting became part of Las Vegas tourism, including a federally funded range. The UFC—Ultimate Fighting Championship—backed by the Fetitta brothers and chief executive Dana White, replaced boxing as the most popular form of fisticuffs, joining NASCAR as a major tourist attraction.

Nevada also looked to the past to appeal to travelers. In 2009 $10 million in federal funds secured by Reid and another $1 million through Lieutenant Governor Lorraine Hunt's efforts led to the reconstruction of the V&T Railway, running from Virginia City. Ely's railroad museum and Boulder City's historic train evoked a key part of Nevada's history. Often accused of imploding history, Las Vegans opened the Smithsonian-affiliated National Atomic Testing Museum; a museum of natural history; an expanded Mormon Fort state park; the $250 million Springs Preserve, a 180-acre array of exhibits and trails, with a new Nevada State Museum next door; the National Museum of Organized Crime and Law Enforcement, known as the Mob Museum, in the city's old federal building; and the Neon Museum next to Cashman Field, providing tours and preserving both signs and the old La Concha Motel, designed by architect Paul Revere Williams.

Gaming: Beyond Nevada

Asian markets had long provided high-rolling gamblers to Nevada casinos, but Macau, a Portuguese colony until China took over in 1999, combined competition and opportunity. Once Macau's government ended Hong Kong billionaire Stanley Ho's forty-year monopoly in 2002, Adelson led the way with the Sands Macau, followed by Wynn, while MGM partnered with Ho. By 2013 Macau's thirty-five casinos produced $45 billion in annual revenue, three times as much as Nevada with one-tenth as many casinos. Investors wanted more: the $4.4 billion Sands Cotai Central opened, with

Wynn planning a $4 billion resort and MGM a $2.5 billion project. But in 2013 federal officials voiced concerns, urging closer regulation of American firms investing in Macau due to fears of money laundering.

Still other sites appealed to Nevada entrepreneurs. Adelson branched out to Singapore and proposed a Spanish Eurovegas of six casinos and eleven hotels. Boyd Gaming bought Peninsula Gaming and its casinos in Louisiana, Kansas, and Iowa for $1.45 billion in 2012. In 2013 Wynn won approval for a $1.2 billion resort in Massachusetts after promising to clean up pollution at a nearby site and give hiring preferences to residents. Indian casinos gained profits and attracted Nevada companies, which obtained contracts for consulting, financing, and management.

With growth came new possibilities for Nevada to dominate gambling markets, production, investment, and technology. As Internet gambling spread, Congress discussed legalizing online poker, while Nevada's three sites reported reaching the $1 million mark in monthly revenue in 2014. NEWave won a contract in June 2013 to supply compliance software to eight Cherokee Nation Entertainment casinos in Oklahoma. Bally acquired SHFL, another gaming manufacturer and, like IGT, kept up with new technology, while Scientific Games, a lottery company, merged with slot maker WMS Industries and then bought Bally for $5.1 billion. According to Bo Bernhard, executive director of UNLV's International Gaming Institute, Nevada had "become an intellectual capital of a global industry, from the invention of the games, the products that drive gambling, all the way up through the corporate level," with the opportunity to dominate the world market.

Seeking Cures, Economic and Otherwise

Nevada had long touted itself for medical tourism; aging baby boomers and the Affordable Care Act of 2010 made the idea more attractive. In 2009 the Lou Ruvo Center for Brain Health opened in Las Vegas with a Frank Gehry–designed eighteen-thousand-piece, twisted-metal facade. The Cleveland Clinic's involvement led to treatment and research in Alzheimer's, dementia, and movement disorders. Comprehensive Cancer Centers of Southern Nevada affiliated with the University of California–Los Angeles for treatment and research, and the Las Vegas Convention and Visitors Authority hired a staffer just for medical tourism. But other

The Cleveland Clinic's Lou Ruvo Center for Brain Health brought leading medical researchers to Las Vegas to study and treat brain disorders and featured the architecture of Frank Gehry, whose design includes 1,999 unique windows and 18,000 stainless-steel shingles. Courtesy of Rex J. Rowley.

efforts failed. MGM executive Jim Murren and his wife, Heather, set up the Nevada Cancer Institute and imported researchers, but it foundered and closed. A different issue—north-south rivalry—affected the University of Nevada School of Medicine. It offered training in Reno and Las Vegas, and media magnate Jim Rogers sought a coordinated health sciences program during his tenure as higher education chancellor (2004–9). But southern Nevadans saw it as UNR's funding problem, not theirs, and pushed for a separate medical school. Meanwhile, rural Nevadans complained about a doctor shortage that the medical school seemed unable to solve.

Nevada's medical community also confronted changes due to "Obamacare." In 2013 Governor Brian Sandoval's decision to expand the state Medicaid program would add two hundred million dollars to its one billion dollars in costs. Only education receives more state funds, but, he said, the move would save money by obtaining federal aid for mental health care. How it might affect other needs remained to be seen: in 2013 Nevada ranked forty-sixth or worse among states in family doctors, pediatricians, psychiatrists, and surgeons per one hundred thousand residents, with a medical school researcher reporting 280,000 more medical appointments a year might take place in the state. Like the federal website, the state's functioned badly during the 2014 rollout, prompting criticism and changes.

Problems with government also affected medicine. In the late 2000s experts found one hundred cases of hepatitis C, one fatal, at Dr. Dipak Desai's Endoscopy Center of Southern Nevada, leading to the doctor's sentencing to life in prison. His influence had helped block investigations, and state health officials had been unable to obtain funds for more inspections. The *Sacramento Bee* reported that between 2008 and 2012, while the state cut spending on treatment by a quarter, to about half the national average, the mental health facility in Las Vegas gave fifteen hundred patients bus tickets elsewhere rather than treat them. In 2013 Lake's Crossing Center in Sparks faced a federal lawsuit over delays in treatment. Controversy continued over the effects of atomic testing and why seventeen children contracted leukemia in the Fallon area from 1997 to 2001: studies cast doubt on a toxic chemical, despite the presence of other diseases often caused by such exposure.

Nevada's desire for limited government produced a different health problem during the Las Vegas building boom. In 2007 and early 2008, twelve construction workers died in eighteen months on Strip construction projects. Workers lacked needed training, the state Occupational Safety and Health Administration apparently succumbed to pressure from contractors, and its federal counterpart loosened safety rules. In June 2008 a strike at the CityCenter project helped inspire improved working conditions at all levels.

In 2001 the *New York Times* said Nevada's rapid population growth and "long legacy of low-tax, libertarian government, rural isolation and a steely tradition of self-reliance . . . left little sense of community to create a huge range of challenges to the state's mental and physical health." Nevada maintained some of the worst numbers of suicides, high school dropouts, pregnant teens, unimmunized children, killings related to domestic violence, health care, smoking, and Medicaid spending. Some problems resulted from transience and lack of community related to fast growth. By 2005 *Wall Street Journal* reporter Christina Binkley noted, several Strip executives lived outside of Las Vegas or escaped to second or third homes: "The fortunes of Las Vegas's gambling leaders may be tied to the kingdom of Las Vegas, but they flee the place with alacrity." In 2009 UNLV sociologists found 60 percent of southern Nevadans moved to their homes from elsewhere in the county—a sign of movement within Las Vegas, not just to and from it.

Gender Issues: Coming a Long Way, a Long Way to Go

Nevada women continued to rise in politics and business. In 2009 Clark County Legal Services director Barbara Buckley became the first female assembly speaker and Marilyn Kirkpatrick the second in 2013. In 2011 Carolyn Goodman defeated Clark County commissioner Chris Giunchigliani, a former assemblywoman and teachers' union leader, in an all-woman election for Las Vegas mayor. While four women followed Miriam Shearing onto the Nevada Supreme Court, three others became federal judges by 2013; Johnnie Rawlinson, Nevada's first woman US district judge in 1997, became the Ninth Circuit's first black woman jurist. Few women rose to the top in the gaming industry, but Elaine Wynn had played a key role in her ex-husband's resorts; Marilyn Winn ran Planet Hollywood, Paris, and Bally's before serving as president of Wynn/Encore Las Vegas; and former Las Vegas mayor Jan Jones became Caesars Entertainment's executive vice president of government affairs and communications. Caesars vice president Marybel Batjer, the daughter of a onetime Nevada Supreme Court justice, worked as Governor Kenny Guinn's chief of staff, among other federal and state posts, before joining California state government.

Other women associated with the resort industry had unhappier experiences. In 2001 veteran bartender Darlene Jespersen sued Harrah's for firing her for refusing to wear makeup. The court held Harrah's did nothing wrong under Title VII of the 1964 Civil Rights Act and Jespersen faced no undue burden due to gender, but the case won attention and encouraged women to stand up for their rights. In turn, in 2001 a group of Las Vegas cocktail waitresses founded the Kiss My Foot movement to fight requirements that they wear high heels, citing injuries and medical expenses caused by being on their feet in uncomfortable shoes. Demonstrations and publicity prompted several casinos to accept their demand.

A 2005 Nevada Women's Fund report pointed out the contradictory lives of the state's women. They still earned less than men, held fewer managerial posts, and had the nation's highest women's mortality rates from lung cancer and suicide; the report concluded they needed more access to child care and encouragement to study math and science. "In the political arena

Nevada has one of the highest rates of women elected to public office, but one of the lowest rates of voter registration and turnout," it said. By 2013 women held half of the state constitutional offices, including one Hispanic, Attorney General Catherine Cortez Masto, who left office the next year due to term limits.

The new century began with troubling signs for LGBTQ Nevadans. Passed overwhelmingly in 2000 and 2002, Question 2 amended the Nevada Constitution to ban gay marriage. While Mormon and Catholic leaders strongly backed it, the issue roiled politics, with a "Marriage Protection Pledge" becoming a litmus test for candidates. The ACLU complained about segregating HIV-positive prisoners and denying medications for them and about the Clark County School District removing mentions of homosexuality from the sex education curriculum. Earlier, the school board banned field trips to an AIDS exhibit at the children's museum.

But the climate improved. Legislators overrode Governor Jim Gibbons's 2009 veto of a bill recognizing same-sex and opposite-sex domestic partnerships. In 2011 his successor, Sandoval, signed a bill protecting the transgender against discrimination in public accommodations, housing, and employment. In 2013 the legislature asked voters to repeal the definition of marriage, and State Senator Kelvin Atkinson won plaudits for announcing his homosexuality, joining four other gay lawmakers. As lawmakers voted, a challenge to Nevada's ban on gay marriage, *Sevcik v. Sandoval,* reached the Ninth Circuit Court of Appeals, which held the law to be unconstitutional. Also in 2013 the Gay and Lesbian Community Center of Las Vegas opened, while Reno's Gay Pride Festival and various organizations served northern Nevada.

Ethnicity in Nevada

Historian Hal Rothman called Las Vegas "the first postintegration city," with a quarter of the people Hispanic, a quarter retired, and little overlap: most Hispanics lived in older eastern and West Las Vegas, and suburban senior communities grew. By 2010 Hispanics numbered 700,000 of Nevada's 2.7 million residents. From 2004 to 2012, the Pew Research Center found, their voter total nearly doubled and, as more Hispanics worked in the resort industry, fed the Culinary Union's power. Reflecting these trends, Democrat Mo Denis became the first Latino state senate majority leader in

2013 and part of a Hispanic caucus that helped pass fifty million dollars for teaching English Language Learners and a driver's authorization card for illegal immigrants to be insured.

These developments reflected Hispanics' influence throughout Nevada. While 80 percent of Nevada's Latinos lived in Clark County, the populace grew across the North, with about 15 percent of the Reno-Sparks area foreign born, mostly Hispanic, by the late 2000s. Cuban émigré Liliam Lujan Hickey introduced Classrooms on Wheels, aiding at-risk families with preschool and parenting; other Latino leaders discussed reviving leadership academies once run by Clark County commissioner Manny Cortez and Senator Harry Reid's longtime chief of staff, Reynaldo Martinez. Hispanics notched several important firsts: Sandoval's election as governor, Oscar Delgado as a Reno councilman, and Isaac Barron as North Las Vegas councilman.

Hispanic power inspired action from Nevada leaders. Reid became a leading backer of immigration reform after trying to end birthright citizenship in 1993 (he called it "the lowest point" of his time in Congress); he also knew Hispanics played a key role in his 2010 reelection and party success. Dean Heller, his GOP colleague, lost the Hispanic vote by 41 percent in 2012 and backed the Senate's immigration reform plan in 2013. Sandoval, who won only one-third of the Latino vote in running for governor in 2010, helped lead a national GOP effort to recruit Hispanic candidates.

At 9 percent, African Americans remained Nevada's second-largest ethnic group. Most lived in Clark County, topping 11 percent of residents by 2012. No other county reached 5 percent, yet African Americans recorded several firsts: in 2002 Joe Neal as first major party nominee for governor; in 2004 the state high court's first member of color, Michael Douglas; Steven Horsford, the state senate majority leader in 2008 and first black Nevadan in Congress, from the new Fourth House District; in 2013 William Horne as assembly majority leader; and in 2014 Richard Boulware as the state's first African American male federal judge. But African Americans held few ownership and executive positions in gaming. Bobby Siller retired as FBI agent in charge, became a control board member, and pressed for more diversity in gaming. In 2001 Detroit businessman Don Barden bought Fitzgerald's and promoted it with his properties around the country.

With the impact of African American voters declining in comparison with that of Latinos, West Las Vegas, populated mainly by both groups, still needed redevelopment. In 2003, after many years of rebuilding efforts, most notably by longtime casino operator Sarann Knight Preddy and her family, the Moulin Rouge burned down, ending hopes it would help lead a West Las Vegas renaissance. In 2008 the Las Vegas City Council supported closing F Street in West Las Vegas to widen I-15, but neighborhood residents protested being cut off. With allies they formed the F Street Coalition, which succeeded in fighting for the street's reopening, with a $13.6 million construction project that began in 2013.

Nevada's Asian population crept toward 10 percent in the 2010 census, a 116 percent increase in the previous decade—the nation's fastest growth rate. Filipinos accounted for much of that, as did Hawaiians, often drawn by jobs in the resort industry. Various groups north and south worked to unify Asian people and overcome their lack of political offices and the tendency of politicians to ignore them. Asians divided more closely by party than Hispanics and African Americans and constituted 12 percent of the Third House District in Clark County, drawing additional notice. Entrepreneurs like Buck Wong and his family at Arcata engineering and Doris and Theodore Lee of Urban Land Company also became leading philanthropists.

Despite sparse numbers (around six thousand in 2010), Basque culture remained prominent. As the sheep industry declined, more Basques became ranch owners. They carved a niche with restaurants in Elko, Fallon, Gardnerville, Reno, and Winnemucca, but the Bilbaos had sold Elko's Stockmen's Hotel, and the Ascuagas agreed in 2013 to sell the Sparks Nugget while remaining as consultants. The Western Basque Festival remains an attraction in Sparks, the Elko Euzkaldunak Club's National Basque Festival turned fifty in 2013, and Gardnerville's song festival celebrates another component of Basque culture; clubs also grew in Battle Mountain, Las Vegas, Reno, and Winnemucca. Others continued to study these activities: the North American Basque Organization serves as a clearinghouse for thirty-eight groups with six thousand members, and UNR's Center for Basque Studies, begun in 1967, continues to conduct research and publish works on Basque culture.

Gold: Boom and Fears of Bust

While gaming generated $10.7 billion in 2011, mining produced $8.8 billion and one-fifth of Nevada's job growth from 2009 to 2012. Nevada yielded up to three-quarters of America's gold, and the 5.5 million ounces of ore dug out of Nevada soil in 2011 fell only 2.5 million ounces short of the Comstock's yield from 1859 to 1881. Multinational Barrick Gold produces half of its gold in the United States, and four-fifths of that in Nevada, while Newmont dug more than 2 million of its 5.2 million ounces in Nevada.

The state's most productive mines dotted the North. Barrick's Cortez Hills, the world's second-largest gold mine, stretched one thousand square miles near Elko. While reserves and prices held up, the need for workers, the world economy, and rising costs affected production. As gold prices septupled from 2000 to 2012, due partly to central banks agreeing to limit sales, mining companies remained hopeful. The Bureau of Land Management approved Canadian Pilot Gold's exploration at Kinsley Mountain near West Wendover. Barrick sent gold for refining to London-based Johnson Matthey in Salt Lake City, Las Vegas contractors provided transportation and supplies, and Searchlight's old Quartette Mine drew interest.

Then the market soured. In 2013, with ore exploration in Nevadan falling by half in eight years, gold prices down $600 an ounce in a year and a half, and an Andean mining investment in trouble, Barrick planned to close its Ruby Hill operation, Eureka's biggest private employer. Barrick's stock fell more than half in six months after former Goldman Sachs president John Thornton, paid $5 million with a $12 million bonus, succeeded company founder Peter Munk. *Forbes* reported management earned $57 million in 2012; Newmont executives made $30 million, up nearly one-third. Whether mining had begun evolving from boom to bust with owners retaining their wealth—as in the Comstock and Tonopah-Goldfield-Ely booms—remained to be seen.

Mining: A Variety of Effects

Other ores glittered, too. Battle Mountain and Ely produced copper, with Nevada Copper's Pumpkin Hollow project at Yerington offering hope for that area. Limestone from Lyon and Elko Counties served the construction trade. Eureka and Tonopah benefited from molybdenite mines for metal alloys and the medical industry, as Clark County did from gypsum and silica sand. One of the world's largest lithium deposits, sixty miles north of Winnemucca, turned out millions of pounds. About 87 percent of Nevada's oil production (down significantly in the past two decades) came from Nye County, mostly in Railroad Valley, and the rest from Eureka. In the early 2010s, the state issued more permits for oil and gas drilling, especially near Carlin and on forty thousand acres of public and private land near Wells.

Mining also drew foreign interest. In 2012 China's Sichuan Hanlong Group, which generated $2.2 billion in molybdenum from ten American mines in 2011, invested in a Molycorp mine the Bureau of Land Management approved near Eureka on Mount Hope for production in 2015. Molycorp had high hopes for its open-pit mine to produce rare earth at Mountain Pass, just southwest of Primm across the California line. Declining market prices and cost overruns limited its success, but studies suggested rare-earth tailings from as far back as the Gold Rush could be used profitably on cellular phones and computers.

How mining—from open pits to the one hundred thousand tons of cyanide used annually—affected Nevada's environment remained an issue. Cleaning up contamination at the shuttered Weed Heights in Lyon County cost millions of dollars and led to a class-action lawsuit and a nearly $20 million settlement for those affected by it. Due to federal rules and dangers to birds, Newmont released one thousand tons of caustic soda into the Lone Tree Mine pit lake near Battle Mountain to balance the pH level. But the Dow Jones Sustainability World Index listed Barrick and Newmont among three hundred global firms leading the way in environmental policy. With mining firms required to file reclamation plans when seeking permits, Barrick plants native flora and contours leach pads and tailing dams to match the geography, set up a farm to collect seeds for planting, and hired Western Shoshone to work it.

Politically, mining remained controversial. Nationally, Senate majority leader Harry Reid blocked revisions to the 1872 mining law. Various critics (who made similar statements about gaming) often complained the industry paid lower taxes than it should, due to the state constitution and lack of legislative support for an increase. But in 2013 lawmakers, including some usually antitax Republicans, backed an initiative developed by former Reno Democratic state senator Sheila Leslie for an amendment to allow higher mining taxes. It barely lost on the 2014 ballot, but legislators took a step that many before them had been unwilling to consider.

The Rural Economy

While rural leaders lamented their diminished influence—by 2013 fewer than 10 percent of Nevadans lived in rural areas, and two state senators represented a dozen counties—their economy retained vitality. Ranches averaged thirty-five hundred acres, third nationally in size. Cattle ranching produced more than 60 percent of agricultural revenue, with Elko second among America's counties in beef cows. Alfalfa hay for farms and ranches remained the top cash crop, along with potatoes, onions, and garlic. The Nevada Agricultural Foundation and state agencies provided various services, including information and grants, to farmers. Dairy farming and manufacturing became more important closer to Reno and Las Vegas.

Diversifying the rural economy remained a priority and a problem. Rural Nevada Development Corporation offices in Ely, Carson City, and Pahrump offered funds for small business and Native Americans. Renewable energy sources offered prospects, as did industrial parks in Meadow Valley and Alamo in Lincoln County. Great Basin College and Western Nevada College, and some College of Southern Nevada services, aided rural areas, but the combination of budget cuts and a new funding system for higher education led to budget problems.

One rural industry, prostitution, prompted both profits and debate. In 2011, calling it a bar to luring capital, Reid urged legislators to ban it, to no avail. Nevada Brothel Owners Association lobbyist George Flint tried to change the rule barring prostitution in counties with four hundred thousand residents, but southern Nevadans blocked him; in 2003 and 2009, he backed taxing the industry, but the legislature refused, apparently believing that to tax brothels would give them too much legitimacy. According to Flint's group, twenty-three legal brothels hosted five hundred thousand customers and earned $250 million a year until the recession halved revenues. Financial issues led to the Mustang Ranch's sale to investor Lance Gilman, who won a Storey County commission seat and planned an industrial park.

Those plans had an impact. In 2014 many Nevadans hailed the interest of Tesla, the electric carmaker, in building a plant in northern Nevada for production of its batteries (and possibly obtaining the lithium for them at a mine in Silver Peak in Esmeralda County). Governor Sandoval called a special legislative session that approved more than $1 billion in tax breaks and other incentives for the facility in Gilman's industrial park. Critics questioned the additional educational and transportation costs that would result and whether the state would make back what it gave away.

Alternative Energy

Since Senators Alan Bible and Howard Cannon unsuccessfully sought federal aid for solar research in 1959, harvesting power from Nevada's sunshine has been a possibility. In the new century, it became a reality. In 2009 Secretary of the Interior Ken Salazar boosted solar-related businesses and programs by pushing renewable energy on federal lands. The BLM approved nine solar projects on 24,000 acres in California and Nevada, with more planned. In 2013 Salazar's successor, Sally Jewell, declared 304,000 acres in six states, including Nevada, off-limits to new mining claims as part of seventeen new "solar energy zones."

By 2013 Nevada boasted several projects operating or planned. Federal officials approved a Korean firm's 350-megawatt solar plant near Boulder City to power up to 105,000 homes. Pioneering "concentrated solar power," with ground mirrors reflecting the sun off of a tower, Crescent Dunes near Tonopah sold power to NV Energy and Ivanpah Solar near Primm to Southern California Edison and Pacific Gas and Electric. With help from NV Energy, Apple would own the Fort Churchill Solar Array near Yerington until NV Energy bought it in five years, while Apple would obtain energy for its 90,000-square-foot data center in Reno. The Public Utilities Commission provided rebates for installing rooftop solar systems, and the gaming industry saw possibilities: MGM announced plans to cover all 20 acres of the Mandalay Bay Convention Center's roof with 20,000 solar panels. But some projects failed, including China-based ENN Mojave Energy's planned solar plant south of Laughlin, and wildlife groups warned of dangers in disturbing or relocating such species as desert tortoises and expressed displeasure that the rays from panels at Ivanpah ignited thousands of birds in midair. The federal government responded with mitigation projects: one Nevada solar project would have to pay fees to help restore land in the nearby Gold Butte area.

Other forms of renewable energy showed promise. A small wind project near Pahrump and a large one near Searchlight suggested more economic diversity and better use of natural resources, as did a geothermal plant at Wabuska in Lyon County, but turbines at White Pine's Spring Valley Wind

Alternative energy sources such as this solar plant in southern Nevada reflected environmental awareness, but also opportunities for profit for the state. Courtesy of Steve Marcus and the *Las Vegas Sun*.

Energy project killed more than five hundred bats in 2013; the operator adjusted the windmills in response. By 2012 Nevada ranked tenth per capita with 3.74 million square feet of LEED-certified green building that year, including a new Las Vegas transit center, North Las Vegas's new city hall, and Nellis Air Force Base's Green Flag training center. NV Energy announced it would close all coal-fired power plants by 2025; as recently as 1980, more than two-thirds of its energy came from coal.

Crisis and Change in Education

Growth exacerbated educational issues. Clark County averaged a new school a month, but overcrowding continued; in 2013 Hispanic enrollment drove the Clark County School District to a record 315,000 students. Educators sought more funds and changed curriculum, but by 2013 only two states had a lower graduation rate (62.7 percent), and the National Assessment of Education Progress found Nevada trailing most states in K–12 reading and math levels; about half of in-state first-year college students had to take remedial classes. The 2010s brought change with the governor empowered to choose the state superintendent rather than the board of education and a new leader in Clark County, but both appointees left quickly. Teachers' unions decried underfunding, and conservative critics blamed their influence for the lack of school choice and failed efforts to deconsolidate the Clark County School District. Yet in the 2010s, a Democratic legislature and Republican governor backed tougher evaluations for teachers, with more grounds for firing and probationary time and class-size cuts for kindergarten.

As at the K–12 level, higher education grew with the population. UNR's enrollment topped 18,000 by 2013, up about 4,000 in a decade, while UNLV's head count reached 27,000 and CSN's 37,000 in 2012. The schools, including Nevada State College, required new buildings to keep up with swelling numbers; UNR added a new Knowledge Center in 2008, while UNLV gained a new student union and facilities for media studies and hotel administration. Faculty and programs at Nevada schools drew national and international attention and funding, but budget and salary cuts made it harder to retain some faculty.

Higher education also faced leadership challenges. Neither successor to UNR's Joe Crowley and UNLV's Carol Harter lasted more than four years as president. From 2000 to 2004, CSN had seven presidents, four of them interim. After Jim Rogers became chancellor in 2004, regents ceded him most authority over system presidents. Rogers pushed UNLV into a $500 million capital campaign and, after rivalries between campuses bred corruption charges, required the entire system to lobby as one, rather than individual campuses striking out on their own. He also had to fight efforts to cut the higher education budget.

Amid cuts and controversy, Nevada found new research opportunities. The Desert Research Institute won more than $390 million in grants and funding in the 2000s. UNLV's partnerships with the prestigious Brookings Institution (Brookings Mountain West) and Lincy Institute increased research and community collaboration. Harter took charge of UNLV's Black Mountain Institute, built on the formation of a "city of asylum" for persecuted writers and resort executive Glenn Schaeffer's endowment of the International Institute of Modern Letters.

Image and Reality

Yet Nevada's image remained something to be both shaped and tolerated. At the 2013 legislature, the *New York Times* reported "a lobbyist courting lawmakers in Stetsons," as though the Old West predominated in Carson City. By 2003 R&R Partners devised a new slogan for Las Vegas: "What happens here, stays here." The most successful campaign in the state's and city's long history of defining themselves, it added luster to the reputation of Billy Vassiliadis, R&R's chief executive, one of Nevada's most powerful lobbyists and political consultants.

Films about and made in Nevada boosted the economy. *The Women* remade the earlier film and play about divorcées in northern Nevada. As the scene of Admiral James Kirk's death, the Valley of Fire became a mecca for *Star Trek* fans. Movies such as *The Hangover* and television shows like *Las Vegas* depicted glitter and fun, while UNLV graduate Anthony Zuiker's *CSI: Crime Scene Investigation* showed a darker side to Las Vegas and proved a ratings and critical success. *The Cooler,* filmed at Reno's Golden Phoenix (now a condo development), depicted Las Vegas evolving from its Mob past into the corporate present. Film festivals drew crowds, and revenue from movies shot in Nevada topped $80 million from 2000 on.

Nevada also latched onto the reality-show genre. Filmed at the Palms, MTV's *The Real World: Las Vegas* drew younger audiences. *Pawn Stars,* based in Las Vegas, became a History Channel hit, spawned imitators and musicals, and made its staff into stars. An HBO reality-style documentary series, *Cathouse,* went "inside" Dennis Hof's Moonlite BunnyRanch in Moundhouse, a few miles east of Carson City. Produced on Comedy Central (2003–9), *Reno 911!* satirized COPS, a reality series with ties to Las Vegas, with a "bumbling group of buffoons and bimbos," as historian Alicia Barber put it. The state film office welcomed it, but some Reno residents resented the caricature—a common theme in Nevada history of reconciling the image used to attract tourists with the reality of living there.

Evolving Politics

Nevada's political culture showed signs of change—which bred further change. Nevada grew less libertarian and more socially conservative due to political polarization, the fast-growing older population, and more prominent social issues. In 2000 Democratic senator Richard Bryan retired after four decades of public service, and former representative Republican John Ensign succeeded him. In the early 2000s, less libertarian Nevadans approved a constitutional amendment barring same-sex marriage and opposed legalizing marijuana. Southern Nevadans approved money for transportation, but not for libraries and the homeless. In 2002, with several of these questions on the ballot and Democrats in disarray, the GOP won all six state constitutional offices, and Republican Jon Porter, a veteran state legislator, captured a newly created House seat.

These events served as a wake-up call and a contrast. Conscious of his narrow win in 1998, Reid developed a close relationship with Ensign, including a deal to let him pick every fourth federal judge despite GOP control (Reid chose then attorney general Brian Sandoval for one of them), which helped both have easy reelections. Reid imported operatives to rebuild the Democratic Party, aided by unions and Hispanics. Voters passed less conservative ballot issues, including a constitutional amendment hiking the minimum wage and a law banning smoking in restaurants and other places that served food. Bar owners objected, but their business suffered less from that than from the recession that began in 2007.

Guinn Versus the Legislature

At the legislature, amid more rigid partisanship, Republican governor Kenny Guinn, a GOP senate led by Bill Raggio, and Democratic speakers Joe Dini of Yerington and Richard Perkins of Henderson still forged compromises. Guinn saw himself as a moderate Republican, pointing to spending cuts of $350 million and privatizing the state workers' compensation system, but sought more education spending and hiked funding for mental health treatment by 300 percent. In 2005 the legislature restructured the Millennium Scholarship program and approved full-day kindergarten for at-risk schools. That year, pressed from his right amid a budget surplus, Guinn agreed to a rebate of some driver's license registration fees.

Guinn's relations with the legislature survived an unusual fight. In 2003 he sought to diversify the tax system to raise about $1 billion, including a hike in what businesses paid per worker and a gross-receipts tax to reduce the state's reliance on gaming and tourism. But passing Guinn's plan required a two-thirds vote of the legislature. GOP senators went along, but in the assembly just over one-third, all Republicans, opposed the measure, advocating one that would produce less revenue (just over $700 million). The session ended with no agreement.

Guinn responded by suing the legislature. The Nevada Supreme Court ruled six to one for Guinn, holding the original Nevada Constitution's guarantee of education for the state's citizens overrode the amendment requiring a two-thirds vote for tax hikes. The legislature met in a special session, and members hoped to settle the impasse. Finally, John Marvel, a rancher from Battle Mountain who represented rural Nevada for three decades, switched to provide the required two-thirds to approve the largest tax increase in Nevada's history. After their controversial opinion, some of the justices retired amid rumors of their certain defeat, and taxes became even more divisive throughout Nevada. Indeed, by 2013 almost a decade had passed since voters in Clark County, the state's most Democratic area, had approved a tax increase that both residents and tourists would have to absorb.

A Changing Electorate, a Controversial Governor

The 2006 election reflected the divide. In the GOP primary for the northern House seat, Secretary of State Dean Heller held off former assemblywomen Sharron Angle from his right and more moderate Dawn Gibbons and then beat conservative Gardnerville Democrat Jill Derby by five points in that district's closest general election ever. The congressman giving up that post, Jim Gibbons, easily won the Republican primary for governor on his anti-tax, antigovernment record. Her long Democratic involvement and a more liberal base propelled State Senator Dina Titus past Henderson mayor Jim Gibson in the primary, but her battles for funding for Clark County hurt her in the North; to win she needed to crush Gibbons in the South. With conservative Democrats unenthused about Titus, Gibbons won, benefiting from a throwback to divisions that once defeated such Democrats as Howard Cannon, for whom Titus had interned.

Yet scandals became the story of the election and its aftermath. After reports that Gibbons hired an undocumented immigrant as a nanny, he faced allegations of assaulting a Las Vegas cocktail waitress; she later sued Gibbons and several others connected to the incident and received a settlement from his political consultant and the Las Vegas Metropolitan Police Department. After the election came a federal probe of payments from a Reno software company and tabloid-style revelations on his personal life, and Elko County's assessor accusing him of trying to use pressure to lower his property tax liability.

His policies proved no less controversial. In 2007, with the building and housing bubbles yet to burst, Gibbons proposed sweeping budget cuts. Most state agencies sliced their budgets by 4.5 percent and businesses received a tax cut, but Democrats won a fight to expand full-day kindergarten. In 2008, with the recession, a shortfall, and the state's Rainy Day Fund of nearly $1 billion expended, Gibbons called a special session, said nothing for days about what he wanted to do, and then blamed lawmakers for causing the budget problems. Lawmakers devised their own approach, based on another 3.3 percent cut.

The 2008 elections swung to Democrats, thanks to the economy and superior organization. At the behest of Reid, now Senate majority leader, the national party enhanced Nevada's role by holding its caucus early in the nominating process. Democrats won the state senate. Titus unseated Porter after three terms in the Third House District. Republicans complained that having to help Raggio fend off a primary challenge from the right from Angle expended resources needed to protect other GOP incumbents. Barack Obama won Nevada's electoral votes over Republican John McCain by 12.5 percent, well ahead of his national margin.

Democratic legislators shaped the budget less than the recession and Gibbons's opposition to taxes. In 2009 he proposed cutting higher education 36 percent and state workers' pay 6 percent. Raggio sought a "sunset" provision, requiring new taxes to be approved again in two years. Gibbons issued a record forty-one vetoes, and, despite Democrats lacking a two-thirds majority in the state senate, lawmakers still overrode twenty-five of them. But by February 2010, with an $800 million deficit looming, Gibbons called a special session. Gibbons and lawmakers agreed to cut education by another 7 percent and to raise fees on mining, banking, and other industries, forcing Gibbons to admit to breaking his "no tax" pledge.

Political Corruption and Ethics

Gibbons's problems fitted a pattern of behavior in Nevada that continued amid the state's growth, cronyism, the gambling culture, and the economic juggernaut making money more plentiful. In 2006 the *Los Angeles Times* suggested that ties to campaign contributors affected how judges ruled and upbraided several jurists for failing to disclose financial links. After two decades as a top lobbyist, controversial due to his clients and his actions, Harvey Whittemore concentrated on developing the Coyote Springs community in Lincoln County until the recession upended his plans. Then, in 2013, a federal jury convicted him of three felonies related to contributing $133,000 to Reid's campaign. According to prosecutors, Whittemore gave money to family, friends, and employees of his Wingfield Nevada Group, who donated it to Reid in their names.

The tawdriest scandal, "G-Sting," enveloped the Clark County Commission. Michael Galardi, the owner of topless clubs, bribed politicians in California and Nevada by providing money and sexual favors. Convicted in 2006, four commissioners went to federal prison: Republican Lance Malone, who lobbied for Galardi after leaving office and paid politicians for him, and Democrats Erin Kenny, an assemblywoman and a candidate for lieutenant governor with close ties to developers; Mary Kincaid-Chauncey, a former North Las Vegas councilwoman and business owner; and Dario Herrera, once considered one of Nevada's brightest political stars, who lost his bid for the House in 2002.

Another scandal led to a first: censuring a state official. Elected Nevada's first female controller in 1998, Kathy Augustine used state workers and equipment on her reelection; the assembly impeached her, but the state senate censured her and let her stay in office. While running for state treasurer in 2006, she died, and an investigation led to her husband's conviction on first-degree murder charges.

Still other scandals demonstrated how politics and personal lives intersected. In 2011, after becoming part of the GOP leadership, Ensign resigned from the Senate. He had an affair with the wife of his chief of staff, Doug Hampton; the couple had been close friends of Ensign and his wife. After Hampton resigned, Ensign helped him pursue lobbying jobs, and his parents gave ninety-six thousand dollars to Hampton and his family. While Hampton received a year's probation for violating federal laws imposing limits on former Senate staffers, the Senate Ethics Committee urged the Justice Department to investigate Ensign, but nothing came of it.

Protecting the Environment: Continuing Battles

By the 2010s 7 percent of the BLM budget went toward rounding up wild horses and burros in ten western states to send to pens for adoption or fenced-in areas in the Midwest; the program's cost doubled from 2009 to 2012. Mustangs on federal land enjoyed protection, but those on state land could be sold for slaughter overseas. With half of the remaining herds in Nevada, state cattlemen's association president J. J. Goicoechea advocated their "being harvested" over being penned; although cattle outnumbered horses nearly fifty to one, ranchers complained they overgrazed.

Meanwhile, Wild Horse Education founder Laura Leigh sued the BLM for more public access to roundups and to stop abuse, which the agency blamed on contract workers. Madeleine Pickens, then the wife of billionaire financier T. Boone Pickens, bought the 14,000-acre Spruce Ranch south of Wells and the 4,500-acre Warm Springs Ranch, hoping to provide a sanctuary. These plans would interfere with existing herds and might expand the population, but they also offered economic potential: Pickens's group opened Mustang Monument, which it likened to a western safari, to tourists in 2014.

Continuing efforts to protect Lake Tahoe bore fruit. The League to Save Lake Tahoe and other environmentalists fought the Tahoe Regional Planning Agency, which they saw as too probusiness. In 2012, after Nevada legislators threatened to withdraw from the compact by 2015 without a new regional plan, TRPA's board approved rules to encourage new infrastructure, make urban areas denser, and remove buildings from sensitive areas. Other efforts also paid dividends: in 2010, with Tahoe's clarity the second worst in forty-five years, the Interior Department provided funding, and the two states agreed on an EPA plan to improve clarity to one hundred feet over the next sixty-five years. By 2012 rules to reduce soil erosion and bans on some watercraft led to substantial improvements. But nonnative fish began moving into the lake, and their potential impact worried researchers. Also, several environmental groups sued to stop the new regional plan, while others accepted it as a means of protecting the lake.

Nevadans also emphasized other environmental jewels. Great Basin National Park's tourist volume reached ninety-five thousand in 2012—about one-third of those visiting Lake Mead National Recreation Area. In 2002 Reid and Gibbons passed a bill increasing Clark County's wilderness by 440,000 acres, including the Sloan Canyon conservation area. The Southern Nevada Public Land Management Act of 1998 led to $400 million for hundreds of trails. The Nature Conservancy kept restoring Carson Valley's River Fork Ranch, while Clark County's Wetlands Park expanded. In 2013 Reid introduced a bill to make almost 350,000 acres of Gold Butte, near the Arizona line, a national conservation area, and the delegation and private citizens sought an ice age park northeast of Las Vegas.

Although Nevada could hardly solve the problem alone, climate change became an issue. Scientists studying the Sierra Nevada warned that the growth zone for giant sequoias could rise hundreds of feet in the next century, endangering existing trees. Research revealed megadroughts from the ninth to twelfth centuries, and again in the thirteenth and fourteenth, and that the late twentieth century may have been a wet period. In 2012 Las Vegas's average temperature reached 71.2 degrees and its average low hit 60.5, both the warmest since the National Weather Service began keeping records, reflecting population growth and its effects.

Warring and Worrying over Water

Worse, Lake Mead seemed to be drying up. Nearly full in 2000, it fell to 42 percent of capacity in 2014. In 2002 St. Thomas, the old Mormon town, resurfaced as the waters fell. More than six hundred businesses that support the river's sustainability formed Protect the Flows, which found Nevada and other states sharing its waters (except California) owed nearly 250,000 jobs and $26 billion in output to the river, which irrigated 3.5 million acres of farmland and served 25 million–plus residents. Lake Mead alone leads to more than 25,000 jobs and nearly $3 million annually.

With 90 percent of southern Nevada's drinking water from Lake Mead, and construction of a new intake tunnel under it to bring more water to Las Vegas, projections looked ominous. A 2012 Bureau of Reclamation study found in the next half century, the river's flow would drop 9 percent and the number relying on it could double to 76.5 million. With Lake Mead's water level at about 1,085 feet in 2014, the federal government would declare a shortage at 1,075 feet, leading to reduced water use. At 1,025 feet, Hoover Dam would stop producing power. In August 2013 then Southern Nevada Water Authority general manager Pat Mulroy suggested the need for federal disaster aid to counter the drought.

In response, Nevada instituted conservation measures and joined other western states in negotiations. In 2007 all seven Colorado River Compact states agreed to let California, Arizona, and Nevada buy water from farmers and decide how to share Lake Mead and Lake Powell water in dry periods. Nevada obtained part of Arizona's allotment under the compact and Utah's portion of the Virgin River. Under a five-year pact between the United States and Mexico, signed in 2012, Mexico would receive US help with conservation efforts and infrastructure such as canals. The SNWA agreed to pay Mexico $2.5 million for 23,700 acre-feet (325,851 gallons per acre-foot), which might raise Lake Mead's level by 15 feet, and additional water from Lake Powell in 2014 and 2015 meant a slow in Lake Mead's decline, but not an end to it.

Another means of bringing water to southern Nevada proved more divisive. The SNWA wanted a 263-mile pipeline to White Pine and Lincoln Counties that would pump up to 27 billion gallons of rural groundwater from four valleys. In 2012 the BLM approved allowing construction on federal land. The state engineer agreed, and the US Fish and Wildlife Service saw no significant effect on a dozen threatened species. Many politicians supported the plan as a way to reduce Clark County's reliance on the Colorado, but critics blasted it. Confederated Tribes of the Goshute Reservation chair Ed Naranjo said, "They're going to let Las Vegas steal our water . . . and decimate our people" by harming the reservation's sacred Nelms Pond and a nursery for the Bonneville cutthroat trout. The project's environmental impact report said at least 137,000 acres of wildlife habitat might change, threatening dozens of species. Indeed, the pipeline united environmental advocates and ranchers, who rarely agreed.

Native Americans

Native American and environmental issues merged at other times. While the Washoe won their fight to protect Cave Rock (see chapter 2), Northern Paiutes benefited from a step in the right direction. By early 2013 the Lahontan cutthroat, once thought extinct, enjoyed a revival. After a scientist found a related group in a creek near Pilot Peak, on the Nevada-Utah line, the US Fish and Wildlife Service brought their eggs to a Gardnerville hatchery and stocked Pyramid Lake. The cutthroats ended up growing five times faster than other trout, and Northern Paiutes and visiting fishermen reported great success. The Northern Paiutes, Western Shoshone, and Washoe continued to work together in the nine-hundred-member Reno-Sparks Indian Colony, on a 28-acre territory in Reno and the Hungry Valley reservation about twenty miles to the north; the colony provided a variety of social and economic development services for its members.

Southern Paiutes found new environmental and economic benefits. While Indian gaming prospered more in other jurisdictions—nationally, revenues in 2011 topped $27 billion—the Moapa Paiutes earned money from their small casino near Valley of Fire State Park. They would also profit from the growing popularity of solar power: in 2012 the Los Angeles

City Council signed a twenty-five-year, $1.6 billion purchase agreement with K Road Moapa Solar, the first plant built on a reservation and designed to produce electricity for nearly 120,000 homes. The 2013 deal to close NV Energy's Reid Gardner plant near the reservation promised to eliminate coal ash that had harmed the Paiutes' health. The Las Vegas band regained 3,800 acres at the Snow Mountain Reservation northwest of Las Vegas and opened three golf courses, profiting from the expansion of tourism.

Less prosperous than other Nevada tribes, Western Shoshone's Te-Moak group of bands at Elko, Wells, South Fork, and Battle Mountain continued in ranching or working for the federal government and operated smoke shops and convenience stores. The Te-Moak Diabetes Program improved members' health and lifestyle. The Western Shoshone also shared other Native Americans' concerns: they objected that the Cortez Hill Mine desecrated a sacred mountain and sought to block a planned mining project at Mount Hope, about twenty miles north of Eureka, because it would affect cultural treasures and natural resources.

The Great Recession

A worldwide recession began in 2008 amid the collapse of major investment firms. Nevada faced its worst economic crisis since the 1880–1900 *borrasca*. Rising land values prompted developers to spend and borrow more, and subprime lending and a buyer's market made it too easy for speculators and lower-income families to buy homes. The construction industry collapsed without new projects to employ workers. After Southern Nevada's median home prices more than doubled from 1994 to 2006, home owners lost $91 billion in equity by 2012. Brookings Mountain West found unemployment up more sharply from 2009 to 2010 in Las Vegas than in any of the nation's one hundred other metropolitan areas.

Nor did Las Vegas suffer alone. From 2006 to 2011, Nevada's job losses paced the nation, and state unemployment rates reached double digits. In a year gaming revenue fell from $1.165 billion to $909.9 million. Mining eased rural Nevada's pain, but Nye ranked as America's fourth-worst county economically. Reno, Fallon, and Fernley joined Las Vegas on the list of the country's highest foreclosure rates, as California's problems and declining tourism afflicted northern Nevada. Empty homes attracted squatters and thieves seeking copper wiring for legal and illegal purposes. Participation in food-stamp programs doubled from 2008 to 2013.

Several troubled projects demonstrated the recession's costs. Boyd Gaming blew up the Stardust to make room for Echelon Place, to open in 2010 with five thousand rooms, 750,000 square feet of convention space, and a 140,000-square-foot casino; instead, its shell sat vacant. In 2006 Phil Ruffin closed the Frontier and then sold to Israeli developers planning a replica of New York City's Plaza Hotel; the recession stopped them. The Fontainebleau suspended construction in 2009, and the Sahara, long on the brink, closed in 2012. Clark County shelved an airport near Primm to relieve McCarran's traffic. Lake Las Vegas filed for Chapter 11 bankruptcy protection in 2008 with debts of $500 million, and its poshest hotel and three golf courses closed. Condominium developments downtown or near the Strip sat vacant. Caesars Entertainment's corporate debt caused concern.

But other plans proceeded. Wynn opened his Encore. MGM built the largest privately funded construction project in US history: its mixed-use 76-acre, $9 billion CityCenter and its four major hotels, condos, and 500,000-square-foot mall, all energy efficient and designed by top architects. MGM brought in Dubai World as a partner and almost entered bankruptcy, but lenders agreed to a funding plan after calls from Reid, the

MGM's CityCenter, opened in 2009, combined hotels and condos, restaurants, and high-end retail and represented a risk during the Great Recession. During its construction, workplace safety became a controversy. Courtesy of Steve Marcus and the *Las Vegas Sun*.

Senate majority leader. CityCenter debuted late in 2009 with about twelve thousand employees and fell short of original expectations, but survived amid controversy over the Harmon, a boutique hotel with no gaming, whose construction defects prompted lawsuits and plans to implode it. After a foreclosure and sale to Deutsche Bank, the $3.9 billion Cosmopolitan opened late in 2010, partnered with Ritz-Carlton, and emphasized hip celebrity chefs and independent rock acts over the usual Strip fare.

Turning and Nonturning Points: The 2010 Election

Nevada's 2010 elections proved historic. Doubting Gibbons's chances, GOP leaders persuaded Sandoval to resign his federal judgeship to challenge him. Echoing Gibbons's antitax views, Sandoval cruised to the general election (the first loss by a governor in a primary) and rolled past Clark County commissioner Rory Reid (the senator's son). Emboldened by the passage of health care reform, the rise of the national "Tea Party" enabled the GOP to regain the House, including a gain in Nevada, where Titus barely lost her reelection bid to former state senator Joe Heck. But Democrats retained a solid assembly majority and one-vote lead in the state senate and carried four of the six state constitutional offices.

Tea Partiers influenced the Senate race, but not as they had hoped. Many pundits wrote off Reid due to his low popularity ratings. Republicans expected casino executive and former state senator Sue Lowden to oppose him, or Danny Tarkanian, the coach's son. But Reid predicted a year before that Republicans would choose Angle and helped her win the primary by targeting Lowden, the front runner, for attack. In the general election, Angle made several gaffes, citing "Second Amendment remedies" for problems and telling a Hispanic student group, "Some of you look a little more Asian to me." Reid carried Clark, Washoe, and Mineral Counties in winning reelection by five percentage points.

Reid's reelection had several effects. Prominent Nevada Republicans like Sig Rogich and Wayne Newton had endorsed Reid before, but Bill Raggio joined them. After the election, GOP state senators ousted him as leader, citing his votes to raise taxes in two previous sessions in addition to backing Reid. Raggio soon announced his retirement as the state's longest-serving legislator ever. And Reid remained leader of his state party, Senate majority leader, a lightning rod, and even more aware of the growing power of Hispanic voters, who gave overwhelming majorities to Democrats.

Laboring to Succeed

The success of Nevada's labor movement varied in the new century. In 2006 the Wynn Las Vegas required dealers to share tips with supervisors and other employees; Nevada's labor commissioner upheld the plan, and dealers voted 444–149 to organize with Transport Workers Local 721. Other dealers stressed working conditions involving secondhand smoke. The tobacco company Philip Morris underwrote a study showing that banning smoking in casinos would cost thousands of jobs and millions in revenue, but in 2009 the National Institute for Occupational Safety and Health found more than half of dealers reported health problems based on poor air quality—from runny noses to coughs and asthma.

While the dealers struggled, the Culinary Union grew. The union backed Wynn on tip sharing, pointing out its contracts included similar provisions —upsetting the dealers, whose lawyer accused the Culinary of repaying Wynn for a ten-year contract, but demonstrating the Culinary's ability to work with ownership. The union's Citizenship Project helped members address immigration issues or work toward citizenship and continued to operate the Culinary Training Academy, training thousands of workers for service occupations and using a federal grant for VESOL—Vocational English for Speakers of Other Languages.

Unions also wielded political power. AFL-CIO director Danny Thompson followed in Claude "Blackie" Evans's influential footsteps in trying to unify Nevada's unions and influence legislators. Las Vegas Culinary leader D. Taylor and political directors Glen Arnodo and Pilar Weiss pushed registration and get-out-the-vote drives, mostly benefiting Democrats, and backed Guinn's tax plan in 2003 against proposals less favorable to gaming. In 2012 Taylor left to become president of the parent union, UNITE HERE. Local president Geoconda Arguello-Kline, a Nicaraguan immigrant who came to Las Vegas in 1983 and worked as a guest-room attendant, then became the first woman and Hispanic to run the sixty-thousand-member union, which included members from eighty-four countries.

The 2012 Election

Reflecting the West's growth and power, all but one presidential ticket since 1948 (1976, the only year Nevada's electoral votes went to the loser) included a westerner. Despite Sheldon Adelson giving an estimated one

hundred million dollars to the GOP nationally, Obama's margin in Nevada—
7 percent—exceeded his national lead. Obama carried Hispanics, 70–25
percent, and the urban counties showed their muscle (Obama won Clark
by one hundred thousand votes, Washoe by seven thousand).

Yet Nevada remained bipartisan. With Hispanic growth and other factors keeping the legislature Democratic, the panel that decided redistricting created two strongly partisan House districts and two divided ones.
The two parties split the House seats: Titus returned in a Democratic Clark
district, Mark Amodei won a full term in the Republican northernmost
counties, Heck won reelection in a GOP-leaning part of Clark County, and
Horsford carried the new Democratic-tilted Fourth District, whose boundaries extended north to Lyon County.

Nevadans waged another hard-fought Senate race in 2012. Senator Dean
Heller sought to retain the seat he had been appointed to against Shelley Berkley, the seven-term Democratic representative from Las Vegas.
A complaint filed with the House Ethics Committee accused her of aiding her husband's medical practice with federal regulators. The committee
report, issued after the election, found no evidence of "special favors or
privileges" for her husband, but concluded Berkley violated House rules by
letting her staff make calls on behalf of her husband's practice—and that
in doing so, she and her aides did what they did for other constituents.
The ethics complaint combined with Democratic "undervoting" for Berkley (while Heller ran six thousand votes behind Romney, Obama outpolled
Berkley by eighty-five thousand) helped Heller win by 1 percent.

Southern Nevada Growth

Southern Nevada went through several major changes in the early 2000s.
Las Vegas showed signs of "Manhattanization," as high-rise condos dotted
the skyline, but often as second or third homes for high-rollers or the well-
to-do. The recession and infrastructure issues (the condos' distance from
stores and schools) ended the movement, at least temporarily. Another
part of the infrastructure, transportation, both improved and fell short: the
bus system grew, adding double-decker, express, and diesel and electric-
hybrid lines, but a monorail unveiled in 2004 only on the Strip's east side
suffered from breakdowns, low ridership, and not extending downtown or
to the airport and went into bankruptcy in 2010.

Although Las Vegas, powered by Summerlin's continued expansion, remained Nevada's largest city, Henderson, North Las Vegas, and unincorporated townships wielded great power. Green Valley and other master-planned parts of Henderson helped it pass Reno in population to be Nevada's second-largest city. In 2003 North Las Vegas's Aliante, a potentially twenty-thousand-resident master-planned area with 420 acres for parks and recreation and with a Sun City, debuted near the beltway. But by 2013, having replaced its old city hall with a new building that won awards for energy efficiency, North Las Vegas teetered on the brink of bankruptcy over such issues as mismanagement of the budget and city benefit packages.

As downtown and its environs aged and wealth flowed to suburbs, casinos changed hands and struggled to compete with the Strip and neighborhood resorts—with varied success. Veteran owner Jackie Gaughan sold his casinos. In 2004 Internet entrepreneurs Tom Breitling and Tim Poster bought the Golden Nugget in Las Vegas and Laughlin from MGM for $215 million, later selling to Landry's Restaurants, which spent $200 million renovating the Las Vegas resort. Binion's closed temporarily and wound up going through two ownership changes, with Harrah's buying it and then selling all but the Horseshoe name and the World Series of Poker. The Lady Luck closed in 2006, but a new owner, CIM Group, finally took over and opened the Downtown Grand in 2013. Las Vegas 51s owners Derek and Greg Stevens bought the Fitzgerald's, changed it to the D Las Vegas, and renovated it; they also became co-owners of the Golden Gate, opened in 1906 as the Hotel Nevada, and teamed with longtime operator Mark Brandenburg on a $12 million expansion and renovation.

A Downtown Renaissance

Known for outrageous public comments, surrounding himself with showgirls, and downing martinis, Mayor Oscar Goodman (1999–2011) pushed the downtown renaissance. He sought a major league sports team and stadium, but urban theorist Richard Florida argued that a city's success in the twenty-first century relied on culture, innovation, and education, and Las Vegas also took that approach. Besides overseeing the Fifth Street School's conversion into an arts complex, Goodman welcomed or encouraged the Springs Preserve, Mob Museum, and Neon Museum. Similarly, downtown Henderson added galleries, murals, and lofts in the Water Street District, while Boulder City added public sculpture to its antique stores and galleries. After Carolyn Goodman succeeded her husband, a nonprofit planned a $45 million renovation of the Reed Whipple Cultural Center to host the local Shakespeare company and other arts organizations. The city also continued to court stadium builders and a major sports franchise.

The sixty-one acres behind the railroad tracks keyed redevelopment. In addition to the Ruvo Center, gaming and business executive Don Snyder volunteered to raise money for a performing arts center. The Donald W. Reynolds Foundation's $150 million donation led to its being named for foundation chair Fred Smith and his wife, Mary. The $470 million center, home to the Nevada Ballet Theatre and Las Vegas Philharmonic, began with a nationally televised gala in 2012. Hoover Dam inspired its appearance, while the directors traveled Europe to gather ideas for the interior and acoustics. A seventeen-story carillon tower with thirty thousand pounds of bronze bells announced events. Next door, a larger Discovery children's museum opened. Just off the sixty-one acres, the World Market Center offered five million square feet of space for furniture companies, joined by Las Vegas Premium Outlets and the IRS and SNWA headquarters.

Tony Hsieh's arrival added to the significance of these developments. A Harvard graduate who helped develop LinkExchange and sold it to Microsoft for $265 million by his twenty-fifth birthday, he invested in Zappos, kept control after selling the online shoe retailer to Amazon for $1.2 billion,

Tony Hsieh's plans for downtown Las Vegas have revolutionized local redevelopment and arts and culture. Courtesy of Zappos.com.

and moved Zappos to Henderson in 2004. In 2010 Las Vegas decided to build a new city hall and sold the old one and adjacent buildings that Hsieh would lease for his company. He began the "Downtown Project" to enhance residential and business density and bought First Friday, the monthly downtown event that draws thousands of residents to galleries, eateries, and clubs. He urged other tech firms to move to the area, creating hopes for a mini Silicon Valley, and devised plans for education, health, cultural programs, and new residences. He supported and invested in Fremont East, a hipster area of galleries and eateries. Nearby apartments and lofts, and the already prominent arts community's continuing growth, created a vibe that fought with and appeared to be defeating the dreariness that had afflicted the area.

Reno, Tahoe, and Tourism

Much as downtown Las Vegas distinguished itself from the Strip, Reno adapted to declining tourism. The end of Northern California's dot-com boom and its growing Indian casinos—especially Thunder Valley near Sacramento and the Red Hawk near Placerville—hurt northern Nevada. The number of Reno's gaming employees fell from twenty-five thousand in 1990 to fewer than fifteen thousand in 2010, with revenue down about one-third and occupancy dipping from 87.2 to 69.6. The county continued to improve its airport, but with fewer flights after American Airlines took over Reno Air and US Airways merged with America West, eliminating two main carriers. Lake Tahoe's gaming revenue swooned, and the recession added to the region's problems, with declining revenues leading to significant cuts in local government. Reno hotel workers, with less unionization in a less vibrant economy, proved likelier to work two jobs than their Las Vegas counterparts.

Yet tourism primed the economic pump. New hotels had been rare before the recession, but several upgraded, and the Reno-Sparks Convention and Visitors Authority attracted events. In 2008 the RSCVA finished the Atlantis Sky Bridge to the Reno-Sparks Convention Center, which joined the Reno Events Center and Reno-Sparks Livestock Center to provide ample meeting space. The Atlantis's $150 million expansion and the Peppermill's $400 million all-suite tower and restaurants helped them become the only Reno hotels to win the American Automobile Association's four-diamond ratings. The Siena, renovated from the old Holiday and opened in 2001, closed in 2010, but reopened as a contemporary boutique resort.

The region also marketed recreation. Reno's National Bowling Stadium remained an attraction, joined by a three-day cycling event, Sparks's Wild Island water park, and the Truckee River Whitewater Park, with kayaking and an annual Reno River Festival that drew thirty thousand visitors annually. The Professional Golfers' Association Reno-Tahoe Open and the Great Balloon Race drew visitors, as did the Reno Air Races, which began in 1964 and survived a crash into the stands in 2011 that killed eleven. The Professional Rodeo Cowboys Association rodeo drew more than one hundred thousand each June, while Hot August Nights emphasized 1950s and 1960s car culture. CommRow featured BaseCamp Climbing, with a 7,000-square-foot indoor park and the world's tallest (164-foot) climbing wall. The Burning Man Festival on the Black Rock Desert also brought tourists and revenue into the area. In 2012 the RSCVA adopted "All seasons, 1,000 reasons" as its promotional slogan, its third in three years, after "A little west of center" and "Far from expected," reflecting its efforts to catch up to "What happens in Vegas," but also emphasizing year-round recreation and fun.

Reno also concentrated on downtown redevelopment, which resembled what happened in Las Vegas—including a vocal mayor. In 2002 Bob Cashell, a former regent and lieutenant governor, won that post. Once owner of a Verdi truck stop that he turned into the Boomtown casino and resort, he ran a number of casinos before succeeding Jeff Griffin. Cashell helped ease infighting and pushed to diversify the local economy while stressing government efficiency and better transportation. The Reno Transportation Rail Access Corridor (RETRAC) solved an old problem: train tracks through downtown, slowing traffic and causing accidents. The project lowered two miles of track in a 33-foot-deep, 54-foot-wide trench, easing flow and making new real estate available for development. New transit centers near Reno's baseball stadium and in Sparks also helped traffic.

Like Las Vegas, Reno emphasized downtown culture, exemplified by the sixteen-million-dollar Nevada Museum of Art building, the River Walk, art produced for the Burning Man Festival, and other innovations. The old city hall became the children's Nevada Discovery Museum. Investors turned three casinos into a hotel and restaurants. Reno planned to turn its 1934 post office into a mixed-use office/bistro/store center. The city welcomed condos, lofts, and galleries: when the Golden Phoenix failed, the Montage Condominium complex replaced it, and the Comstock Hotel reappeared as the Riverwalk Towers. In 2009 Reno's downtown stadium for the AAA Aces aided redevelopment: the area behind right field, "the Stockade," had once been the red-light district.

Arts, Media, and Culture

Increased interest in the arts in urban areas demonstrated Nevada's cultural vibrancy. State museums, libraries, and cultural agencies suffered funding, staff, and programming cuts, but residents welcomed numerous touring and local events; attended one of many film festivals dotting Nevada; visited history museums in Caliente, Tonopah, Boulder City, and Fallon as well as children's museums in Reno, Las Vegas, and Carson City; and frequented Lake Tahoe's annual Shakespeare festival or the regular performances mounted by companies in Reno and Las Vegas, where book festivals became community events. In 2012 Las Vegas's art museum, closed due to financial problems in 2009, returned in UNLV's Barrick Museum, and the BLM's twenty-million-dollar California Trail Interpretive Center opened near Elko with its 1,000 square feet of murals and a sculpture of a Great Basin Native woman. Elko's National Cowboy Poetry Gathering kept growing, as it celebrated its thirtieth annual performance in 2014 with more than fifty poets and twenty-five musicians, including nearby resident Waddie Mitchell, a rancher and poet.

Nevada continued to produce varied authors who looked at their state in diverse ways. Young Nevada writers joined longtime voices with new fiction, with works by Tupelo Hassman and Ben Rogers focusing on the Reno area and Claire Vaye Watkins examining several aspects of Nevada life. Gregory Martin's *Mountain City* evoked his family's life in a tiny town north of Elko. Las Vegas native Charles Bock won prizes for his debut novel, *Beautiful Children,* and resident Laura McBride's depiction of the community in *We Are Called to Rise* garnered national attention. Las Vegan H. Lee Barnes wrote fiction and nonfiction about Vietnam, where he served in the war; *The Lucky,* a novel modeled on Horseshoe owner Benny Binion; and creative nonfiction. William L. Fox's prose and poetry about Nevada provided new ways of looking at the landscape. Authors associated with UNLV's creative writing program published a variety of Nevada-related material.

Nevada's journalism evolved and won honors. In Las Vegas, in 2005, the *Sun* became a section of the *Review-Journal* in connection with the joint operating agreement that the owners of the two newspapers had signed to enable the *Sun* to keep publishing. The Greenspun family invested in in-depth reporting and the Web, winning the 2009 Pulitzer Prize for Public Service for a series on safety issues in Strip projects, but the recession forced the *Sun* to cut back. KLAS-TV-8, a Las Vegas television station, won a Peabody Award in 2008 for work by reporter George Knapp and photojournalist Matt Adams on the proposed water pipeline, and the station's investigative unit took numerous national honors. All newspapers concentrated more on the Web, including rural weeklies, and Twitter became an important way for Nevadans to try to keep informed.

The (Slow) Economic Recovery

Nevada's recovery lagged behind most states, especially in tourism-dependent southern Nevada, but in late 2012 a Brookings Institution report suggested Las Vegas had begun to recover. Although the report ranked Las Vegas at 194 among the world's 300 largest cities, it showed Las Vegas rebounding from 298 in 2009. Las Vegas home prices dropped 11.2 percent in 2011 but went up 16.3 percent in 2012, the biggest turnaround of any metropolitan area, and the continuing rise paced the nation. Double-digit unemployment continued until a December 2012 report showed it at 9.7 percent statewide—but higher in Las Vegas and Reno and among Hispanics, while Elko's gold mining boom kept its rate to 6 percent. By early 2014 Las Vegas ranked as the nation's top area for undervalued homes. In 2013 casino revenue topped $11 billion, still nearly $2 billion below 2007 levels, with Clark County rising and Washoe going up for the first time in seven years. While a record 39.7 million visited Las Vegas in 2012 and Strip gambling revenue in February 2013 peaked at $696 million, tourist spending per trip dropped from $1,318 in 2008 to $1,021 five years later. By early 2013, 35,000 southern Nevadans worked in construction, around 30 percent the number in 2006. By August 2014 statewide unemployment had dropped to 7.6 percent, the lowest total in six years.

Hopeful signs continued in 2012 and 2013. Tourist volume remained high. Las Vegans reported $6.3 billion from conventions and trade shows in 2012. Federal spending still provided billions of dollars, with F-35 fighter jets coming to Nellis and Predator drones at Creech at Indian Springs. The

150,000 visitors for the Las Vegas Motor Speedway's NASCAR weekend and the 115,000 in Las Vegas for the Electric Daisy Carnival, some coming through McCarran International Airport's new $2.4 billion domestic and international terminal, testified to the impact and variety of tourism. High-tech and its benefits continued, with Switch Communications becoming Nevada's first data and technology storage center for casinos and housing UNLV's newly acquired Intel Cherry Creek supercomputer and Zappos and Hsieh reshaping downtown Las Vegas. Northern Nevada welcomed Apple's $1 billion data center for its "cloud" service in a technology park east of Sparks and its business and purchasing center in downtown Reno.

The Strip and the construction industry showed vigor. By 2014 boutique properties led the way—MGM Morgans Hotel Group opened the Delano Las Vegas at THEhotel, Caesars converted the old Barbary Coast and Bill's Gambling Hall into the Cromwell and added the Nobu Hotel in a tower at Caesars Palace, and SLS turned the Sahara into a mixed-use resort, aided by a federal program encouraging foreign investment in job creation. MGM slated a five-story, $100 million club/restaurant; a $350 million, 20,000-seat arena; and a $100 million outdoor plaza with a beer garden, shops, park, and food stands. Caesars Entertainment changed the Imperial Palace to the Quad and unveiled the "Linq," a $500 million–plus shopping and dining area with a 550-foot observation wheel. At the Strip's less prosperous north end, in addition to the SLS, Malaysia's Genting Group bought Echelon Place and planned Resort World Las Vegas with a China theme, including a Great Wall and live pandas, a 3,500-room hotel, and a 175,000-square-foot casino. The continued success of nightclubs catering to younger crowds suggested changes in the industry and potential for still greater profits: one club owner said, "Half of Steve Wynn's profit comes from the night clubs. Gambling is an amenity now."

Nevada at 150

In 2014 Nevada marked its sesquicentennial by looking back and looking ahead. Longtime residents often lament how much has changed, but many benefited from Nevada's greatest growth spurt ever—and suffered as the economy crashed. Plans for new properties and mines promised prosperity, but not a return to the earlier boom or its accompanying housing bubble; demographers predicted continued population growth, but at a much slower pace. Several initiatives suggested that Nevada had great potential in global and technological areas: Hsieh and Switch Communications in Las Vegas, Apple and Tesla in the Reno area, and the continued growth of data warehousing and gaming manufacturers like IGT and Bally. In an age of technological advances and telecommuting, Nevada, once the center of new inventions in mining and still in gaming, had always been a twenty-four-hour state that invited the world to visit. The gaming industry continued to dominate the state politically and economically, much as mining once did.

Granting the importance of these changes, other developments suggested links between the past, present, and future. Two new legislative caucuses reflected Nevada's evolution. A Hispanic caucus reflected the US Census Bureau's projection that by 2043, no ethnic group in America would be large enough to be called a majority and fitted with Nevada's experience with immigrant populations. A Clark County caucus sought to unite the more than 70 percent of the legislature representing Nevada's largest

Artist Ron Spears painted a portrait of Valley of Fire for Nevada's sesquicentennial postage stamp, unveiled in May 2014. *From left:* Lieutenant Governor Brian Krolicki, Senator Harry Reid, Governor Brian Sandoval, former representative Jim Bilbray (a member of the US Postal Service board of governors), Senator Dean Heller, Myron Martin of the Smith Center for the Performing Arts, and Postmaster General Patrick Donahoe. Courtesy of L. E. Baskow and the *Las Vegas Sun.*

metropolitan entity—much like the Comstock in the nineteenth century and the Reno area for a significant part of the twentieth. In May 2013 investor Warren Buffett's announcement that he would buy NV Energy thrilled financial experts as a sign that Nevada had matured enough to interest major investors—like hopes that the Corporate Gaming Act of 1969 would attract Wall Street money and much as mining, railroad, and gaming magnates have greatly influenced Nevada from its beginnings. After the winter of 2011 proved to be the fourth warmest in more than a century, ski resorts reported problems maintaining snowpacks as climate change reshaped the globe, and battles over water and the environment continued, Nevadans could remember that their state's geologic past shaped the mining industry that made statehood possible and the geography that determined settlement and helped promote a tourist economy.

In 2014 residents could detect one, two, or three Nevadas. The three encompassed Clark County, Washoe County, and the rural areas; the two could be defined as the Las Vegas area and the rest of the state. Often, they seemed to have disparate needs and desires and differed politically, economically, ideologically, socially, and culturally. But whether urban or rural, northern or southern, they shared the characteristics of always being settled and resettled, serving as a pit stop or an obstacle en route to somewhere else, an attraction for those hoping to try their luck in the ground or at the tables, a beneficiary and a victim of outside interests ranging from the federal government to businesspeople. Together they formed—and remain—one Nevada.

SUGGESTED READINGS

Andersen, Jim. *Lost in Austin: A Nevada Memoir.* Reno: University of Nevada Press, 2009.

Binkley, Christina. *Winner Takes All: Steve Wynn, Kirk Kerkorian, Gary Loveman, and the Race to Own Las Vegas.* New York: Hyperion, 2008.

Blythin, Evan. *Vanishing Village: The Struggle for Community in New West.* Las Vegas: CityLife Books, 2010.

Borchard, Kurt. *Homeless in Las Vegas: Stories from the Street.* Reno: University of Nevada Press, 2011.

———. *The Word on the Street: Homeless Men in Las Vegas.* Reno: University of Nevada Press, 2005.

Brents, Barbara G., Crystal A. Jackson, and Kathryn Hausbeck. *The State of Sex: Nevada's Brothel Industry.* New York: Routledge, 2009.

Bubb, Daniel K. *Landing in Las Vegas: Commercial Aviation and the Making of a Tourist City.* Reno: University of Nevada Press, 2012.

Chung, Su Kim. *Las Vegas: Then and Now.* 2nd ed. San Diego: Thunder Bay Press, 2013.

Cobb, Neal, and Jerry Fenwick. *Reno Now and Then.* Reno: University of Nevada Oral History Program, 2008.

Divich, Kurt. *The Smith Center for the Performing Arts: A Dream in the Desert.* Las Vegas: Stephens Press, 2012.

Franci, Giovanna. *Dreaming of Italy: Las Vegas and the Virtual Grand Tour.* Reno: University of Nevada Press, 2005.

Huber, Nicole, and Ralph Stern. *Urbanizing the Mojave Desert: Las Vegas.* Berlin: Jovis, 2008.

Huddy, John. *Storming Las Vegas: How a Cuban-Born, Soviet-Trained Commando Took Down the Strip to the Tune of Five World-Class Hotels, Three Armored Cars, and Millions of Dollars.* New York: Ballantine Books, 2008.

Miech, Rob. *The Last Natural: Bryce Harper's Big Gamble in Sin City and the Greatest Amateur Season Ever.* New York: Thomas Dunne Books/Macmillan, 2012.

Moss, P. *Blue Vegas.* Las Vegas: CityLife Books, 2009.

———. *Vegas Knockout.* Las Vegas: CityLife Books, 2012.

O'Brien, Matthew. *Beneath the Neon: Life and Death in the Tunnels of Las Vegas.* Las Vegas: Stephens Press, 2007.

———. *My Week at the Blue Angel, and Other Stories from the Storm Drains, Strip Clubs, and Trailer Parks of Las Vegas.* Las Vegas: Stephens Press, 2010.

Pierce, Todd James, and Jarret Keene, eds. *Dead Neon: Tales of Near-Future Las Vegas.* Reno: University of Nevada Press, 2010.

Raento, Paulina, and David G. Schwartz, eds. *Gambling, Space, and Time: Shifting Boundaries and Cultures.* Reno: University of Nevada Press, 2011.

Rothman, Hal K. *Neon Metropolis: How Las Vegas Started the Twenty-First Century.* New York: Routledge, 2003.

———. *Playing the Odds: Las Vegas and the Modern West.* Albuquerque: University of New Mexico Press, 2007.

Rowley, Rex J. *Everyday Las Vegas: Local Life in a Tourist Town.* Reno: University of Nevada Press, 2013.

Schumacher, Geoff. *Sun, Sin, and Suburbia: The History of Modern Las Vegas.* Las Vegas: Stephens Press, 2012.

Schwartz, David G. *Cutting the Wire: Gambling Prohibition and the Internet.* Reno: University of Nevada Press, 2005.

Sheehan, Jack E. *Skin City: Uncovering the Las Vegas Sex Industry.* Las Vegas: Stephens Press, 2005.

Simich, Jerry L., and Thomas C. Wright, eds. *More Peoples of Las Vegas: One City, Many Faces.* Reno: University of Nevada Press, 2010.

———, eds. *The Peoples of Las Vegas: One City, Many Faces.* Reno: University of Nevada Press, 2005.

Zuiker, Anthony E. *Mr. csi: How a Vegas Dreamer Made a Killing in Hollywood, One Body at a Time.* New York: HarperCollins, 2011.

INDEX